The Hindu Religious Tradition

The Hindu Religious Tradition

The Hindu Religious Tradition

A Philosophical Approach

Pratima Bowes

Routledge & Kegan Paul

London, Henley and Boston

First published in Great Britain in 1977
by Routledge & Kegan Paul Ltd
39 Store Street
London WC 1E 7 *DD*

Broadway House
Newton Road
Henley-on-Thames

Oxon RG9 1EN *and*
9 Park Street
Boston, Mass. 02108, *USA*

Set in 10/12 *pt. Times Roman*
and printed in India

ISBN 0 7100 8668 7

To
Dipali Nag

Preface

I shall in this book treat religious belief and behaviour not as divinely disclosed knowledge but as a characteristic kind of human viewing of reality. What is called 'reality' is no one thing, it is given to man in a variety of ways as different aspects of it make different impacts on man and elicit characteristic kinds of response. Some of these characteristic impacts and responses give rise to what is known as 'religion'. I shall thus treat religion on a par with other characteristic kinds of human beliefs and activities, such as science, art etc., and not as something with a special guarantee attached to it. That is, whatever value religion has will be seen to derive from human attempts to comprehend reality in a characteristic way rather than from revelation in a narrow sense. (All understanding may be said to be revelation in some sense.) The diversity of the Hindu religious tradition and its multiple forms within this characteristic approach seem to me to require this treatment.

To say that religion is a human way of experiencing reality however is not to say that the religious approach is purely subjective, entirely a human construction, having no objective reference beyond the fact of experiencing. For barring what are called illusions, hallucinations and fancy, experience is usually understood to involve not only an experiencer, but also something that is given to be experienced, something that can be experienced by more than one person. Whether or not an experience is of this nature can be found out by investigating whether there is a language that deals with it, a language that is used inter-subjectively in a meaningful manner with the understanding that what is being talked about is given. We know that religious languages do exist and that these are used by religious communities despite the fact that since reality is viewed from the religious point of view as transcending the spatio-temporal limitations of ordinary experience all human beings do not automatically share religious experience as they do sense experience; (religious perception needs the adoption of a specific point of view). There are no doubt some people who believe that religious experience is to be categorised as illusion, hallucination or at any rate as no more than psychological experiencing. But

to approach religion from the human angle is not necessarily to
subscribe to such a view, even though seen from the human angle
it is easier to recognise that religion can easily become a focus
for illusions, hallucinations and delusions. To say that religion
constitutes a human approach to reality is then not to say that
there is no reality to which this approach can be appropriately
made. It is however to say that human knowledge in the field
of religion is fallible, subject to modification, correction etc.,
in the same way as knowledge elsewhere and that likewise this
knowledge must be understood in relation to the purpose and
point of view involved in making whatever claim is being made.
(All human knowledge is relative to a purpose and point of
view.) That is, the validity of any claim made within the sphere
of religion can only be evaluated when seen in the context of a
framework of reference which is necessarily involved, not
independently.

Religious knowledge suffers from several possible complications. Human beings experience reality from many different
points of view and as the same man has all these experiences,
in real life these are not always kept separate in logically water-
tight compartments. Sometimes the same facts are experienced,
and described, at the same time, from more than one point of
view, which are mixed together – either because this is required
for an understanding of what is going on or because of confusion
between some apparently similar features. This happens more
often in the sphere of religious experience where imagination
can have a relatively free scope because it lacks the kind of
check that limits sense experience. Thus we find that religious
experience can get mixed up with magic to a greater or less
degree, because both magic and religion are freed of the space-
time-cause framework of the normal business of life. (Perhaps
an element of magical attitude is present in all religious ritual,
but magic by itself is not religion. However, as magic is based
on a belief in non-physical forces operating in the universe its
link with religion is understandable.) Also beliefs which normally
belong to social customs, and which men hold because they
belong to a certain social milieu, and even superstitions rooted
in hopes and fears that have nothing to do with religious reality
can attach themselves to religious viewing of reality and become
a part of what is believed to be religious experience. All this

becomes understandable when religion is viewed as a human enterprise, subject to human failings, and related to human hopes and fears. Anyway, these complications sometimes tend to make religion a source of superstition and consequent enslavement of mind rather than of integration and enlightenment. Nevertheless it will not do to say that religion is nothing but magic, superstition, and sanctified social custom; the very fact that we have these different terms and that they are not synonyms show that they do not have the same reference, however difficult it may be in real life to keep these separate or even to decide in a particular case which is which.

I have used the expression 'the Hindu religious tradition', rather than the more common 'the Hindu religion' or 'Hinduism', since the religious beliefs and practices of the Hindus do not have a compact and unified character that can be packed under one doctrine or dogma. This tradition includes widely different beliefs, doctrines and practices including forms which elsewhere would be thought to constitute different religions. Indeed what is called Hinduism contains within one fold all *types* of religious beliefs to be found in different religious communities in the world. Hence it is best understood as a tradition rather than as a religion. This is not to say that as a tradition it does not have peculiarities of its own which make it unique in the same way as all religions are thought to be unique. What these peculiarities are I shall be exploring in this book, and these will emerge in course of my treatment of various types of approach to religious reality that we find in this tradition. I have tried to understand these approaches in terms of purposes, within the general religious outlook, that men have in mind in embarking on a religious search and in terms of levels of integration that it is the function of religion to bring about.

There is much in this complex tradition, which by itself constitutes a whole religious world in miniature, so to say, that one may find magical, superstitious and rather futile, but also much, according to me, that is of value from a philosophical point of view. It is to these aspects that I shall mainly concentrate my attention, as the title of this book would indicate.

PRATIMA BOWES

Contents

		Page
Preface		vii
I	WHAT IS THE HINDU RELIGIOUS TRADITION?	1
II	SOME RELEVANT HINDU BELIEFS	43
III	RELIGIOUS REALITY AND LEVELS OF INTEGRATION IN THE HINDU TRADITION	81
IV	POLYTHEISM	101
V	NON-DUALISM	135
	UPANISADIC NON-DUALISM	135
	NON-DUALISM OF SAMKARA	163
VI	SAMKHYA-YOGA PERFECTIONISM	179
VII	DEVOTIONALISM AND QUALIFIED MONOTHEISM	199
	DEVOTIONALISM: A DISTINCTIVE APPROACH	199
	VAISHNAVISM, SAIVISM, SAKTISM	217
	(a) VAISHNAVISM	219
	(b) SAIVISM	235
	(c) SAKTISM	250
VIII	TRUTH AND THE HINDU RELIGIOUS TRADITION	269
IX	MORAL AND SPIRITUAL VALUES IN THE HINDU TRADITION	291
X	CONCLUSION	307
	INDEX	316

What is the Hindu Religious Tradition ?

This study of the Hindu religious tradition is not a sociological enquiry and it is not my concern here to give factual information about current religious beliefs and practices of the people who are known as Hindus. But it will help us to understand the peculiar features of this tradition if we ask how and why this tradition came to be what it is. This requires us to have a brief look at the culture and history of the people known as Hindus to whom this tradition is confined, unlike Buddhism, Christianity, and Islam which are found among people of different culture groups. But from a philosophical point of view the value of the concepts involved should not be thought to be bound up with the fortunes of the Hindu peoples, their achievements and failures, and the Hindu religious tradition as I see it may be worthwhile studying even if the people known as Hindus altogether cease to exist.

Most of the literature that is relevant to the study of the Hindu religious tradition from a philosophical point of view was written during the period when Hindu culture and civilisation were still vital enough to be creative: I mean the period previous to the Muslim conquest of India. (Religious movements of a devotional sort continued to erupt here and there even during the period of decay of Hindu civilisation lasting over several centuries.) It is difficult to put a precise date on anything Hindu, but I would say that Hindu culture has gone through a process of gradual degeneration and decay over the past seven or eight centuries. And this means that despite an unbroken physical continuity of the culture known as the Hindu over thousands of years, there is a serious gap in it in terms of creative achievements, which makes the pre-Muslim Hindu culture quite a different thing from the culture of the Hindus in recent centuries. It is important to say this as it is fashionable to make Hindu religion responsible for the low level of attainment of the present-day Hindu society – in terms of modern civilisation – whereas to my mind it is the overall decay of Hindu culture, in its political, social, economic, and intellectual dimensions, that caused what is called 'the Hindu religion' to degenerate into the negative elements that are so often deplored as inimical to progress. A philosophical study of this tradition shows that these negative elements do not constitute the essence or the message of some entity called 'the Hindu religion'. The domination of the Hindu mind by these elements is rather a sign of decadence of Hindu culture and the degeneration of its religious tradition consequent upon the general degeneration of the culture of which it forms a part. It is because this 'religion' has functioned only in one cultural context, namely the Hindu, that it is particularly easy to fall into the trap of trying to explain the shortcomings of modern Hindu society as a function of its religion. This is a temptation to which western commentators, especially if they are committed Christians, have been particularly prone. This even tempts people to interpret ancient Hindu scriptures in the light of what they believe are serious defects in the modern Hindu way of life, by reading into them beliefs which arose much later in socio-economic-cultural circumstances that are quite different from those in which these books were composed.

There is in any tradition, including the Hindu, a great gap between what books say and how people who claim allegiance to these books behave. But the gap in Hindu culture I am talking about is over and above this universal gap to be found in all cultures. This extra gap was created by a long period of actual decay in cultural vitality and gradual erosion of civilised standards, both in aspiration and achievement, in manifold aspects of Hindu civilisation and society. It seems to me that even before the Muslim power arrived in India the seeds of decadence that Hindu culture nurtured within itself had already grown to some proportion and this was shown in the total inability of Hindu society to defend itself against aggression, not just military aggression but aggression against its cultural forms, such as the temples – and yet defence against aggression and maintenance of the righteous order of society is a recognised duty of the kshatriya according to Hindu scriptures. But actual loss of power and subjection to an alien culture that was rigidly monotheistic – which believed itself to possess absolute truth revealed by God, that can be imposed on people, if necessary, against their will – and therefore intolerant of Hindu culture, which stands at the opposite pole of rigid monotheism, effectively sealed the process of decay.

There is no dispute about the fact that the Hindus, like other ancient peoples, built a highly developed civilisation. This was not a spiritual civilisation in the sense that it is not at all the case that all Hindu endeavours were concentrated on other worldly achievements. On the contrary, it did manage to produce a degree of material wealth that was generally recognised to be high in the ancient world, according to the standards of those days, quite apart from the fact that material progress and prosperity were explicitly recognised by this culture as amongst the legitimate goals of human endeavours.[1]

Indeed it can be argued that it was the reputed material wealth of India that invited continual foreign aggression throughout Indian history, eventually causing its downfall. But apart from material wealth it produced aesthetic, religious, philosophical and scientific (or protoscientific) works of considerable merit during the period of its progress. All this was possible despite Hindu religious beliefs and practices which are nowadays thought to be antithetical to progress in this world. However, Hindu culture harboured the seeds of decadence within itself, and this was the caste system.

Now the caste system was probably a fairly reasonable solution to the challenge that was thrown up by the peculiar social situation which happened to develop in ancient India. This was a confrontation between peoples belonging to different races, colours, cultures, and degrees of civilisation. These peoples belonged to at least three distinct groups: (1) the aborigines or tribal peoples of India who are said to be of the same racial stock as the Australian aborigines and whose culture was of the same level; (2) the Dravidians. Nobody knows for certain who they were, although some scholars believe that they were some sort of Mediterranean people who had entered India at an early date. Whoever they were, they were different from the aborigines and they belonged to a highly developed urban civilisation, that of the Indus valley, although it may well be the case that some mixture between the Dravidians and the aborigines had already taken place before the Aryan entry; (3) the Aryans, who had a highly developed language, great

[1]See *Arthasastra*, *Laws of Manu*, and *Mahabharata*.

mobility (peculiar to nomads), and probably use of metals which
gave them material advantage over the Dravidians, although
their civilisation at the time of entry into India (believed to be
between 2000–1500 B.C.) was not comparable to the Dravidians
in other respects, in the building of planned cities, for instance.
In a situation where all these peoples were thrown together,
there could be four possible solutions to the challenges involved :
(1) virtual extermination by one race of others, as happened in
North America; (2) imposition of the culture of the dominant
group over the rest, as happened in South America; (3) absolute
equality of all races in all matters, which the world is yet to see;
(4) the caste system, which instead of destroying the principles
of social groupings, customs, and organisations of the constituent elements tried to bring them under an overall order, which
yet made room for these differences and kept the elements
separate as far as possible. There may already have been in
India, before the arrival of Aryans, the custom of hereditary
groupings of people performing different functions and following
different customs of marriage, food etc., derived from a tribal
past, and the aborigines may already have been recruited to do
dirty jobs, the tribal organisation of society ensuring that they
were kept as a group distinct from all others. On this was
superimposed the Aryan varna system, dividing the functions of
the society into four categories, and hierarchically arranging
them in order of importance as (1) studying, teaching, sacrificing,
(2) political and military, (3) economic, and (4) menial. This
allowed inclusion under the idea of one function of multitudinous
caste-like distinctions that already existed. A function, say that
of sacrificing or fighting, when treated as one caste could accommodate within itself the so-called sub-castes with their internal
exclusiveness. The whole thing could then be brought under the
idea of fourfold division of society.

The racial prejudices of the Aryans and the Dravidians must
have found the caste system a great blessing because it allowed
different racial and cultural elements to be put into different
slots of castes and sub-castes and yet managed to create some
kind of a functioning unity. The aborigines had little say in the
new emerging society and they were kept out of the idea of
order by treating them as outcastes, possibly because the
differences between the Aryan–Dravidian and the aborigines

were much more pronounced ethnically and culturally than between the Aryan and the Dravidian. Racial prejudice is a fact, but in view of the fact that the Dravidian civilisation was of a high order and that it was spread over an extensive area the usual story that the Dravidians were made into sudras can hardly be believed. The Aryans could hardly have managed that, in view of the large Dravidian population, and the Dravidians must have contributed to the higher functions of the new society as much as the Aryans. But as one function could include numerous endogamous and exclusive castes (or sub-castes, depending on one's system of classification) there could be both Aryan and Dravidian brahmans, that is, people doing the same kind of job, teaching, sacrificing etc., who would yet remain distinct as social groups (that is, there could be two sub-castes of brahmans between whom there would be no intermarriage and inter-dining, thus helping to keep the ethnic groups separate). Nevertheless, fusion of cultures and races did take place — if the Dravidians were a Mediterranean people and not a noseless black race mentioned in the Vedas, which description was perhaps aimed at the aborigine rather than the Dravidian, there would not be very pronounced differences between the two races — and such a thing was inevitable in view of the fact that there was some kind of idea of one society. And this obliterated the memory of racial distinctions from the minds of the Indians while perpetuating social customs some of which might have originated in the need to keep races separate (such as creation of exclusive sub-castes within one caste in order to accommodate endogamous groups).

To criticise the caste system is not the same thing as saying that the Hindu society should have been egalitarian rather than hierarchical. Hierarchy is not the same thing as caste and many hierarchical societies have existed without the benefit of caste. Caste means the division of society into thousands of exclusive little units, whereas hierarchy, such as that of fourfold varna, if it did function, would have meant different functions differently valued in terms of prestige, which theoretically, at any rate, could be open to all sections of the populace. Anyone showing intellectual, ethical, and spiritual excellence would be highly honoured as a brahman irrespective of his parentage, and the story of Satyakama in the Upanisads points to such a state of affairs. But what ultimately prevailed in India was hierarchy of caste (which suited the need of keeping ethnic groups separate), fixed according to birth (a brahman remained a brahman even if he did no teaching or sacrificing; and a kshatriya, even if he taught, remained a non-brahman), and the whole thing was confused because caste was discussed under the concept of varna, when these two institutions stand for totally different things.

The varna–caste confusion meant that the device of keeping people separate did not function perfectly, and intermarriages were all the time taking place, giving rise to the inevitable mixing of cultures and races. And up to the time of Mahabharata, at any rate, the caste system was not envisaged as an insurmountable barrier between different hereditary groups – this is what it largely became at a subsequent time – and it was flexible enough to allow intermarriage between different varnas (castes?) as well as the following of a profession other than a hereditary one (Krishna was supposed to have said that one's own duty means one's caste duty, while there are numerous examples in the *Mahabharata* of people doing other things). Significantly, Vyasa, the compiler of the *Mahabharata*, was said to have a sudra mother, so had the grandfather of the royal cousins between whom the Kurukshetra war took place. To cite a historical case, the Maurya dynasty, one of the most famous in ancient India, was founded by a sudra. One can easily multiply instances.

Thus races and cultures got mixed in India. In view of the actual practice of mixing in the early days, one would have thought that with the progress of Hindu civilisation the tribalism of caste would give way to a more integrated society, as happened with civilisations elsewhere where different tribes mingled to make one nation. This could have happened had the teachers and moral leaders of Hindu society undertook to preach in favour of the transformation. But this did not happen because very powerful vested interests in the system, especially for the brahman, had been created. The highest caste, the brahmans, had virtual monopoly over all intellectual, cultural, and religious functions of the society and one of the ways in which they could perpetually secure their hereditary position of power was to preach the inviolability of the system itself, no matter what obtained in practice. The brahmans did certainly exploit the

opportunities accorded to them by this monopolistic situation
to the fullest extent possible. Not only had they no interest in
preaching the desirability of a more integrated people, say,
through the fusion of hundreds of sub-castes into one caste – the
sub-caste problem was not even mentioned in the literature–
thereby making the varna system more of a reality, even if
operating on a hereditary line instead of being open, the fusion
of castes was held up by them as a disaster of cosmic dimension
which men must avoid like plague. In the earlier literature, the
Vedas and the Upanisads, the system does not appear to have
been finally fixed, the varna idea, as distinct from caste, still
retaining some applicability. The kshatriyas were teaching and
preaching during Upanisadic times, and there is even the story
of Viswamitra, a kshatriya, becoming a brahman, no doubt in
teeth of great opposition. But this certainly suggests that a
varna could be fixed by function and not by birth. By the time
the law books began to appear (300 B.C.?) the brahman law-
givers were insisting that maintaining the purity of the system
was the greatest of duties of all men. So through the constant
preaching of the brahmans, the law-givers, and the intellectual
leaders of the society, the system itself began to assume more
and more importance in the Hindu mind, until it was finally
frozen despite the fact that by then people had totally forgotten
what it was originally meant to accomplish.

The freezing of the caste system was to my mind a sign of
decadence that was overtaking Hindu culture; it was closing
in instead of being open to fresh challenges. (To be fair, we
should remember that by the time Hindu culture was overrun
by Islam it had had a run of at least 2,500 years, if we count
its beginnings from the entry of the Aryans into India; if we
count the Dravidian civilisation as part of Hindu history it
becomes much more ancient.) According to the caste system
the brahmans were the intellectual, moral, and spiritual leaders
of the society, besides being in charge of its priestly functions.
It was the duty of the kshatriya to rule, to protect the righteous
order of the society, to defend it against aggression, and generally see to the social well being of men.[2] The administration
and organisation of the social order was the province of the

---

[2]See *Arthasastra* by Kautilya and *Laws of Manu.*

kshatriya, and even the brahman came under his jurisdiction in this regard; (the king could even decide as to the relative status of different orders of brahmans). Also it was directly under the patronage of the Hindu kings that the intellectual and cultural life of the Hindu society flourished, via the courts and assemblies where public debates and discussions took place – assemblies of different sorts are mentioned in Sanskrit from the time of the Vedas – and later via the temple which became the centre of the cultural activities of the Hindus. These centres for the dissemination of cultural values through the patronage of the kings were very important for the vitality of Hindu civilisation, for it did not have a church or any other comparable institution through which direct preaching could take place. According to Hindu scriptures, dharmasastras, arthasastras etc., it was the duty of the king to secure all that was necessary for the moral and physical health of the society, and a part of this consisted in maintaining brahmans through gifts etc. This power of the king over the brahmans did put some restraint on brahman activities, which were extremely potent in their influence over the minds of men, just as the intellectual and spiritual leadership of the brahman caste did something to check the secular power of the king.

At the time of the Muslim invasion, which began around 1000 A.D. and continued in various waves through several centuries, the Hindu kings miserably failed to carry out the caste duty the scriptures had enjoined on them, to protect society against aggression. It does not seem that any serious attempt was at all made on the part of the Hindu kings to combine forces against aggression, unlike earlier times when Chandragupta (a non-kshatriya) did succeed in raising an army and defeating the Greeks left in India after Alexander's invasion. Nor does it seem that the brahmans, the intellectual and moral leaders, were in any way perturbed at what was taking place, including attack on temples, and no attempt was made on their part to understand what was happening, let alone provide any kind of leadership, against the crisis that was overtaking Hindu civilisation. And after the consolidation of Muslim power in India, the brahmans seem to have concentrated their energies on tightening up caste rules, on devising elaborate rules against pollution (*Laws of Manu* lays down no general prohibition against inter-dining of castes), and generally on framing various restrictive injunctions about what a Hindu must not do if he is not to lose caste. Thus both the brahmans and kshatriyas, the secular and religious leaders of the Hindus, miserably failed Hindu society, and as the common people had always been told that their responsibility did not extend beyond their caste duty it probably never occurred to them to even bother. That the whole thing came down like a pack of cards shows how utterly inadequate the idea of building a society on the basis of caste functions was in meeting the new challenges that were now facing the Hindus.

Thus the caste system, although probably once a reasonable solution to a difficult problem, eventually barred the door to further development of society by making it utterly immobile – thereby contributing to the undoing of Hindu civilisation. In a society where it is, theoretically at any rate, open to anybody to function in any capacity, intellectual, religious, economic, or military, original thinking and leadership in the management of the affairs of the society can come from anyone belonging to any stratum of the society. In a society where people's duty is defined strictly in terms of caste, there exists no impetus for involvement, on the part of the general populace, in the affairs of the society, beyond their own restricted sphere of interest. Where nobody but a brahman is supposed to think and nobody but a kshatriya is supposed to fight aggression, the failure of one caste in respect of the function that belongs to it means the failure of the whole of the society, since others who are potentially capable of providing leadership and supplying the necessary energy to deal with the problems involved are brought up to think that such things are none of their business. The same is true of the economic functions of the society, which were concentrated in the hands of one caste. Had these been open to anyone, new thinking and new methods of organisation of trade, industry, and agriculture might have been available; but they were not, and Hindu society remained stuck at the economic level of feudalism, even though according to some authorities there was enough capital accumulation in Hindu society to have made development of large scale production possible.

As political and economic power passed over to Muslim hands, the main source of stimulation and dissemination of Hindu culture, centred around courts, assemblies, and temples maintained by kings, dried up. So did patronage to brahmans, and Hindu society was left without any leadership, either secular or spiritual. There was also the fact of direct and continued aggression on Hindu institutions, particularly temples, the vital centres of Hindu civilisation, by an intolerant and alien culture which refused to be absorbed into the general body of the Hindu society, as all other peoples who had come into India throughout history (of which there were a great many) were absorbed. Of course, in course of time when a great many Hindus had been converted to Islam there was some accommodation between Islamic and Hindu cultures, even synthesis in some respects, but monotheistic Islam remained strongly antagonistic to polytheistic Hinduism. During the long centuries of Muslim rule, Hindu culture, by and large left without the leadership of Hindu kings on whom it had always been dependent, went steadily downhill, although, unlike Buddhism, it did not physically disappear.

It was recognised as early as the time of the Mahabharata that the Hindu culture and social order were dependent on the function of the king. As is said in the *Mahabharata*, 'Santi Parva', 'All the duties, principle and subordinate, of the three orders are dependent for their observance upon the duties of the kshatriyas. The duties in respect of the four modes of life, those of yatis, O son of Pandu, and the customs relating to the conduct of men in general, are all included in kingly duties. If the functions of royalty are disturbed, all creatures are overtaken by evil. Without the protection of the king all other eternal duties of men suffer destruction.'[3] And the only leadership that came from the brahmans was restrictive and negative, more and more rules by which to bind the minds of men to superstitious practices of various sorts.

To give an example of inversion of Hindu values by brahmans: The ancient Hindus had maintained trade relations with the West and had travelled to Greece and Rome. They had also travelled to China and had later on even founded kingdoms in the Far East. But during the negative phase of Hinduism I am

---

[3] *Mahabharata*, Santi Parva, trans. P.C. Roy, p. 143.

talking about, the brahmans ruled that anybody who crossed the sea would become an outcast, and this meant the end of overseas trading activities of Hindus.[4] And if there were a few brahmans here and there who were assiduously memorising the Vedas or writing commentaries on scriptures, such isolated activities did nothing for the general mass of the Hindu people and their cultural nourishment. I do not wish to idealise the ancient culture of the Hindus and suggest that there were no superstitious rules and prohibitions at all in Hindu culture before the breakdown; but there was enough vitality and health in society to keep these purely negative elements within reasonable proportions, whereas during the long centuries of Hindu decay these came to occupy the centre of the stage in the Hindu drama, so to say. All that was vital to being a Hindu, according to the brahmans from mediaeval times onwards, was not to eat beef, not to marry or dine outside one's caste, not to deviate in the slightest detail from elaborate ritual observances which had come to cover all of life and from rules against pollution. It is impossible to believe that classical Hindu civilisation was built by men whose mental horizons did not extend beyond thoughts of pollution and ritual purity. But this is what Hinduism had more or less come to mean by the 18th century.

The British occupation of India prolonged the period of decay, but by the time the British arrived in India the Hindus generally had fallen to such oblivion of the positive contents of their own tradition that the British orientalists had to take it upon themselves to tell the Hindus about their own tradition. There is no doubt that it is the labour of the western orientalists that made the Hindu scriptures generally available to the Hindus themselves. To quote J. Muir, 'My primary object in this volume, as in its predecessor, has been to produce a work which may assist the researches of those Hindus who desire to investigate critically the origin and history of their nation and of their national literature, religion and institutions, and may facilitate the operations of those European teachers whose business it is

---

[4]They ruined the trading caste, the vaishyas of Bengal, by pressurising them into becoming sudras. This may have had something to do with the lack of business ability of the Bengalees, in contrast to other peoples of India who did manage to retain a trading caste, the Gujratis and the Marwaris. See N.K. Dutta, *Origin and Growth of Caste in India*, Vol. II.

to communicate to the Hindus the results of modern enquiry on the various subjects here examined.'[5]

The Hindu society, although now politically independent, has not yet recovered from this long process of decay of Hindu civilisation, and this gap I have talked about has not yet been bridged. This cannot be expected to happen soon, either, particularly through a democratic process, considering the enormity of the problem – poverty, overpopulation, caste divisions, and mass illiteracy. Nor has Hindu society as a whole adjusted itself yet in its intellectual and emotional orientations to the altered picture of society where the traditional concept of performance of duties according to caste can no longer be of vital significance, and it may be some time before new social values that are needed in the altered perspective of life take root; (deeply rooted attitudes can change only through radical change in the social pattern of existence). In short, Hindu society has not yet found its feet in the modern world with its altered perspective. So what I have to say about the values of the Hindu religious tradition cannot automatically be transferred on to the scene of the present-day Hindu society. Indeed, some of the insights that I shall be talking about may even appear to be totally absent in modern India, and this includes not only religious but social and moral values as well.

To give some examples of values that were once held in high esteem but are practically non-existent now: The Vedas show delight in and adoration of a great many things in man's environment, rivers, trees, mountains, animals etc., and these are treated as sacred. In so far as the Vedas are claimed to be a part of the Hindu tradition (indeed its foundation according to the traditional account) it will be justifiable to claim that this religious tradition treats nature as sacred and as organically related to man. But this does not mean that Hindus today behave towards nature in accordance with this insight. No doubt many Hindus even today believe that the river Ganges (and others) is sacred, and so are the cows (and other animals). This belief, however, is now purely ritualistic – one dips in the Ganges to wash away one's sins on 'holy' days, and one adorns the cow

[5]Preface to the first edition, *Original Sanskrit Texts*, Vol. II, Amsterdam, Oriental Press, 1967.

on a certain day of the year with garlands and vermilion and gives it special attention. Such ritualistic degeneration of the Vedic worldview contains nothing of the tender concern shown in innumerable verses of the Vedas towards man's natural and animal environment. Indeed, for a Hindu belief in the sacredness of the Ganges is perfectly compatible with polluting it in the most merciless manner and the sacredness of animals with their utterly callous treatment (except on prescribed 'holy' days). Many writers have commented on the unhygienic, insanitary, and unaesthetic mode of life of the Hindus, and this they somehow take to be an inherent or intrinsic function of the Hindu civilisation or even religion itself, which supposedly failed to attach any importance to conditions of life here on earth.[6] But this is a misconception and if we read the *Vishnu Purana* we find that a good deal of concern is shown there for cleanliness and sanitary habits. 'A man should not void impurities of nature either in the courtyard of his house or in any place where there is the print of a man's foot. Nor should he pass excrement in a ploughed field, or a pasturage, or in the company of men, or on a high road, or in rivers and the like, which are holy, or on the bank of a river or in a cremation ground.[7] Other ancient texts lay stress on cleanliness, environmental as well as domestic and personal, and the *Kama Sutra* emphasises the importance for a civilised man to live in aesthetically pleasing surroundings both natural and artistically created. These considerations do not have much importance for the Hindus now, as is evident from the dirt, filth, squalor, and consequently unpleasing appearance of Hindu places of habitation, including the temples. It is the *Vishnu Purana* again which shows that the Hindu attitude to animals has not always been ritualistic (in the *Rigveda* one even prays to Rudra for their happiness and well-being), for there a householder is required to provide food everyday for birds and beasts, this constituting a normal part of one's everyday duty, appropriate to the second stage of a man's existence. What all these show is not that the Hindu civilisation (and religion) failed to develop certain human values essential for a satisfactory existence of men here on earth, but that a great

[6] V. S. Naipal, for instance, in his *Area of Darkness*, p. 199.
[7] *Vishnu Purana*, trans. Manmatha Nath Dutt,

many values once cherished in this tradition have been subsequently lost. No doubt poverty and overpopulation add to lack of standards, but the major cause of this loss is the gap in the maintenance and furtherance of civilised values that I have talked about.

Of course, it must be admitted that in classical Hindu civilisation, as in other ancient and mediaeval civilisations (with only a limited amount of wealth to distribute because of their relatively primitive techniques of production), high culture and refinement were confined to the upper castes or classes, while the majority of the populace remained not only unlettered but also lacking in opportunities for gracious living. The situation was probably even worse in Hindu India than elsewhere because of the arrogance of the upper castes, especially the brahmans, who thought that it was right and proper that the lower castes should be left without the benefit of high culture. With the advent of the modern age in Europe and its vastly potent industrial techniques for creating wealth on a mass scale, it was possible to spread the fruits of civilisation among the common people in the west; but India failed to enter this phase of history and Hindu civilisation, instead of progressing through the creation of new economic, social, and political institutions as happened in Europe, began to regress, thus losing a good deal of its old values even among the higher castes, instead of being able to spread them throughout the different strata of the population. This is the explanation for the disarray of Hindu affairs and for the apathy and indifference of the Hindu masses (the Muslims in India share the same fate) who have remained without the benefit of modern education (as well as of ancient high culture). To say that all this is the result of Hindu religion is to utter a tautology, if 'Hindu religion' means the whole Hindu way of life including the caste system; it is false if by 'Hindu religion' is meant a specific body of doctrines about religious reality, (supposedly preaching total unconcern about the world and human society), as I hope to show.

My object in talking about the degeneration of Hindu civilisation is this. The downfall of Hindu culture, of which the present condition of the Hindus is a legacy, is a socio-economic-political phenomenon, and it should not be explained as a function of Hindu religious beliefs, however, fashionable it may be to do so. The key concepts of Hindu culture and religious tradition were arrived at quite early and these were compatible with the progress of Hindu society, both materially and intellectually. Contrary to accepted opinion, the Hindus did achieve considerable success in certain fields of scientific knowledge[8] and they have a rich philosophical tradition in the proper sense of the term – in the sense in which this term is understood in the west – apart from a religious one. The value of the religious ideas in the Hindu tradition should therefore be judged independently of the fortunes of the Hindu peoples, despite the fact that the peculiarity of this tradition can be best understood by reference to certain characteristic facts of Hindu history. Let us now have a brief look at the tradition to see how it came to be what it is.

The term 'religion' may be used in more than one way; it may mean the whole way of life of a people, because in the culture concerned no clear-cut distinction has been made between beliefs and practices which are specifically religious, that is, concerned with questions of ultimate reality and man's relationship with it, and other expressions of life, social, economic, political, aesthetic, and the like. But the term 'religion' may also be narrowly defined and used exclusively to refer to ultimate reality, and when so defined the beliefs involved are not thought to be necessarily tied up with any specific social, political or economic arrangement, although in no culture are religious beliefs totally divorced from other forms of life. Take, for instance, the coronation ceremony in England. This is primarily social or political in nature, but it has also a religious aspect. Nevertheless, it is not an integral part of the Christian religion and no mention need be made of it in an account of Christian beliefs, and if a western society ceases to have a king it would not be thought that it would thereby cease to be Christian. In some societies, however, this kind of clear-cut distinction between the religious and the social may not have been made (although I am not saying that it cannot be made), and the ceremony of installing a chief to his office of authority in some tribal society may appear to be as much a religious business as a social one.

[8]See B. Seal, *The Positive Sciences of the Hindus*. Also, *A Concise History of Science in India*, Chief Editor, D.M. Bose. Published by National Commission for the compilation of the History of Science in India, New D elhi.

One may then be tempted to cite this ceremony as part of the religious belief and practice of the tribe concerned, particularly if the tribe itself has not separated its religious beliefs from its social practices. If this is done, we must remember that here the term 'religion' means the whole way of life of a people with which religious beliefs are thoroughly intertwined, rather than belief specifically about the nature of ultimate reality. But even in a culture where clear-cut distinctions do not exist, it is possible to separate, analytically, specifically religious beliefs (narrowed down to questions of ultimate reality) from other beliefs and practices. If this is not done and the term 'religion' is used to refer to the whole complex of beliefs and practices of a people, then the explanation of certain characteristic features of this way of life by means of its religious beliefs and practices becomes a tautology.

The term 'Hinduism' as it is sometimes used is more a name for the whole cultural tradition of the Hindus than for beliefs which are narrowly religious. Hindu culture does possess literature which is specifically religious in nature, as distinct from political, aesthetic, philosophical etc., and yet in the culture as a whole no clear-cut distinction between religion and other forms of life exists, since all forms of life, social, political, economic, and so forth in the classical Hindu culture have been conceived to have a religious dimension. It is this state of affairs which makes it possible for people to talk about Hindu religion in terms of Hindu social customs. There exist books where accounts of such things as various Hindu customs, some purely superstitious in nature, connected with the birth of a child, for example, are given as a description of the Hindu religion. But these customs are a part of Hindu culture, whether or not one approves of them, and they are more social than religious in implication, except for the fact that social customs of this sort also involve elements of religious practice (in much the same way as does the coronation ceremony, for instance). But a social practice, however, invested with a religious significance as well, does not become religious belief as such, and we ought to be clear what we are describing when we describe practices of this nature as Hindu religious belief.

Or take again the opinion often expressed that the caste system is the centre of the Hindu religion and that the breakdown of this system means the end of this religion. As a matter of fact, the caste system is a particular socio-economic arrangement (which, however, has not remained an unchanging entity throughout Hindu history) under which Hindus have traditionally lived, but it would be a mistake to think that this system was introduced into the Hindu society by something that may be referred to as 'the Hindu religion'. (It is doubtful if this expression, as distinct from the expression 'the Hindu religious tradition', has any precise application.) One of the first references in Hindu literature to division of society in classes or castes (it is not clear which it is at this stage) is found in the Purusasukta of the *Rigveda*. This hymn says that the brahmans came out of the mouth of the sacrificed Purusa, the kshatriyas from the arms, the vaishyas from the thigh, and the sudras from the feet. But obviously the brahmans etc. already existed as social entities – an arrangement to which the hymn gave religious sanction. It is not at all the case that these divisions were created because the hymn said this must be done to carry out divine commands. All that the hymn does is to sanctify an accomplished social fact, which came into being independently of religious beliefs. In a society where some kind of easily recognisable distinction exists between religion and other beliefs and patterns of behaviour, as in western culture, a social arrangement such as the class system, even though approved by the Christian church at certain periods of western society, is not thought to be central to Christian beliefs. The kind of interweaving of religious and other forms of life that we find in Hindu society is not present in religions which have been introduced into a society through the teachings of a particular founder who had access or claimed to have access to a special truth, thought to be different from what the society in general believed in, either through personal enlightenment or revelation from God. I mean religions which are not the result of crystallisation of wisdom to which myriads of men have contributed over a long period of time, but were introduced into a society through special preaching, which required the rejection of at least some of the ways, beliefs and customs hitherto prevalent in the society in question. A religion which is founded in this fashion does not have the same kind of organic relationship to social practices as has a religion which has just grown out of a way of life and crystallised over a long period of history through the collective search of many men, never having been introduced into the society by anyone in particular at any particular time, as is the case with the Hindu religious tradition. This organic relationship is expressed through the fact that all forms of life in the traditional Hindu pattern have a religious dimension, one of the functions of religion having been to sanctify the ways of society and make them part of a 'sacred' tradition. However, it is possible to separate Hindu religious beliefs from Hindu culture in general, but even if we do this it will still be the case that we have to contend with several distinct types of beliefs and practices within the Hindu fold. These are not just sects that have branched off from one central body of doctrine or dogma originally preached by one person, and they would have been called distinct religions in themselves had they not all formed part of one distinctive cultural tradition.

This is why I believe that it is better to talk about the Hindu religious tradition than about the Hindu religion, thought to be a uniquely identifiable entity. Many writers on Hinduism have remarked about the profusion of forms and the tremendous diversity amongst them that characterise this religious tradition and yet they have referred to it as one religion, presumably because this diversity is held together by means of certain cultural factors whereby it does manage to appear as one entity. One of these is the caste system, under which all Hindus had traditionally lived no matter what the details of their religious beliefs, and in so far as this has been given a religious dimension it has somehow created the idea of a community even while dividing the society into little factions. The other is the doctrine of the law of karma and rebirth. This is really a metaphysical doctrine about the mechanism according to which everything happens in the world and its repercussion on human fortunes. Again, because of the religious dimension of this doctrine, it brings all Hindus within a common pattern of belief. Still another is the philosophical theory that all doctrines and beliefs are different formulations of one Truth expressed at different levels and in accordance with the different orientations of the people concerned who hold these beliefs. This sanctions diversity while at the same time making for the unity of the tradition as a whole. But before I go into the question of the unity of the Hindu religious tradition, I wish to talk about its diversity a little more and investigate why it is what it is.

The Hindu religious tradition has no founder – except a purely mythical one like the god Brahma, stories about whose activity began to appear at a certain point in the growth of this tradition. It did not even have a name of its own until one was given to it by non-Hindu observers. In the Hindu literature people refer to their religious tradition as *sanatana dharma* or eternal religion, which is hardly a name since religion according to the Hindu definition of this term can only be eternal. Ancient Indians had thought that their religion had always been there, and so it had in a sense, never having had any official beginning and never having been introduced through special preaching at any particular time.

Already in the *Rigveda*, which the tradition looks upon, along with three other Vedas, Brahmans, Aranyakas and Upanisads, as the foundation of all Hindu religious beliefs, the poets talk about still more ancient seers from whom they have heard thus and who are mentioned with admiration. But historically speaking the Vedas are not the sole source of the Hindu religious tradition. The tradition grew over a long stretch of time – and being a tradition it is still open – the beginnings of which are lost in antiquity by a slow process of accumulation, amalgamation, and refinement of beliefs and practices found in at least three distinct ethnic and culture groups already mentioned – the Aryan, the Dravidian, and the aboriginal tribal. These people happened to come together in India through historical circumstances and their ways of life gradually blended or were accepted as distinct and coexisting trends, to produce a composite and complex tradition. At no stage of the gradual shaping of this tradition was any belief or practice violently, (by which I mean through special effort requiring a total change in one's way of life), introduced or violently overthrown, although fighting over territory between different groups went on.

The blending of traditions took place through the gradual social process of originally distinct beliefs mutually influencing one another in course of coexistence, or through sheer acceptance of other peoples' beliefs as distinct elements in a complex social fabric. It seems to me that this was possible because all the cultures that were involved in this process allowed polytheism, whether or not they could be called pure polytheism, that is to say, lacking in all conception of the unity of religious reality. The Vedas certainly do not preach pure polytheism, for the conception of the unity of one reality manifesting itself in diversity is very much there. But the practical concern of the Vedas was the adoration and worship of the diverse manifestations of this reality in order that a good life may be obtained here on earth and in heaven afterwards, hence they can be called polytheistic. Polytheistic gods are certainly differently conceived in different cultures, but no matter how conceived in detail they are usually expressions of important human concerns with which men everywhere have to come to terms, such as life, death, suffering, sex, power – natural, social, and moral – and so on in one form or another. Polytheistic cultures can thus find their own gods or something very similar to them in other peoples' gods; (the Greeks, for instance, found Heracles in Krishna and Dionysus in Siva in India). This allows mutual influence and blending of cognate ideas between polytheistic cultures, cultures which have not been historically founded by anyone and which because of the multiplicity of their own beliefs do not demand adherence to any particular body of truth from everyone. Because of a lack of consciousness of a historical beginning of the belief held, which did not have to establish itself through gaining ascendency in course of active struggle over rival beliefs previously held by a people, there is less identification in polytheistic cultures with a definite and particular history of belief to which anything belonging to another definite and particular history is felt to be necessarily alien. Coexistence, mutual influence, and sometimes eventual synthesis is thus made possible between polytheistic cultural traits, including religious beliefs.

As already mentioned, there were three culture complexes involved in the process of accumulation and amalgamation that made the Hindu tradition. First, the tribal peoples, of whom there were many distinct groups in India, as mentioned in the *Mahabharata*. It is impossible to say how much influence was exerted by tribal beliefs and practices on the general body of the Hindu tradition, but to the degree that tribal groups contribute to the general composition of the Hindu population their ways of life also form a part of the composite tradition of the Hindus. Perhaps the tribal groups were not assimilated to any extensive degree, and even today there are many tribes in India who exist in varying degrees outside the Hindu pale. In any case, even when assimilated they constituted the lowest stratum of the Hindu society and seldom rose to positions of influence, unlike the Dravidian stratum of the people of India who perhaps blended with the Aryans much more easily, and significantly contributed to the development of the Hindu tradition. Nevertheless, the Hindu society probably did not remain immune to tribal ways, particularly at the village level, and some of these came to be a part of the huge and amorphous body of beliefs and practices that constitute the Hindu religious complex. It is generally thought that the Dravidians were accepted in the Hindu society as sudras, but this is highly implausible. As the Dravidian civilisation is now generally reckoned to have been more developed than that which the Aryans brought into India, it is unlikely that the kings, priests, teachers, and other skilled men of this civilisation, which, as recent archaeological researches show, was extensively spread over India, were everywhere reduced to menial service. They must have contributed to the higher functions of the new society that was coming into being, and were thus drafted into higher castes as well as into the lowest. The stories about Asura kings in the *Mahabharata* indicate as much (asuras were believed to be the opponents of the devas, who probably represent the Aryans).

The religious beliefs and practices of all the three peoples were an aspect of their life style and culture, their manners, customs, forms of social relationships, and so forth, and these did not exist as an independent body of doctrines on their own which could be taken over and imposed on others in isolation. So what followed from the coexistence and mixing together of cultures and races was a huge, uncoordinated, and enormously complex corpus of beliefs and practices – that is, a cultural tradition with many sub-traditions, and of this religion only formed an aspect. In course of time, similar trends coalesced to form more profound conceptions, and originally distinct trends either blended together to produce fresh ones or just continued to exist side by side, often with apparent contradiction. The result is that every shade of religious belief and practice

found anywhere in human communities, magic, animism, polytheism, a qualified version of pantheism, monism, theism and
even a qualified version of monotheism can be found within the
religious tradition of the people who are called 'Hindus'. All
of these can claim to be a genuine part of the tradition, in so far
as a tradition is one that is lived by people, but none of these
can claim to represent it in any exclusive manner.

The fact that the Hindu religious tradition has slowly
developed through what we may in this context refer to as a
natural process of social growth is reflected in the circumstance
that there is no Hindu church through which doctrines and
practices are propagated, not even an institutionalised and
organised clerical order with authority to decide what is or what
is not in accordance with Hindu beliefs. Indeed, whatever
beliefs and practices can be found amongst the population
called 'Hindu' can be thought to be a part of this tradition,
although not every stratum of the population was 'Sanskritised'
to the same degree, especially as Sanskritisation[9] happened
not through conversion but through slow assimilation of beliefs
and ways of living. And it is this state of affairs which makes
it extraordinarily difficult to say what 'the Hindu religion'
consists of, or even to decide what is meant by the term 'the
Hindu religion'. This is difficult even in respect of the written
tradition of the Hindus, but once we step out of that into the
body of beliefs and practices lived by all the people who are
called Hindus it becomes impossible to size it up. Added to
this is the difficulty that the term 'Hindu' also means a culture
and not just a religion, and it is perfectly possible for someone
who belongs to this culture but discards all religious beliefs
to call himself a Hindu. There are Hindu atheists and materialists
in India today as there were in 600 B.C. There was a time when
it was obligatory on all who belonged to this culture to adhere
to a caste pattern of life. But it is possible for individual Hindus
now to discard all of the things that traditionally form part
of the concept of belonging to a caste and yet remain a Hindu;
(this is different from saying that the caste system has lost its
hold on the Hindu mind, generally speaking). But even in respect

[9]This term is used to refer to the process whereby Aryan values were
assimilated by the non-Aryan strata of the Hindu peoples.

of Hindus who hold religious beliefs of some sort, there is no particular article of faith that can be said to be obligatory on all Hindus as the divinity of Christ is obligatory on Christians.

Perhaps some would say that it is obligatory on all Hindus to accept the authority of the Vedas, since those in ancient India who did not do so were branded as non-believers, (not non-Hindu, since the term 'Hindu' did not then exist). The trouble is, however, that lower caste and illiterate Hindus are generally not acquainted with the sacred literature (sruti) of the Hindus, and they probably have not even heard of the Vedas. And even though literate Hindus may assert that the Vedas constitute sacred literature, the number of Hindus who know what these books actually contain are extremely few indeed. And since the educational system of modern India makes no provision whatsoever for Hindus to come into contact with these books, even education does not help so as far acquaintance with written religious tradition is concerned.[10]

Belief in the sacredness of the Vedas (the term in this context includes the Upanisads), however, is a part of the written tradition, and many Hindu writers have traditionally claimed that the whole of this tradition, its beliefs, and practices have been derived from the Vedas. Some even claim that the Vedas constitute revealed literature. Now the Upanisads talk about Brahman and its identity with Atman, but nowhere in the discussions has it been suggested that this understanding has come to the sages from some source other than their experience. To say that this literature along with the rest of the divisions of knowledge possessed by Vedic men, (such as logic, grammar etc.), has been breathed forth by Brahman, as does Brihadaranyaka, hardly amounts to claiming revelation in the normal sense in which this term is understood in a religious context. The experience of the identity of Atman with Brahman may not be ordinary experience, and in some Upanisads it has been explicitly stated that man's Self (Atman) must reveal itself, it cannot be grasped by man's ordinary intelligence. But this Self-revelation is something quite different from what is called

---

[10]As a matter of fact, most Hindus probably believe in karma and rebirth, but as Buddhists and Jains believed in these as well, these cannot be treated as the hallmark of Hinduism, nor is it the case that a Hindu will cease to be a Hindu if he discards belief in karma or rebirth.

'revelation from God' in monotheism. As for the Vedas themselves, these consist of hymns addressed to gods by men who
mostly represent powerful natural phenomena, such as the
sun, the wind, lightning, fire etc. They also include abstract
functions such as moral and physical law, friendly compact,
liberality, speech, faith, and so on. There are also many Vedic
hymns in praise of various things and objects, not only natural
objects such as rivers, trees, and mountains, but also artifacts
such as the kettle-drum, the plough, the sacrificial post, and
the altar. The Vedas show a keen sensitiveness to man's natural
(in which animals are included) and social environment, and
these are treated as sacred, but they contain no injunction or
command from gods to men, nor do they contain any suggestion
to the effect that God, or a god, actually appeared before a
poet and revealed his nature to him. If these hymns contain
anything about the nature of gods, it has very much the appearance of human conception about this supposed nature and
not that of direct disclosure received from above. Sometimes,
no doubt, Vedic poets claim to be inspired by divine speech,
conceived as the goddess Vac, or some other divine power, such
as Indra, Agni, Prajapati, and so forth, in the way Homer and
Hesiod claimed to be inspired by the divine Muse. There is
one hymn in the *Rigveda* which hints that the truth the poet is
concerned with needs more than ordinary human intelligence
to fathom it, and even then it is not being explicitly claimed that
this truth has been revealed by God. More often, however, the
poets simply said that they searched their hearts and found the
truth there rather than that they received it from an external
source.

The fact that the Vedas contain a good deal of puzzlement
over the nature of truth and that some of the hymns even despair
of the possibility of men and even gods ever solving the mystery
of divine reality makes it impossible to believe that the poets
are claiming that anything was disclosed to them by an act of
revelation from above. Take, for instance, the following verse
from the *Rigveda* (I.164.4-6):

Who had beheld at birth the primal being?
Unripe in mind, in spirit undiscerning, I ask.
I ask unknowing, those who know the sages, as

one all ignorant, for sake of knowledge.
What was that One who in the unborn's image
hath stabilised and fixed firm these world's six regions?

Or:

Ye shall not find him who produced these creatures
another thing has risen up amongst you.
Enwrapt in mystery cloud, with lips that stammer,
hymn chanters wander and are discontended.

(*Rigveda*, X.82.7)

So they ask men,
'Ye thoughtful men inquire with your spirit'.

(*Rigveda*, X.81.4)

The famous Nasadiya Sukta (*Rigveda*, X.129.6–7) ends thus:

Who knows for certain? Who shall here declare it?
Whence was it born, and whence came this creation?
The gods were born after the world's creation,
Then who can know from whence it has arisen?

None knoweth whence creation has arisen,
And whether he has or has not produced it
He who surveys it in the highest heaven
He only knows, and haply he may not know.

And the *Rigvedic* hymn, X.121, contains this refrain, 'which god should we worship with our oblation?'

I do not wish to suggest that the *Rigvedic* poets do not offer various answers to these fundamental puzzles, but their answers constitute human attempts (however inspired we may think these are) at solving the ultimate mystery rather than revelation in any literal sense from God to the effect that His nature is such and such. Another difficulty is that many Vedic hymns concern matters of social rather than of religious interest, such as descriptions of marriage ceremonies, financial ruin caused by gambling, expression of desire for shining in disputation in learned assemblies, importance of giving gifts and so on, besides spells and charms of the *Atharva Veda*, and one wonders what is being revealed through these hymns except men's thoughts about the life they live.

Indeed the tradition itself does not even have one consistent idea about the nature of this revelation. One version of the sacredness of the Vedas is that these were revealed by Brahma (although his name does not even appear in the four Vedas) a particular god of the Hindu pantheon, to the first man Manu, who then revealed these to others, though even here there are several variations on the same theme. The other is that the Vedas contain truths that are eternally revealed, they were not revealed by anyone to anybody in particular at any one particular time, and the Vedic poets, through the purity of their hearts and the enlightenment of their intellect, just discovered the truths that are always there.

As for the whole of the tradition being derived from the Vedas, the three most important figures in the present Hindu pantheon, Siva, Krishna, and Kali or Durga (or the mother goddess with some other name) do not appear in their present form in the Vedas, although Siva and Krishna are foreshadowed in the relatively unimportant Vedic divinities, Rudra and Vishnu, and the mother goddess probably in the goddess Vac in the *Rigvedic* hymn X.125, where she is spoken of as the power behind the Universe. The ideas of these gods and goddesses as found now incorporate many things which are non-existent in the Vedas, the concept, for instance, of incarnation, or the use of the phallic symbol to represent god Siva's creative function. It is thus obvious that Vedic ideas have amalgamated with non-Vedic beliefs to produce the composite conceptions of important Hindu divinities. So the claim that the whole of the Hindu tradition can be found in the Vedas, whether or not the Vedas were 'revealed', cannot be accepted in a literal sense. Let me give another example to show that not all of what the Hindus believe today comes from the Vedas. The cows are generally treated with great respect in the Vedas, but this attitude of respect and veneration is extended to a great many other things as well, both animate and inanimate. Indeed there is hardly any human activity, natural object, or phenomenon which has not been treated in this reverential way in the Vedas. The laying of the foundation of a house is treated as a sacred activity, for instance. But there is no prohibition on the eating of beef to be found in the early books of the *Rigveda*.[11] Quite the contrary. According to descriptions given in the Vedas beef was being eaten even by priests on important sacrificial and ceremonial occasions. Yet 'not eating beef' became almost the defining characteristic of the Hindu religion at some stage, and this was claimed to be so by people who at the same time declared that all their beliefs came from the Vedas.

Nevertheless there is a sense in which the Vedas can be said to be the basis of the Hindu religious tradition, if not in all its details, in its orientation and philosophy at any rate. One of the characteristic facts of this tradition is its multiplicity of approaches to the divine and its use of a variety of models and pictures in elucidating the nature of divine reality. And this is already found in the Vedas. For the Vedic poets continued to make ever-fresh attempts at penetrating the divine mystery, and in course of this long quest produced every possible model that man can use in his search for the divine – polytheism, a qualified version of pantheism, monism, and even a qualified monotheism. This was possible because Vedic hymns were composed over many centuries by many people who give expression in these hymns to their very human attempt at comprehending the nature of divine reality. They do not expound a particular doctrine about this reality revealed to and shared by all in common. But the Hindu tradition, despite its multiplicity, does also show unity, as all traditions must. And this also comes from the Vedas, where it is explicitly declared that the truth is one, but sages call it by many names (*Rigveda* I.164). Not only do the Vedas proclaim this unity, they give expression to it in the way they conceive of the gods. Vedic gods are incompletely personified, and one of their important characteristics is that they frequently take on one another's function, the result being that differences between them do not appear to be final or clear-cut. The Vedic poets find it easy to address one god by the name of others. To quote *Rigveda* (II.1.3-4):

Thou, Agni, art Indra, the Hero of heroes

[11]Such is the ignorance of the Hindus in respect of their sacred literature that this revelation comes as a shock to most.

thou art Vishnu of the wide stride, adorable
thou, Brahmanaspati, art the Veda-knower, the wealth-finder
thou, the sustainer, unitest us with wisdom.

Thou, Agni, art King Varuna who upholds the law
thou as Mitra, wonder-worker, art to be worshipped;
thou art Arya man, Lord of the virtuous, delighting all,
thou art liberal Amsa in the assembly.

Again, *Rigveda* (III.54.17):

Great and lovely, O Poets, is this trait of yours
    that all you devas exist in Indra.

or *Rigveda* (VI.9.5):

A steady light, swifter than thought, is stationed
among the moving things to sow the way;
all the devas, of one mind and like wisdom,
proceed devoutly to that One intelligence.

Vedic gods easily merge into one another, so that one god,
Mitra-Varuna, is made out of two gods, Mitra and Varuna, and
they are even merged altogether and the result is referred to
either in the singular as all-god, or in the plural as all-gods.
Thus even while Vedic gods are conceived as separate entities,
they are also believed at the same time to be somehow one. The
Rigveda says this in so many words (III.55.1): 'Great is the
single Godhood of the devas.' This idea was later developed in
the Upanisadic doctrine of one reality manifesting itself in
diversities in different names and forms, and it is precisely
through means of this doctrine that the Hindu religious tradition, at least in so far as it is a literate tradition, has managed
to maintain itself as one tradition, despite its multiple origins
and the extreme diversity of its doctrines.

The traditional Hindu belief that all that one finds in the
Hindu religious tradition is derived from the Vedas has worked
for unity in another way. Even when some god or religious idea
has come from a different source, an attempt has been made to
show that this is nothing but a variant of something that is

contained in the Vedas, and the Vedas are versatile enough to lend themselves to this approach. For instance, various mother goddesses which belong to the popular religion of the Hindus at the folk level are most probably goddesses which were being worshipped by the people of India even before the Aryans arrived on the scene. In so far as the spread of the Aryan culture happened through accommodation, rather than by a total replacement of beliefs and customs, a claim was made at some stage that these goddesses, who remained in the form in which they had hitherto existed, were manifestations in different name and form of the Vedic mother goddess (a mother goddess, although not particularly prominent there, does in fact appear in the Vedas). The anthropological term 'Sanskritization' even though in the reverse, may be used in this connection to describe the process whereby things originally not belonging to the Vedas have been legitimised in their name.

Thus the idea that the Vedas are the sole source of the Hindu religious tradition is a myth, but the use of this myth was badly needed to give coherence to a diffused and many-faceted tradition that would altogether lack any semblance of unity otherwise. I am here using the term 'myth', not in the sense of a pure fiction that ought to be discarded, but in the sense of a presupposition that is made to function in such a way that a tradition and history are seen not only as one but also as sacred in its terms. In this sense a myth cannot be said to be simply true or false, since its function is to create a certain approach to facts which are transformed in the very process of approaching them in this manner. For instance, even if Siva, as he is conceived and worshipped by the Hindus, did originally belong more to the pre-Vedic culture of India than to the Vedic, as many scholars insist, the fact that the patronage of the Vedas was extended to Siva via the cognate conception of Rudra in the Vedas does actually make it possible for him to eventually belong to the Vedic tradition, in so far as the Hindu tradition is claimed to be Vedic, irrespective of his origin. It is in this way that the Vedas have acted as the foundation of the Hindu religious tradition rather than by supplying all the actual details of beliefs and practices of all subsequent times. Of course, as a matter of fact, a great deal of Hindu religious practices and not only its philosophy are still Vedic; Vedic sacraments are still in use, and although Hindu worship is now more tantric than Vedic it does contain various Vedic elements as well. But this by itself would not have created one tradition had the Hindus not seen all things that belong to their tradition as one, through using the idea of their origin in the Vedas.

But the fact that the Vedas, acting in this capacity, can legitimately be claimed to be sacred to the Hindu tradition does not make the compositions that constitute the Vedas and Upanisads other than so many attempts on the part of the human mind to comprehend the mysteries of reality as approached from a religious point of view. The Vedic seers may well be described as religious geniuses, and like all geniuses they were no doubt inspired, particularly when they found all that goes to make life 'sacred' via the conception of gods, but what they uttered were their own thoughts. If these can be said to be revealed truths, they are so only in the sense that the discovery of a scientific genius can be said to be a revelation. It is when we see the Vedas as human search for truth that their peculiar character as scriptures – I mean the fact that every shade of religious belief and attitude is contained therein and has in actual fact been legitimised in their name – can properly be understood and appreciated.

It is usual for people who become acquainted with the Hindu tradition via the Upanisads to believe that the Hindu religion has no room for a Personal God and that it stands for pantheism or monism that advocates an impersonal principle or force as the ultimate reality in which love has no place. This is a misconception. Already in the Vedas the gods were being addressed as our father, mother, brother, friend, saviour, and protector, and love was not only being offered to gods, acknowledgement of receiving it from them was also being made. But alongside this conception of gods being related to men in terms of human values, there is another mode of thought which treats of divine reality as a supra-personal (rather than impersonal) conscious principle, and it is out of desire for manifold expression that arose in this conscious principle that creation is said to have come about (*Rigveda*, X. 129). That is, the story of creation is being envisaged not in terms of man's needs but in terms of the need for divine reality to project itself in multiplicity. This, however, does not at all mean that human values have no place in this divine act of self-expression, for there is nothing that is outside of it. These values are then embodied in the conception of gods. The term 'deva' comes from the root 'div', meaning to shine, and this makes a deva or a god 'a shining being' (in other words, an embodiment of a human value). Anything that is brilliant, especially powerful or potent in the scheme of human life, whether that is a natural or a social fact, is called a god in the *Rigveda*, and such a deva enters into relationship with humans, (indeed without this relationship, which allows that men can approach the devas and via them the facts of life, it will be pointless to talk about them). But the *Rigveda* also conceives of God, the creator, and not just gods, and as creator He certainly is related to man in a most intimate way. To quote *Rigveda*, III, 54, 5-8 :

What pathways leadeth to the gods? Who knoweth this
    of a truth? and who shall now declare it?
Seen are their lowest dwelling places only, but
    they are in remote and secret regions.

All things they part and keep asunder; though bearing up
    the mighty gods they reel not
One is lord of what is fixed and moving, that
    walks, that flies, this multiform creation.

And :

Him we invoke for aid who reigns supreme,
    the lord of all that stands or moves, inspirer of the soul.
                                                (*Rigveda*, I.89.5)

The Upanisads continued to use both these languages, of a Personal God, and of the supra-personal non-dual essence of the universe. But in the period of the Brahmans, the literature that comes between the Vedas and the Upanisads, some important changes in belief had begun to take place. These books developed the idea of the magical potency of sacrifice, the acts by which men were supposed to get in touch with the gods, to such a degree that the priests had begun to claim that the gods could be compelled to act as men wished them to, (indeed it is pointless to project gods unless it is thought that they could be persuaded to act as men wish), if the ritual was correctly performed. The result was that the gods lost at least some of their importance, and this was usurped by the priest via his ability to handle power. This process of gradual loss of status for Vedic gods continued in the Upanisads, where both gods and rituals were accorded a place of secondary importance, interest being concentrated on the *understanding* of the essence of the universe and its actual realisation in man's own being. In accordance with this shift of interest the Upanisads talk not so much of gods, nor even of God, (although these concepts are not altogether absent), but of Brahman and Atman. The choice of the term 'Brahman' as different from God is significant, since through it an entirely different mode of approach, different from that of man's hopes and wishes, is made to the comprehension of divine reality. As projected beyond the terms of the specifically human need for love and protection, it becomes beyond description, and such concepts as our father, lord, saviour, or protector are no longer felt to be adequate to catch the immensity of divine reality. In order to lead man beyond his human concerns as embodied in the term he uses, Lord God, to describe divine reality, language of a most paradoxical kind is used to point to Brahman, (not to describe, because the inexhaustible immensity of Brahman cannot be described). Brahman is greater than the greatest and smaller than the smallest. It is the most far and the most near. It is 'within' us and outside us, and so on. But what Brahman is can be realised through man's own Self, the infinite and eternal essence that is already in man. The human personality, as we normally think of it, that is to say as bereft of this infinite and eternal essence, is a limited being, conditioned by its own name and form. To see the infinite in oneself is to burst the bonds of finitude and this is described under the metaphor of rivers entering the sea. This metaphor has been badly handled by commentators, who have jumped to the conclusion that what is being advocated is the loss of the reality of man and his merging into some impersonal pool. But the river entering the sea is supposed to become the sea by losing its individual name and form, and it is said in the Upanisads that he who knows Brahman becomes Brahman. The best indication of what becoming Brahman means is given in such terms as 'being', 'consciousness' and 'bliss'. So ultimately we do come back to human values, but these values are now seen in their cosmic dimension and not in a purely human context, (where they come tied up with the fulfilment of human needs and hopes).

But the concept of a supreme Personal God on whom man can centre his need for love and devotion is just as much a part of this complex tradition as anything else, and this is represented by devotionalism which perhaps developed outside the official sacrificial ritualism and mysticism of the Vedic aristocracy. For the Vedas may contain the concepts of God and love, but their orientation is not devotional. This trend in the Hindu tradition has probably come from the common people, whether Aryan or non-Aryan, and it is possible that the common people of India, even in Vedic times, followed a pattern of life that was somewhat different from that of the more sophisticated Aryan aristocracy about whom we hear in the Vedas and Upanisads. They had their own mode of approach to the divine, and devotionalism was probably the main expression of their religious sentiment. This sentiment of devotion may have been directed to a variety of gods, but these eventually crystallised into three main gods, Siva, Krishna, and Brahma, the last having been replaced at some point by a mother goddess Kali or Durga.

Devotionalism led to theism and even to a qualified version of monotheism. Monotheism in the Hindu context is qualified, for the tradition is such that any one of the three figures around whom religious devotion is centred can be treated as the Supreme Divine Being. Also belief in one God is not thought in this tradition to contradict the worship of many gods. Even monotheism could not be exclusive in the Hindu tradition because of the diversity of sources from which different conceptions of gods came, sources which all found a place within the totality of a tradition that is agglomerative rather than exclusive. This probably could not have happened if the development of this tradition was directed from one centre, but there was no such centre.

As the conceptions of these monotheistic gods came from different sources we find in Hindu myths and legends many instances of quarrels among sects trying to prove the supremacy of their own god over that of others. But characteristically the quarrel was over who should reign supreme rather than who should reign in an exclusive manner. Again characteristically, the philosophers took a hand in these disputes and settled the question by saying that the concepts of Siva, Krishna, and Kali (or Brahma) are different expressions of the same supreme divinity who is, in his unmanifested form, beyond description. This did not altogether stop sectarian bickerings, (hardly any of it exists now), but it made it possible for all these concepts of God to find a place within one tradition.

To mention just one or two more trends within the tradition, what we have discussed of the tradition so far agrees that there is one universal religious reality, whether we call it Brahman or God – Siva, Krishna, or Kali. But there had been people within the tradition who did not find it necessary to use any concept of universal import to give expression to their religious quest. This trend comes from Samkhya philosophy, which postulates that there is not one but two eternal principles, matter and spirit, and the spirit it talks about is not universal, the same Self that is in everyone, but a multiplicity of them, each eternal, and in its true essence, free of the spatio-temporal conditioning of the mind–body system. The religious aim of man here is simply to realise his spiritual freedom, not unity with God, not identity with Brahman. This spiritual freedom of man is lost through ignorance of man's true nature and ignorance consists in accepting the mind–body system as one's true being. Strange as it may seem this philosophy too claims to be derived from the Vedas, although this has been contested.

There are also men within the tradition (without this, however, being a part of the written tradition) who are imbued with a great love of God but who refuse to give any definite name to their God or to clothe Him in any kind of dogma or doctrine. They are called 'Bauls' and they reject all kinds of ritualistic worship followed by the orthodox Hindu of the Sanskritic tradition. This is a relatively modern phenomenon originating in the ranks of the lowest classes and castes of society who have no use for the Vedas or the conventional ritualism of the Vedic tradition. Indeed the Vedic tradition was deliberately barred from them by the dictates of the brahman law-givers. The Baul approach is one of direct communion with God and its simplicity and beauty is often found very attractive, even by the sophistica-ted upper castes. An attitude of mind which does not accord much importance to dogmas and doctrines regarding the nature of religious reality is, however, fairly common, even amongst people in the tradition who speak in the name of the Vedas, however much their lives may be hemmed in by superstitious ritualism of a social kind. As there are so many doctrines within the Vedic tradition itself, none of which taken by itself is thought to be obligatory on anyone who calls himself a Hindu, their importance has been compared to that of a ladder which we must use to get to the top of the roof, but having got there discard as no longer being of any use. In view of this fact that no particular trend within the Hindu tradition could be allowed exclusive validity, since they all speak in the name of the Vedas – amongst the learned, at any rate – it can easily be seen that the so-called revealed truths of the Vedas do not function here in the same way as do revealed truths in other religions. It seems to me that the Vedas have authority in the Hindu religious tradition primarily in the sense that it is by means of using this idea of the sacredness of the Vedas that the whole of this diffused and rather far-flung tradition can be kept together and sanctioned, that is, the Vedas can be appealed to by everyone as they cannot be used to prove that any particular doctrine held by anyone within the tradition, or way of approach to the divine, is false, not even the Baul approach; for there are many statements in the Vedas and Upanisads to the effect that the divine is beyond name and form and that ritualism is an unsafe craft in which to cross the ocean of this world. But to accept in this sense the authority of the Vedas for the Hindu religious tradition does not imply that God told the Hindus and only the Hindus what to think of Him and what not to think and that what this is can be found out from the Vedas. The Vedas certainly contain religious insight of a rich and varied kind – insight which cannot be sized up exclusively within one dogma or doctrine – which men of genuine spiritual enlightenment arrived at, and in so far as this is the case their value as religious literature does not have to be denied (embodying man's search for the divine and his attempt at finding an answer to the great riddle of life).

The Hindus did think of religious reality in a variety of modes and it seems that they were willing to try any concept or approach to see if it was going to get them any closer to the mystery which fascinated them. The Hindu attitude seems to be that the more the ways in which we, with our inevitable limitations, try

to fathom that which is all and beyond, the better is our chance
to catch a glimpse of it in its inexhaustibility. Even if the thoughts
of Hindu thinkers do not represent direct disclosures from above
they are certainly very valuable as expressions of manifold human
endeavours to penetrate the mystery of divine reality.   This
should not be taken to imply that what the Hindus say about
religious reality cannot have any truth in it. But this truth is a
human truth, and it belongs to the same order as truth in the field
of any other human endeavour such as art or science. Hindus
themselves do not claim exclusive validity or truth for any of
their doctrines and accept them all as different approaches to
the same Truth which in its inexhaustibility transcends man's
capacity to finally size it up in conceptual terms. In view of the
plurality of their own tradition this is the only way in which the
problem of truth could possibly be handled. I shall discuss this
issue more fully in a subsequent chapter.

This non-exclusive attitude Hindus have extended to religions
other than their own, and if the Hindus in recent centuries have
made any contribution to the Hindu tradition – and being a
religious tradition rather than a religion it is still open – it is in
asserting that all religions are so many different ways of reaching
the same religious reality. I do not mean by this that the roots
of this attitude do not lie deep in the tradition right back to the
Vedas, for it does, but there has not been much occasion in
ancient India to refer to religions other than the Hindu. (According to some interpretations a sneering attitude is shown in a few
Rigvedic hymns towards the worship of the phallus, but as this
symbol got assimilated into the mainstream of the tradition the
antagonism could not have been that deep.) This occasion was
presented to Ramakrishna,[12] the nineteenth century Hindu
saint, and he made acceptance of other religions an explicit
part of his teaching, claiming that they all reveal the same Truth
in different ways. And to show this acceptance means that he
personally, whilst still remaining a Hindu, adopted the Christian
and Islamic concepts of God and their mode of worship in his
search for religious reality; and this he claimed showed him that
all paths lead to the same divine consciousness, provided the
search is genuine, which is what ultimately matters.

---

[12]See *The Gospel of Sri Ramakrishna*, trans. Swami Nikhilananda.

I am not, however, saying that all Hindus do in fact – meaning at the level of practice – accept other religions on an equal footing with their own. What I am concerned with is the written tradition, what the books say, and with the teaching of people who are accepted in the tradition as wise, (there were mediaeval saints also who preached that all religions convey the same truths after Islam has entered India), and what is allowed Hindus consistently with their tradition. There is in all traditions a gap between what the ideal sets forth and what obtains in reality, and my object is simply to get the ideal straight. When it came to practice, Hindu sects did quarrel amongst themselves about the question of the supremacy of their own God over others, and such quarrels sometimes led to violence. No doubt most Hindus, like other human beings, prefer what they are used to and they are likely to quarrel if this preference is called into question. Also there was some quarrel between Hindus and Buddhists in India. But Hinduism and Buddhism existed side by side in India, influencing each other well over a thousand years, despite squabbles in some quarters, until the arrival of Islam, when Buddhism succumbed to the pressure and disappeared.[13] There could not be a deliberate and large-scale campaign carried out by Hinduism against Buddhism (or anything else) if for no other reason than this, that there was no Church or a comparable organised body to do the campaigning, quite apart from the fact that the Hindu mind, being used to a variety of beliefs within his own tradition, is not, by and large, passionately aroused at the thought of the existence of rival beliefs. Individual instances of intolerance and violence apart, (as distinct from organised violence as a deliberate policy), and no doubt some of this can be found in the long history of India, the fights between Hindus and Buddhists were academic, over points of philosophy rather than of practice and faith, and such academic fights considerably enriched the Indian philosophical tradition.

Academic mud-slinging can, however, be found in plenty amongst schools of philosophy in India which were all officially

---

[13]Buddhism, unlike Hinduism, was organised in institutions like churches, monasteries and universities, and the destruction of these institutions meant the disappearance of Buddhism as a religion.

in the believers' camp, (the Buddhists were branded by brahmans as non-believers because of their rejection of the Vedas as the source of religious authority). And if the Hindus called the Buddhists names, the Buddhists were not slow in retaliating. Debates and disputes in learned assemblies were a regular feature of intellectual life in India, right from Vedic times, (there is even a prayer in the *Rigveda* for intellectual brilliance in assembly), and this can hardly be called religious intolerance. Hindu academic attacks on Buddhism and its assimilation of elements of Buddhist beliefs in the characteristically Hindu way no doubt made Buddhism lose the intellectual prominence it had once enjoyed in India and it was already in decline, relatively to Hinduism, even before the advent of Islam. But it cannot be said that such attacks constituted persecution of Buddhists by the Hindus. According to the concept of Rajdharma (the duty of the king or state) in ancient India, kings were supposed to maintain ascetics and mendicants of all descriptions, whether they belonged to their own or 'heretical' orders, and as far as one can gather from the *Arthasastra* of Kautilya and edicts of Asoka, this was what was generally practised, though here again exceptions can no doubt be found.

As the Hindu religious tradition itself was so diffused and many-sided, and as it functioned by acceptance and incorporation of diverse beliefs and practices, it did not find it impossible eventually to suggest that Buddha himself was one of the incarnations of God, or to incorporate some of the Buddhist concepts into its own systems. Because of the multiplicity and plurality of their own tradition, most Hindu thinkers seem to be able to take differences of belief in their stride and not get unduly excited over them, particularly since their own tradition stresses knowledge of God in the sense of actual experience and not in the sense of correct statements about His nature.

But what I have particularly in mind in talking about this particular feature of the Hindu religious tradition are various statements to be found in Hindu religious scriptures which allow a Hindu to accept all conceptions of God and all paths of approach to Him, (that is, differences of belief and practice) as different but equally valid expressions of the same fundamental search. Indeed if a Hindu understands the significance of his own tradition, where many gods and many paths do as a matter

of fact co-exist, and where all of these are recognised as legitimate, he ought to be able to accept, (and I think that most
Hindus do as a matter of fact accept this *in theory*, at least),
that this applies outside his own tradition as well. For when the
'sacred' books talk about differences in name and form, they
do not mean differences to be found *within the Hindu tradition*,
for the concept of a Hindu tradition, as opposed to a non-
Hindu one, did not then exist. When they talked about differences they no doubt meant differences they knew about, but the
general tenor of their statements makes it clear that they were
not talking about any specific set of differences, but about the
fact of difference as such. And there is no reason why this should
not be taken to mean differences wherever they are to be found,
within and across traditions. As a matter of fact, there is a
verse in the *Atharvaveda*[14] (VII.52), which does suggest that the
Vedic poets meant to include people other than themselves in
their thoughts.

Let us have concord with our own people
and concord with people who are strangers to us;
Asvins, create between us and the strangers
a unity of hearts.

May we unite in our hearts, unite in our purposes
and not fight against the divine spirit within us.
Let not the battle cry rise amidst many slain
nor the arrows of the war-god fall with the break of day.

Here it is being explicitly recognised by the Vedic poet that
the divine spirit within the strangers and themselves is the same,
so there should be concord.

I shall now give a few quotations from Hindu books as examples of what I have just said. To quote the *Atharvaveda* (IV.16.8) :

Varuna is that which exists alongside
Varuna is that which exists crosswise
Varuna is of our own land, He is of
foreign land. Varuna is divine, he is human.

[14]*Hymns from the Vedas.* A.C. Bose, p. 205.

'Varuna is of foreign land' cannot mean that other people actually accept this name as the name of their God, or that they conceive their God exactly as Varuna is conceived under another name. The point is that difference in name or conception is unimportant, and while divine names and corresponding beliefs are different divine reality is the same towards which they are all directed. What matters is actually to be in touch with this reality, and one can do so, for Varuna is divine but he is also human. In the *Gita* this is expressed in a different way by saying that God lives in the heart of each man.

This point about the relative unimportance of name and form is explicitly made in *Rigveda* (I.164.46). Here it is said that one should try to know the divine reality, to which many a name may be ascribed, and not get stuck at the level of names only, for differences of name, in this instance, do not make for differences in reality.

They call him Indra, Mitra, Varuna, Agni, and
he is heavenly nobly winged Garutman.
To what is one, sages give many a name
They call it Agni, Yana, Matarisvam.

Again, says *Rigveda* (X. 114.5), 'The wise poets with their words shape the one Being in many ways'.

The *Bhagavadgita*, which is itself an attempt at synthesis between the Upanisadic approach and the devotional one, recognises the fact of diversity of beliefs and paths and accepts them as legitimate. While advocating a personal God, Krishna, it at the same time allows man to follow the path of knowledge, which consists in the contemplation of Brahman, only this is qualified by saying that this is a much harder path. It also recognises that people may worship God under some other name and form than Krishna, but this will not in any way jeopardise their chance for liberation. Indeed, Krishna says in the *Gita* that in whichever way a devotee worships God, in the same way does he, Krishna, make himself available to him. This is why the *Gita* can be used as a religious scripture by all sects in India. To quote (7.21), 'Whichever deity a devotee wishes to worship with dedication, in the same divinity do I make his devotion unwavering.' The same sentiment recurs in verses (4.11) : 'However men approach me, even so do I welcome them, it is my path, O Partha, that men take from every side.' Again, says Krishna, (9.23) : 'Dear Kaunteya, those who with real devotion worship other gods, they do in fact worship me, even if that may not be in accordance with prescribed acts.'

This makes it clear that the *Bhagavadgita* is not insisting, even when putting forward the idea of Krishna as the supreme God, that all men who seek God must do so under the name and form of Krishna. As the divine reality is the same towards which all religious search is directed, worshipping other gods will in effect mean worshipping Krishna himself, when by Krishna is meant not a particular name and form, but divine reality itself (as disclosed to Arjuna in its universal form).

The Hindu scriptures do not insist that in order to be a true believer a particular body of doctrines and God with a definite name and form must be adopted and that anything other than what is being recommended must be rejected. Instead the *Rigveda* says (X.63.2) :

All your names devas ! are worthy of our homage worthy of our praise, and worthy of our worship.

And says the *Bhagavatam:* 'Like the bee gathering honey from different flowers, the wise man accepts the essence of different scriptures and sees only the good in all religions.'[15] Even the insistence on the Vedas in the written tradition does not amount to much, since the Vedas have been found by the Hindus to be consistent with every form of belief that can be possibly held by man. Indeed, the concept of a false god seems to be foreign to this tradition and attack on other people's religious beliefs and practices (as distinct from philosophical disputes) not very common even in secondary Hindu scriptures (some of it can be found in the Puranas), while it hardly exists at all in the primary sources of Hindu beliefs, the Vedas (except for one or two possible references to phallus worship), the Upanisads and the *Gita*.

It would be a pity if this is taken to mean that my purpose here is to glorify the behaviour of the Hindus who by no means live up to the possibilities that their tradition offers (although in

[15] *Srimad Bhagavatam*, trans. Swami Prabhabananda, p. 216.

this particular respect they behave better than in others). My only concern is with the highest possibilities of man that can be conceived in accordance with the positive contentions of this religious tradition and acceptance of other people's religions and ways of life as just as valid as one's own seems to me one of these.

CHAPTER II

Some Relevant Hindu Beliefs

It will perhaps be useful here to consider certain general Hindu beliefs which have an intimate bearing on Hindu religious thinking. These are : (1) Hindu cosmology, the conception of space, time, and life as infinite and not produced by any once-for-all act of creation; (2) the doctrine of Karma and reincarnation; (3) the concept of varnasrama dharma, or four ends and stages of life, and (4) the doctrine of adhirakiveda or competence.

Many non-Hindu writers on Hinduism have been appalled by the boundless fancy and extravagance of imagination displayed by Hindu myths and legends. Some of this distaste for fancy is cultural and it arises out of an inclination to take everything said in an extremely literal fashion, which is how western intellectuals usually judge the meaning of a statement made. Because the Hindu tradition does not insist on applying rigidly clear-cut categories in the field of religious thinking, Hindus often do not look at religious statements made from the point of view of finding out whether they are to be labelled as 'fact' or 'fancy', and they will claim that certain facts can be best conveyed through the use of fancy. For instance, giving extra limbs, heads etc., to images of gods and goddesses may be a means of conveying the message that even though they are being conceived under the image of man they remain enormously more endowed with power than human beings. Thus the question whether the god Brahma, who as portrayed in images looks like a man in every other respect, does in actual fact have four heads, one in each direction, east, west, south, and north, or whether it is just a piece of fancy is a question that a typical Hindu does not feel called upon to settle. He is content to let this image perform the job it is supposed to perform, that is, convey the suggestion that the creator god is all-seeing, without caring much about the logical distinction between 'fact' and 'fancy', that is, whether the heads are literally there. An illiterate Hindu will no doubt normally take the heads as actually there, but a sophisticated Hindu will calmly accept the factual non-existence of these heads and, indeed, if need be, of Brahma himself, and yet find the employment of this image meaningful. He will therefore continue to talk about the four heads of Brahma in appropriate contexts without feeling that he is indulging in pure fancy.

The underlying belief seems to be that images and statements can perform the job of making us see things in a certain light, even if we have not antecedently decided as to the level at which these are to be interpreted, that is, they do their work without any conscious reflection on our part as to exactly how they are to function. Since it is admitted in this tradition that meaning is partly symbolic, sometimes at any rate, if not always, and that this symbolic meaning can be conveyed to us even if we ourselves believe that the meaning is literal and do not quite understand its symbolic function on a conscious level, it is not essential that a clear-cut separation between the literal and symbolic elements in a statement should be made at the outset before we understand what it means. At any rate religious meanings do not have a fixed character and the same statement may operate at different levels and yield different meanings even to the same person, if he is prepared to allow this to happen.

However, there is a sense in which this charge of unrestricted imagination is justified, for not only are there an endless number of tales, each with many different versions and with different embellishments, to be found in a profusion of scriptures, both primary and secondary, in the Hindu tradition, but the tales themselves are progressively blown beyond all proportion as we move from book to book (showing an insatiable desire for further and further magnification of possibilities). Take, for instance, the story of Krishna's exploits with women. In the *Vishnu Purana* this has no great importance, and all that is mentioned in this *Purana* is that whilst still a boy Krishna assumed the appearance of a youth and danced with a multitude of cowherd girls, fulfilling their romantic urge towards him (as a part of divine bestowing of favours). As we move from *Vishnu* to *Bhagavat Purana*, a time-span of four centuries, the Hindu myth makers display an inordinate desire for further and further magnification of Krishna's exploits. In the *Bhagavat Purana*, apart from having several wives and sporting with the gopis (cowherd girls), Krishna is also portrayed as carrying off sixty thousand women at one go, and his exploits in this direction are in other Puranas embellished beyond recognition compared to the rather innocent story of the *Vishnu Purana* – where the idea that the incarnate God can be all things to all beings, including love between sexes, first takes shape. Whatever may be the full explanation of this tendency for imaginative extravagance, it ties up with the Hindu desire to operate with a huge canvas and on a vast scale which inclines them to push thought to the furthest limits of all possibilities.

This tendency is shown abundantly in Hindu cosmology, as in all activities and doctrines. One of the reasons no doubt is the importance in the Hindu tradition of the concept of limitlessness (ananta). Freedom from limitations involved in all name and form is an integral part of the Hindu concept of fullness and perfection and a liberated man is supposed to achieve this limitlessness here on earth. As Troy Wilson Organ remarks, 'The high value placed upon the absence of limit is witnessed in many facets of Hindu culture: detailed sculpturing of temples, the music that seems to go on interminably, the cyclic theory of time, the lack of interest in originations and eschatologies, the open canon of scriptures, the unwillingness to draw sharp lines between animals, men and gods, and the effort to see conflicting philosophies as compatible doctrines.'[1] Although Hindu cosmology was purely mythical, (that is, it was not arrived at through a process of serious scientific or rational thinking), it comes surprisingly close in some respects to modern scientific theories about the extent of the universe and its duration in time, through letting the imagination have limitless freedom to play with vast expanses of space and time. It was because the canvas was so vast that the Hindus could even anticipate the evolutionary doctrine and say that life has passed through 8,400,000 species before it took the form of human life. 'According to some Hindu commentators of scriptures a jiva is granted a human body only after going through 8,400,000 previous incarnations of lower forms of life– 2,000,000 as plant, 900,000 as an aquatic, 1,100,000 as an insect, 1,000,000 as a bird, 3,000,000 as a cow and 400,000 as

[1]*The Hindu Quest for the Perfection of Man*, p. 146.

a monkey.'[2] This again shows the huge scale on which everything is conceived in the Hindu scriptures.

The reason why I am discussing all this here is this. There
are trends in Hindu thinking which are not satisfied by putting
forward as the end of man's aspiration a heaven which men
may attain through God's grace and where they would live
under his loving care in perfect harmony, (although this model
is certainly present in the Hindu tradition). To my mind this is
because the goal appears limited in the background of the
vastness of space and time – (men may inhabit different uni-
verses during different periods of their progress towards limitlessness) – with its millions of forms of life, in the context of
which the eternal human drama takes place, according to the
Hindu tradition. Hindu aspiration has been, at least one typical
Hindu aspiration, to be unlimited beyond all bonds of finitude,
and this can only be attained by identification with the universe
and its ground, not by living in heaven. This desire for bound-
lessness is shown in all Hindu speculations, myths and legends,
and generally in the extravagance of their imagination.

According to the Hindu tradition there is no such thing as a
once-for-all creation at a particular time from which progress
towards a definite end, again once-for-all, can be calculated.
The movements of things in time is in a circle and not in a
straight line, and if there is a built-in tendency in things to
progressively get better, there is also the tendency to progressively deteriorate when a certain height of perfection has been
reached. But when things have touched bottom there will
inevitably be an upward movement as there will be a downward movement once perfection has been reached. This gives us
the doctrine of a cycle of four yugas : Krita, the golden age
when everything is pretty well perfect and men behave like
saints; Treta, when there is one-quarter imperfection; Dwapara,
when imperfection equals perfection; and Kali, the most degenerate age when things are three-quarters imperfect. After the
completion of a cycle of four yugas everything is supposed to
start getting better and reach perfection but thereby also inevitably introduce the downward process of degeneration. So the
universe cannot be said to have any absolute beginning in time

[2]*The Nature of Hinduism*, Louis Renou, p. 67.

or absolute end, and the movement from beginning to end is always complemented by a fresh beginning. This is so because the ground of all existence is eternal and this moves from an unmanifested state to manifestation and then back to the unmanifest state again, and this process goes on being repeated. I shall now quote from the *Vishnu Purana* to show how all this has been mythically conceived.

Vishnu being the source of all existence is both its material and efficient cause, the material potentiality of the world is there eternally – it is called Pradhaha or Prakriti – but only in creation does it take a manifested form. The first step towards manifestation takes place when the pure potentialities (essence) of the elements, called tanmatras, ether, air, light, water, and earth emerge. These being pure potentialities are not yet endowed with qualities. 'Having combined therefore with one another they assumed through their mutual association the character of one mass of entire unity and from the direction of Spirit, with the acquiescence of the indiscrete[3] principle, intellect and the rest to the gross elements inclusive formed an egg which gradually expanded like a bubble of water. This vast egg, O sage, compounded of the elements and resting on the waters, was the excellent natural abode of Vishnu in the form of Brahma, and there Vishnu, the lord of the universe, whose essence is inscrutable, assumed a perceptible form, and even he himself abides in it in the character of Brahma. . . .In that egg, O brahman, were the continents and seas and mountains, the planets and divisions of the universe, the gods, the demons and mankind.'[4] This one egg develops into the earth as well as other regions in space. The earth is composed of seven continents and seven oceans. The account is mythical, and continents and oceans are imagined to encircle one another, the oceans being composed of milk and butter, treacle etc., the last being of fresh water. 'Beyond the sea of fresh water is a region of twice its extent, where the land is of gold and where no living beings reside. Thence extends the Lokaloka mountain which is ten thousand yoganas in breadth and as many in

---

[3] that is, the principle of materiality.

[4] *Vishnu Purana*, Vol. I, pp. 38–40, in collected works of H.H. Wilson, Vol. VI (London, Trubner & Co. 1864).

height; and beyond it, perpetual darkness invests the mountain all around; which darkness is again encompassed by the shell of the egg. Such Maitreya is the earth, which with its continents, mountains, oceans and exterior shall is fifty crores (five hundred million) of yoganas in extent.'[5]

But besides the earth, there are other regions of the universe that evolve out of one egg. There are seven regions below the earth called Atala, Vitala, Nitala, Gambhastimat, Mahatala, Sutala, and Patala, where dwell Danavas, Daityas, Yakshas, and snake gods. Below these are twenty-eight hells. There are also spheres above the earth. 'The sphere of the earth (or Bhuloka) comprehending its oceans, mountains and rivers, extends as far as it is illuminated by the rays of the sun and moon, and to the same extent both in diameter and circumference the sphere of the sky (Bhuvar-loka) spreads above it (as far upwards as to the planetary sphere or Swar-loka).'[6] Then follows a description of planets and stars covering millions of leagues, the furthest of which is called Dhruva (the pole star). 'Above Dhruva at the distance of ten million leagues lies the sphere of saints (or Mahar-loka), the inhabitants of which dwell in it throughout a kalpa (or day of Brahma). At twice that distance is situated Jana-loka, where Sanardana and other pure-minded sons of Brahma reside. At four times the distance of the last two lies the Tapaloka (the sphere of spiritual heat), inhabited by deities called Vairajas and who are unconsumable by fire. At six times the distance (or twelve crores – a hundred and twenty million leagues) is situated Satya-loka (the sphere of truth), the inhabitants of which never again know death.'[7] Again, 'The region which extends from the earth to the sun, in which the siddhas and other celestial beings move, is the atmospheric sphere which also I have described. The interval between the sun and Dhruva, extending fourteen hundred thousand leagues, is called by those who are acquainted with the system of the universe, the heavenly sphere. These three spheres are termed transitory. The three highest, Janas, Tapas, and Satya, are

[5]*Vishnu Purana*, Vol. II, in collected works of H.H. Wilson, Vol. VII, pp. 204–205.

[6]*Ibid*, p. 224.

[7]*Ibid*. p. 227.

durable. Mahar-loka, as situated between the two, has also a mixed character, for although it is deserted at the end of the kalpa it is not destroyed. These seven spheres, together with the Patalas, I have thus, Maitreya, explained to you.'[8]

But space is infinite and the system of the universe which has just been described comprising different spheres is not the only system in creation. 'The world is encompassed on every side, and above and below by the shell of the egg (of Brahma) in the same manner as the seed of the wood apple is invested by its rind. Around (the outer surface of) the shell flows water, for a space equal to ten times (the diameter of the world). The waters again are encompassed exteriorly by fire, fire by air, and air by ether, ether by the origin of the elements (Ahamkara) and that by intellect. Each of these extends ten times the breadth of that which it encloses, and the last is encircled by (the chief principle) pradhana, which is infinite and its extent cannot be enumerated. It is therefore called the boundless and illimitable cause of all existing things, Supreme (nature) or Prakriti, the cause of all mundane eggs, of which there are thousands and tens of thousands, millions and thousands of millions, such as has been described.'[9]

Thus by sheer force of imagination the ancient Hindus arrived at the idea of an infinite universe and of the existence of millions of systems in it. As J. Muir[10] remarks, the compilers of Puranas in reality knew nothing of any part of the world except that immediately around them, let alone of different systems of universe. But it seems to me that their boundless fancy and exaggerated imgination did serve them well in this instance, for they came closer to an appreciation of the vastness of the universe and of the existence of an infinite number of systems in it than is generally to be found in mythical accounts.

But the scale is vast not only in terms of space, it is vast in terms of time as well. 'Affecting the quality of activity, Hari, the lord of all, himself becoming Brahma engaged in the creation of the universe. Vishnu with the quality of goodness and of

[8]*Ibid.*, p. 231.

[9]*Ibid.*, pp. 231–232.

[10]See *Original Sanskrit Texts*, (Amsterdam Oriental Press, 1967), Vol. I, p. 504.

immeasurable power preserves created things through successive ages, until the close of the period termed a kalpa, when the same mighty deity, Janardana, invested with the quality of darkness, assumes the awful form of Rudra and swallows up the universe. Having thus devoured all things and converted the world into one vast ocean the supreme reposes upon his mighty serpent couch amidst the deep. He awakens after a season, and again as Brahma becomes the author of creation.[11] Vishnu is indeed the universe and the source of the universe, so 'Vishnu as creator creates himself, as preserver preserves himself and as destroyer destroys himself at the end of all things.[12] Then follows an account of the measure of time during which creation and destruction take place. These times are vast and they are calculated according to three different systems, that of Brahma, of gods and of men. Gods live in a different world from men, so their system of calculating time is not the same as man's, and Brahma being the creator calculates time on yet another scale. '...Six months form an Ayana (the period of the sun's progress north or south of the ecliptic) and two Ayanas compose a year. The southern Ayana is a night and the northern a day of the gods. Twelve thousand divine years each composed of three hundred and sixty such days constitute the period of the four yugas or ages. They are thus distributed: the Krita age has four thousand divine years, the Treta three thousand, the Dwapara two thousand, and the Kali age one thousand. So those acquainted with antiquity have declared. The period which precedes a yuga is called a Sandhya and it is of as many hundred years as there are thousands in the yuga; and the period that follows a yuga, termed the Samdhyamsa, is of similar duration. The interval between the Sandhya and Samdhyamsa is the yuga denominated Krita etc. The Krita, Treta, Dwapara, and Kali constitute a great age or aggregate of four ages, a thousand such aggregates are a day of Brahma; and fourteen Manus reign within that time. Hear the division of time which they measure: seven rishis, certain (secondary) divinities, Indra, Manu, and the kings, his sons, are created and perish at one period, and the interval called

[11] *Vishnu Purana*, Vol. I, p. 41, Wilson, Collected Works, Vol. VI.
[12] *Ibid.*, p. 42.

a Manwantara is equal to seventy-one times the number of years contained in the four yugas, with some additional years; this is the duration of the Manu, the attendant divinities and the rest which is equal to 852,000 divine years or to 30,672,000 years of mortals independent of the additional period. Fourteen times this period constitute a Brahma day, that is, a day of Brahma, the term (Brahma) being the derivative form. At the end of this day a dissolution of the universe occurs when all the three worlds, earth and the regions of space are consumed with fire. The dwellers of Maharloka (the region inhabited by saints who survive the world), distressed by heat, repair then to Janaloka (the region of holymen after their decease). When the three worlds are but one mighty ocean, Brahma who is one with Nanayana satiate with the demolition of the universe sleeps upon his serpent bed – contemplated as the lotus born by the ascetic inhabitants of Janaloka – for a night of equal duration with his day; at the close of which he creates anew. Of such days and nights is a year of Brahma composed and a hundred such years constitute his whole life.'[13]

According to Wilson we have in the first place a computation of the years of the gods in the four ages as:

Krita Age	4000	
Sandhya	400	
Samdhyamsa	400	
	————	4800
Treta Age	3000	
Sandhya	300	
Samdhyamsa	300	
	————	3600
Dwapara Age	2000	
Sandhya	200	
Samdhyamsa	200	
	————	2400
Kali Age	1000	
Sandhya	100	
Samdhyamsa	100	
	————	1200
	Total	12,000

If these divine years are converted into years of mortals by multiplying them by 360 (a year of man being a day of the gods) we obtain the years of which the yugas of mortals are respectively said to consist:

4800 × 360	1,728,000
3600 × 360	1,296,000
2400 × 360	864,000
1200 × 360	432,000
Total	4,320,000
	= A Mahayuga

Thus 4,320,000,000 years (that is, a Mahayuga × 1000 = 4,320,000,000 in human years) constitute a day or a night of Brahma.

There are two terms used in respect of dissolution in the Puranas, dissolution (pralaya), which happens at the end of a day of Brahma, and great dissolution (mahapralaya), which happens at the end of a life of a particular Brahma (who has a lifetime of 100 years). It is not clear what is dissolved at each period, maybe pralaya affects only our system in the universe and mahapralaya all the millions of systems. Anyway, dissolution is conceived to be both partial and total. But as we have seen creation starts again and thus the universe goes on without any real beginning or end, despite periodic dissolution partial or total – for dissolution is only a reabsorption of the manifested stuff of the universe into the primal potentiality of the Prakriti (principle of materiality) which constitutes the lower nature of Brahma or Vishnu and not total annihilation.

All this of course is purely mythical and, there is no doubt, a product of fantastic imagination. Nevertheless it can be so interpreted as to be not too far off from some modern cosmological speculations. According to some authorities the present universe was created as zero time some 13 aeons past (13,000,000,000 years ago) when the 'matter and energy of the universe were actually and literally squashed together into one huge mass' which the Belgian astronomer G.E. Lemaître called the cosmic egg.[14] Also, the Hindu theory of the eternality of the universe is supported by the law of conservation of energy which implies, as Asimov says, that the substance of the universe is essentially eternal.[15] Asimov suggests that the substance of the universe before the formation of the cosmic egg might have existed in order that it could remain stable over countless aeons, in the form of an exceedingly thin gas. 'The universe would then be the kind of empty space that now exists between the galaxies and that is certainly stable.'[16] This has its counterpart in the Hindu conjecture that at the time of the great dissolution everything goes back to the primal Prikriti (the potential state of the material universe, avyakta Prakriti) which, so long as it remains in a state of equilibrium or stability has no visible manifestation. According to the scientific view we are considering, that is, of the hyperbolic universe, 'The universe starts in a state of virtual emptiness, goes through a phase of contraction to maximum density and then through a phase of expansion to emptiness again. We do not have to puzzle ourselves over a cosmic egg that exists to begin with and then after an indefinite period of stability, suddenly exploded. Instead the cosmic egg becomes a momentary object placed midway in eternity.'[17] This contraction and expansion may mythically be labelled as the day and night of Brahma or his birth and death. According to the hyperbolic universe thesis what is eternal is emptiness. 'It begins with an empty universe with a thin gas, presumably hydrogen. It ends as an empty universe filled with innumerable white dwarfs. There is a definite beginning and a definite end and we inhabit the brief interval of time during which the universe deviates for an instance from its eternal emptiness.[18] This is not so according to the Hindu account, for although it is emptiness at the night or death of Brahma, and it lasts a long while, equal to the period of duration of creation, Brahma himself is dissolved into Brahman or Vishnu, who potentially holds within himself eternal possibilities of manifestation. These appear, disappear, and reappear

[14]See *The Universe*, Isaac Asimov (Pelican), p. 236.
[15]*Ibid.*, p. 236.
[16]*Ibid.*, p. 244.
[17]*Ibid.*, p. 245.
[18]*Ibid.*, p. 245.

in cycles without ever being exhausted. So hopefully another cosmic egg will be formed and creation will repeat itself. If, as Asimov says, the substance of the world is eternal then given enough time – if there is no such thing as end of time, millions and billions of years are available – there is no reason why another cosmic egg cannot form itself.

The Hindus mythically anticipated another scientific doctrine, that of evolution, not only progressive origination in higher and higher forms of all living things, but also the origination of life from matter. This again they could do because according to the Hindu tradition all is Brahman, from inanimate matter to divinities in heaven in different name and form. 'The various stages of existence, Maitreya, are inanimate things, insects, fish, birds, animals, men, holy men, gods and liberated spirit, each, in succession, a thousand degrees superior to that which precedes it, and through these stages the beings that are either in heaven or in hell are destined to proceed until final emancipation be obtained.'[19] According to the Hindu tradition there are 8,400,000 forms of flora and fauna, and the same class of being, the jiva, occupies these species, as all life is constituted of one principle, including human life. A human life is obtained only after life has travelled through all the previous stages of existence in the shape of lower forms of life.[20] Man's superiority to other forms of life, including that of gods, lies in his capacity to consciously seek liberation, that is, integration with the non-dual essence of existence beyond the particularities of name and form. This the gods, being steeped in pleasure, or animals, being non-self-conscious, cannot do. Nevertheless he occurs in a continuous series of manifestations of essentially the same life principle (this being in the ultimate analysis an expression of Brahman in the world of multiplicity).

We can now have a look at the Hindu doctrine of the law of Karma and reincarnation. One of the important concepts to be found in the Vedas is rita, cosmic law or order. This was later transformed into the concept of dharma. According to this concept, not only is the universe law-governed, everything has its own nature or dharma (law of its being) and this makes it

---

[19] *Vishnu Purana*, Vol. II, p. 221, Collected Works, Wilson, Vol. VII.
[20] See pp. 45-46.

function in a particular way expressive of its inner being. So nothing that happens just happens, it has a cause or rationale that explains why it happens. In the Vedic period rita although conceived to be eternal, was also thought to have a divine upholder in the form of Indra, Varuna, Agni, or some other deity. But when the concept of dharma took shape this external support was discarded and dharma was thought to function by its own inner dynamics.

One of the obvious facts of life is differences and inequalities between men, differences in caste status and inequalities of natural endowment as well as of the amount of suffering and enjoyment that men undergo. This cannot be a matter of chance or haphazard arrangement if everything is governed by law. The caste system itself is an example of order in society, so a man's duties and obligations as determined by his caste becomes a part of the general concept of lawfulness or order. These along with his natural endowments determine a man's dharma, what he is and how he functions and fares in life. This dharma, expressing the law of a man's being is not something that is imposed on him from the outside, on the contrary, it is a result of his own karma or action. In other words, the assumption is that it is not an accident that men are born into different heredity and environment as a result of which they fare differently in life; the differences are expressions of the functioning of a law, the law of karma.

But actions performed by men in this life cannot account for the differences in their heredity and environment (caste status etc.) which appear to be given before any action takes place. So the karma that determines man's dharma in this life can only be the karma of a previous life. That is, there must be rebirth according to karma to explain different fortunes of men in this life.

It may well be that belief in rebirth came first and the law of karma was produced as an explanation of this belief rather than that the Hindus came to believe in rebirth because the law of karma required it. But both concepts are tied up with the idea of dharma or law and what I am concerned with is the rationale of these concepts in relation to one another rather than their exact chronological sequence (this in any case will be conjectural considering the paucity of historical data). For rebirth, too, no

matter how this idea came to be there, was required by the idea
of dharma. In the early Vedic age the result of good and bad
action performed by men was enjoyment of heaven and suffering
in hell in a straightforward manner, and rebirth on earth was
not thought of. Some commentators believe that this idea does
occasionally appear in the Vedas, but there is in the *Rigveda*
only the vaguest of hints about the possibility of return and no
unambiguous reference to a belief that people actually are being
born again. In a funeral petition in *Rigveda*, 10.16.3, it is
requested that the vital principle of the deceased should go to
heaven, or to earth, or to the waters, or abide in the plants,
and in hymn 10.14.8, the soul of the deceased is asked to return
home again. There is also a petition to Agni that the spirit of
the dead be again associated with the body. But no firm belief
that people do, as a matter of fact, get born again is to be
found. By the time of the Upanisads, when the concept of
rebirth came into its own, the enjoyment of pleasures in heaven
was no longer thought to be the most desirable thing for man
to aspire after and in its place was put up the ideal of identity
with Brahmana, which represents a state of bliss and not of
fulfilment of pleasures. Indeed this state is to be achieved here
on earth by going beyond the limitations of pleasure and pain.
This was not something that many men could be seen to enjoy
in actual fact and the concept of rebirth was badly needed to
ensure that the goal remains achievable by all, no matter how
many births were going to be needed for this purpose. If there
is only one birth a lot of people were bound to end by not
achieving their full potential and this would be a waste and
contrary to the concept of order. This idea was also needed to
explain why only a few people desired liberation and even fewer
achieved it in any generation of men, and this is where it
connects up with the idea of dharma of a man's being – those
who seek liberation in this life have gradually over many past
lives worked for it and thereby achieved necessary samskaras
(drives, desires, inclinations formed out of impressions generated
by action) for seeking this particular goal. Without rebirth
through which the necessary samskaras can be slowly accumulated it will be a matter of chance as to who seeks liberation
and who does not, and this the Hindu mind was unwilling to
accept. This desire may of course be generated in man by God's

grace, but even when grace is brought in in Hindu thinking, it is not thought to be capriciously bestowed, being related to the worthiness of the recipient, who must love God enough to be capable of receiving grace. The presence of such love of God in a man is again not a matter of chance, it is a result of his own actions in this and past lives.

Now the question is, how exactly does the mechanism of karma function, and what does it mean to say that one is reborn in another life? In the Brahmanas, the literature that followed the Vedas, we come across the concept of redeath rather than rebirth. The idea of rebirth becomes important at the time of the Upanisads. 'Accordingly as one acts, according as one behaves, so does he become in the next life. The doer of good becomes good, the doer of evil becomes evil. One becomes virtuous by virtuous action, bad by bad action. Others, however, say that a person consists of desires. As is his desire so is his will, as is his will so is the deed he does, whatever deed he does, that he attains.'[21] 'The individual soul roams about in reincarnation according to its deeds.'[22] 'The soul being overcome by the bright or dark fruits of action, enters a good or an evil womb.'[23] And this is how the functioning of the law of karma is brought to bear on the social order. 'Those whose conduct has been good will quickly attain a good birth, the birth of a brahmin, the birth of a kshatriya, or the birth of a vaishya. But those whose conduct has been evil will quickly attain an evil birth, the birth of a dog, the birth of a hog or the birth of a chandala.'[24]

But how exactly does the mechanism of karma function and what precisely is the entity that is reborn? The law of karma says that the fortunes of a man in this life, the sort of person he is, and his enjoyments and sufferings are the results of his action in a previous life. Actions are normally generated by desires, and desires are fed by feelings of attraction and repulsion. Performance of actions thus generated feeds back the system of desires out of which they arise in the form of an unconscious drive or tendency (called vasana or samskara in Sanskrit) that takes root in the personality. Indeed desiring itself when

---

[21] *Brihadaranyaka Upanisad*, 4.4.5, trans. Radhakrishnan.
[22] *Svetasvatara Upanisad*, 5.7, trans. Hume.
[23] *Maitri*, 3.2, trans. Hume.
[24] *Chandogya*, 4.10.7, trans. Radhakrishnan.

produced out of instinctive attraction and repulsion, even when
not followed by overt activity would in this context qualify as
action, inasmuch as this too would strengthen impressions and
sow the seeds of future happenings. The law of karma determines
not only what sort of person one is going to be, it also determines
what sort of things are going to happen to one, determining
the amount of pleasure and pain that will befall him, so that
actions done and desires felt in this life can be balanced out by
counterhappenings in the future. And one's birth and circumstances will be such that these counter possibilities generated
could be actualised. The sum total of these tendencies and
possibilities as accumulated at the end of a life – the seeds of
another life urge – constitute what is called the subtle body which
is psychic in nature (the psychic is constituted of subtle matter
according to the Hindu tradition and it is to be distinguished
from consciousness called 'cit'). This subtle body is not
destroyed with the destruction of the gross body at death when
it takes up another gross body. The innate capacities of this
gross body and its circumstances will be in accordance with the
tendencies and possibilities that have been built up and that
now have to be actualised in this life.

There are several questions that may be asked of this account.
It may be felt that it may be all very well to explain my
present fortunes by action in a previous life, but how
about that life itself. How is that to be accounted for, and
if that is also the result of a still previous existence and
its karma, what about the beginning of the series? A man
cannot be said to have created by his own action what he was
at the beginning of the series, and thus the law of karma only
pushes back the problem and does not solve it. The Hindu
answer to this normally is that there is no such thing as the
absolute beginning of a series. Souls are eternal, they do not
start their career at any particular point in time which will
constitute the beginning of a series from scratch. Even during
dissolution unliberated souls are not destroyed but remain in a
potential state along with their karma to start again with a new
system of creation. This answer seems unsatisfactory to me for
it is not entirely clear who or what is reborn and where in this
account of being born again the concept of an eternal soul
fits in.

When it is said that Mr. X will be born again in a future life to enjoy or suffer according to seeds sown in this life, it is clear that the man born in the future will not literally be Mr. X but a different person altogether, say, Mr. Y, who will not even have any memory of what happened to Mr. X. In what sense then are Mr. X and Mr. Y the same person? Now, according to Hindu doctrines the nature of man is complex, composed as it is of several different components: (1) one of the components is provided by what are called the elements, water, air, fire, ether, and earth. Man's body, like everything material, is composed of these elements. This part of man is called the bhutatman (elemental or physical self); (2) another component is the vital spirit (prana) that animates the physical self and directs its activities; (3) the third is provided by intelligence and mental faculties (buddhi, manas, ahamkara). These are responsible for intelligent apprehension of what there is, and for feelings of pleasure and pain. These last two, sometimes together, sometimes separately, are called the jivatman, that which makes for the ego or individuality in man. They are still material in nature, although a good deal more subtle than the elements. But apart from these, there is also the eternal self or the divine essence (Atman or Paramatman) in man consisting of pure consciousness, according to some accounts at any rate.[25] (According to some Atman has consciousness, according to others it is consciousness.) This consciousness as caught in the jivatman (the psycho-physical self) makes man consciously aware of his individuality and so Self is often identified with self. But these two are in fact separable. What is eternal in man is the Atman or Self, and not the jivatman or self, which is a temporal manifestation of the lower (apara) nature of Brahman and is subject to eventual destruction. It is clear that the bhutatman, the gross body, does not transmigrate, since it is completely destroyed at death. It may be said that it is the jivatman that transmigrates, but the individuality feeling of Mr. Y, that is, his ego, being different from the individuality feeling of Mr. X, it cannot be said that Mr. Y and Mr. X have literally the same jivatman. Since Mr. Y, his jivatman, is constituted by the subtle body formed as a

[25]Consciousness is to be distinguished from the mind, the characteristic of which is intelligence but not self-consciousness awareness.

result of activities of Mr. X, all that can be said is that the jivatman in Mr. Y is causally dependent on the jivatman of Mr. X, being part of the cause-effect series that is continuous between Mr. X and Mr. Y, indeed between many other jivatmans, if transmigration is a fact. Mr. X and Mr. Y are then the same person only in the extended sense of being part of a causally continuous series of states and events. Therefore when rebirth of the same person is talked about, what is involved is the movement of a life urge in different forms in a continuous series where a succeeding configuration is causally dependent on the one that precedes it. When human beings are said to be reborn as animals or gods as a result of bad or good actions, this life urge must be thought to include animals, men and gods in a sliding scale of the same vital principle in different forms.

However, it may be said that this difficulty of not having an absolutely identical entity throughout affects not only the concept of the same person being reborn in different lives, it also affects any one life (that which is normally recognised as one life). *Srimad Bhagavatam* was already aware of this problem: 'Like the flame of a lamp or the current of a river, the bodies of creatures, with the imperceptible passing of time, are in constant motion. Hence they are in a sense continually born and continually dying. Is the flame of the lamp one and the same as before? Is the current of water one and the same always? Is man, if identified with the body, the same man today that he was yesterday?'[26] Mr. X himself is the same person throughout his present life only in the sense of being a causally continuous series of states and events, for nothing in him remains identically the same from birth to death. However, one could reply that his faculty of memory constitutes a unity out of the series which is unavailable between Mr. X and Mr. Y. It is this memory that explains Mr. X's sense of identity. The *Bhagavatam* has a reply to this also. Memory is a function of a particular mind-body complex with the destruction of which it too is destroyed. 'At the moment of death the sum of all the experiences of life on earth comes to the surface of the mind – for in the mind are stored all impressions of past deeds – and the dying man then becomes absorbed in these

[26] *Srimad Bhagavatam*, trans. Prabhabananda, p. 272.

experiences. Then comes complete loss of memory. Next there arises before man's mind the vision of his life to come, a vision regulated by his impressions of past deeds; and he no longer recollects his life on earth. This complete forgetfulness of his past identity is death.

'His complete acceptance of another state and identification with a new body is said to be his birth. He no longer remembers his past life, and, though he has existed before, he considers himself newly born.'[27] In any case, the trouble with memory is that it is not continuous and it does not cover the whole of the series that belongs to any one life. Mr. X does not remember everything about himself, particularly states and events that occurred during infancy or in his pre-natal condition, but he still accepts these periods of his life and the totally forgotten events that happened to him afterwards (we remember only a fraction of what actually happens to us) as part of *his* life.

Perhaps the answer to this is that there is enough memory available in any one life to make us overlook the gaps and accept continuity of a whole life on trust. That is, we can give a reasonable meaning to the concept of the same person (unity of a continuous series linked by memory) even though there is nothing that remains absolutely identical throughout his whole life, and even though there are gaps in memory. How can we talk about Mr. X and Mr. Y being the same person when there is no memory at all to link the two lives?

The Hindu answer to this may be twofold: (1) one is the claim that some people do remember some events of their previous life. Also, it is claimed that through the development of certain psychic powers by means of Yogic disciplines such memory can be made available, just as forgotten events of this life may be made available through special psychoanalytical techniques. Acceptance of this claim is necessarily a matter of faith, since conclusive proof is unavailable, and therefore it is of not much value in a philosophical analysis of what it means to say that the same person is reborn in another life. (2) The other answer may be that if we are going to accept continuity of a series from conception to death as the meaning of being the same person, and this is all that is strictly available even in the case of one

[27] *Ibid.*, pp. 271–272.

life, then this can be extended over several lives. Although in the case of one life memory does help to create a *feeling* of unity in respect of a continuous series, this memory has gaps and the fact of the continuity is not dependent on the feeling of unity that memory creates. Suppose a sixty-year-old man sits down to remember all that has happened to him throughout his life, he will only come up with bits and pieces of discontinuous items and by no means the whole lot of states and events that have gone into the making of his life. Therefore the continuity of the series of states and events between conception and death of a single life cannot strictly be made dependent on memory. If so, the continuity of the series between Mr. X and Mr. Y is not impaired by the lack of memory between these two lives.

However, this makes Mr. X and Mr. Y the same person in a highly eccentric sense, even if we accept the fact of continuity between their two lives entirely on trust – that of being two different parts of a continuous series of states and events. This may not be exactly what the Hindus mean when they talk about a person being reborn. But this turns out to be the only acceptable sense, though it need not seriously worry them, because they believe in any case that all things in the world are continuous, being expressions of the same divine essence in different name and form.

We have seen in discussing personal identity that memory is important only in so far as it allows a person to experience a feeling of unity with regard to a continuous series of states and events which is one's own life. But a feeling of unity with a continuous series, some chunks of which constitute other lives, as normally regarded, may be there without the benefit of memory. If Mr. Y who is a Hindu believes that he had a previous life or is going to have a future one, even if he has no awareness whatsoever of what these past and future lives are like considered as a specific configuration of states and events, and that he is the same person migrating between the three (and many others extending backwards and forwards), then it can constitute a recognisable use of the term 'same', *if we concede that there is in fact continuity of series* between these lives without the benefit of memory linkage. (This does not matter since Mr. Y is not insisting on memory.)   Although Mr. Y does not remember his past life and he will not remembert his present life when he is reborn in the future, it is part of his belief that events in 'his' past life, whatever they were, must have been of a nature to ensure the present events, and events in 'his future life, whatever they are going to be, will be of a nature that is entailed in present events. A particular chunk, out of a causally determined continuous series, that is linked by memory and is recognised in ordinary usage as being the same person is, according to this extended usage, also the 'same' person as another chunk out of the same series similarly linked by memory, even without the benefit of any memory linkage between the two chunks.

It may seem ridiculous to base the meaning of 'being the same person' on belief for which there is no evidence, that is, when we cannot prove that there 'actually is continuity as we can when memory is available. But it seems to me that we do sometimes accept belief of this nature as sufficient ground for using the expression 'the same person'. Take the following case: Mr. X says that he is the same person today as he was on 25 August 1971, although he passed the whole of that day in a state of unconsciousness as a result of an accident the previous day. No doubt in this case the evidence of other people is available, but I doubt if Mr. X believes what he does about his being the same person because of this public evidence.

The other element that can literally be the same between a succession of lives is the Atman. Atman is eternal and unchanging, but it can now inhabit one body, now another,[28] and being identical it can provide the element of sameness in lives that are in other respects different. But if the law of karma is functioning then the bodies inhabited by the same Atman must be causally linked. So it cannot be just the Atman that transmigrates, it must also be the subtle body that provides the causal linkage between one gross body and another. However, in so far as Atman is identical between different bodies in successive lives, these bodies can constitute the same person in a much more straightforward sense than in the other interpretation. This will do for Hindu theistic systems which believe that each man's self, although an

---

[28]This is to be understood metaphorically, for Atman is non-material, and to say that it inhabits a body is to say that it functions through the medium of a particular body.

expression of divine Self that is in everything, is a distinct entity by itself and remains distinct even in liberation, so a succession of lives can be inhabited by an identical entity. Atman of course is eternal, so it is reborn only in the sense of coming to inhabit a different body, and it must be the subtle body that is the carrier of karma, not the Atman (since it is unchanging).

In the context of Hindu thinking, however, it is somewhat difficult to give a precise content to the idea of a distinctive and individual Self (as opposed to self the jivatman) in each man. For the particularity and distinctiveness of an empirical person, his individuality or ego, is provided by the jivatman element in man and this perhaps is true of the theistic systems as well. The jivatman element is material and when this is separated from the Atman the basis for individuality or particularity seems to be lost. If the Atman is to provide the element of sameness between successive lives, and if it is to be conceived as different between different series forming a chain of lives, it must itself possess individuality in addition to the individuality of the jivatman. What this individuality consists of is not clear. Perhaps it consists of just being a distinct centre of experience, although there is no difference of content (this belongs to the jivatman) between the experience that is one Self and another. For what is normally thought to constitute individuality – distinctiveness of a person's physical and mental attributes and the unity of his experiences as forming a particular history – is believed to belong to the jivatman. In any case, this Atman must be thought to be a substantival entity if it is to retain individuality when the jivatman is destroyed, as it must be when karma is finished.

But non-theistic Hindu systems do not believe in a substantival Self. For advaita Vedanta, for instance, Self in man is just the function of Pure consciousness, which is the same for each man, and therefore in such a system personal distinctiveness cannot be explained in terms of it. It is not as if consciousness is some sort of ghostly substance which is enclosed in successive bodies, this substance in different men being as distinct from one another as their minds and bodies are. It is an identical function of self-manifestation and it gets individuated only through being reflected in the jivatman component of the personality. It has no substantival character of its own. So here the concept of the same person being reborn through successive lives can only be explained in terms of the causal continuity of the jivatmans in these lives.

I said earlier that the Hindus refuse to answer questions about the beginning of a series of lives before the accumulation of any personal karma, when the fortunes of a man cannot be explained by his previous life. For them lives have always been in circulation without any absolute beginning, and even a new system of creation after universal dissolution is not an absolute beginning but a link in a continuous and cyclical series of beginnings and ends. I also said that this answer does not really face the problem involved. But what I am going to say about it is related to another problem relevant to the Hindu concept of rebirth, and I shall discuss that before dealing with the question of beginning. A man is reborn in accordance with the good or bad action of his previous life and according to some Hindu accounts, if this action is bad enough he will go down the scale and be born as an animal, and if it is good he will go up and be born as a god or some such higher being in another sphere. A god or an animal cannot achieve liberation, and one must finally be born as a man to realise this state. But the problem is how can a life which has been downgraded to the level of an animal or upgraded to the level of a god be born again as man; and in any case the very idea of man being reborn as an animal is found objectionable by many who do not find the idea of rebirth as a man totally unacceptable. (The problem of transmigration between lives of gods and man does not arouse much criticism, since the existence of gods in another sphere is not taken seriously, and this part of the doctrine is treated as fanciful and quietly ignored.)

Granting for the moment that rebirth as an animal is possible, the problem is this – an animal's karma has not the same quality as that of a human being. How can it then be upgraded into a human life (presumably the upgrading would have to happen according to the animal's karma)? In answering such questions the Hindus had to develop very elaborate theories as to how the law of karma functions. No human being is either all good or all bad. A life gets upgraded or downgraded in the scale as a result of the accumulation of some specially good or bad karma. But besides this special accumulation there is always the load of ordinary karma which is kept in store for the time being and which comes into effect only after the special merit or demerit has been exhausted in a higher or lower birth. So the upgrading of an animal is the result not just of its own karma as an animal but of the accumulated but unspent karma of previous life. The same with higher life. A higher life is reborn as a human life not as a result of its karma but as the result of the unspent accumulated karma of a previous human life. There is this need to be reborn as a human being, as gods being steeped in pleasure cannot achieve liberation. A man hankers after a life of pure pleasure such as gods are believed to enjoy, so he can get it as a result of very good karma. But as this is not the end of life, which consists in union or identity with Brahman (or God), he must be reborn as a man to achieve this. So a human life is the most valuable of all lives despite the fact that higher beings enjoy incomparably more pleasures.

But apart from such doctrines the idea of an exchange between animal and human life is not unacceptable to the Hindu tradition in so far as it is believed that all lives, including those of gods, form a continuous series and that a life must travel through lower forms before it takes the human shape. So the possibility of an animal life being upgraded to a human life is not contrary to the dharma of things (the law according to which things happen). Indeed, according to some Hindu scriptures, not only life but all existence is continuous – from the insentient to the sentient, from the ' sentient to the intelligent, and then to the conscious – all of this being the manifestation of the same divine essence in greater or less degrees. Man contains within himself all the levels of development conceived as different layers of which he is composed. He has the bodily self (food body) and above it the vital self composed of the life principle; then the mind self composed of mental functions; then knowledge self composed of consciousness, and finally bliss self.[29] There is a steady progression from matter to life, from life to mind, from mind to consciousness, and finally to bliss of self-realisation. In any case, the principle of life is continuous between plants, fish (and other aquatic creatures), worm, bird, animal, and man, and accroding to the Puranas, as we

---

[29] See *Taittiriya Upanisad*.

have seen, it has travelled 8,400,000 species before reaching man in a continuously evolving series. So man, far from being unique, is a culmination of the development of the vital principle that travels through various forms.

This idea of continuity and progressive development is shown in the doctrine of the ten avataras (incarnations) of Vishnu; fish, tortoise, the boar, man-lion (an intermediate creature between man and beast), the dwarf (not yet a full-sized man), and the best men of exceptional qualities. So an interchange of human life with that of an animal is not thought to be an impossibility, according to the Hindu way of thinking about life. There is some difficulty, however, with the theistic doctrine of an individual Self in each human being that can inhabit different bodies. The animal has a mind self (that is, it is intelligent), but no knowledge self composed of consciousness. Self in man, however, is precisely this consciousness or an entity endowed with consciousness. What happens to it when a life that was human is reborn in an animal form? If the eternal Self, consisting of consciousness, is what ensures that successive lives are of the same being, then when a man is reborn as an animal, it ought to be endowed with consciousness as well to ensure that lives involved are of the same being. As this is not the case, it seems to me that theistic doctrines have to deny that a man can be reborn as an animal. Or perhaps, despite its individuality, this consciousness can be veiled over by the grossness of the animal's psychophysical organism.

This particular difficulty can be avoided if the idea of being the same is explained in terms of the causal continuity of a series of mind-body selves, and this may happen between animal and human lives. According to the Samkhya and Vedanta Schools in the Hindu tradition the mind-body self in man is so subtle that it reflects the consciousness-self in it, but the animal mind-body self is not subtle enough to do so. Man is not unique in so far as his mind-body is concerned and this he shares with the animals; he is unique only because he has an extra dimension, consciousness-self and the possibility of bliss. In this pattern it is the mind-body self that is reborn and it is this which provides for causal continuity and the element of 'sameness'. So when a human being is reborn as an animal presumably his mind-body self becomes relatively gross and the life involved does not any longer reflect consciousness. But when this life is reborn on the human plane after the bad karma has been exhausted it acquires the necessary subtlety and comes to have a consciousness-self reflected in it.

I think that the question about the beginning can now be tackled. The Hindu doctrine that there is no absolute beginning only means that the Universe is eternal (rather, the potentiality for it), despite periodic dissolution and if there is a movement from the sentient to the insentient during dissolution it is always followed by a counter-movement from the insentient to the sentient during creation. But when the sentient principle moves from the plant onwards to the human during a particular cycle of creation there must be a moment when a human life appears on the scene from a pre-human predecessor and it is the dharma and karma of this predecessor that must determine the quality of the particular human life involved and not the karma of a human being. The predecessor's life will have to be close enough to make this possible, that is, the development from animal to man has to be in a minute gradation of closely resembling capacities and the first beginning of human life will have to be similar enough to the animal to make transition possible. But a human life is endowed with consciousness and thus with freedom and so it soon begins to acquire and accumulate karma of a different kind eventually leading to greater differences between the two forms of life. Naturally the same drama of development of life has been enacted during a previous kalpa (cycle of ages) and as there is continuity not only between all life but also life and matter as well, there is no absolute beginning of anything only if we accept that which comes before something in a causal chain as part of its history. Human life when seen to be continuous with other forms of life has no absolute beginning. It does, however, appear to have a beginning as a human life, at a particular kalpa, at any rate, and the beginning of this life must be thought to be determined by the karma of non-human forms of life. In so far as the doctrine of karma which determines rebirth is a causal idea this should be acceptable. But then it cannot be said that all that befalls a human being is determined, always and everywhere, by his own karma, if this is to be interpreted narrowly. Also, if we refuse to talk about beginnings we shall have to use the language of an eternal movement of life through successive stages, its reversion back to non-life and a new start from there again, rather than eternal human life. And although the Self is eternal, this by itself does not make a human being who is born and who dies. I have already discussed the difficulties of trying to explain the rebirth of the same person in terms of it. In the non-theistic pattern it is not even necessary to try to explain the concept of the same person in terms of this eternal Self.

I am sure that when the Hindus talk about rebirth they imply much more than has been suggested here, causal continuity between different forms of life. For what is being reborn is not really the 'same person' in any normal sense of this phrase but the life principle itself, so to say. But if they want to insist on the possibility of rebirth as animals this is all that can be meant. However, there is good a deal in Hindu doctrines, particularly that of non-dualism, which affirms that all that there is shares the same essence, the differences being of name and shape and work,[30] with which the meaning of rebirth I have suggested here is consistent; whether or not this is how the question is viewed in actual fact, by most Hindus.

Another question that is often asked about the law of karma is this. If the function of the law of karma is to give a deterministic account of how and why things happen as they do there is no such thing as freedom of will and man becomes a plaything in the hands of destiny represented by his past karma. As present karma which is going to build the seeds of a future life is determined by past karma there is absolutely no way of breaking out of the chain and radically altering matters. This however is not meant to be the case. Man is said to be able to achieve liberation and earn it by working for it; if past karma determined everything no sense could be given to the repeated assertions in Hindu scriptures that liberation can be achieved by effort.

Past karma does in fact determine a great deal in man, the tendencies, dispositions and capabilities of a man, his status and achievement, the amount of pleasure and pain he will suffer in life, and so on. There is no doubt that most things most men do

---

[30] *Brihadaranyaka*, I.6.3, trans. Radhakrishnan.

are a function of these factors which create feelings of attachment and repulsion, the driving forces behind action. But man is
not only a jivatman he is also an atman and as such has consciousness and freedom, even if it is true that most men most of
the time act at the jivatman level. He can thus exercise choice
if he so wishes, that is, refuse to act under feelings of attachment and repulsion and learn to perform detached actions instead. Indeed it is in this that the unique position of man lies, his
capacity to achieve liberation. A detached action does not
accumulate karma because it does not involve desire, the prime
force involved in life urge, and it is by performing detached
actions that man can begin to regulate his own possibilities and
so his own karma, instead of being regulated by it.

Past karma, it is said, is to be found in a man's life in two
forms. (1) Karma in respect of which the die has already been
cast and which has begun to produce appropriate results. Nothing can be done about this part of karma, and no matter what
a man does now, things will happen in the way laid down by the
law of karma, so to say. (2) Stored-up karma which has not yet
been drawn upon and has remained, as yet, in the form of pure
possibilities for the future. The future effects of this part of
karma can be changed or mitigated by action now, if this is of
a counter-balancing nature, and it is up to the agent to undertake such action. He can at least make a beginning now and if
he cannot achieve very much in this life, the pressure of his past
karma being too great in relation to his capacities, there is a
succession of lives available for him to go on trying. As nothing
is ever lost he can eventually move close to the goal. Thus it is a
mistake to believe that the law of karma must make one a fatalist, if by a fatalist we mean someone who says that everything
is laid down and nothing whatever can be altered by effort.
This law of karma certainly inclines one to accept a good deal
of the suffering in this life as a result of one's action in a past life,
and this may be a bad thing as it makes one put up with in-
justice, but it certainly leaves the future open to effort, in
theory at any rate. Indeed it seems to me that the law of karma
is just as capable of producing a sense of responsibility about
one's own destiny as fatalism, and if the present day Hindus
interpret the law of karma in a fatalistic manner, the reason
for it ought to be sought elsewhere – such as grinding poverty,

economic backwardness of the society as a whole, total lack of opportunity for an individual to achieve anything very much in life, and so on – rather than in the intentions of the law itself.

But what about attitudes to other people's fates, fortunes and sufferings? If this is all a result of karma then perhaps people should be left to suffer, and nothing ought to be done to help anyone. I do not see that this follows. The law of karma may be a moral law, but only in the sense of having moral repercussions – people enjoying and suffering as a result of what they do – it is not moral in the sense that it is a good thing that things happen in this way (one can of course take up this attitude if one likes, but one does not have to). If the law of karma can be interfered· with in respect of one's own life (effort towards liberation will be impossible without the possibility of such interference) and this interference is possible because man is not just a cause-and-effect system belonging to nature (Prakriti) but also a Self (Purusa) who can enjoy freedom from this system if he decides to achieve this freedom through effort, then I do not see why we should take the attitude that the law of karma should be left to take its full toll when other people are concerned – even if we believe that everything that happens to a man is *uniquely determined* by his actions in a previous life, as we need not. All that would happen, when the working of the law of karma in a person's life is interfered with by actions of other people rather than of himself, is that this would have no effect on his future life which would still be determined by what he does in this life himself and not what other people do to him.

There is only one sphere where, traditionally speaking, the Hindus have brought in the law of karma to justify other people's suffering and inaction in respect of this suffering. This is the sphere of caste, and the sufferings and injustices inflicted by this system on the underprivileged. The Hindus have done so not out of respect for the law of karma but in order to justify privilege. Had the law of karma not been available as a justificatory doctrine, something else would have been used to the same purpose. Suffering brought about, say, through disease has not been left without medical attention in Hindu India on the ground that this is only the law of karma operating and one must not interfere with this law. This is because even though one may be said, generally speaking, to suffer as a result of one's actions it is not the case that any particular and fixed kind and degree of suffering is entailed in any particular karma and the law can only operate within a certain range of possibilities and not in a uniquely determined manner which enables us to connect, say, suffering X, with its specific kind and degree, with action Y.

For what karma determines in the first instance is one's psychic and physical endowments which placed in a certain environment will work themselves out in a certain manner that is in accordance with the operations of this law. But the environment in which one is placed is not entirely a product of one's own karma, it is a joint product of the karma of countless men who interact with one another. So if this environment (not only social, but also political, economic, and even physical) is seen to inflict suffering on people which can be alleviated through appropriate changes there is absolutely no reason why someone who believes in the law of karma and rebirth must adopt the attitude that nothing must be done to change things for people who suffer. Compassion and charity being virtues which are required from a religious point of view, one can in any case try to help people who may be legitimately said to be suffering through their own fault. But a social institution being the result of the karma of many people, its limitations may inflict on a person suffering which is not the exclusive result of his own karma. This kind of operation of the law is possible because man is by nature a social animal and is not an isolated individual. This social dimension of the law of karma has not received any attention in the Hindu tradition because it could make one critical of the caste system. Of course not all suffering can be eliminated by social action but this is no reason why one should not try to eliminate by social means sufferings which are the result of inadequate and unjust institutions and which themselves have been brought about by social action. That the caste system is not necessarily tied up with the law of karma and rebirth is shown by the fact that Buddhism believes in this law just as does Hinduism, but unlike Hinduism it does not believe in caste. And the belief in this law did not make it impossible for Buddhism to develop the ideal of Boddhisattva, the man of universal compassion and friendliness, who would postpone his own liberation for the sake of liberation of other people. The failure of the Hindu tradition to develop this ideal seems to me a serious short-coming of this tradition.

The intentions of the law of karma and the doctrine of re-birth in a religious context are to lead men beyond a condition-ed existence geared to thoughts of pleasure for the ego to infinitude and experience of bliss. Liberation means libera-tion from limitations of finitude represented by the mind-body system (that is, the jivatman) with which a man normally iden-tifies himself. The mind-body system acts on the pleasure-pain principle and is limited within the confines of a particular ego. The recognition of the divine essence, the atman, in oneself enables one to go beyond the limitations of the ego and through identification of one's own self with the divine essence in every-thing achieve infinitude, perfect harmony and bliss of being that pleasures are unable to provide. The doctrine of rebirth, according to karma, allows a series of lives progressively to work for the achievement of this state. Unfortunately in some Hindu writings, emphasis at some stage began to be placed on what liberation is from rather than what it is for. Liberation is liberation from rebirth, no doubt, but this is because rebirth happens only when there is desire for pleasure and desire for pleasure keeps one confined to the personal ego. This means failure to achieve integration with the divine essence in oneself and in everything else. Thus liberation from rebirth is incidental to liberation for integration with the divine. But if one talks only of liberation from rebirth, birth itself must be presented as so full of suffering that any sensible man would naturally want to escape from it. This is how the problem is presented in some Hindu works, *Samkhya* for instance, or the *Maitri Upanisad*. This distorts the original idea found in early Upanisads which talked of liberation in terms of attaining Brahman and in no way indulged in pessimistic sentiments about the sorrowful pros-pects of this life. However, if birth is feared it is also seen as an opportunity for further progress and liberation can be guaran-teed to all only through the prospect of this continued opportunity.

That the concept of liberation is not an off-shoot of a

pessimistic valuation of the world–this is how it is so often presented by commentators – is shown in the traditional Hindu
concept of four ends of life and that of asrama dharma, that is,
the concept of duties according to the stage of one's life.[31] The
four ends are morality or righteousness (dharma), material gain
(artha), pleasure (kama), and freedom or liberation (moksa).
All of these are legitimate and valuable goals for a creature
with a nature that is human, and the goal of liberation, it is
recommended in the Hindu sastras, should usually be adopted
only after a normal life of other ends has been fully lived and
all one's debts to gods, ancestors, parents, other human beings
and sub-human animals have been paid. As these four goals
cannot all be simultaneously achieved, life was thought of as a
journey divided up in asramas or stages in which different goals
can be set for special attention. Although dharma (morality)
is a concept that runs through the whole of life, preparation
for a life of dharma and training in it take place at the first
stage of life called brahmacharya (studentship). The student's
life is visualised as a life of discipline and study preparatory
to entering the second stage, that of the householder. At this
stage, which officially lasts till one has grey hair, wrinkles, and
grandchildren, pursuance of pleasure and material gain becomes
legitimate objectives *ideally* in accordance with dharma, although books on pleasure and gain realistically admit that this
ideal cannot always be achieved. Indeed, the duty of increasing
material wealth on the part of a householder, particularly a
vaisya, the third caste in the social hierarchy whose duty it
was to engage in agriculture, trade, commerce, etc. (the economic function of the society) was explicitly recommended in
dharmasastras (law books) so that the householders could
maintain by alms giving both the mendicants, the people at the
last stage of life, and the students.

As for pleasure, if the manifold world is an expression of
divine essence, as we are told in all Hindu scriptures, then the
enjoyment of this world, even as a individual ego, is part of
this scheme of divine self-expression in multiplicity and, therefore, perfectly legitimate. The second stage of life is thought to

[31]See *Laws of Manu, Kama Sutra* by Vatsayana, and *Arthasastra* by Kautilya.
Various translations available.

be the proper time for the pursuance of pleasure as well as the time for doing one's duty by society by performing jobs that belong to one's own caste. The law books which dealt with social aspects of dharma, duties, obligations etc., not only did not undervalue this stage, some of them, Manu, for instance, went to the extent of saying that this is the most excellent order of all. The third stage is the stage of retirement from the pursuit of pleasure and wealth when one is advised to turn one's attention to the cultivation of the Self within or to God. The fourth stage, for which the third stage is a preparation, is the life of a mendicant who has cut his ties with all these worldly and egocentric goals and who, established in freedom from the ordinary requirements of life, can treat the whole world as his habitation. The life of a mendicant is recommended in ancient books to a man in the fourth stage of life, as this life was thought to be best suited to the living of non-attachment in practice, since a mendicant does not have anything to call his own, not even a fixed habitation which man at the third stage (Vanaprastha or forest-dwelling) still enjoys. But the sign of freedom or liberation is not in mendicancy as such, which, in India at any rate, has never been a particularly difficult way of life to adopt, alms-giving being a part of a householder's dharma but an attitude of mind which makes no distinction between mine and thine and which can look upon the whole world as one's own, or as belonging to God. Mendicancy adopted as a 'profession' – and for the vast majority of the mendicants, it is probably no more than a profession – is, something quite different. Anyway the ideal is freedom from the limitations that comes from thinking of oneself as an ego, distinct from other egos, and there is no bar on achieving this state of mind without mendicancy. In fact, a mendicant can be quite as attached to his way of life as the householder to his and such a mendicant is just as close or far from liberation as a householder is.

It is true that with the distortion of the concept of liberation within the tradition from a positive ideal of liberation for – this being a state of mind one should enjoy while in this world – to a negative concept of liberation from rebirth, the original insight into the beauty of life in all its forms including sex and the value of pleasures that comes from the enjoyment of this beauty – embodied in the concept of four ends of life – began to be lost in certain circles. Teachers belonging to these circles began to preach that renunciation of this world and the adoption of the life of an ascetic or that of a mendicant is the only worthwhile goal, suggesting thereby that those who are not engaged in asceticism were wasting their valuable time on worthless objectives. This attitude to my mind is contrary to the widely prevalent belief to be found in all types of Hindu scriptures, that all that there is, is an expression of the divine essence. A corollary of this belief is that all that there is can be looked upon as sacred and this was the prevailing opinion in the Vedas where even trees, mountains, rivers, and animals were deified, in most early Upanisads and in the *Gita* – books which are thought to be sources of the Hindu tradition. But the ideal of liberation from rebirth, considered as the end of all one's aspirations in this world, must paint the world in as dark a colour as possible, so that all men's energies could be concentrated on not getting born again in such a dreadful place, and this was done in many secondary Hindu scriptures. To ensure that one is not born again one must cease to have desires, and the best way to ensure this is to have as little involvement in the affairs of the world as possible – contrary to the advise of Krishna in the *Gita* – in short to renounce the world. If this is what men at all times should desire, then it is nonsense to talk about stages of life and it was pointless for Brahman to have manifested itself in manifold names and forms. I am not suggesting that the positive ideal of liberation altogether disappeared from the tradition but it was certainly overshadowed in certain very influential circles by the negative ideal of not getting born again and during the long centuries of degeneration and decay of Hindu culture it was this negative ideal that came to grip the Hindu mind.

However, I think that because of the Hindu acceptance of the concept of stages of life which make individuals at different times of their lives ready for the pursuit of different goals, there is a way of interpreting Hindu teachings about renunciation such that it could be said that a teacher was talking only to those who were ready to adopt it and not to all and sundry, irrespective of their stage of life and readiness. That is, he was only aiming at people who were at the appropriate stage, the fourth, and some people can be at this stage even quite early in life, if we combine the idea of stages of life with that of rebirth and law of karma. The concept of stages of life is a schema which could be followed in one life or over several lives rather than a description of four parts of an actual life lived in any one birth. What I am saying is that the idea of asrama or stage of life should be given a much more extended meaning than the usual interpretation which suggests that one completes all the four stages and achieves all the four ends in the span of one lifetime. If this did happen then there would not have been anybody left to be reborn. As rebirth does happen according to the Hindu tradition, not everybody does, in fact, traverse all the four stages in one life. Indeed, according to Hindu scriptures themselves, it takes many lives to achieve liberation. If so, the idea of stages of life should also be seen in relation to a whole series of lives through which one passes before liberation is attained. The schema of four ends and stages of life only sets forth what life is for and how to fulfil all its potentialities in graduated stages. How one jiva (life urge) passing through a succession of lives works this out is a different question. So in any generation of men people will be found who, although of the same age, belong to different stages of life and the vast majority of any generation of men will end their lives as householders. Some people may even remain at the first stage of brahmacharya (student) all through their lives. People, who are not at the appropriate stage, arrived at over a course of several lives, no matter what their age, are not ready for liberation and for them renunciation is not the end. But those who renounce at an early age are at the appropriate stage, as is shown by their readiness to do so, so when liberation is said to be the ultimate goal of life it is not being preached in the context of Hindu beliefs, that everybody everywhere should be engaged in it.

Indeed, if rebirth is a fact then everyone cannot be engaged in the quest for liberation and there will be only some people at any one time who are at an appropriate stage to be actively engaged in it as a goal to be obtained here and now. If this was not so, all those vast periods of time, through which a cycle of creation has to pass – giving a series of lives belonging to one life-urge, a long stretch of time in which to be liberated – would be quite inexplicable. Thus even when liberation is preached to all the law of karma (and rebirth) ensures that only those who are at the appropriate stage, and they can be of any age, will take any notice. This being the case there must be other worth-

while ends which fulfil human potentialities and which people
who are not engaged in liberation can work for, such as prosperity (artha), pleasure (kama) and righteousness (dharma), and
these were, in fact, recognised by the tradition as worthwhile
human objectives. The doctrine that Hindu culture went down
through preaching moksa then bases itself on a simplified version
of the Hindu intellectual or religious tradition, which, contrary
to some opinion, is very realistic and seldom refuses to acknowledge facts of life. (Indeed, what it suffers from is the opposite
tendency, to accept all facts indiscriminately.) The fact that the
vast majority of men of any one generation do not desire moksa,
let alone to be actively engaged in it, shows that they are not
at the appropriate stage and this can be explained by the law of
karma and rebirth.

These doctrines imply that human beings to be found on earth
at any one time, instead of all being made exactly the same in
respect of their hopes, aspirations, capacities for achievement,
etc., belong to different stages of intellectual, moral, and spiritual
development. As all these lives have been in circulation over
many rounds during which their karma may have moved them
backwards and forwards in many ways, and away from or towards
the goal of liberation, the level at which they have started this
life is a resultant of many forces, determined by karma of many
lives, so it is not the same for all men. Many men in their
present life will not find the idea of liberation attractive in any
way. Indeed they may even find it positively repugnant and they
may have to live for pleasure, etc., over several lives before the
idea begins to look tempting. Some, however, may have already
advanced towards it to such a degree in a previous existence
(or existences) that nothing less will make sense in this life.
Hence, the importance in Hindu scriptures of the doctrine of
adhiraki-bheda (differences in readiness and competence). This
explicitly acknowledges that the doctrine of renunciation should
be preached only to the competent, that is, those whose have the
required emotional, moral, intellectual, and spiritual readiness
(possibly acquired over many lives).

Not only life-long renunciation, there is nothing, and no
teaching, which, according to the Hindu doctrines, is supposed
to fit everyone, hence the profusion of forms. The doctrine of
karma and rebirth postulates that human beings at any one

time are a different stages of emotional, intellectual, moral, and spiritual development and their orientations in these matters can be different from one person to another.[32] This is why there have to be different models and pictures of divine reality, with form and without form, to be used in our approach to it, and different paths, those of love, action, knowledge and meditation, to be followed, in accordance with one's taste and aptitudes. The use of one model, however elementary one may think it is for oneself, may help another to advance towards the next stage, whereas an unsuitable model, however 'advanced' in itself, may be positively harmful because the individual concerned is not ready to respond to it in the right way and this may hinder his spiritual progress altogether.

So teaching and practice must be relative to personalities in order that people may derive maximum benefit from their religious life. It is the task of a guru (spiritual teacher) to help one to find one's level (provided of course gurus of real wisdom are available). Unfortunately the guru ideal has also been badly exploited and it has helped to produce excessively docile, timid and unthinking human beings for whom the ritual of veneration for the guru has come to occupy the greatest significance in life. Anyway, a man who cannot be his own guide must seek guidance somewhere and ideally it should come from the guru; and the guru, ideally, is not supposed to impose a uniform pattern of thought and practice on everyone. In the Hindu tradition even the same man can use different pictures and paths at different times, if he so wishes. Some men are so constituted that they prefer to think of the divine as formless, while others can make sense of the divine only by attributing to it many forms in their absolute perfection and the Hindu tradition allows one to choose one or the other according to one's inclination. For the divine is everywhere, in everything and in oneself as well as being transcendent and this is what has to be realised. It matters little whether one does this by thinking of the divine as formless or as possessed of perfect form. But it may matter to a man, whether he is to adopt one

[32]This idea was used to justify the hereditary caste system, one's birth in a certain caste being determined by one's own karma. Unfortunately, human beings are always capable of using a good idea to a bad end.

or the other picture. For if he adopts a picture which is opposed to the emotional and intellectual cast of his personality, the result will be negative, so a man must adopt, in his attempt to integrate himself with the Divine, the kind of picture to which he can respond. The picture of the Divine as formless Brahman present in everything as its innermost essence may be the right picture for one man, but a man of bhakti, that is, of another kind of emotional and intellectual orientation, may find this quite unacceptable. What suits him is the loving adoration of a Personal God who made the world and by whose grace immortality in heaven can be achieved. These differences in disposition are explained in the Hindu tradition by the law of karma.

CHAPTER III

Religious Reality and Levels of Integration in the Hindu Tradition

It is often believed that to talk about religion is to talk about God, the transcendent person, who has created this world, also of man's relationship to God as one person to another. This view is biased in favour of one form of religion, that is, monotheism. There exist religions which operate without the concept of God (conceived to be an absolute and infinite person) such as Buddhism and even though this concept is not absent from the Hindu tradition, there exist in it a good many other forms along with monotheism that equally qualify as religious belief. In these forms an absolute distinction typically made by monotheism between the creator and the created, and the sacred and the profane, does not exist. Instead of the divine reality being thought to be the transcendent source of all creation – when thought of as the source rather than as the ground this reality may be thought of as a person – it is often treated here as the transcendent-immanent essence or ground of all existence; and as such the whole of reality becomes in some sense an expression of divine reality. But it becomes so only when looked at in a characteristic way – one that relates in one way or another to a search for what is of abiding significance as opposed to what is merely transient and short-lived. This characteristic way includes man's concern about his own ultimate nature that extends beyond his physical being, his attitude towards life and its possibilities here on earth as upheld by values and principles that range beyond, his relationship to other human beings and the rest of the cosmos, all being seen as integral to an abiding process, and last but not least his thought about the ultimate ground of all existence and value and the relatedness of everything to this ground. If we do not prejudge that any one particular form, such as monotheism, is the valid form for conceiving the reality that is dealt with in religion but investigate the whole spectrum of forms that actually exist in order to find a possible common reference, we can think of religion as a point of view from which reality is viewed and explored in characteristic ways that set the ultimate and enduring terms of reference of all existence and value, human and non-human. Reality as viewed in these terms may be called 'religious reality' and the concept of God as found in monotheism represents but one of the forms in which this reality may appear to man.

Now to use the term 'reality' is normally to indicate that there is something there which has an independent and objective existence as opposed to being a subjective construction that exists only in the mind. It is a common prejudice in modern philosophy that it is only by means of the senses (and thought exercised in respect of what is revealed through the senses) that objective reality is caught hold of, any thought that is not backed up by sensory material is not thought about reality, it is just a matter of human imagination and fancy. So the term 'religious reality' will perhaps not be acceptable to some as indicating something given. But if we look at actual human life and experience and the ways in which human beings get to know things in practice – and there is really no other place than experience from which to start thinking – we find that all sorts of capacities, perceptual, conceptual, imaginative, intuitive, and even affective are being used by man to discern what there is. None of these capacities is infallible but none can be said to be always wrong either. So there is no reason why the senses should be thought to have an exclusive claim in the matter of revealing reality, considering that they are as human as these other capacities. Not only are the senses not infallible they have to be trained to find the kind of perceptual qualities that belong to the human world and this training essentially depends on the use of language that fixes similarities and differences between things by conceptual means. The claim that only the senses reveal reality is based on an *a priori* assumption that what can be given or got at can only be sensory material, it cannot have a nature that is accessible to thought (or feeling) without the aid of sensation. Such a claim, besides being an *a priori* prejudice, is belied by any developed language where what most words refer to are not sensory qualities and it would be absurd to say that what most of language is talking about is not reality but subjective fancy. The fact is that there is no way of judging what the nature of reality is like except as it happens to be revealed in experience, and what is revealed is essentially dependent upon our capacity to receive it. This is as much true of sensory reality as of any other. As reality has to be given in experience (to appropriate faculties) for us to find it, we must start with experience in our investigation of what there is and if we do this we can have no ground for denying that our conceptual, imaginative, and intuitive faculties are just as much capacities to reveal reality as are perceptual faculties. (This does not mean that they cannot go wrong.) So I shall take the fact that people do claim religious experience and the fact that there exist religious languages that are inter-subjectively shared by a group of people in a meaningful manner as sufficient justification for the use of the term 'religious reality'. That this reality is not accessible to sensation simply means that this is not sensory reality, it does not mean that it cannot be given. And the fact that not everyone uses religious language, unlike sensory language, does not show either that it cannot be given. For this may only mean that some people do not use their capacity to receive intimations of religious reality, either because they are not interested or because they are deficient in the kind of sensitivity that is required to look at things from the religious point of view. Religious reality is given but it cannot be revealed to one unless one takes up the religious point of view from which a certain kind of search for significance, that involving the ultimate and the enduring, makes sense. Not only that, as religious reality is not one thing amongst other things but is the infinite and absolute source or ground of all things this point of view has to be further mediated by the use of models which give this reality a discernible shape. Only thus can it be related to familiar spheres of experience and talked about in a community of people. To expect that religious concepts will make sense as dealing with objective reality without all this understanding having to be brought to bear on it, is to show total unawareness of what religion is about. (The problem of models via which religious reality is mediated will be talked about later in the book.)

I have said that we have to start in all enquiry about reality with man and his experience. Now man is a highly complex being, with interests and purposes that are of different kinds and his explorations of reality, that which he finds to be given to him in experience are mediated by these interests and purposes constituting different points of view. One kind of concerns and purposes leads man to adopt the commonsense framework or point of view which enables him to find certain things, another the scientific point of view which discloses quite different things. Both commonsense qualities and scientific entities are given, but they are found to be given only through the adoption of a particular point of view from which characteristic facts are revealed. Among these concerns as a complex being is man's concern about the ultimate terms of reference of his being and behaving and this concern becomes religious when it is tied up with his search for something that is of abiding significance, something that just is, absolutely, beyond generation and destruction, something that needs no support but can support everything else as its source or ground. When that which is given in experience includes man's own nature that is capable of imaginative reflection and intuitive apprehension a question can arise as to how that which is limited and finite can come to be or exist on its own. (This question is not necessarily consciously formulated. But the mind can have problems and concerns and seek answers to them without being self-consciously aware that there is a specific problem to which a specific answer is being given.) And it arises because all things finite and limited are found to be dependent for their existence and function on other things. If instead of accepting this as a fact not to be probed further, man goes on to adopt the religious point of view from which the question about the ultimate is asked, he opens himself up for a reality of another kind. This reality can only be conceived as infinite and absolute, something that can be the basis for all existence and value, being above the limitations – spatio-temporal and causal – of finite reality. This reality may indeed be a mystery in some sense, and yet, since it is conceived to be self-existent, its existence is not felt to be as mysterious as is the existence of the finite – which is not self-explanatory – without the support of the infinite.

I have said that this reality is conceived, but conceiving is typically a human way of exploring what is given (without the exercise of this capacity not even sensory qualities would be

known in the form in which they are known to human beings).
Man explores reality in a variety of ways through a variety of
conceptual schemas that have evolved through his attempt
to deal with the pressures that his specific types of concerns and
questions bring to bear on him and these constitute different
points of view from which and through which what is given
appears to him in characteristic ways. This is true not only of
religious reality but a good many other things as well that are
considered to belong to human experience. An objection may
no doubt arise here. How can man who is a finite and limited
being conceive of something that is infinite and unconditioned.
This objection, however, does not hold in respect of the Hindu
tradition. If according to this tradition it is true that man is,
from some point of view, finite and limited, it is also true that
he has an infinite essence in him – religious reality in this tradition is not a reality apart but is something that permeates
everything as its transcendent-immanent ground – in the form of
consciousness or Self, which when freed from the limitations of
a particular mind-body that constitutes a particular ego, can
be seen to be absolute and infinite. Consciousness in this tradition is not conceived to be the function of the brain, it is conceived to be an independent reality of its own, called 'Self',
which is infinite and unconditioned in its nature but which
when limited by a particular mind-body complex takes on the
appearance of a finite consciousness owned by a finite ego.
Man is thus both finite and infinite, the infinite in him being
veiled over by the finite, and it is because man has intimations
of this dual nature in himself that he can ask the kind of
question that is formulated from the religious point of view.
Furthermore since according to this tradition religious reality
is not a reality apart, but reality as viewed in a characteristic
manner, man is never really divorced from it in actual fact,
whether or not he realizes this to be the case.

What I have said so far may suggest that religion is an intellectual enterprise, something concerned with fundamental
puzzles and their answers. But what I have done so far is to
talk about the terms of reference of the religious point of view –
which indicate the area where religious reality is to be
located – as reflected on by philosophy. Religion as practised by
man is also, and most importantly, a search for integration with

religious reality. For the practical religious impulse is based on a feeling or awareness, not necessarily consciously formulated, that living acquires its deepest significance or its fullest potential, when it is linked or integrated with its source or ground in a conscious manner. From the point of view of religious practice it is this feeling of integration that brings to man a sense of the ultimate and abiding significance of his own being and it is this kind of concern that defines the possibility of man's taking up a religious point of view.

In the Hindu tradition religious reality, which in its character as infinite and absolute has no definite shape, is approached in a variety of ways through the use of a variety of models that are conceived in relation to the particular interests and purposes through which religious search is mediated for people of different kinds and temperaments. These approaches take the shape of polytheism, non-dualism (or monism), samkhya-yoga perfectionism and monotheism (with three variants) all of which are accepted as valid approaches to religious reality inasmuch as integration with religious reality is sought by different people at different levels and dimensions. This is possible because religious reality, that which is absolute and eternal, is conceived here not as something apart from and transcendent to the relative-temporal, but as its transcendent-immanent ground so that everything partakes of its essence and so contact with it can be made at different levels. Hence all things, and not necessarily only things human, can be the symbol of religious reality, as all of reality becomes religious reality when looked at from the religious point of view. Which symbol (or symbols) one adopts depends upon the background of needs and experiences that leads one to look for religious reality. I shall, in the chapters that follow, deal with the different approaches here mentioned, but in the rest of this chapter I shall talk about different levels and dimensions of integration with religious reality and this will involve me in talking also about the different functions that religion performs in this tradition.

An examination of the Hindu tradition, which has managed to retain within one fold many types of religious perception and insight, shows that the human need for integration with religious reality operates on three different levels and in two different dimensions. These levels are cosmic, social, and individual, three planes of existence to which man can believe himself to belong, and the dimensions are the temporal and the timeless, that is, the here and now values of everyday life, such as are involved in the practice of polytheism, and eternal values embodied in the quest for immortality, such as we find both in monotheism and monism. The classical Indian tradition produced a multitude of myths, symbols, rituals, and philosophies which function on different planes and cater to these diverse needs of integration felt by men of widely different religious temperament and orientation. Prominent amongst these differences are a temperament which seeks integration through knowledge, or an understanding of the ultimate nature of reality, and a temperament which wants to achieve this primarily through emotion. The former leads one to explore what we may call 'spiritual ontology' and the latter to faith and devotion, inspired by a spirit of dependence on and sense of surrender to some power beyond oneself. However, these two different approaches are recognised by the Hindu tradition equally as religious quests, for the purpose of spiritual ontology is not to gain information but to achieve integration.

I do not wish to imply that the quest for integration on the part of an individual may not involve all of these levels, or that these are kept distinct and separate in the tradition in a logical manner, (or even that they have been consciously thought out as distinct aims). Indeed they are often mixed up together, and concepts that can be said to have distinct logical functions have been used across recognisable boundaries, giving rise to the charge of inconsistency or contradiction. I am making the distinc- tions clear-cut in order to bring out the point of using different kinds of language in respect of what, the tradition agrees, is the same religious reality.

At the cosmic level the quest is for integration with all exis- tence, natural, animal and human, all of which are seen to be the expression of an eternal divine essence, and as such non- different from one another. And this is embodied in the contem- plative search for Brahman, the Supra-Personal Absolute of the Upanisads. Brahman literally means 'the immensity', that which is all and beyond all, being its inexhaustible source, and the quest is to know and feel one with it, that is, to. be integrated with the source and all its manifestations. This is why the language used for this quest in the Upānisads is 'becoming Brahman', and it is said that he who knows 'I am Brahman' knows truly, for he realises his oneness with this-all. Time and time again in the Upanisads Brahman has been described as 'this-all', and this has led many western commentators to describe the belief involved as pantheism, but if it is pantheism it is pantheism with a difference. Brahman may be this-all, but it is also beyond this-all, and Brahman has been described as 'not this and not that', as in the *Brihadaranyaka Upanisad*, to bring this out.

According to *Mundaka* II.2.11, 'Brahman indeed is this immortal. Brahman before, Brahman behind, to right and to left, stretched forth below and above, Brahman indeed is this whole world, this widest extent,' and yet, says *Katha* (v. 15), 'There the sun shines not, nor the moon, nor the stars; lightnings shine not there, and much less earthly fire. From His light all these give light and His radiance illumes all creation.' (Máscaro). Thus Brahman may not just be this-all, but to see religious reality as this-all is to be identified and integrated with the whole of existence. This is made possible through conceiving of Brahman as Self with which man's self is identified, (in the sense of not being different from it). As in the *Brihadaranyaka* (ii.5.15), 'verily, this Self is the overlord of all things, the king of all things. As all the spokes are held together in the hub and felly of a wheel, just so in this Self, all things, all gods, all worlds, all breathing things, all these selves are held together.' The point is to realise infinity in one's own being through integration with the Infinite because, as is said in the *Chandogya* (VII.23), 'Where there is the Infinite there is joy. There is no joy in the finite, only in the Infinite is joy; know the nature of the Infinite, where nothing else is seen or heard or known, there is the Infinite. Where something else is seen or heard or known, there is the finite. The Infinite is immortal, but the finite is mortal.' Again,

> 'But the Infinite is above and below, North and South and East and West.
> The Infinite is the whole universe.
>
> I am above and below, North and South and East and West. I am the whole universe.'

From this cosmic point of view man accepts everything, not

just what human beings consider to be good because it fulfils the
purpose of ministering to their happiness, but literally everything.
This has been expressed in *Yajurveda*[1], Ch. 39, where Rishi
Dadhyac in a mood of cosmic expansion blesses everything:

'Blessed be the vital breaths with their controlling Lord, blessed
be earth, blessed Agni, blessed the mid-region, blessed the air,
blessed the sky, blessed the sun';

and so it goes blessing everything and wishing,

'on me be bestowed the animal's elegance of form, the flavour
of food, and fame and grace, on me a blessing,'

until it comes to

'a blessing on grief, a blessing on grieving,
a blessing on the sorrowing, a blessing on sorrow,'

and finally,

'on heaven and earth may there be a blessing.'

When man has integration of this kind in mind, he views
religious reality not as a Personal God who has created the
world specifically to confer happiness on man, but as something
that is beyond personality and beyond man's need for happiness, being the inexhaustible source of all possibilities that
man, in so far as he is finite, may judge good, bad or indifferent
depending on whether or not it makes him happy. But the man
in search of infinity has no concern for happiness, for as the
Brihadaranyaka says, 'the world is his ... indeed he is the world
itself'.

But the search for cosmic integration may also operate at a
lower level of generality, where manifold powers of nature
expressing cosmic order and harmony (called rita) are conceived
as various divinities. Man finds his unity with nature through
adoration of and ritual sacrifice to divinities representing various
functions of nature and through these with cosmic order itself

[1]*Hymns from the Vedas*, A.C. Bose, p. 349.

that unites heaven and earth. This unity can be experienced, and all things, rivers, mountains, trees, animals, can be adored as sacred, as they have been in the Vedas. To quote *Rigveda* (1.164.33), 'The heaven is my parent and progenitor: the navel of the earth is my kinsman, the spacious earth is my mother.' In the hymn to the Earth,[2] *Atharvaveda* (XII. i. 25-26), the poet says,

'Thy fragrance that is in men and women
and the majesty and lustre in males
in the hero and the steed,
and the radiance that is in the maiden
unite us with these, O earth.

Rock, soil, stone, and dust
Earth is held together and bound firm
To her my obeisance, to gold-breasted earth.'

This is what is said in loving adoration of Ushas the goddess of dawn (*Rigveda* V. 80.2),[3] who prepares men for their day's task:

'The lovely Ushas rouses up the people
Makes the paths easy to tread, and goes forward
She, great, all-impelling, rides her great chariot
And spreads the light before the day's beginning.'

Thus the need for integration may be felt not just with the totality of the cosmos or the essence of it, but with its various differentiated forms of splendour and excellence through which the cosmos effects him in his day-to-day existence. Man is a part of nature, and plants, animals, men, and gods belong to one family. Knowing this man can be united with all that exists. At this level of integration man does not transcend finitude but feels replenished by favours that come to him from different quarters, the sun, the moon, fire, air and lightning, rivers, trees, mountains, and also animals. And he is grateful that life is good, as is expressed in so many hymns

[2]*Ibid.*, p. 369.
[3]*Ibid.*, p. 271.

of the Vedas. To quote a verse from *Rigveda* (I. 89.8):[4]

'May we, devas, hear with our ears what is good
and holy ones! see with our eyes what is good
and praising you with steady limbs and body
enjoy the divinely bestowed term of life.'

Polytheism as a specific approach to religious reality has also another kind of integration in view. It is integration with life itself as it exists in time and its ordinary values that men look for via their own desires – values such as health, wealth, success, long life, brilliance, and happiness here on earth, rather than with that dimension of existence which transcends time as is important in monism and monotheism.[5] It is for these things that polytheistic gods are approached and worshipped. But it is a scheme in which all men are included, prayer being normally of the form 'Give us'. Even when it is framed as 'give me', polytheistic prayer is communal, in which a lot of people join together. Polytheism thus expresses a belief that it is a good thing for men to enjoy health, wealth etc., which can be seen to belong to a sacred complex by looking upon them as gifts from gods. Lakshmi, the goddess of wealth, when collectively worshipped, is more a celebration of wealth as a good thing for all men to enjoy rather than an expression of a selfish desire to appropriate it for oneself. When seen in this way that which men naturally desire becomes a part of a divine plan for human beings here on earth. One thus becomes integrated with desires and their functions, indeed with the normal and everyday business of life itself, not only by seeing it as shared by other people but also as a part of a reality bigger than man, from which it derives its sanction. Polytheism is thus a religious affirmation of life in its everydayness, via the concept of gods who guarantee human values.

But the search for the sacred, and integration with it may also be stimulated by man's social existence, that is, man as a being bound not only by laws and customs but also by love and

[4]*Ibid.*, p. 111.
[5]This desire for integration with values that exist in time in polytheistic worship can be contrasted with the quest for immortality, that is, integration with the timeless, which figures prominently in monism and monotheism.

affection to other human beings – when this is seen not as a passing phenomenon but as grounded in an enduring value that transcends any particular man or epoch. This dimension of the sacred is expressed in diverse ways both through belief and practice. One of these is cosmogonic myth or belief in sacred history. This latter may be traced to actual historical events and persons (raised to the dimension of the sacred) as in monotheistic religion, or to a beginning which cannot be traced to any identifiable historical occurrence and yet in so far as it is believed in it performs just the same function of conferring sacredness on a community. An example of this is the Purusa-Sukta of the *Rigveda* (x. 90), according to which the whole of existence, including gods, men and their social functions such as is involved in the idea of four categories (varna), has been created out of the sacrificed limbs of the primeval self, three-quarters of whose being however has remained beyond manifestation. So man's social existence is not just a convenience, it is in accordance with divine self-expression and therefore sacred.

To this approach to the sacred also belong symbols such as our father, mother, friend, moral governor, protector etc., under whose love and care all men are united, in the language of the *Rigveda*, as of one mind. Indeed human family and society here on earth is a copy of divine family and society in heaven. Father Sky and Mother Earth are the parents both of men and gods, of whom there are several groups – as there are different tribes of men on earth – such as Adityas, Vasus, and Rudras, the semi-divine Angirasas and lower deities such as Ribhus, Apsaras, and Gandharvas. They have different functions, and yet they help one another, and work in perfect harmony such as can be expected from human beings on earth. This need for accord has been emphasised in *Rigveda* (10.191.2.4): 'meet together, talk together, let your minds apprehend alike...common be your intention, common be the wishes of your hearts, common be the thoughts so that there may be perfect union among you'. The same has been emphasised in the *Atharvaveda* (III.30.1,2,7):

'Freedom from hate I bring you, concord and unanimity,
Love one another as the cow loveth the calf that she hath borne,

One-minded with his mother let the son be loyal to the sire
Let the wife, calm and gentle, speak words as sweet as honey
    to her lord.
With binding charm I make you all united and obeying
One sole leader and one-minded
Even as the gods who watch and guard the Amrit
At morn and eve may ye be kindly hearted.

Sacredness of man's social values has been expressed in hymns such as these:

Agni men seek thee as a father with their prayers
Win thee, bright formed, to brotherhood with holy acts
Thou art a son to him who duly worships thee
A trusty friend thou guardest from attack.

(*Rigveda*, II. 1.9)

The *Rigveda* speaks thus of Mitra, the god who watches over truth-speaking and sincerity between man and man:

He is the dearest friend of mortals
Let us not anger Varuna nor Vayu, nor him
The dearest friend of mortals, Mitra

(*Rigveda* VII. 62.4)

Indra is invoked thus:

Our Saviour Indra, our Protector Indra
easily called at each call, Hero Indra
We call on the mighty, much-invoked Indra
may he bless us the bounteous Indra

(*Rigveda* VI. 47.11)

Again:

Mighty Indra with the sweetest of songs
I catch thy garments hem, as a child the father's

(*Rigveda* VIII. 70.5)

Indra is not only loved, he also loves:

> We, Indra, we, loving thee,
> with oblation sing our songs
> and thou, our Treasure, lovest us

(Rigveda III. 41.7)

To Pushan a hymn of praise is offered using the imagery of love
between man and woman:

> Accept with love this my song, be
> gracious to my worshipful thought
> as a bridegroom to his bride.

(Rigveda III. 62.8)

Finally a prayer for strength so that one may cultivate universal
friendliness:

> Strong one make me strong!
> may all beings look on me with the eye of friend
> may I look on all beings with the eye of friend
> may we look on one another with the eye of friend

(Rigveda X. 85.42)

In later Hinduism the picture of eternal life as living in the
presence of Siva along with other liberated souls, such as is used
by Southern Saivism in the Hindu tradition, is inspired by
thought of the sacred in man's social existence which, divested of
all its limitations and imperfections, will be reproduced on an
eternal plane. This picture in its turn can inspire a loving bond
between people who share a common life here on earth and who
will again be equal participants in an eternal life hereafter.

To this dimension of approach to the sacred also belong such
things as communal prayer, ritual, sacrament and various other
religious observances and ceremonials that bind the members of
a community together as a group by virtue of their sharing in
activities that are felt to be deeply meaningful. It seems that at
least one of the functions of religious rites and festivities is
social, that is, to enable people to integrate on a social plane
through activities that are thought to have enduring significance,

going beyond the life of any single individual. When occasions for social gathering, such as are connected, for example, with birth, death, marriage, etc., are seen to have an extra dimension through rites being sanctified in the name of a divine being who is our common father, protector, or whatever – to say this is really to say that forms of man's social existence are sacred – they can bring people more closely together than does a purely social occasion, such as a dinner party.

Public religious ceremonies and celebrations of holy days of various descriptions perform a social function in another way. They provide occasions for public merry-making and rejoicing and raise collective enjoyment of life to the sacred dimension. They also contribute a style to a people's way of life and its cultural expressions such as music, dancing, painting, sculpture, etc. This is a vital social function, particularly in societies where mass entertainments through mass media do not exist, and where religious ceremonies are the main venues for corporate enjoyment and creativity. And because of the undercurrent of the sacred dimension on which such activities and performances are believed to be based, they add an extra touch of meaning beyond that of utility to social undertakings in which men jointly participate or in which one man's creative endeavours are directed towards the enjoyment of others. In all human cultures cultural activities of men and their social forms had originally been inspired by the thought of the sacred, for it is only thus that they could be accepted as of enduring value and an enrichment of man's social life. Thus even while contributing to entertainment, public ceremonials of a religious character can provide a deeper bond between participants, actors, and onlookers alike, than perhaps does a purely social occasion for fun that is divested of all connotations of the sacred.

A great deal in Hindu religious life has this social function of creating cohesion in the Hindu way of life. The Hindu tradition does not have a church or an organised clerical order – Hindu priests function in a purely private capacity and have no institutional status as an organised body – institutions through which religious communities can be integrated in the social sphere. But the social dimension of Hindu religious tradition in the form of rites, rituals, ceremonies, and festivities – of which there is a good deal more in Hinduism than in any other religion – functions in a diffused way to integrate people in a community. Religion in its aspect of social practice manifestly becomes a part of a culture giving a certain style and pattern to social forms of communion and communication, and these serve the cause of integration. What are called Hindu manners, morals, and customs are expressions of Hindu culture in its social aspect, but these have acquired a religious connotation through the viewing of man's social life as sacred. But they should be seen to be what they are, as social phenomena touched by a religious approach to the fact of man's social existence rather than as the essence of Hindu religion itself. To this aspect of Hindu religious tradition belongs also the institution of caste. Traditional Hindu culture is unthinkable without caste, but what is called the Hindu religion can surely discard certain forms of social integration it has hitherto used, no matter for how long a time, and institute others in their place. For even if a religious approach to social existence says that such existence is sacred, it need not insist that institutions through which men give shape to this existence, according to needs of space and time, are permanently fixed. And indeed this much has been admitted in the *Mahabharata*, Santiparva (188.16) : 'There is no difference amongst the four varnas. This world is Brahman (belongs to Brahman), because it was formerly created by Brahman and later reduced to different varnas by their diverse actions. 'Caste is so pervasive a fact in Hindu social and cultural life that one may find it impossible to imagine a 'Hindu way of life' without it. But this only means that Hindu culture, as it has hitherto existed, is unthinkable without it. But no culture that has a history is a fixed entity and its social and economic institutions, which are what caste is, remain subject to change, however difficult it is to visualise change in respect of something that has enjoyed a long life running into thousands of years. But caste as an institution had not remained an identical entity throughout these years, and it kept changing shape until it was finally frozen during the long centuries of decadence and decay of Hindu culture. Caste is a social and economic arrangement that was created by men under certain challenges; it can be changed by pressure from certain other challeges that come to them under widely different circumstances.

The need for not identifying, as is so often done, the social aspects of Hindu religious tradition with the whole of this tradition is particularly important, as this tradition allows cosmic and self-integration, besides social integration, as legitimate objects of man's religious quest. In these contexts, as is explicitly recognised in the tradition, manners, morals, customs and caste lose their significance. No doubt for the vast majority of the Hindus the level of social integration remains the most important aspect of man's religious quest. But this need not be so, and an understanding of the religious quest in the Hindu tradition need not concentrate on its social dimension, except of course when the problem is approached from a sociological or anthropological point of view. As approached from a religious point of view, Hindu religion must not be equated with its social forms, however these may be invested with a sacred aura, as this would mean a failure to recognise other ways of approach to the divine that form an integral part of Hindu tradition.

I have already discussed the quest for cosmic integration in the Hindu tradition. Now a few words about self-integration. When the religious impulse in the Hindu tradition in inspired by a quest for self-integration, where man seeks the sacred through an understanding of the deepest and the most enduring stratum of his own being, it is the concept of 'Atman' or 'Purusa', in English 'Self' with a capital S, that becomes the ultimate term of reference in man's religious search. 'Self' means the infinite and eternal essence in man, represented most often in the tradition by the principle of consciousness that functions in all men, and although each man may be conceived as a separate Self, as is done in Samkhya, its essence is not thought to differ between man and man. This essence is to be separated by a process of contemplative self-discipline called 'Yoga' from all that is limited, finite and transitory in man's being, that is, his physical and psychic being. The reason why this has to be done is this. Man normally takes his physical and psychic being, which are conditioned and limited by other physical and psychic facts, as the whole of himself, and this keeps him from understanding that there is within him an immortal essence that is not increased or diminished by facts of pleasure or pain – these being what normally determine what man will or will not seek.

Although achieving self-integration means in this context being established in one's immortal essence, it also involves that through an intensive process of discipline man comes to a better understanding of his physical and psychic being as well. So integration·means integration with the whole of man's being, physical, psychic and spiritual. Underlying man's physical and psychic being are what are called in Sanskrit 'samskaras' or 'vasanas' – that is, unconscious drives, impulses, reflexes, etc., both physical and psychic, which regulate a man's functioning as an ego without his realising that this is so. Man comes to a true understanding of these when he comes face to face with the resistance that these forces generate whenever he makes an attempt at control. But mastery of these forces can be achieved and pressed to the service of what is autonomous and undecaying in man. When this happens, man becomes master of himself and he is no longer a slave to the forces of nature, represented by the ego's demand for satisfaction. To be liberated means to know that the satisfaction of the ego's demands is not the final word in man's quest for self-fulfilment. This understanding, which has to be lived in order that it may be gained, cannot be conferred on man from an external source, it has to be achieved by man himself. So the concept of 'Self', the immortal essence in man himself, remains the most important concept in this context.

This is a religious quest in so far as it is directed to what is immortal and of ultimate value. That this is to be found in man's own being does not make this approach any less religious, for it is not the finite and limited ego, subject to spatio-temporal conditioning, that is the object of man's quest in this context of self-integration, but that which is infinite and eternal and so divine in man himself.

This quest for self-understanding on the part of man as a being of a certain kind may remain a thing on its own, as it does in Samkhya, or it may become an ingredient in all search for religious reality, whether this is conceived as Supra-Personal Absolute or a Personal God. The trouble with man, as it is conceived in the Hindu tradition, is not so much sin as ignorance, and ignorance is not only ignorance about the nature of ultimate reality, it is also ignorance about the possibilities of man as a being of a distinctive sort. For man as an expression of the divine creative energy is potentially divine, and it is because of this that he can relink himself with the divine source via his capacity for self-conscious understanding. This does not happen because man accepts himself as limited by his own particular system of desires generated by his physical and psychic being. Knowledge of one's true nature, that is, the fact that one is not only a physical and psychic being but also spiritual and, in that capacity, free, is essential for achieving unity with the source. As this will not happen as long as man's physical and psychic being remains in control, self-understanding cannot be divorced from the understanding of the divine source.

Self-integration, social integration and cosmic integration may remain exclusive goals, but they may not, and in the Hindu tradition one of these often shades into the others. In the Upanisads search for the Self ultimately ends in the realisation that it is identical with Brahman, the Supra-Personal Absolute, and in the *Gita* and the Tantras generally knowledge of God leads to a fuller understanding of oneself as a free agent. Nevertheless the impulse for these three different types of integration has produced different kinds of models and concepts that are used in the Hindu tradition in its quest for the divine. When man thinks of himself as not just a social being, bound by love and affection to other human beings, but as a part of the cosmos and its manifold forms of expression with which he feels himself to be in harmony or in a state of rapport, he formulates the sacred in supra-personal terms, such as Brahman in the Upanisads. When, however, man's social existence as a being amongst other beings who share his distinctive nature is the point of departure, the model he uses is that of a creator, the Lord, father or mother, through whose love and care human beings are to be united in an eternal life of bliss. But when the religious quest is inspired by the mystery of man's own being he uses the concept of Atman, or Self, as his model, although very often this Self is seen to be non-different from Brahman, the divine immensity, as in the Upanisads, or united with God, the Ultimate Person, as in the *Gita*. Nevertheless, when the stimulus for the religious quest comes primarily from man's need to understand himself and to be integrated with the fullest and highest possibilities of his own being, the picture of eternal life that he projects is not that of living in the presence of God but that of transcending finitude and the limitations of the human condition – the strife, the dualities, the contradictions, and the suffering that these engender.

Religion thus performs the function of integration in the Hindu tradition in the same way as in other traditions. But religious reality is here approached from more than one point of view and the nature of integration sought for is also multiple. It may be felt that all these approaches cannot be equally legitimate and that only one of these can be valid, since there can be only one truth about religious reality. Now by 'truth' may be meant the truth of a statement, or it may mean 'being', as in 'God is the ultimate Truth'. The being of religious reality is what it is, it is the infinite and eternal source of all existence and value, and the Hindu tradition acknowledges that it is always the same no matter what we say about it. But when by 'truth' is meant truth of the statements that we make about it, it cannot be maintained, according to this tradition, that there is only one truth. For religious reality, being the infinite and ultimate essence of all existence and value cannot be comprehended in its totality by conceptual means, as concepts function by the negation of their contrary. All man's conceptual formulations of religious reality, as of everything else, are from a certain framework of enquiry, and this determines which symbol or symbols are going to be used by man when he tries to illuminate its nature. I have said that the type of integration a man is looking for may well determine his framework of enquiry and hence his choice of concepts, gods, Brahman, Lord God, or Atman. There have been thinkers belonging to this tradition who have insisted that all of these are different descriptions of the same ultimate reality but this can be the case only if these descriptions are models under which one tries to view ultimate reality as determined by the purpose one has in mind in embarking on a religious search. As far as this tradition is concerned it cannot be said that there can be only one purpose behind man's search for the divine, for the tradition incorporates all the four types of purpose I have here discussed. This is because there is no authority within this tradition, such as a church or a particular sacred book or group of books, preaching only one type of doctrine that can be appealed to in finding out what is or is not a religious search.

CHAPTER IV

Polytheism

Hindu polytheism has its roots in the Vedas and however one may feel about the Hindu claim that all forms of belief and practice found in their tradition have their origin in the Vedas, there is no doubt that the theory and practice of polytheism at its best can be found there. So I shall mainly concentrate on the Vedas, despite the fact that present-day Hindu polytheism differs substantially from Vedic polytheism in both theory and practice. Polytheistic gods worshipped today by Hindus are by and large different from those mentioned in the Vedas. (But as nothing in the Hindu tradition is ever discarded Vedic gods have been retained as unimportant functionaries such as doorkeepers in Hindu temples or as guardians of the quarters and so on.) The Vedic Indians did not have temples and their gods were not represented in images. Their worship consisted in the singing of hymns and chanting of sacrificial formulae by people who took soma, a liquor or drug that helped to produce a state of transport, accompanied by ritual sacrifice in the form of offerings of clarified butter, soma and such other stuff on to fire, enclosed in a specially built altar. The importance of fire lay in this, that it could act as the symbol that links heaven and earth (the sun is a form of fire in the sky) and ritual sacrifice was a form of reliving the link that binds these two together. Present-day polytheistic Hindu worship consists of offerings of food, water, light etc., to an image of a god or goddess, accompanied by incantations and prayers, who it is hoped will look kindly upon the worshipper. (Sometimes, however, an act of worship is just an expression of adoration and devotion.) It is conceived differently from Vedic worship in so far as it does not involve the Vedic idea of rita, a universal cosmic order to which both gods and men belong and of which the gods are the upholders, helped no doubt in their task by human offerings, particularly that of invigorating soma during ritual sacrifice.

The theory and practice of sacrifice in the Vedas was consciously based on the idea of cosmic order which it is the function of sacrifice to symbolically reproduce via the mediation of

Agni (the fire god). This is why an act of sacrifice on the part
of man was believed to strengthen the creative potencies of
gods. Present-day Hindu Puja is an act of adoration or of
supplication to gods and goddesses who are not believed to be
dependent on man's activities even though they are pleased
at the homage paid to them by men; and if men do not
honour gods it is they themselves who lose out, not the gods.
This was not so for the Vedas. In the Vedas, gods depend on
men in the same way as men depend on gods (not, of course,
to the same extent), in so far as the gods are conceived to
subsist by virtue of ritual offering. 'It is sacrifice, O Indra,
that made thee so powerful when thou didst split the dragon'
(*Rigveda* IV. 32.12). Vedic worship thus involved an element
of participation on the part of the humans in the task of the
gods, despite the fact that gods were conceived to be in a position to offer men various boons, such as health, wealth, long
life, intellectual brilliance etc., while present day Hindu polytheistic worship consists entirely of passive offerings suggesting
a one-way dependence of men on gods for worldly fortunes.

Although polytheism is a distinct religious outlook it cannot
be found on its own in the Hindu tradition, even if it can be
found elsewhere (which is now questioned by anthropologists).
The same god, say, Siva or Krishna, who is worshipped by
some Hindus as the sole Lord, may be treated by others as one
god among many. That is, the same god may be treated either
polytheistically or monotheistically, and this is true of the
Vedas as well. The Purana stories treat Krishna and Siva at
both these levels, and this is apt to confuse one unless one is
aware of the different conceptual models involved. A god conceived polytheistically is a powerful being and as such an object
of respect, adoration or propitiation, but he is neither all-
powerful nor all-perfect, as 'our sole Lord or Father in Heaven'
is conceived to be. So when a Purana story shows Siva, for instance, as subject to human emotions and even liable to be affected by bad karma, he is obviously being fitted into a polytheistic model and not being treated as (for the time being, at
any rate) our sole Lord. But as the Hindu tradition does not
insist that the concept of a god must belong exclusively either
to a polytheistic complex or to a monotheistic one, the same
Siva is elsewhere conceived as not only free from such human

limitations, but beyond all dualities and even beyond the capacity of our language to fathom his mystery. This is the case in the Vedas as well. Rigvedic Indra leads men in battle against their enemies and is helped in his task by various secondary divinities; he braces himself by quaffing quantities of soma and bragging about his superhuman powers. The same Indra suddenly becomes rather remote as the sole lord of the cosmic order, full of majesty and matchless splendour, and pure and stainless he becomes the inspirer of men's souls.

As western investigators who translated the Vedas were expecting polytheism to be pure, unmixed with any element of monotheism, – since by definition polytheism and monotheism are logical incompatibles and one can be arrived at only by leaving behind the other – they were somewhat baffled by the phenomenon that polytheistic gods such as Indra, Varuna, and pretty well everyone else, were sometimes addressed as the highest and the best, occasionally even as the king, the creator, the lord and so on, apparently suggesting the status of the God of all gods. Max Müller then had to invent a new term (actually he borrowed it from elsewhere) 'henotheism' to describe the tendency in the Vedas to elevate a god who normally occupies no higher position than that of one among many to the position of the supreme being. This could not be called monotheism, because the occupation of the supreme position by one god did not mean that others were discarded, nor did the god himself permanently remain in this position of glory, and others were accorded the same treatment some time or other. Many commentators thought that this was evidence of logical confusion, produced by the inability of the Hindus (or the Vedic Indians) to arrive at the One True God, as did the Jews. The Hindus got stuck at a half-way house position, so to say, and did not quite get there despite some attempts, hence the mix-up.

The fact is that in the Vedas, as in the rest of the Hindu tradition, polytheism and monotheism were not treated as logical incompatibles; they embody two different outlooks on the divine, one sees the many in the One, while the other sees the One in the many, embodied in various objects of concern to life here on earth. Wisdom consists in not totally rejecting either of these outlooks, as both are equally legitimate ways of searching for the divine, which it will be inadequate to finally characterise as one or the many, since in the Hindu tradition it is 'the all'. Being 'all' the divine can be seen in either of these ways, depending on the vantage point from which one starts one's looking and searching. If one's purpose is to adore the many as manifold expressions of the divine, especially as these impinge on what man values in life as objects of his immediate concern here on earth, that is, all that goes into making life full of the magnificence that man can be grateful for, then one sees the divine splendour in the many and speaks the polytheistic language. If one's purpose is not so much to adore life in its multiplicities, as to seek specifically the one principle that permeates all and to glorify its creative function rather than the splendour that belongs to the created realm, one sees the divine as the one beyond the many and speaks the monotheistic language. (One can even speak the monistic language if one sees the divine beyond all, and yet present in all, although the interest even here is on the one rather than the many.)

According to the Hindu tradition one way of seeing the divine need not exclude the other. The two languages are not logically exclusive, as they are adopted from different points of view and serve different purposes, but it is perfectly permissible to adopt the one mode of seeing in preference to the other and use language accordingly, so long as no attempt is made to debar anyone from using the other language. This is what explains the existence of both polytheistic and the so-called henotheistic language in the Vedas, for the question is not whether there is only one God or many gods, but what language – of God or gods – fits this specific context of viewing the divine. It may be felt that we cannot treat both languages as equally legitimate, since God exists but gods do not, being nothing but products of human fancy. But there are people, and their number is on the increase, who object not only to the language of gods, but also to that of God, conceived as a Person, who they believe is equally a product of human imagination. So instead of prejudging that it is the language of God that accurately reflects the state of affairs as it is, it may be permissible to enquire into both the languages to see the vision of the divine that they embody. Also, it may be permissible to think of the divine as not only the Lord who created the world, but also in terms of powers and potencies in this world that constitute so many manifestations of this divine creative principle in man's life, not only man's physical environment, such as the sun, the moon and the rain, but also his social relatedness and moral possibilities inherent in his belongingness to one order along with the rest of the things in the created realm— things such as are expressed in concepts like charity, friendship, love, speech, moral law, and spiritual light. Henotheism is then not a confused half-way house between polytheism and monotheism proper. It is an expression of the attitude of mind which is prepared to use either of these languages and switch from one to the other according to need. The divine or religious reality (or reality conceived from the religious point of view) is strictly speaking neither one nor many, it is the inexhaustible source of all possibilities – both of existence and value. But man can see it as one (or not-two, as the Hindu choice of term goes) or many or as both.

Polytheistic gods belong to a specific complex of beliefs and attitudes to life and they must be conceived to be close to man in order to fulfil their function – of being the embodiment of something that is important to the question of living man's life here on earth, something that is an object of man's immediate concern and that man pursues as being desirable or recognises and accepts as a fact, even though it may not be particularly pleasant, such as suffering, disease, or death. There are stories of gods in Hindu Puranas who display some human weakness and even get punished for it, and such stories are to be found in all polytheistic cultures. Even so, their status as gods remains undiminished, for it seems to me that this is a device by which gods are humanised and brought close to man. Man must be able to look up to his gods, so they must excel him in many ways, yet they must not be so remote as to make any genuine communication impossible, as would be the case if they were perfection incarnate and unable to sympathise with human weaknesses. As the polytheistic approach to the divine is rooted in man's involvement with the objects of his immediate concern, or with life in its everyday setting, these weaknesses are important for man to recognise.

There is not much myth-making in the Vedas, and Vedic gods do not stand out as clear-cut persons, unlike Greek gods or later polytheistic Hindu gods. Even so, the goddess Dawn takes pride in showing herself to admiring men, behaving just like a beautiful woman conscious of her capacity to captivate, or she gets married to Soma. Varuna, the moral god, employs invisible spies everywhere, so that he may know what is going on when two men confer in secret. This kind of language helps man to find his affinity with his gods, who are the embodiments of his values, and to create the image of one world in which gods and men participate without any great difficulty of mutual understanding. Of course, if a god behaves too much like a human being, having no greater power than man has, he loses his status as a god, for a god must be, in some ways at least, more than a man. Nevertheless, this belonging together of gods and men in one world, and the perception of life that goes with it, is the impulse behind polytheism. Men and gods are in fact said to be brothers, born of the same parents, heaven and earth, so gods cannot be unconcerned with what is going on here. This thinking of gods in human terms has been continued in present Hindu polytheism. The goddess Durga is thought, at the monotheistic level to be the creatrix, the supreme source of all manifested energy, but at the polytheistic level she is fondly imagined to have come back, during the Durga Puja festival, to earth to visit her parents, and for the three days of her stay she is treated as an honoured but intimate and beloved guest. So honouring Durga is a way of honouring values of human relationship as well.

The gods are close to man and are intimately involved in human weal and woe; this involvement is their *raison d'etre*. They can be asked for various things that men cherish, health, wealth, glory, fame, etc.,—asking gods for these things is vindicating them as human values; they can be appealed to for protection against sin and evil, disease, and death – to do this is not only to show dislike of these facts but at the same time their acceptance as unavoidable facts of life. Indeed, it looks as if man has a right to ask for gifts and protection from his gods, for they make human life what it is, and he can even show disapproval of gods if they fail to do what they are supposed to do for human good. In *Rigveda* (5.83.10) a rishi gets rather annoyed with Parjanya, the rain god, and tells him where to get off. 'You have rained down rain, now kindly check it.' In book VIII, (1.14), another rishi shows discontent with

Indra's niggardliness : 'If I, oh Indra, were like thee, the single sovereign of all wealth, my worshipper should be rich in kine.'

Polytheistic and monotheistic attitudes are so interwoven in the Hindu tradition that even the same man who gives monotheistic honours to Krishna, for example, in one context, may treat him polytheistically in another, and imagination is allowed freedom to function at will at different levels, according to mood and context. So it is not so much the case that there are polytheistic and monotheistic gods, there are polytheistic and monotheistic attitudes to divine reality, and accordingly two kinds of language in respect of it.

The use of both these languages is possible because in the Hindu tradition no *absolute* distinction has been insisted upon between the divine and the created (or human), the sacred and the profane, although this distinction is certainly to be found there. To say that this distinction is not absolute means this : that which is the transcendent source of all existence and value is at the same time the immanent essence of all things in the universe. The distinction between the sacred and the profane emerges from the way we look at what there is, as linked or not linked with the source. It does not lie in two totally different orders of being which remain absolutely distinct under all circumstances and like oil and water cannot mix. This perception of the fundamental unity of the divine and the created, or the sacred and the profane, is what is expressed in the Purusa myth of the *Rigveda* (X.90). Three-quarters of the sacrificed Purusa (Person or Self) is outside the created realm, it is transcendent to the world and is unmanifested therein, but it is a quarter of the same Purusa that becomes, as a result of the sacrifice, the natural world, gods, men and everything else that belongs to the manifested world. We may call the transcendent three-quarters 'the divine' and the manifested quarter 'the created', and it will be a valid distinction for certain purposes. But the essence of the manifested is not different from the essence of the transcendent, and we can see this if we know how to look, and so it will be in order to treat the manifested as sacred[1] as well. Thus, to a discerning mind, the many of the

---

[1] I am using the term 'sacred' in this way: to treat something as sacred is to see it as possessed of value for its own sake, just for being what it is, when this value is thought to be linked with an inexhaustible source in which all things have their being and meaning.

manifested world can be the bearer of divine essence, and this seems to be the meaning of Vedic polytheism. Polytheism is an attitude of mind which delights in the many – in the diverse manifestations of divine power and potency in this world of man's immediate concern, having ultimate bearing on things that men value in life and take pleasure in, whereas monism or monotheism delights in the one. Both attitudes are to be found in the Vedas, but it is via the polytheistic attitude that Vedic poets mostly give expression to their perception of the divine, and as a result Vedic hymns convey a tremendous sense of joy in living, in all men's pursuits, in all things of this world, in fact in everything that moves or moves not.

So the question in the Hindu religious tradition is 'Shall we see the divine as the one or as the many?' – and we can do both as the Vedas do – and not 'Is the divine one or many?' That this is the proper question is shown by a story in the *Brihadara-nyaka Upanisad*. Yajnavalkya was asked by someone how many gods there were. He gave this apparently baffling answer: three and three thousand, three and three hundred, thirty-three, six, two, one and a half, and one. The answer makes it clear that we can find as many gods as we like depending on our terms of reference. (Yajnavalkya explains in what sense gods could be said to be thirty-three, three etc.) And we can find gods because they are embodiments of human values, values which can be treated as sacred by accepting them as gifts from the gods that are worth praying for and being grateful for.

The way the Vedas treat the gods shows that they are not believed to be fixed entities, literally inhabiting some place called the heaven, (some gods belong to heaven, some to atmosphere, and some to earth.) Gods are born just as human beings are born – and if they achieve immortality that is by drinking soma, and it has been said in hymn X.129 that they are later than the world's production. This certainly represents an important trend of thinking about the gods in the Vedas. A poet in the *Atharvaveda* even goes so far as to say (XI.8.32):

Therefore whoever knoweth man regardeth him as Brahmana's self
For all the deities abide in him like cattle in their pen.

Perhaps some Vedic poets had a vague understanding that gods are born out of men's minds. And yet, according to the Hindu way of thinking, this will not mean that gods are *purely* imaginary and being fictions ought to be discarded. According to this tradition there is a correspondence between the macrocosm and the microcosm, and forces which generate gods in men's minds also represent powers and potencies that regulate the world outside. Let us take as an example the fire-god Agni. Agni is a god because fire as the source of heat and light is a thing of great human value that adorns every home. Man's valuation of heat and light may be a subjective thing, but the power and potency that make men value heat and light is there and is not a matter of human imagination only. Again, Agni is a suitable symbol for moral purity, one of the functions of fire being purification. It is also the symbol of spiritual illumination, when the inner light in man is approached under the metaphor of physical light. There is then such a god as Agni, for to treat Agni as a god is to say that heat and light, moral purity and spiritual illumination are dear to man and that which symbolises all this is possessed of divine essence. All these things will not be values for men unless they conceive of these as values; nevertheless it is power that is seen to be in the nature of things, as looked at from the physical, moral, and spiritual points of view, that makes it possible for man to perceive these as values. So god-making is not a purely imaginary process.

In so far as polytheism is a version of theism, a suitable description for it is not deification of a lot of ordinary things of this world mistakenly believed to be divinities by the primitive mind, it is seeing that divine essence – that which is the source of all value and existence – is manifested in things that men are immediately concerned with and which they value as fulfilling the possibilities of life on earth. So god-language can be a shorthand expression for this perception which is given concrete embodiment in the personalities of gods. It need not be thought to be a product of exaggerated fancy coupled with lack of 'information' about the one true God.

So Agni as a god is a fiction if we mean by the reality of such a god that we can go up to heaven or wherever and meet some person face to face who will fit a certain description. He is not a fiction if the godhood of Agni consists in his function of acting as a symbol for heat and light, purity and illumination, that men may come to value and consider as sacred. That Agni is not meant to be an individual person having fixed characteristics that cannot be identified with someone else's is shown by the fact that suddenly Agni is addressed as 'Thou art Mitra, thou art Varuna', etc. Again, it is the function of Agni, so far as his divinity is concerned, that is important and not his personality, which appears in effect to consist of his function, and some other god-concept may also fulfil the function of symbolising what Agni stands for. The Sun can take on the function of giving men heat and light, Indra, Varuna, or someone else may confer moral purity or spiritual illumination. Agni's function can be taken over by other gods – and Vedic gods constantly take over one another's function – without any diminution of his divinity, for his divinity is his function and this remains no matter what the name under which it is performed.

Agni is both physical heat that sustains the body and spiritual illumination that sustains the mind. So worship of Agni is adoration of values of life as well as of mind.[2]

Thou Agni art the protector of the body, protect my body,
Thou Agni art the bestower of long life, bestow on me long
                                                                            life,
Thou Agni art the bestower of intellectual brilliance, bestow
                                                    on me intellectual brilliance;
Whatever Agni is deficient in my body, make that complete
                                                                            for me.
                                                    (*Yajurveda*, vs. 3.17)

Since Agni we through tapas, are
kindling the fire of the spirit
may we be dear to the veda
long-lived and bright in intellect

                                                    (*Atharvaveda* VII.61.1)

Agni is the symbol of the wonder of life itself.

Thou wondrous one! Lord of wonders who makest us

[2]All quotations henceforward will be taken from *Hymns from the Vedas*, by A.C. Bose, unless otherwise mentioned.

perceive the wonder that's most splendid, life-giving,
give treasures, beautiful and great, including many sons,
with brightness, O beautiful one! to thy singer.

(Rigveda VI.6.7)

And finally Agni Vaisvanara (universal) is identified with the
divine itself, in man and outside man.

A steady light, swifter than thought, is stationed
among the moving things, to show the way;
all the devas (gods) of one mind and like wisdom
proceed devoutly to that one intelligence.
My ears strain to hear, my eyes to see
this all-spreading light lodged within my spirit,
my mind roams afar beyond its confines
what shall I speak, and what indeed shall I think?

(Rigveda VI.9.5-6)

Once the symbolic character of Agni is recognised, he can be
prayed to for anything, for concord in assembly, for purification from sin, protection from enemies, good homes, wealth,
progeny, glory, and certainly bliss, indeed for all that man finds
valuable in his individual and social existence, and the Vedas
are full of hymns to Agni to this effect.

The Vedas as religious scriptures are often undervalued, since
poets here mostly express their adoration of things of this
life, and not only for intellectual and spiritual illumination.
Some people even try to find hidden and esoteric meaning in
these verses and to show that when the poets are asking for
wealth they mean spiritual and not material wealth. This pre-
supposes that there is something wrong with man's adoration of
life and his valuation of what can be thought to be its treasures,
health, wealth, fame, glory, pleasure, long life, children, social
concord, friendship, freedom from sin and evil, and so on, even
when these are seen to be divine splendours on earth. But this
judgment can only be passed in the light of an alternative
system of valuation that deprecates or depreciates all that man
generally finds to be of value. But when things which men treasure in life are seen as manifestations of divine splendour on
earth and so holy, I do not see why man's desire to participate

in this splendour and enjoy the magnificence of life as gifts from gods should be found embarrassing to a religious mind except on some alternative understanding of the divine that has no relationship to things that pertain here. But the Vedic Indians did not have this alternative conception. This is how a kshatriya prays in *Yajurveda* (vs. 20.25):

> Thou art tejas (energy) give me tejas.
> Thou art virja (manliness) give me virya.
> Thou art bala (strength) give me bala.
> Thou art ojas (power of spirit) give me ojas.
> Thou art manyu (wrath) give me manyu.

The poets find the world itself as holy, so there is no sense of guilt about enjoyment of life.

> Where spiritual and ruling power (brahmana and kshatra)
> move together in unity,
> that world I know as holy
> where devas with Agni dwell.

Where there is unity amongst men and where the gods dwell is a holy world, meaning that in a well-ordered peaceful society values men live by, such as life, health, strength, intelligence etc., are sacred, that is, to be thought of as divine gifts to men. To see them as sacred is to view them differently from the profane attitude which believes these values to be based on nothing but desires of human individuals. The sacred attitude, expressive as it is of a religious world view, sees human desires in the totality of the life of man in its relationship to other lives, embedded as all these are believed to be in one source of existence and value.

   The Vedic poets not only found their pursuit of health and wealth and other good things of this life as holy activity, they also took the whole of their environment, natural, animal, and social as sacred. Gods, men, animals, and insentient objects belong together in a universal cosmic order (rita), and so the relationships involved are organic. Nature is bountiful and she offers men various covetable gifts, light, heat, water, air, lightning, the sun, the beautiful dawn, and many other things besides. So these can be imagined as divinities and praised, adored and prayed to in appreciation of a full life.

> Waters! you who are health-giving
> give us energy so that we may look on great delight.
> Give us a share of your most beneficent sapidity
> like mothers longing with love.
>
> (*Rigveda* X.9.1-2)

> The treasure of immortality
> Vata (air) that lies hidden in thy home,
> Give us of it, so that we may live.
>
> (*Rigveda* X.186.3)

Earth herself is a goddess. She is adored for her gifts, admired as the source of sustenance, and at the same time she is an object of tender concern so that man may not injure her by thoughtless actions. I shall now quote several verses from the Atharvavedic hymn to earth (XII), as I find it particularly expressive of the organic view I am talking about:

> Truth, eternal order that is great and stern
> consecration, austerity, prayer and ritual
> these uphold the earth,
> may the Queen of what has been and will be
> make a wide world for us   (1)

> Earth in which men of old before us
> performed their various work,
> where devas (gods) overwhelmed the Asuras (demons)
> Earth, home of kine, horses, birds,
> may she give us magnificence and lustre.   (5)

> Mother of all plants
> firm earth upheld by eternal law
> may she be ever beneficent and gracious to us
> as we tread on her   (17)

> Whatever I dig from thee earth
> may that have quick growth again,
> O purifier, may we not injure thy vitals or thy heart.   (35)

> Earth in which there are cities, the work of devas
> and fields where men are variously employed
> Earth that bears all things in her womb
> may the lord of life make her graceful for
> us from every side.   (43)

> Earth, my mother! set me securely with bliss
> in full accord with heaven, Wise one,
> uphold me in grace and splendour.   (63)

The rivers too are treated as sacred, and Saraswati is addressed thus (*Rigveda* 1.164.49):

> That breast of thine which is exhaustless, health-giving
> by which thou nursest all that is noble
> containing treasure, bearing wealth, bestowed freely,
> lay that bare Saraswati, for our nurture.

And the sage Viswamitra approached the two rivers Vipas and Suturdri with these words (*Rigveda* III.33.9-10):

> Sisters may you listen well to the poet
> who with wagon and chariot has come from afar,
> bow down quite low, be easy to cross
> stay rivers, with your streams, below the axles.

The rivers answer thus:

> Yes, singer, we will listen to thy words,
> as with wagon and chariot thou comest from afar.
> I will bend before thee like a nursing mother,
> I will yield to thee like a maiden to the suitor.

There is concern shown for animals, who are sometimes treated as sacred, in man's relationship to gods.

> Mountain Lord, we speak to thee with blissful words
> so that all that is moving and living
> may, free from disease, have happiness of heart.
> (*Yajurveda*, vs. 16.4)

Indra is king over all
may there be grace on the biped, grace on the quadruped.

(*Yajurveda*, vs.36.18)

The poet prays that the cows may have good pasture and drink
pure water, and as the bringer of good fortune, they are praised
as 'To me the cows are Bhaga (a god), they are Indra'. The
close relationship between men and beasts is acknowledged in
the hymn to the earth already mentioned:

Born of thee, on thee move mortal creatures
Thou bearest them, the biped and the quadruped.

All that are born of earth share the same fire and are closely
related.

There lies the fire within the earth and in plants
and waters carry it.
There is fire in stone
there is a deep fire within men
a fire in the kine
a fire in the horses.

(*Atharvaveda* XII.19)

This attitude which recognises the interrelatedness of man's life
with his environment is extended to objects that men themselves
create. A house where a man lives is an important element in
his life, so it has to be consecrated and blessed in the name of
Lord of dwellings. The tools of men's trades are important;
they are not just inanimate objects but extensions of man's personality and so fit for his concern in the form of adoration,
consecration and blessing.

It is easy to deride this attitude as naive, primitive, and
superstitious. An enlightened attitude is supposed to find that
there is nothing sacred about rivers and trees, houses, and
ploughs; they are useful for men and their value lies in utility
and nothing more. Hence to look upon them as anything more

is superstitious. But this so-called superstitious and primitive attitude to man's environment is a part of a world-view, an organic conception of life and its relatedness to the universe and a valuation of this relatedness as fulfilling for man. That this attitude is found more often among men who are said to be primitive than among men who are said to be enlightened does not in the least prove that an atomistic and utilitarian conception of the universe is right and an organic and reverential approach is wrong. Anyway, this organic world-view is embedded in the Vedic conception of rita – cosmic order or lawfulness, that displays itself not only in nature but in man's social, moral and personal life.

> Firm-seated are the foundations of Rita
> in its lovely form are many splendid beauties.

(Rigveda IV.23.9)

All things of the manifested universe, including gods, are expressions of this order, even though gods are at the same time said to be its upholders (not creators). This is only to be expected, for the function of gods is precisely to be upholders of all that is valuable for man, including order. Everyday the sun rises in the east bringing men warmth and light, and a new lease of life, so to say, and just as regularly the beautiful dawn heralds his approach, preparing man for his day's task, with her alluring charm and grace.

> The Sun shining on all crest by crest
> the lord of what moves and what stands still,
> the seven sister bays bear the chariot
> for the well-being of men.

(Rigveda VII.16.15)

> Admit us Ushas (dawn) to thy grace
> that's marvellous and most far famed.
> Give us thy earthly nurture, Daughter of the sky,
> so that we may rejoice.

(Rigveda I.90.6)

And to Agni:

> Thou by the law hast spread about
> flowering and seed bearing plants and streams of water,
> thou who generatest the matchless lightnings in the sky
>
> > (*Rigveda* II.137)

To say that the work of the sun, dawn and the like is divine activity is to show appreciation and gratitude for the order that makes possible the bounties of nature and the regulated rhythm of man's life.

This order is shown in man's social and moral life as well. Society was ordered in classes or castes, dividing amongst men all the jobs that need to be done, and a poet in the *Rigveda* prays that this order may be blessed by the gods.

> Quicken the power of knowledge (brahman) and rouse the
>   intellect.
> Quicken protective power (kshatra) and rouse up peoples.
> Quicken the milch-cow to put strength in people.
>
> > (*Rigveda* VIII.35.16-18)

Again:

> Give lustre to our Brahmanas
> give lustre to our kingly men
> give lustre to our Vaishyas and Sudras.
>
> > (*Yajurveda*, vs.18.48)

And, although later in the Hindu tradition the brahmans claimed that the sudras must not hear the Vedas, this is not what the Vedic poets themselves thought (the brahmans, still later, went to the extent of claiming that everybody else but themselves were sudras).

> So that I may speak the blissful word to the masses of the
>   people
> to the Brahmana and the Rajanya (kshatriya)
> to the Sudra and the Vaishya
> to our own men and to the stranger.
>
> > (*Yajurveda*, 26.2)

Indra, the kshatriya par excellence among the gods, is the creator of the social order, and he creates this by killing Vritra, forces of obstruction and evil in social life. A prayer to Indra says:

> Go forward, meet the foe, conquer,
> thy thunderbolt cannot be resisted.
> Indra, manliness is thy strength,
> destroy Vritra, win the waters,
> acclaiming self-dominion.

> (*Rigveda* I.80.3)

And by establishing order Indra caters for the well-being of men:

> Bestow on us, Indra, the best of treasures,
> the efficient mind and great brilliance,
> the increase of wealth, the health of bodies,
> the sweetness of speech and fairness of days.

> (*Rigveda* II.21.6)

And says *Atharvaveda* (XIX.15.4):

> Lead us to a free world, wise one,
> Where lie divine lustre, sunlight and security.
> Valiant are the arrows of thee, the powerful,
> We will take to their vast shelter.

The order of social life depends on right conduct and friendliness between men, so Agni and Varuna and Mitra (the god of friendly compact) are prayed to ensure that men keep to the right path. Varuna is also invoked so that men may find release from a sense of sin and guilt.

> Agni, make me have good conduct (su-carita)
> bar me against bad conduct (dus-carita).

> (*Yajurveda* vs.4.28)

> The great ruler of all these worlds
> beholds as if from near at hand,

the man who thinks he acts by stealth
the devas know of this of him.
When one stands or walks or moves in secret
or goes to his lying down or uprising,
when two sitting together take secret council
King Varuna knows, being there the third.

(Atharvaveda IV. 16.1-2)

Again to Varuna :

What sin we have ever committed against our
intimate, Varuna, against a friend or a companion,
at any time, a brother, a neighbour, a stranger,
that, O Varuna, loose from us.
If, like gamblers at play, we have cheated, whether
in truth, or without knowing, all that lose from us,
O god, so we may be dear to thee, O Varuna.

(Rigveda X, 117, 7-8, trans. Macdonald)

Mitra too is important :

He is the dearest friend of mortals:
let us not anger Varuna, nor Vayu, nor him,
the dearest friend of mortals, Mitra.

(Rigveda VII. 62.4)[3]

From trouble caused by men the Lord preserve us
from woe sent by his friend, let Mitra save us

(Rigveda IV. 55.5)[3]

From an attitude of appreciation of order in society as sacred,
it was easy to shift to the attitude that a particular order found
in a particular society at a particular time – which is devised
by men to cope with certain challenges inherent in the situation,
in this case the caste system – was divinely instituted. Unfortunately that step was taken, and in course of time the system took
on the appearance of an unalterably fixed order that belongs to
the very nature of society as such.

[3]These two verses are quoted from P. D. Mehta, *Early Indian Religious
Thought*, p. 46.

The Vedas thus seem to me a homage to the plenitude of life paid by men who had not taken life for granted and who were still excited by its wonders, as looked at from a religious world-view; and the powers and potencies of generation, order and harmony that make this plenitude and delight possible are treated by them as divinities. While the Vedas do sometimes talk about heaven where men shall continue to enjoy the felicities that life has to offer, they show a good deal more concern about life on earth where they desire to spend a hundred autumns with all their powers of body and mind intact. The understanding of immortality by Vedic men is not necessarily bound up with a future life in heaven. There is a sort of immortality for men in the fact of biological succession, so a poet prays, 'may I be immortal through my children'. Also there is immortality for man in the quality of his experience and not merely in indefinite continuation, 'O men, you are born for perfection' says a Yajurvedic poet, and the most famous prayer in the Vedas, the Gayatri Mantra, asks for illumination of the intellect (the key to immortality). Later in the *Brihadaranyaka Upanishad*, light or illumination is explicitly identified with immortality, so runs a prayer :

Lead me from darkness to light
from unreality (untruth) to the real (truth)
from death to immortality.

To quote A. C. Bose, 'As *amritasya putrah*, son of (heir to) immortality, the Vedic sage considers himself to be "a brother of Devas" (*Rigveda* VIII. 83.8). As such he would make a heaven of the earth and live like a Deva. This he strives to do through worship and good life : "We have become the children of Prajā-pati (the Lord of life), Devas ! We have attained heaven, we have become immortal", declares a Yajurvedic sage after a yajna (sacrifice, *Yajurveda* vs. 9.21). Not only immortality but also mortality (mrityu) is the shadow of God, says the Rigvedic sage (*Rigveda* X. 121.2).'[4]

Christian commentators on Vedas such as Griswold, Bloom-field (and others), and recently Dhavamony, in his *Love of God according to Saiva Siddhanta*, have found in Varuna, in his

[4]*Hymns from the Vedas*, p. 334.

capacity as a god who upholds moral law and to whom man prays for deliverance from sin and guilt, the potential 'one true god', who, unfortunately for the Hindu religion, failed to materialise. This to my mind shows a complete failure to comprehend how the idea of divinity functions in the Vedas. Sin and guilt and feelings of inadequacy which these produce are important facts of human life, and so is the need for fair and friendly dealing between men. In a polytheistic culture, the human impulse towards the overcoming of the sense of sin and inadequacy and towards the recognition of all men, including strangers, as brothers, (and the acceptance of these as social and moral values), is bound to be associated with a particular god or treated as a sacred function; (other gods than Varuna have been said in the Vedas to be the moral guide, Agni, for instance, or Rudra). But in a polytheistic culture which is concerned with 'worshipping' the ordinary values of life, as looked at from a religious point of view, this particular divine function (that of morality) does not have the exclusive or the overwhelming importance that it has in purely monotheistic religions. Moral values are among the most important values that men recognise anywhere; but polytheism, in the Vedas at any rate, is more an expression of joy and delight in life, looked at as a wondrous and precious gift from the gods, than of sin, guilt and inadequacy, even though no human being can be free of these feelings, and Vedic Indians were not, as shown in the conception of Varuna. What comes through from a reading of the Vedic hymns, however, is an attitude that is thrilled with life and eager to participate in its beauty and splendour, not one that is solemn, self-righteous, or sanctimonious, which an exclusive preoccupation with morals tends to generate. The Vedas show an attitude of affection towards all that pertains to man's life, friends, family, neighbours, strangers, animals, insentient nature, and they take it for granted that this is only 'natural' for man, but it would be totally incongruous with the Vedic poets' perception of life, if they were to exalt freedom from sin, or love of neighbour, as the 'virtue'; one should live for, to please God or to attain immortality.

This perception of life is shown in the conceptions of two of the most important deities in the Vedic pantheon, Indra, and Soma. Indra as the ideal kshatriya (the Hindus ought to take

note that the most dearly beloved of all Vedic gods was a kshatriya and not a (*brahman*) is the embodiment of vigour, strength,
vitality, courage, and leadership, of unlimited bounty, magnificence and beauty, that is, of all those qualities which go to
build a heroic conception of life. The Vedas leave no doubt that
Indra, the darling of Vedic Indians, is the most prominent of all
deities, one who is looked up to as a model more often than
anybody else :

> For each and every form he is the model
> it is his form that is to be seen everywhere.
> Indra moves multiform by his creative charm
> the bay steeds yoked to his car are a thousand.
>
> (*Rigveda* VI.47.18)

Since Indra stands for the very life urge itself in its heroic
dimensions, the acceptance of Indra is acceptance of life itself
in all its dynamism. To my mind, what is significant for the
development of post-Vedic Hindu culture was not, as is often
remarked by Christians, the relegation of Varuna to the position
of the 'lord of waters' (for his moral functions survived by being
taken over by other gods), but the degeneration of Indra in the
Puranas into a ludicrous and laughable figure, shorn of all
majesty, dignity, and glory. Some of the majestic conception of
life that Indra stood for no doubt survived in the Krishna
legends, but in a rather diluted fashion. Krishna of the Puranas
does not stand for a heroic vision of life quite as unambiguously
as did Indra of the *Rigveda*.

The same attitude of acceptance of life as delight is shown in
the conception of Soma, a god to whom the whole of the 9th
book of the *Rigveda* was devoted. Soma is the personification of
a liquor or drug taken by participants in ritual and offered by
priests to gods to augment their efficiency. Soma produces
ecstasy, transport, and delight, besides contributing to health,
vitality, and vision, and the fact that Soma was treated as a god
shows the Vedic perception of life I am talking about.

To quote *Rigveda* (1.91, trans. Griffiths) :

> Thou Soma art pre-eminent for wisdom
> along the straightest path thou art our leader.

Our wise forefathers by thy guidance, Indu,
gained for themselves among the gods great virtues. (1)

Thou by thy insight art most wise, O Soma,
strong by these energies and all possessing;
mighty art thou by all thy powers and greatness,
by glories art thou glorious, guide of mortals. (2)

Soma be happy in our heart as milch-kine in the grassy
   meads,
As a young man in his own house. (3)

O Soma, god, the mortal man, who in thy friendship hath
   delight,
Him doth the mighty sage befriend. (14)

Soma, wax great, from every side may vigorous powers unite
   in thee.
Be in the gathering-place of strength. (16)[5]

Again (*Rigveda* VIII. 68, trans. Griffiths) :

This here is Soma, ne'er restrained, active,
all-conquering, bursting forth,
Rishi and sage by sapience. (1)

All that is he covers over, all that is sick he medicines
the blind man sees, the cripple walks. (2)

Gracious, displaying tender love, unconquered, gentle in thy
   thoughts,
Be sweet, O Soma, to our heart. (7)

It is Soma who confers immortality (*Rigveda* IX.188.3, trans.
Griffiths) :

[5]Quoted from Mehta, pp. 55, 57.

For verily Pavamana (Soma) thou hast, splendidest
called all the generations of gods to immortality.

In the context of such a perception of life the god who represents protection against sin, guilt, and inadequacy, however
important this function may be for the well-being of mortal
man, can hardly be said to have the potentiality of becoming
the 'one true God' – even if we believe that there is room for
the concept of 'the only true God' in the Vedas at all. In the
Vedas no one god, not even beloved Indra, to whom the
majority of the hymns of the *Rigveda* have been addressed, has
been allowed the distinction of 'the one true God', although
many gods, including Indra, have been treated monotheistically
as well as polytheistically. Gods in the Vedas, including such
important gods as Indra and Varuna, have remained manifestations of divine power and potency in human living, and divinity
itself has been conceived both monotheistically and monistical-
ly, either as the supreme being, the lord, creator, etc., or as the
divine 'it' or 'that' which necessarily remains beyond man's
conceptual formulation. But what is important in the Vedas is
its polytheism – its perception of life itself in all its diversity
here on earth in religious terms. A religious outlook is relevant
to the living of men's life here on earth in respect of all that
concerns life, not just in respect of morality. Certainly our
awareness of religious reality is pertinent to our relationship
with other people, but it is also relevant to the perception of life
itself as a thing of glory and beauty, just for its own sake and
not for the sake of some other purpose that may be achieved by
using processes of life here on earth, such as salvation after
death. In a polytheistic culture perception of life in aesthetic
terms is just as valid as its perception in moral terms. A religious attitude to the multiformity of life needs no other justification than the intensity of man's awareness and enjoyment of
the processes of life itself as they are lived, and his response to
them as sacred – processes such as suffering and sex, desire,[6]
longing and love, interdependence with environment, openness
to beauty, in sights, sounds and rhythms (all these being incorporated into ritual), and so on. It also involves awareness of
death and its final acceptance as that which completes life

---

[6]Desire was conceived as a god in the *Atharvaveda*.

(perhaps rather reluctantly). So we find hymns to death as well as
to life :

> As we Adityas! are men
> with death as our companion
> graciously lengthen our life
> so that we may live.
>
> (*Rigveda*, VIII. 18.22)

> Honour with thy oblation Yama (the god of death) the king,
> the son of Vivasvat, the gatherer of men,
> who travelled to the lofty heights beyond
> and searches and finds the path for many.
>
> (*Rigveda*, X.14.17)

Finally (*Rigveda*, VII.59.12) :

> To Tryambaka, our offering,
> to the fragrance bearer, the increaser of nourishment,
> may he release me like a cucumber from its stem
> from mortal life, not from immortality.

Very often Vedic hymns are represented by commentators as
just so many aids to ritual, in course of which they are to be
sung and recited. Ritual certainly plays an important part in
religion, but one has merely to read the hymns to see that they
could not have been conceived merely as aids to ritual. Indeed,
Vedic ritual, before it degenerated into the ritualism of the
Brahmana period, seems to me to be the expression of the same
world-view as Vedic poetry. This ritual consisted of acts of
sacrifice and its function was to relink heaven and earth, the
sacred and the profane, through the mediation of Agni, the fire
god who belongs to both realms. The Vedic Indians believed
that the whole of the cosmos, including gods, men, animals,
and insentient objects belong to one sacred system and this was
maintained by the activity of both gods and men. Sacrifice is
a means of consciously participating in this order through symbolically re-enacting it. The integral and organic relationship in
which man stands to the universe somehow gets dimmed in the
everydayness of his life, causing him to fall from grace or to

feel cut off from the sources of sustenance. That is, man is apt to suffer from a sense of sin, impurity, inadequacy or incompleteness when he fails to experience his rootedness in the order that links heaven and earth. The ritual of sacrifice helps to bring back to man a renewed sense of wholeness and integration of life with the sources of its sustenance *via* divine mediation (Agni, the god of fire) – so it was thought to purify and ennoble men. 'With sacrifice I purify both earth and heaven', says one hymn. 'May Agni take away from us all these our evil acts, our hateful days', says another. The integrative function of ritual may even make one feel that one has become a god, so it is said in a hymn: 'Vouchsafe, O Indra, that we may be You', or 'let this mortal clay be the immortal god'. At any rate, at the end of sacrifice and prayer, one returns to the original sense of wholeness, purity and sinlessness, feelings that are vitally important for man's mental health. So the poet declares, 'we have won and prevailed this day, we are made free from sin'. Vedic ritual does not seem to overshadow Vedic perception of life, rather it forms an integral part of the same vision. I have no wish to suggest that everyone in Vedic society understood the potentials of polytheism at this level. No religion realises its full potential in practice on a mass scale. Nevertheless it is there to be explored and this is what I am trying to do.

This close relationship between ritual and vision was lost when Vedic ritual degenerated into excessive ritualism in the period of the Brahmanas that preceded the Upanisads. These books relegated the Vedic gods, who for Vedic poets were embodiments of religious reality in its manifold aspects, to a rather insignificant position, and made correct performance of ritual the central fact in the expression of man's religious impulse. It was not so much the direct participation of the sacrificer as the activity of the priests which dominated the centre of the stage in this new development of ritualism. The priests devoted themselves energetically to the elaboration of sacrifices in their minutest details, and these grew to extraordinary proportions at the hands of people who seemed to have lacked the vision and understanding of the Vedic poets about man's relationship to religious reality. And they made ritual, which had been suitably magnified to serve their vested interest in the practice of religious craft, the very centre of religion, claiming that the slightest deviation from the elaborate arrangements involved would constitute a grievous sin, or at least make the whole thing lose all efficacy. Naturally, this enabled the brahmans, the hereditary custodians of the knowledge of sacrifice, to become experts in their drafts, which nobody outside the closed circle of know-how could question. This closed expertise helped to maintain the position of the brahmans in Hindu society as the most venerable caste with a 'divine' right to dictate to the people how they should live. No wonder that sacrifice itself was claimed in these books to have a magical potency of its own, able to secure various results and compel gods to comply with man's wishes, with the result that the priest, the wielder of magical power, came to occupy the most exalted place in the whole business.

No doubt all ritual has a 'magical' aspect in so far as it involves the belief that certain activities carried out by men will be efficacious in integrating them with forces outside themselves. It may well be that this magic works through auto-suggestion rather than through actual manipulation of forces outside men, as magic proper is supposed to be able to do. Anyway, it seems to me that an element of magic, however we are to interpret this term, is an integral part of all ritual practice. But it becomes superstitious when elaborate magical manipulation of various symbols, set up to make it appear that ritual is a thing on its own, becomes the centre of religious activity, carried on by priests on behalf of other men, and when such activity is believed to have potency in satisfying men's desires almost independently of what they do.

One of the reactions to this aberration was the Upanisads. But Upanisads were taught only to the select few, so the overshadowing of Vedic gods by Brahmanical ritualism meant that the Vedic tradition came to lose by and large (although not entirely, as some of it was continued in the Hindu doctrine of *lila* which I shall discuss later) the Vedic vision of life, and what took its place was superstitious manipulation of supposedly symbolic activities, which must all be done according to a very precise and rigidly prescribed formula (prescribed by the brahman caste itself). And because ritual became a thing on its own, requiring the services of several classes of expert priests and lasting perhaps a few days, months or years, as the case may be, the question of symbolically reliving the wholeness of life through ritual became quite secondary.

This superstitious attitude to ritual, along with a tendency to expand it into intricate details of ever-growing fineness, became a permanent feature of Hindu religious practice, generally speaking at any rate. As the Brahmans had monopoly over all intellectual and religious functions of society, according to orthodox accounts which they themselves propagated, they succeeded in creating an attitude that looked upon performance of ritual itself (for which the service of a priest is essential) as a thing of great merit and its non-performance a mortal sin. As long as Hindu culture remained creative there arose from time to time people of vision who reacted against this excessive ritualism and who called for a return to a more direct approach to the divine. But during the long period of Hindu decadence, especially after the Muslim take-over, when Hindu society had lost its nerve and its vitality, ritualism came into its own and virtually dominated the religious practice of the Hindus. As a result, Hindu religion in the mass became almost synonymous with superstitious do's and don't's of which there were a great variety. This was a price that the Hindu society had to pay for the existence within the tradition of a hereditary class of priests, whose livelihood depended on an ever-expanding field of ritual practice that would cover a man's life from birth to death. (Indeed it extended even further, from conception to years after death.)

The Vedic sacrifice not only became very elaborate, it also became very costly. Later in the Hindu tradition another form of worship called 'puja' took the place of sacrifice, but it too remained elaborate and costly and often a strain on one's financial resources, particularly as there are a great many festivities in the Hindu religious calendar, gathered in form every possible source. This happened despite the fact that Krishna in the *Gita* and many saints within the Hindu tradition preached simplicity and directness of devotional activity. As birth, death, marriage, etc., are religious occasions, they too involve elaborate and costly ritual and festivities, and because of the undercurrent of a superstitious attitude to ritual a Hindu feels absolutely obliged to carry these on, as they always have been, even at the risk of financial ruin.

The Hindu fondness for ceremonial observances, which are

partly social and partly religious, has become insatiable, so it seems, through a process of social conditioning running into thousands of years. A Hindu, while keeping all his traditional forms of celebration, will eagerly add to them such typical western observances as birthday and marriage day, and while these are purely social functions in the west, they soon begin to acquire a religious overtone in the Hindu context. Many Hindus observe Christmas day, on the side, so to say, by feasting, and they would have happily incorporated a good deal of Muslim ritual had such a move not been strongly opposed by Islam. A Hindu can change his traditional practices by adding to it new material that may be derived from non-Hindu sources – the more the merrier – but the traditional Hindu attitude is that nothing must ever be discarded that has once formed a part of its tradition. And this particular characteristic reflects the process by which what is now called 'Hinduism' itself came into being.

As pointed out in the Introduction, the Hindu tradition, including its religion, is an amalgamation and synthesis of different kinds of beliefs and practices held by at least three different kinds of ethnic and culture groups – the Aryans, the Dravidians, and the Aborigines. This means that Hindu polytheism grew into something different from Vedic polytheism. The Aryan penetration of India did not mean that the beliefs and practices of people who were already in India were overthrown. The Aryan religion was not a proselytising one, as polytheistic religions generally are not, and the Aryans made no attempt to convert everyone to their faith.[7] Instead, in course of time Aryan beliefs and practices assimilated a great deal from other strands of thought and practice, both Dravidian and aboriginal, and some Vedic ritual and philosophy percolated down to the masses through sheer coexistence. The common culture now called 'Hinduism' was gradually born – through spontaneous processes of social functioning rather than through deliberate preaching or teaching on a mass scale, since Hinduism does not have institutions through which mass preaching can be carried on.

Indeed, the Vedic Aryans were not even interested in mass conversion. On the contrary, they were quite reluctant to share their religion with the non-Aryan common people of India, who

[7]The concept of conversion does not exist in the Hindu religious tradition.

were branded as sudras and thought not to be fit for the Vedas. So folk religion remained a thing different from the religion of the Aryan aristocracy, which in course of time incorporated within itself a good deal of Dravidian aristocracy as well (the Dravidians had built a high civilisation in India before the Aryan entry). As the brahmans made no attempt to change the beliefs and practices of the common people of India, they continued to have their own gods and goddesses and their own method of worship, and in course of social interchange between the different peoples in India some of these entered into the Vedic fold and changed its character. So was born Hindu polytheism as distinct from Vedic polytheism, with its somewhat different corpus of gods and goddesses and its different method of worship. Even then a distinction remained within Hinduism between what have been called 'high' and 'low' cultures -- the high culture being much more Vedic in its orientation than the low, which retained folk gods and goddesses and non-Vedic ritual practices almost in their original form. And despite the fact that constant interaction and synthesis between these two has been a feature of the Hindu tradition, a distinction between the high and low culture of the Hindus still remains, in however attenuated a form.

However, even folk religion in India had the benefit of the Vedic philosophy that all deities men worship are expressions, in different names and forms, of the same divine power, and it was through this philosophy accepted by all people of India, who are now called 'Hindus', that some kind of unity was arrived at amidst the tremendous diversity of belief and practice – originating in different cultural and racial sources – that even today characterise the Hindu tradition. This explains why Hindu polytheism presents a picture of an amorphous mass that is prolific, unsystematic, and out of control, especially to people who are brought up in a neat and tidy system of monotheistic belief and practice. But it has also given the Hindus a liberal outlook that does not want to attack other peoples' beliefs and practices because they are different from their own.

Hinduism has retained within itself all kinds of beliefs and practices, from the most profound religious philosophy to gross superstitious magic, that were found amongst all the peoples who go to compose the Hindu population. In fact the name

'Hinduism' was devised by non-Hindus as a collective designation for this mass of material, some amalgamated and synthesised, some still retaining distinct and separate traits. Literate and high caste Hindus generally think of Hinduism as religious philosophy that is derived mainly from the Vedic sources, and they are rather shocked when western observers insist on describing folk superstition and magic as Hinduism. As far as they are concerned the essence of Hinduism lies in its philosophy and in its expressions in Hindu high culture. They overlook the fact that religion is something that is lived by the people, and as lived by the common people of India it is Hindu ritualism rather than Hindu philosophy that dominates their life. As the elaborate ritualism of the Brahmans was further expanded by incorporation of material from non-Aryan sources, the Hindu tradition has come to have a huge, unwieldy, wasteful, costly, and extravagant apparatus of ritual practice, with a built-in tendency to grow rather than to diminish. And there is no doubt that it is this which looms larger in the average Hindu mind than philosophical doctrines. As there is no pruning mechanism within the Hindu system there exists no device for deliberately simplifying it, and any attempt at reform ends by creating a new sect, thereby adding to its complexity rather than simplifying it for everyone. The Hindu tradition can change only in the way in which it came into existence – through changes brought about in the general structure of the society people live in.

Present-day Hindu polytheism, as I said before, is rather different from Vedic polytheism, although its gods and goddesses perform more or less the same functions as Vedic deities. Apart from the fact that the Hindu approach to gods and goddesses is overlaid with the minutiae of ritualism and a superstitious approach to formalities of worship, the long decadence that the Hindu culture has suffered on all its fronts, social, economic, and intellectual, has meant that the Hindus have, by and large, lost the heroic and the organic vision of life that we find in the Vedas. Hindus no doubt still venerate mountains, rivers, trees, and animals, but such veneration is often more ritualistic than an expression of an organic vision. It is as if, as far as the majority of the Hindus are concerned, at any rate, polytheism has been mechanised and is running on its own steam, so to say, minus the understanding of the holiness and sacredness of life in all its manifold expressions. Not that this would be denied by literate Hindus who are acquainted with their written tradition, but it is doubtful if this understanding directs the Hindu perception of life to any significant degree. And as long as Hindu society does not recover from its abject material poverty, it can hardly be expected that the Vedic vision of the beauty and splendour of life will mean anything very much to the average Hindu. Unfortunately for the Hindus they do not even get to know the Vedas, despite the fact that their tradition is supposed to be derived therefrom. The four Vedas remained the exclusive property of a handful of brahmans who memorised them from generation to generation from the earliest times and it was not until quite late in the history of Hinduism that they were written down. Even so they remained out of bounds for the vast majority of Hindus, not only because of the attitude of the brahmans, who had come to acquire a proprietary right over this literature, but also because of the archaic Sanskrit in which these books were written. Today people other than brahmans can read the Vedas, but the only people who do are a handful of scholars with specialised interest in ancient Indian culture. They are supposed to be sacred for Hindus, but they are not read by them as other sacred books are read, for instance, the *Bible* by Christians and the *Koran* by Muslims. So it is far from the case that Hindus automatically inherit Vedic wisdom, even if this wisdom is to be found in books that Hindus call their own.

Present-day Hindu polytheism does, however, perform its social function of acting as a source of collective enjoyment and entertainment that is integrative despite ritualism, and as the Hindu masses have little to look forward to in life, perhaps this social function is not unimportant. Also it helps people to accept facts of life and to be reconciled to them, even if it does not infuse them with the idea that life is a precious gift from the gods. And perhaps, when all is said and done, it does, in an unconscious way, still express something of the Vedic joy of life – or at least involvement with life – since polytheistic worship *is* an affirmation of the values of life here on earth.

It is usual for people who hold an evolutionary theory o truth to believe that polytheism constitutes a primitive stage in the development of religious consciousness and that it is ultimately rejected in favour of monotheism, which represents the highest religious truth. I have tried to say that polytheism and monotheism (or monism) represent two entirely different kinds of impulses in man's approach to the divine and that they should not be viewed as alternatives competing for man's exclusive acceptance. Polytheism is a religious outlook that sees the one as reflected in the many interests that belong to life on earth, and it cannot be outgrown as long as man retains any sense of value as regards his immediate concerns. One may not be permitted to use the language of gods any more, but gods were symbols through which man's perception of the values of this life and his adoration and admiration of these as divine gifts were being expressed. The rejection of polytheistic beliefs and practices as required by monotheism does not result in man's abandonment of his preoccupation with what immediately affects him. He may not find anything sacred in the ordinary activities of life any more, but he can be, just the same, passionately attached to health, wealth, success, glory and so forth, without however the benefit of seeing them as part of an integral and religious world-view. Also it is perfectly possible, and it frequently happens, to make a god, say, out of efficiency or whatever, wi hout one's realising that this is being done, because the language of gods is not being used any more. Indeed, all that polytheistic men worshipped, health, wealth, prosperity, power, fame, glory, social concord, and moral virtues, are still being worshipped by men today, minus of course the gods. Because the language of gods is not being used any more, one is not aware that some of these things are being treated as almost sacred, that is, possessed of an intrinsic worth that gives meaning and significance to life. And the same goes for polytheistic religious festivities and rituals. One may get rid of them, thinking that they are superstitious, even while they mean no more than life-affirmation (such as the festival of spring etc.), but other things which are of no greater intrinsic merit, and perhaps less creative and integrative in their effects, soon fill up the vacuum – such as television, bingo, betting, and so on. A polytheism which has not got out of hand by being excessively prolific, wasteful, and extravagant, can, so it seems to me, supply a religious world-view to man's pursuit of life and happiness – and not just of virtue and salvation after death – here on earth and make it integrative and wholesome. As polytheism is not an alternative to monotheism the practice of polytheism does not require us to deny the unity of religious reality, as was made quite evident in the Vedas.

CHAPTER V

Non-dualism

Upanisadic Non-dualism

Vedic polytheism, as we have noted in the preceding Chapter, degenerated, via the activity of the priests, into a system of elaborate and extravagant ritualism. Gone is the spirit of wonder and puzzlement over ultimate questions, also the sense of mystical communion with life and nature to be found in the Vedas. Instead we find in the books called Brahmanas that dull, dreary, and hairsplitting discussion over the minutiae of sacrificial practice has now become the sole concern of religion.

The Upanisads are a reaction against this tendency, to be found more or less in all religious traditions, to petrify living experience and means of communion into a thing in itself that has moreover been converted into an expert activity to be followed according to strict rules. These rules are the province of the experts, the brahman priets, who in the case of Hinduism have a hereditary right in expertise. It is significant that quite a few of the Upanisadic sages belonged to the kshatriya class whose function in the social system, as defined by brahmans, came to be political and military and not intellectual or spiritual. Perhaps the caste system was, to some degree at any rate, still functional at this stage and the brahmans had not yet succeeded in giving a purely hereditary meaning to one's role in life in society. In any case, this is evidence that there were people in Vedic society who felt that brahmanical ritualism did not satisfy their religious quest and who branched out into reflection on their own, whether or not this was specifically thought to be their job.

The role of the kshatriyas in the Upanishads should not, however, be exaggerated, for there are famous brahman sages in the Upanishads who reacted in the same way as did the kshatriyas. The brahman caste supplied both the priests and the intellectuals whose business it was to think. It is not that intellectuals did not have vested interest or that the brahmans did not use their monopolistic position in matters of thought in furthering their own privileges. They had even declared themselves to be gods on earth and exempt from many duties and obligations that were binding on lesser mortals. In almost all Hindu books that came out of brahman hands it is tirelessly preached that the brahmans are superior beings and must be given the supreme position of honour on all occasions, even if individual brahmans had nothing to show in terms of character and achievement that they deserved it. Nevertheless the intellectual class does seem to be able to throw up people from time to time whose horizon of thinking reaches beyond that of their immediate interest or that of their class or caste. So we find that in Hindu writings a critical trend of thought does persist which propagates the idea that one becomes a brahman not by birth but by intellectual, moral and spiritual achievements and that even a sudra is a brahman if he shows these.[1]

There were brahmans in the Upanisads who were willing to learn from the kshatriyas on spiritual matters. (In the *Mahabharata* a brahman was even sent to learn from a sudra.) In any case, the Upanisadic sages declared that formalities of ritualism were an unsafe raft; moreover, this was for people who aspired for nothing more than pleasures in heaven, not for those who sought the supreme illumination attainable by man, that is, moksa. However, although the impulse behind the Upanisads is a search for genuine religious experience and illumination, characteristically these books do not condemn ritualism out of hand, nor do they try to establish a different concept of religion altogether. As remarked earlier, it seems that nothing is ever to be entirely discarded, even if it is not thought to be of much value by the thinker concerned, for the mere fact that it exists is perhaps taken to be evidence that it is of some value to some people. The Upanisads give ritual a secondary or unimportant place or they just show indifference to ritual practice, there is no question of any suggestion that Vedic rituals should be replaced by their own findings. Indeed such is the Hindu attachment to whatever exists in the tradition that the sages, instead of suggesting that elaborate ritualism should be abandoned, take enormous trouble in giving a symbolic interpretation to ritual, such

---

[1]*Mahabharata* (Anusasana Parva, 14.3.6) A man whether he be a brahman, kshatriya, vaishya, or sudra is such by nature—the kshatriya or vaishya who lives in the condition of a brahman by practising the duties of one attains to brahmanhood—this is my opinion.

as the Asvamedha sacrifice in the *Brihadaranyaka* – the head of the horse is to be meditated upon as the dawn and so forth – so that the entire sacrifice is reinterpreted into a cosmic symbolism for meditation. The sage then could accept the sacrifice, suitably reinterpreted in his own mind, as significant, but such reinterpretation meant nothing to the ordinary man in the street whose approach to ritual remained superstitious as ever.

I said in the section on polytheism that this is a religious attitude that sees the one in the many. The inherent danger of this approach, if this were to be the only religious attitude available to man, is that a man may become absorbed in the many as many and he may lose the insight that the religious worth of the ordinary values of life lies in their being understood as expressions of divine essence in the field of multiplicity. When this happens pursuit of life and happiness is transformed from a sacred to a profane activity, because they are no longer linked with the source from which, speaking from a religious point of view, all values are derived. Also polytheistic religious practice then becomes a conventional following of traditionally done activities – more social in their implications than religious – rather than an actual means of integration with the divine source.

What then is needed is the counterbalancing wisdom that searches for the one in the many, and this seems to be the religious impulse behind monism or monotheism. I am using the term non-dualism (advaita) rather than monism in expounding the Hindu tradition, as it happens to be a better description of Hindu thoughts in this matter. There is a subtle difference in philosophical implications of these two terms 'monism' and 'non-dualism'. 'Monism' may be thought to have a numerical implication, one as against the many, and here unity may appear to be numerical. 'Non-dualism' has no numerical implication, things are not different from one another, or not two, from the point of view of seeing the divine essence present in all things, but their numerical manyness need not be in question in any way. The Upanisads concern themselves with the non-dual divine essence of the universe, but they in no way reject the numerical manyness in order to preach non-dualism. No doubt a very influential Hindu thinker, Samkara (8th century A.D.), had tried to show that the Upanisads declare the world to be illusory (maya), but this, according to me and many others in the

Hindu tradition, constitutes a gross misinterpretation of what these books actually say. An examination of these books shows that the religious impulse of the sages is here directed to exploring the non-dual essence of the universe rather than, as in the Vedas, to an appreciation of the sacredness of the many as divine expressions in the context of immediate human concerns. Nevertheless the Upanisads are replete with statements to the effect that all that there is is an expression of Brahman, the divine immensity, and these directly contradict the illusion doctrine foisted on the Upanisads by Samkara.

Because of the wide acceptance of Samkara's interpretation of the Upanisads as *the* interpretation, it became fashionable to hold that the Upanisads show world-weariness and that their message is life negating. Often this interpretation is accepted because it provides an easy explanation of the present state of Hindu society in disarray, steeped in poverty and large-scale apathy among the masses about their environment, physical, social, economic, and moral. The principal Upanisads do not say that the world is steeped in misery, except for Maitri, which is post-Buddhist and is obviously influenced by the Buddhist dictum that everything is suffering (sarvam duhkham). In both *Brihadaranyaka* and *Taittiriya* Upanisads it is said that life is good and full of bliss, but ordinary human bliss is as nothing compared to the bliss of Brahman, which is equal to human bliss multiplied many hundred times. 'If one is healthy in body, wealthy, lord over others, lavishly provided with all human enjoyments, that is the highest human bliss. This human bliss multiplied a hundred times makes one unit of the bliss for the fathers who have won their world.'[2] Thus it goes on multiplying this bliss by hundred many times over until we come to bliss of Brahman. Similarly in *Taittiriya*, 'Let there be a youth, a good youth, well-read, prompt in action, steady in mind and strong in body. Let the whole earth be full of wealth for him. That is one human bliss. What is a hundred times the human bliss that is one bliss of human fairies...'[3] This Upanisad too multiplies human bliss many hundred times before we come to bliss of Brahman. So

[2] *Brihadaranyaka Upanisad*, IV.3.33, in *The Principal Upanisads*, trans. Radhakrishnan, p. 266.

[3] *Taittiriya Upanisad*, II.8.1, Radhakrishnan, pp. 550–551.

one does not seek Brahman because one thereby escapes the sufferings of this world, rather one seeks it because its bliss is incomparably more than that of ordinary human bliss. *Taittiriya* also says
that out of the bliss of Brahman all things arise, they live by it
and also in the end also disappear into it. One could cite innumerable verses from the Upanisads to make the point that according
to these books life is fundamentally good rather than fundamentally bad, (as Edgerton remarks in his *Beginning of Indian
Philosophy*). I shall give just one more example from the
Brihadaranyaka in support of what I have said. Expounding the
significance of the Gayatri Mantra of the *Rigveda* it says: "Then
he sips it (saying), 'Oh that adorable light: the winds blow
sweetly for the righteous, the rivers pour forth honey. May the
herbs be sweet unto us, to earth hail. Let us meditate on the
divine glory: may the night and the day be sweet. May the dust
of the earth be sweet .May heaven, our father, be sweet to us,
to the atmosphere, hail. May he inspire (illumine) our understanding. May the tree be sweet unto us. May the sun be sweet,
may the cows be filled with sweetness for us, to the heaven,
hail.' "[4]

The Upanisads do not say that a man of knowledge will dissociate himself from all activities in this world, as Samkara insists
in his interpretation of the *Gita* in accordance with what he
believes the Upanisads preach.[5] This will be generally evident
from the quotations I shall give from these books in this chapter
quite apart from the fact that the Upanisadic sages themselves,
whether they were brahmans or kshatriyas, were very much active
in the world. Let me just give here one or two quotations to
illustrate what I mean. 'Truly it is life that shines forth in all
beings. Knowing him the wise man does not talk of anything else.
Sporting in the self, delighting in the self, *performing works*, such
a one is the greatest of the knowers of Brahman.'[6] 'Now this self,
verily, is the world of all beings. In so far as he makes offerings
and sacrifices, he becomes the world of the gods. In so far as
he learns (the Vedas) he becomes the world of seers. In so
far as he offers libation to the fathers and desires offspring,

[4]*Brihadaranyaka*, VI.3.6, Radhakrishnan, pp. 318–319.
[5]See *The Bhagavadgita* with the commentary of Sri Samkaracharya, trans.
A. Mahadeva Sastri.
[6]*Mundaka*, 3.1.4, Radhakrishnan, pp. 687 (emphasis added).

he becomes the world of the fathers. In so far as he gives shelter and food to men, he becomes the world of man. In so far as he gives grass and water to the animals, he becomes the world of animals. In so far as beasts and birds, even to the ants, find a living in his houses, he becomes their world.'[7] Here it is being explicitly said that one can search for identity with the Self through identity with all created realms (since Self is all beings) and one at least of the ways of experiencing this identity is through offering service to creatures of these realms. I fail to find any suggestion in these books that a man of knowledge would be contaminated by action in this world, as Samkara suggests. No doubt the Upanisads insist that in order to be liberated one must attain knowledge of Self, mere action is not enough, but this is different from saying that knowledge of Self necessarily means dissociation from action, as Samkara does. To quote the *Brihadaranyaka* again: 'If anyone, however, departs from this world without seeing (knowing) his own world, it, being unknown, does not protect him, as the Vedas unrecited or a deed not done do not (protect him). Even if one performs a great and holy work, but without knowing this, that work of his is exhausted in the end. One should meditate only on the Self as his (true) world. The work of him who meditates on the Self alone as his world is not exhausted for, out of that very Self, he creates whatsoever he desires.'[8] And the second verse of the *Isa Upanisad* advises one to pursue both work and wisdom. 'Always performing works here one should wish to live a hundred years. If you live thus as a man, (meaning seeing the world as enveloped by God, as said in the first verse), there is no other way than this by which karman does not adhere to you.'

The Upanisadic sages show no sign of weariness with the world, and when it came to questions of practical living they were no less aware of worldly values than other people. Indeed they were being very handsomely rewarded by kings for their disputations in learned assemblies, and once the king Janaka offered to give a thousand cows with ten gold coins tied to each horn to the most wise brahman present in the assembly. Yajnavalkya, one of the most famous of all Upanisadic thinkers, if not

---

[7] *Brihadaranyaka*, I.4.16, Radhakrishnan, pp. 171–172.
[8] *Brihadaranyaka*, 14.15 trans. Radhakrishnan, p. 171.

the most famous, asked his disciple to take the cows home. He was then naturally questioned by others whether he thought himself the most wise. To this he replied, 'We bow to the wisest Brahmana, but we just wish to have these cows.' On another occasion when Yajnavalkya came to Janaka at his court, the latter said to him, 'Yajnavalkya, for what purpose have you come – wishing for cattle or subtle questions?' Yajnavalkya said in reply, 'For both, your majesty.'

It is also not true, as many Hindus fondly believe, that the sages, the teachers of the Upanisads, were living in forest dwellings in a state of poverty and simplicity. Some of the teachers of the principal Upanisads were actually kshatriyas, and they were preaching whilst still engaged in governing their kingdoms. Yajnavalkya, a Brahman, was certainly not a forest dweller before his renunciation. He was very much in society, in constant touch with kings and assemblies. He had two wives and enough material wealth to worry about a just distribution of this between his two wives before he left for the forest. And he is certainly not the one exception to the general rule of poverty and simplicity. The *Brihadaranyaka* Upanisad tells this story. The king Pravahana Jaivali asked Svetaketu (who had been taught by his father, Gautama) various questions to which he did not know the answers. The boy went back to his father and complained about not having been taught properly. The father, a brahman, decided to seek instruction from the king and approached him. The king offered to give him riches instead. To this Gautama replies: 'It is well known that I have abundance of gold, of cows and horses, maidservants, retinue and apparel. Be not ungenerous towards me, sir, in regard to that which is the abundant, the infinite, the unlimited.'[9] This certainly contradicts the traditional picture of an Upanisadic sage living in a forest in utter simplicity and poverty.

Here is a teacher's prayer from the *Taittiriya* Upanisad which further supports my contention. 'Bringing to me and increasing always clothes and cattle, food and drink, doing this long, do thou, then, bring prosperity in wool along with cattle. May students of sacred knowledge come to me from every side. Hail. May students of sacred knowledge come to me well-equipped. May students of sacred knowledge come to me self-controlled. May

---

[9] *Brihadaranyaka*, VI.2.7, Radhakrishnan, p. 311.

students of sacred knowledge come to me peaceful. Hail.'[10] Then
there is this instruction to the student at the end of his studies,
who was not being exhorted to live a life of poverty and simplicity. 'Having taught the Veda the teacher instructs the pupil.
Speak the truth, practise virtue. Let there be no neglect of your
(daily) reading. Having brought to the teacher the wealth that
is pleasing (to him), do not cut off the thread of the offspring.
Let there be no neglect of truth. Let there be no neglect of virtue. Let there be no neglect of welfare. Let there be no neglect
of prosperity. Let there be no neglect of study and teaching.
Let there be no neglect of duties to the gods and fathers.'[11]

It is a mistake to believe that the Upanisads show complete indifference to the affairs of men in relation to life on earth. Indeed
in most principal Upanisads, desire and its satisfaction is thought
to be important enough to be talked about, and here and there
the old attitude that sacrifice can help man to obtain his desires
reappears. Doubtless man's understanding of this world is being
said to be lower knowledge in relation to knowledge of Brahman
which is higher. Nevertheless this lower knowledge, which
includes not only the four Vedas but also history, ancient
lore, sciences etc., is said to be breathed forth by Brahman, and
it is neither dismissed as unnecessary nor treated as unimportant. Quite the contrary. The importance of food as being vital
even for the higher functions of man such as thought is fully
acknowledged in *Chandogya* and *Taittiriya*. In the *Chandogya*
Upanisad the sage Uddalaka instructs his son Svetaketu to
refrain from food for fifteen days and then come back and talk
about the Vedas. The fast makes Svetaketu unable to answer
the questions put to him by his father, who then says, 'Just as,
my dear, of a great lighted fire a single coal of the size of a
firefly may be left which would not thereafter burn much, even
so, my dear, of your sixteen parts only one part is left and so
with it you do not apprehend (remember) the Vedas. Eat, then
you will understand me.'[12] Says *Taittiriya*, 'From food, verily,
are produced whatsoever creatures dwell on the earth. Moreover, by food alone they live. And then also into it they pass
at the end. Food verily is the eldest born of things. Therefore

[10]*Taittiriya*, I.4.2, Radhakrishnan, p. 530.
[11]*Taittiriya*, I.2.1, Radhakrishnan, p. 537.
[12]*Chandogya*, VI.7.3, Radhakrishnan, p. 543.

it is called the healing herb of all. Verily those who worship Brahman as food obtain all food.'[13] *Taittiriya*, indeed, includes our understanding of the constitution of things, arising out of combination (of elements) under sacred knowledge. 'Now next we will expound the sacred teaching of combination under five heads, with regard to the world, with regard to the luminaries, with regard to knowledge, with regard to progeny, with regard to oneself. These are great combinations they say.'[14] Admittedly the knowledge that is imparted under these heads is rather unsatisfactory, nevertheless it is thought that these problems should be discussed and understood in order that a man may have a good life here and hereafter. 'These are the great combinations. He who knows these great combinations thus expounded becomes endowed with offspring, cattle, with the splendour of Brahma-knowledge, with food to eat, and with the heavenly world.'[15]

It is universally acknowledged in the Upanisads that it is out of the natural elements such as air, fire, water etc., and their natural ways of functioning that all things have been constituted including the intellectual capacities of the human mind, even if it is true at the same time that it is out of Brahman (Self) or Being that elements come forth. 'From this Self verily ether arose, from ether, air, from air, fire, from fire, water, from water, the earth, from the earth, herbs, from herbs, food, from food, the person.'[16] In most principal Upanisads there is a certain amount of discussion about the material constitution of the world of which a knowledgeable man is expected to be aware. The *Brihadaranyaka* (V.5.1) even goes to the extent of saying that in the beginning water alone existed, that water produced the real and Brahman is the real. It is not that Brahman is produced from water, the universal principle of physical existence, but the thinker concerned does, like Thales in Greece, envisage water as the universal principle of all natural phenomena. All this is not found to be in any way antithetical to the major quest of the Upanisads — search after higher knowledge of nondual Brahman. Raikava, a rather eccentric sage, declares in the

[13]*Taittiriya*, II.2.1, Radhakrishnan, p. 543.
[14]*Ibid.*, I.3.1, p. 528
[15]*Ibid.*, I.3.6, p. 529.
[16]*Ibid.*, II.3.1, p. 542.

Chandogya that it is air which is the universal principle of the natural world, while the *Katha Upanisad* suggests that is fire. In the *Chandogya* it is postulated that in the beginning there was only Being. From Being fire was produced, from fire, water, and from water, earth. Another thinker in the *Chandogya*, Pravahana Jaivali, speculates that space is the final habitat of all things.

The quest for the sacred knowledge of Brahman in the Upanisads thus did not mean a total lack of interest and curiosity in the normal life of man and the constitution of his natural habitat, just as the recognition of the sacredness of the many in the Vedas did not mean that the ultimate unity of all things was ignored. To see the many as one a man could not stop at the many as many, each different from the other, he must view them in the light of some principle which enables him to overcome the differences (not different or not two). But this does not make the differences unreal or non-existent, even from the point of view of the ultimate non-dual essence that permeates them all, and this quite clearly seems to me the message of the Upanisads. No doubt certain facts can be ignored from a certain point of view as not being relevant to what is being looked for, and differences are not relevant to finding the non-dual essence, so they may be said to be unreal from this point of view, but only in a metaphorical sense when 'unreal' means 'not relevant', so might as well be said not to exist, (unreal, *as it were*). But 'unreal' is a dangerous term, and it is not used by the Upanisads themselves. Samkara's introduction of the term 'unreal' in respect of the world, even when qualified as 'from the ultimate point of view', has succeeded in seriously misrepresenting what these books are about. I shall talk about this more later in this section.

In many Upanisads, *Brihadaranyaka, Prasna, Taittiriya* etc., it is said that in the beginning Brahman was alone without a second he (or it), then desired to become many and having created the world entered into it, or, according to a different version he projected the world out of himself. The many then is not different from Brahman because it is an expression of Brahman's substance or essence and not something that stands over against it. 'As a spider moves along the thread, as small sparks come forth from fire, even so from this Self come forth all breaths, all worlds, all divinities, all beings. Its secret meaning is the truth of truth.

Vital breaths are the truth, and their truth is it (Self).'[17] [A distinction is being made here between the true or the real (satya) and the truth of the true or real of the real, and not between the real and the false, as the maya doctrine would have it.] This is repeated in the *Mundaka* 'As a spider sends forth and draws in (its thread), as herbs grow on the earth, as the hair (grows) on the head and the body of a living person, so from the imperishable arises here the universe.'[18] The *Brihadaranyaka* says that in the beginning this world was only the Self in the shape of a person. 'He verily had no delight, therefore he who is alone has no delight. He desired a second. He became as large as a woman and a man in close embrace. He caused that Self to fall into two parts. From that arose husband and wife'[19] and so on. This clearly sets out that the Self made himself into many for the sake of delight. Similar ideas are found in other Upanisads. Says Aitareya, "The Self verily was (all) this, one only in the beginning. Nothing else whatever winked, He thought, let me now create the worlds.'[20] And *Taittiriya* adds, 'He the (Supreme Soul) desired'. Let me become many, let me be born. He performed austerity. Having performed austerity he created all this, whatever is here. Having created this, into it, indeed, he entered. Having entered it he became both the actual and the beyond, the defined and undefined, both the founded and the unfounded, the intelligent and the non-intelligent, the true and the untrue. As the real he became whatever there is here. That is what they call the real.'[21]

This makes it perfectly clear that everything here is real, and it is real because it is an expression of Brahman. In the *Brihadaranyaka* the many are called 'the real' and the one is called 'the real of the real' (Satyasya satyam). That is, the many are manifestations of the one, but the Self as one remains the essence of the many, without which they would not be at all. Even in the face of this Samkara claims that the Upanisads preach that the world is an illusion (maya), at best a mixture of truth and untruth, and only Brahman is real from the ultimate point of view. So

[17]*Brihadaranyaka*, I. 1.20. p. 190.
[18]*Mundaka*, I. 1.7, p. 673.
[19]*Brihadaranyaka*, I. 4.3, p. 164.
[20]*Aitareya*, I, 1.1, p. 515.
[21]*Taittiriya*, II. 6.1, p. 548.

he rephrases the distinction and, instead of using the Upanisadic
language of the Real of the real, which is contrasted with the
merely 'real', he uses instead the language of the real and the false
(illusory), even if he concedes that the false is not unreal at the
phenomenal level, which itself, in any case, is a product of ignorance. The very need for such rephrasing shows – since one's perception of reality is very much bound up with the term one uses –
that he does not see the world in the way the Upanisads see
it.[22] If there is an ultimate point of view from which the world
is unreal, literally and not just metaphorically (meaning, does not
exist, *as it were*), the phenomenal reality of the world does not
particularly help, and those who treat the world as real in its
phenomenal character of multiplicity, even if they take it as
manifold expressions of Brahman, are still under ignorance and
illusion. Also, one who accepts that there is an ultimate point of
view beyond the phenomenal level even if one has not attained
this point of view, can be inclined to treat the world as of no
consequence even at the phenomenal level, which is in any case
a product of ignorance, so one is told. To do this is to reject
the wisdom of the Vedas, also of the Upanisads. The followers
of Samkara, of course, stress that one should not treat the world
as unreal at the phenomenal level, but the fact that this danger
is implicit in the doctrine, considering the way that it is phrased,
shows the importance of using language in such a way that needless confusions can be avoided. 'Real of the real' of the Upanisads
is an admirable expression which does not incline one to treat
the world as without ontological substance at any level, and if
Samkara believed that the world should not be treated as unreal
at the phenomenal level, which is the level at which almost all
of us live almost all the time, he should have used the Upanisadic
expressions, 'the real' and 'the real of the real', instead of intro-
ducing his own distinction between the false and the real.

There are, of course, a few passages in the Upanisads, notably
Brihadaranyaka and the *Chandogya*, where it is suggested that
duality is seeming (*iva* – as it were), and these passages can be
made to yield the illusion interpretation. But as these passages are
few they should be understood in such a way as does not make
nonsense of the vast majority of the pronouncements of the

[22]This is also shown in his rephrasing of the distinction between the higher
and lower knowledge of Brahman, as the Upanisads put it, into knowledge
and ignorance (avidya).

Upanisads, instead of our trying to twist almost the whole of the Upanisads in order to fit them into an illusion interpretation, suggested by a few passages, when these can just as well be explained without the concept of illusion. The Upanisads repeatedly assert that Brahman is this all; the illusion doctrine says that all this has been falsely imposed on Brahman by the ignorance-soaked human mind, and Samkara twists the meaning of Upanisadic pronouncements in order that they may yield the meaning he wants.

In *Brihadaranyaka*, book IV, section 3, Yajnavalkya is explaining what the experience of Brahman – which as an experience transcends the duality of subject and object because it is an experience of Brahman as essence (Self) rather than as multiplicity – is like. He says, 'As a man when in the embrace of his beloved wife knows nothing within or without, so the person when in the embrace of the intelligent self knows nothing within or without.'[23] As the overcoming of duality in love and the experience of unity or identity achieved therein does not mean that either the husband or the wife ceases to exist as a distinct person, so the experience of the realisation of Brahman as Self, which is the same as one's own essence, does not mean that the world of multiplicity, including the mind-body components of one's own personality, physically disappears as multiplicity (because it is not experienced), leaving only a unitary substance called Brahman. All that it need mean is that the actual experience of Brahman as Self, the essence of all existence, is such that it does not involve any awareness of multiplicity, and this is bound to be the case as this essence is the same in all. Later on in the same section Yajnavalkya continues, 'Verily, where there is, as it were, another, there one might see the other, one might taste the other, one might speak to the other, one might touch the other, one might know the other.'[24] Here it seems to me that the expression, *as it were*, on which the whole suggestion of illusion hangs, is just a manner of speaking which emphasises the fact that consciousness of duality is necessary for us to see the other etc. Where this consciousness is overcome, as in the non-dual experience of Brahman as Self (identical with Self in oneself), one does not see the other etc., and not that there is no other at

[23]*Brihadaranyaka*, VI.3.21, p. 262.
[24]*Ibid.*, IV.3.31, p. 265.

all in the world for us to be able to see it, (which is to say that it is illusorily posited there by ignorance). This is made clear in the next quotation. 'For where there is duality, as it were, there one sees the other, one smells the other, one tastes the other....But where everything *has become just one's own self* by what and whom should one see, by what and whom should one smell,...'[25] etc. That what is in question here is the nature of the experience of Brahman as Self rather than ontology (whether the world is there or not there) is made clear in the following. 'Only by the mind is it to be perceived. In it there is no diversity. He goes from death to death, who sees in it, as it were, diversity.'[26] It is only by the mind that one has the Brahman experience as Self or essence of all existence, and such experience, by definition, has no diversity in it (for Brahman experience is the experience of the non-dual essence of the universe). Anybody who sees *only* diversity goes from death to death, if overcoming death is dependent on Brahman experience. (Anybody who has this experience is not limited to the seeing of diversity only.) So one can treat diversity *as if it were only seeming*, in order to prepare oneself for the supreme experience. But the ontological status of diversity is not thereby affected. I think that the following two verses from the Katha make the same point about the necessity of overcoming diversity by means of one's mind in order to be in a position to perceive the non-dual essence. 'Whatever is here that (is) there. Whatever is there, that, too, is here. Whoever perceives anything like manyness here goes from death to death.'[27] 'By mind alone this is to be obtained. There is nothing of variety here. Whoever perceives anything like variety goes from death to death.'

The ultimate experience according to the *Brihadaranyaka* is an experience of identity between Atman (the Self in oneself) and Brahman (the Self in everything), as a fully realised love experience is an experience of identity between husband and wife. In that supreme experience everything becomes just one's own self (*where everything has become just one's own self* by what and whom should one see etc.) as the Upanisad explicitly says. But there cannot be this process of becoming one with everything

---

[25]*Brihadaranyaka*, IV.5.15, p. 286, (emphasis added).
[26]*Ibid.*, IV.4.19, p. 277.
[27]*Katha*, II.1.10, p. 634.

unless everything that is being referred to is physically there for one to become one with. Becoming one does not mean that that which one becomes one with is *physically* appropriated into one's own self at the moment of identity experience – so that it, ontologically speaking, altogether disappears out of existence and is put back into existence again when this moment is over – for one does see diversity again when identity experience has come to an end. Nor can it mean – if we are to take seriously various pronouncements of this Upaniṣad to the effect that everything that exists has been breathed forth by Brahman – that everything was never there except as projected by one's ignorance. The ignorant sees *only* diversity, because he never attains to the supreme illuminative knowledge or experience of the unity of essence that runs through everything, but that does not mean that it is only the ignorant who sees diversity and the wise does not. The wise too sees it, but at the manifold expressions of Brahman. Only, at the moment of illumination, he experiences nothing but the non-dual essence of everything, that is, Brahman as Self and not the multiplicity that constitutes manifold expressions of the essence (as not-self). As it is the task of the Upaniṣads to tell us about the non-dual experience of unity or identity it is only to be expected that this aspect of the matter, and not the diversity, will receive special attention. But there has been no denial of diversity, as such, from any point of view, phenomenal or ultimate, if such a point of view is ontological rather than psychological. Psychologically one can say multiplicity disappears *as it were*, because it is not experienced.

Let us now see what *Chandogya* has to say on this issue. In chapter VI, section 1, Uddalaka asks his son Svetaketu, who has returned home at twenty-four years of age, after having completed his Vedic studies, whether he knows that by which 'the unhearable becomes heard, unperceivable becomes perceived, the unknowable becomes known'. Svetaketu admits that he does not, and the following instruction is given him to impart this knowledge. 'Just as, my dear, by one clod of clay all that is made of clay becomes known, the modification being only a name arising from speech, while the truth is that it is just clay';[28] and after adding various other things to this effect he concludes, 'This, my dear, is the teaching.' This one thing in the next section is called Being alone, one only without a second, and later on it is identified with the subtle essence that is in man (as well as in everything else) as his Self. It seems to me clear that if what one is wanting to know is that one thing of which everything is made, it is only natural to emphasise that the one reality in all things made of clay is clay and not their differences in size, shape etc., which make us give them different names in language. The truth about all things made of clay, notwithstanding their different appearances, is only just clay if what we are interested in knowing is the common essence of all things made of clay, and it is made abundantly clear in the context of the discussion involved that this is the point of interest. In another context it will be quite important to explore the differences as designated by name and form, that is, if we want to use something made of clay for the purposes of arranging flowers it will not do to get hold of something called a coffee-cup. That the level where differences of name and shape justly fit is not unreal is made clear in the following quotation, even if it is true that understanding of things at this level will not give us an actual experience of Brahman as the non-dual essence of it all (that is, as Self). 'Verily a name is Rigveda (so also) Yajurveda, Samaveda, Atharvana as the fourth, the epic and the ancient lore as the fifth, the Veda of the Vedas, the propitiation of fathers, the science of numbers, the science of portents, the science of time, logic, ethics and politics, the science of gods, the science of weapons, the science of serpents and the fine arts. All this is mere name. Meditate on the name.'[29] The fact that one is being asked to meditate on what is being said to be mere name shows that the expression 'mere name' does not mean unreality. Further, 'He who meditates on name as Brahman becomes independent as far as name goes, he who meditates on name as Brahman.'[30] There is, of course, something greater than the name (the realm of multiplicity differentiated by means of names) involved in our understanding of Brahman and Sanatkumar,

[28]*Chandogya*, VI, 1.4, p. 446–447.
[29]*Ibid.*, VII, 1. 4, p. 469.
[30]*Chandogya*, VII, 1. 5, p. 469.

the expounder of the doctrine, goes on to explicate it as speech, mind etc., finally arriving at the infinite in which the real happiness of man lies. This includes everything, 'it is below and above, behind and front, south and north. It is indeed all this world.' Here again there is no suggestion that the world is illusory. Quite the contrary.

Finally the *Svetasvatara*, where the term *maya* is actually used. But I see no reason why this term here should be translated as illusion where 'illusion' necessarily bears an ontological significance (of not being there at all). In the *Rigveda* this term is used to designate Indra's occult power that creates manifold forms out of one. This power may appear to us as magical (in so far as magic *appears* to create many out of one) but what the *Rigveda* itself stresses is the creative potentiality of divine power to pour forth many out of one, without any connotation that what is being created in this fashion is an illusion. Let us now see what the *Svetasvatara* has to say. 'The Lord supports all this, which is a combination of the mutable and the immutable, the manifest and the unmanifest. And the soul not being the Lord is bound because of his being an enjoyer. By knowing God (the soul) is freed from all fetters.'[31] This is followed by, 'What is perishable is the *pradhana* (primary matter), what is immortal and imperishable is Hara (the Lord). Over both the perishable and the soul the One God rules. By meditating on Him, by uniting with Him, by reflecting on His being, more and more there is a complete cessation from the illusion of the world.'[32]

Now the Sanskrit *visva-maya*, which is here translated as 'illusion of the world' obviously does not mean what Samkara means by 'illusion', which is that the word is a projection of ignorance and is imposed on to the reality of Brahman, for God, Hara, is here made the Lord over the perishable world. What is meant by *maya* here is more properly delusion, a psychological rather than ontological term, that which fetters man, namely, the ignorant belief that man can find ultimate fulfilment through satisfaction of ordinary human desires, geared *solely* to the perishable world of multiplicity. This is a delusion despite the

---

[31] *Svetasvatara*, 1.8, p. 714
[32] *Ibid*, 1.20, p. 715

fact that the world of multiplicity is very much there and unlike the *maya* of Samkara it does not have an ontological connotation, that is, projecting of a non-existing world as existing which is found to be non-existing from the ultimate point of view. It is because the world exists that it can fetter man's mind and produce, through ignorance of the knowledge of God, the false belief that man can live his highest possibilities in terms of the world alone. So, 'By knowing God, there is a falling off of all fetters, when the sufferings are destroyed, there is cessation of birth and death.'[33] To be free of maya is to be free of fetters or delusion about the possibilities of happiness solely through the things of this world, not to be free of the belief that the world exists at all except as a projection of ignorance. Says *Svetasvatara*, 'The Vedas, the sacrifices, the ritual, the observances, the past, the future and what the Vedas declare, all this the matter sends forth out of this, in this the other (the individual soul) is confined by maya,'[34] that is, by a false belief or delusion as to what these things can do for him. Further, 'Know thou that prakriti (nature) is maya, and the wielder of maya is the great Lord. The whole world is pervaded by beings that are parts of him.'[35] If the things of this world are parts of God, then the fact that prakriti is maya shows that maya cannot mean, ontologically speaking, that whatever is maya is illusory. It can only mean what maya means in the Rigveda, magic-like creative potentiality of divine power that can breathe forth multiplicity out of its own being.

As to the nature of religious reality there are three types of statements to be found in the Upanisads. (1) Brahman is a suprapersonal divine principle that is beyond all characterisation by attributes (Nirguna Brahman). The usual translation of Brahman as 'impersonal absolute' is thus a mistake, since Brahman is definitely said to be beyond attributes, including those designated by such terms as 'personal' and 'impersonal'. According to this trend of thinking Brahman is referred to by the neuter 'it' or 'that'. (2) Brahman is the ultimate person, God or Lord, in respect of whom the personal 'he' is used rather than the neuter

---

[33] *Svetasvatara*, I.11, p. 716.
[34] *Ibid.*, IV. 9, p. 714.
[35] *Ibid.*, IV. 10, p. 734.

'it' (Saguna Brahman). (3) Brahman is in everything as its innermost essence and we can best convey what this essence is by such terms as being (sat), consciousness (cit) and bliss (ananda). However, these are not descriptions and no description is adequate. We may of course use such predicates as 'the infinite' or 'the all' in talking about Brahman, because these predicates do not circumscribe Brahman in any way. From the ultimate point of view, from which Brahman is everything and beyond, the opinion that Brahman is personal – if this is to mean that everything that is not a part of the concept of personality is to be excluded from Brahman – is just as one-sided as the view that Brahman is impersonal, if this is to mean that personal attributes cannot belong to Brahman. This means that neither the language of 'he' or 'it' can have any exclusive claim to be the true description – since there is no such thing as the true description – and both can be used in respect of Brahman.

Indeed both the so-called impersonal and personal languages are used sometimes in the same Upanisad and even in the same verse, and nowhere is to be found any quarrel amongst the Upanisadic sages as to which is the true or better language, such as developed in later times between Samkara and Ramanuja, who unlike the sages themselves had definite doctrines to preach about the nature of religious reality. The theory that Brahman when understood in relation to the world is to be thought of as God whilst in Its *true essence* Brahman is impersonal – the suggestion being that God talk is for inferior minds steeped in ignorance – is again not to be found in the Upanisads. As far as the Upanisads are concerned, the true essence of Brahman does not exclude the world, and they take great pains to declare that Brahman is this all. The insistence that Brahman is impersonal as against personal is just as much dogma as the contrary insistence that Brahman can only be personal and the Upanisads preach no dogma. And as they see the world as a manifestation of Brahman, the language of God or Lord is, according to them, perfectly legitimate for anyone who wants to use it, with this proviso, that whether or not religious reality is to be thought of as a person this reality is immanent in everything down to sticks and stones and must not be made wholly transcendent to the world, standing over against it and excluding the world from its true being.

In this the *Gita* follows the Upanisads. For although the major interest of the Gita lies in putting forward the image of Krishna as a personal God, it allows at the same time that those who wish to follow the path of knowledge rather than of bhakti (devotion and love) may with perfect legitimacy use the non-personal model of Brahman in their religious quest. And although Krishna is a personal God, according to the *Gita*, he is present in the heart of every man as well as in everything in the world which constitutes his lower nature (apara prakriti). The personal-impersonal distinction has nothing to do with whether or not religious reality is to be thought of as immanent in the manifested world. So ultimately it becomes a question of personal preference, based on one's cast of mind, whether one is to use the one language or the other in integrating oneself with religious reality. A predominantly intellectualist cast of mind may find the transpersonal or impersonal language more congenial to itself, whereas a devotional cast of mind may prefer the language of Lord God. And there is no reason why we should say that the one cast of mind is superior to the other. The Upanisads use both the models and leave one free to choose, if one must choose, not being happy about using both, unlike the Upanisads themselves. Let me now give a few quotations from the Upanisads to substantiate what I have just said.

'In the beginning this (world) was only the self in the shape of a person. Looking around he saw nothing else than the self. He first said, "I am". Therefore arose the name of I.'[36] 'At that time the Universe was undifferentiated. It became diffentiated by name and form (so that it is said) he has such a name, such a shape. Therefore even today this (universe) is differentiated by name and shape (so that it is said) he has such a name, such a shape. He (the self) entered in here even to the tips of the nails, as a razor is (hidden) in the razor-case or as the fire in the fire source.'[37] This is followed by the impersonal 'that' language. Brahman, indeed, was this in the beginning. It knew itself only as "I am Brahman". Therefore it became all.'[38] In the next verse the 'he' and the 'that' are used together in the same

---

[36] *Brihadaranyaka*, I.4.1, p. 163.

[37] *Brihadaranyaka*, I.4.7, p. 166.

[38] *Ibid.*, I.4.7, p. 166.

context (as indeed in the one just quoted). 'Verily in the beginning this world was Brahman, one only. That being one did not flourish. He created further an excellent form, the Ksatra power, even those who are, ksatras (rulers) among the gods... etc.'[39]

Now for some examples from other Upanisads. 'Bhrigu, the son of Varuna, approached his father Varuna and said, "Venerable Sir, teach me Brahman". He explained to him this: matter, life, sight, hearing, mind, speech. To him he said further, "That verily from which these beings are born, that by which when born they live, that into which when departing they enter, that seek to know, that is Brahman".'[40] The same Upanisad uses the personal language in another place. 'He (the supreme soul) desired, Let me become many, let me be born, He performed austerities...' etc.[41] The Isa starts by unambiguously using the language of God: '(Know that) all this, whatever moves in this moving world is enveloped by God. Therefore, find your enjoyment by renunciation. Do not covet what belongs to others.'[42] Yet later on the language used is more suitable to an impersonal or transpersonal principle. '(The Spirit) is unmoving, one, swifter than the mind. The senses do not reach It as It is ever ahead of them. Though Itself standing still It outstrips those who run. In It the all-pervading air supports the activities of beings.'[43] The *Kena* Upanisad brings out that Brahman is beyond all description and therefore, according to it, the controversy whether to call Brahman personal or impersonal is of no consequence. 'There the eye goes not, speech goes not, nor the mind; we know not, we understand not how one can teach this.'[44] 'Other, indeed, it is than the known and also it is above the unknown. Thus have we heard from the ancients who have explained it to us, that which is not expressed; through speech, but by which speech is expressed; that verily, know thou is Brahman — not what (people) here adore.'[45] So any claim about

[39] *Ibid.*, I.4.11, p. 169.
[40] *Taittiriya*, III.1.1, p. 553.
[41] *Ibid.*, II.6.1, p. 548.
[42] *Isa*, I.1, p. 567.
[43] *Isa*, I.4, p. 570.
[44] *Kena*, I.3, p. 582.
[45] *Ibid.*, I.4–5, p. 582.

being able to give a definite description should be abandoned. 'I do not think that I know it well; nor do I think that I do not know it. He who among us knows it, and he, too, does not know that he does not know.'[46]

Katha refers to Brahman as a person yet formless. 'Beyond the manifest is the person, all pervading and without any mark whatever. By knowing whom a man is liberated and goes to life eternal.'[47] *Svetasvatera*, too, uses both languages: 'Higher than this is Brahman, the supreme (the great) hidden in all creatures according to their bodies, the one who envelops the universe. Knowing him, the Lord, (men) become immortal.'

The explanation for the use of a variety of languages is that these books are concerned with religious experience and illumination and not with dogma. This experience is ultimately beyond expression in language, apart from the fact that the texture of one person's experience of that which is all and beyond all may conceivably differ from that of another. So if one is going to express this experience, 'identity with Brahman' may be just as adequate as 'union with God', where both Brahman and God are understood, as in the Upanisads, to be non-dual in the sense of including all, as well as to be both immanent in and transcendent to the world. It is because Samkara and Ramanuja have doctrines to preach about the nature of religious reality that they emphasise passages which lend themselves to their own dogma while ignoring others or reinterpreting them. I may seem to be supporting Ramanuja against Samkara when I say that from the ultimate point of view the world is an expression of Brahman and that it is not illusory, but this must not be taken as involving me in saying, in the manner of Ramanuja, that Brahman must be conceived as a personal God, Vishnu, or that the ultimate religious experience can only be union with God and not identity with Brahman. One may find that the category of personality is restrictive, since this would seem to exclude the world from being a manifestation of Brahman as distinct from being a creation out of nothing. Ramanuja no doubt said that the world and the selves constitute the body of Brahman as a Person, but a being with a body like this is a person in a highly eccentric sense and it

[46]*Ibid.*, II.2, p. 584.
[47]*Katha*, II.3.8, p. 644.
[48]*Svetasvatera*, III.7, p. 727.

seems to me to make little difference as far as the ontological question of the nature of such a reality is concerned whether it should be described as a Person or as transpersonal.

The nature of religious experience, even if one accepts the world as real (in so far as its essence is Brahman in the form of Self), may well be identity with Brahman. For Brahman experience, as distinct from the intellectual understanding that Brahman is the non-dual essence of the manifested world, may well be one in which all sense of duality, including the sense of one's own existence as a separate entity, may be completely overcome.[49] This does not mean that one who experiences identity ceases to have existence as a person, for identity is identity in respect of one's essence Atman or Self, which is no different from the essence of Brahman. Says Yajnavalkya in allaying the misgivings of Maitreyi, who is bewildered by hearing that in Brahman experience all consciousness ceases. 'Verily, when there[50] he does not see, he is, verily, seeing, though he does not see for there is no cessation of the seeing of a seer, because of the imperishability (of the seer). There is not, however, a second, nothing else separate from him that he could see.'[51] For if the experience is specifically of the identical essence that is in everything, including oneself, then so far as this experience is concerned there is nothing else separate from him that he could see.

Nevertheless, the experience of integration with religious reality may not take the form of experience of identity. Some people describe their religious experience as union with God wherein one retains a sense of one's separateness as a distinct entity and I see no reason why this should not be accepted as just as genuine and valid as experience of identity. Religious reality is what it is, but one's experience of integration with it may be expressed either in terms of identity or of union. As both these kinds of experience happen there is absolutely no ground, other than dogma, on which to declare that the one or the other is the

[49] That is, Brahman experience may be an experience in which there is no subject standing over against the object of experience and all that one is left with may be experience of Reality which Vedanta philosophy designates as Being, Consciousness, Bliss.

[50] Radhakrishnan adds in brackets (in the state of deep sleep), I do not think that there need necessarily be any reference to deep sleep here.

[51] *Brihadaranyaka*, IV.3.23, pp. 263–264.

genuine religious experience, as some people do.

What then is the meaning of moksa, the key term in the Upanisadic search for religious reality? Moksa means liberation from finitude and so from the processes of birth and death that finite beings are subject to. Human beings identify themselves with an egocentric system of desires, which keeps them confined to the narrow compass of their particular and individual lives. Desire, as Sartre says, means a lack or gap which has to be overcome, but as long as desire continues or sense of lack persists, so does finitude. Desire also involves frustration and suffering which are inevitable features of a finite existence. It is because man identifies himself with a particular system of desires that he fails to realise that there is also in him an infinite and eternal principle, that of consciousness, called Atman or Self, which is in fact identical with Brahman conceived as Being, Consciousness, and Bliss. Liberation from finitude can be achieved by transcending desires, and such transcendence means not only transcendence of suffering but also of ordinary egocentric joys of life that fulfilment of desire brings.

It is possibly because the Upanisads talk about transcendence of desires that they have been characterised by many commentators as pessimistic and life-negating, and search for moksa has been thought to be motivated by a desire for escape from suffering and frustration. There is no doubt that search for moksa may be motivated in this way or that a man may embark on a quest for moksa because he feels that life has no beauty or pleasure to offer which makes it worth living and cultivating. But even though this may be true of some Hindu thinking on life, which became particularly prominent at a later stage of Hindu history (there are pessimists to be found everywhere), I do not think that there is any justification for reading this back into the early Upanisads themselves. Transcendence of desires in the Upanisads is not motivated by a desire to escape suffering; the motive lies rather in overcoming egocentricity, since transcendence includes both sufferings and joys that go to define an ego. The Upanisads do not say that life holds forth no beauty or pleasure worth having; what they say is that the bliss of Brahman is many hundred times more than what satisfaction of ordinary human pleasures can offer. As for pessimism, if we mean by it the thought that satisfaction of ordinary human pleasures does not realise the highest possibilities of man, which is bliss, nor does it enable him to experience infinitude and eternity – and this man is capable of experiencing here on earth, according to the Upaniṣads – then these books are pessimistic. The Upaniṣads are life negating if we identify life with ordinary desires, but if the life of man is also to include the possibility of bliss and the experience of identity with all existence then, as these things are the goal of man in mokṣa, as far as the Upaniṣads are concerned, it is a state not of negation but of fulfilment.

There is of course to be found a certain tension in the Upaniṣads between two ways of viewing Brahman. One says that Brahman includes everything, from the life of man to sticks and stones, and according to this way of looking at Brahman everything can be said to be sacred – an attitude that we also find in the Vedas. But the Upaniṣads also say that Brahman is identical with ῾Atman, the Self in man – and it is only Self that can be the non-dual essence of everything – and this may lead one to conclude that nothing but Self is to be valued in any way. I personally believe that the point of specifically identifying Brahman with Atman – when it has been said repeatedly that Brahman is everything – is this : Brahman experience, that is, the actual realisation of the presence of Brahman in the world, is possible only on the part of man, even if everything is Brahman, and that too only because man is a conscious being. Consciousness, divested of all its particularities, is, according to Hindu thinkers, an infinite and eternal principle, so a man who consciously experiences Brahman finds at the moment of his experience that his consciousness or Self, that which is the essence of his being, is nothing other than Brahman, the Reality. This Reality may be everything, but it is only as Self that it may be thought to constitute the non-dual *essence* that permeates the world of multiplicity. This realisation need not lead one to deny all reality or value to things in the world other than the Atman or Self, and the Upaniṣads do not do that. Nevertheless if Self is the non-dual essence of all things then one can perhaps legitimately take up the attitude that it is the realisation of Self that matters, everything else is of no consequence. So some people in the Hindu tradition have thought that this Self is to be realised by severely dissociating it from everything that is not Self by means of asceticism. Asceticism may mean just a definite pro-

gramme of discipline which cuts out enjoyment of ordinary
pleasures of life because it is in the way of liberation from finitude, without it being the case that he who embarks on a programme of asceticism necessarily believes that there is anything
sinful or undesirable about pleasure as such. But there can be an
ascetic attitude to life itself, constituting a total orientation of a
person, and this does fail to find any beauty in life (in its desires
and pleasures), and does not just consider pleasure a hindrance,
which is what a programme of asceticism, as a path of discipline,
need involve. The Upanisads themselves do not exhibit an
ascetic attitude to life which finds something wrong with the
very idea of pleasure – I hope this has been made clear by quotations – nor do they paint life in dark and dismal colours (except
for Maitri). But they do not solve the tension either between the
two languages, everything is Brahman and only the Self is Brahman, the non-dual essence, and this tension persists throughout
the Hindu tradition, in the form of two opposed approaches to
life, called the way of enjoyment (pravritti marga) and the way
of restraint and renunciation (nivritti marga). Consequently we
find in the Hindu tradition intense asceticism and a negative
attitude to life and its beauty on the one hand, and on the other
unrestrained enjoyment found not only in the extravagance and
abandon of countless Hindu festivities, both social and religious,
in the lush and luxuriant imagery of Hindu art and literature,
but also in the conception of one at least of the major Hindu
gods, Krishna, who savours life on all its fronts to the fullest
degree and with the greatest enjoyment. Those who have found
the whole of Hindu culture life-denying have done so only by
concentrating their attention on a small segment of it.

As I said, the principal Upanisads themselves do not preach
asceticism (and they certainly show no repugnance at the idea of
enjoyment), as does Yoga, and at this period of Hindu culture,
at any rate, renunciation of ordinary pleasures of life was to take
place only at the third stage of life. It is, to my mind, perfectly
consistent with the attitude of the Upanisads to value things of
this world if they are taken as manifestations of Brahman, provided it is understood that such valuation by itself will not lead
to an actual experience of Self, the non-dual essence. For this
one must concentrate on the Self itself and follow a definite path
of discipline. The Upanisadic answer to this problem was the

scheme of dividing life into different stages, some to be devoted to things of this world, some to Self-realisation. The dominant conception of liberation in the Hindu tradition at some stage came to be 'not being born again', which is certainly a negative idea, and it suggests that life itself is to be feared rather than savoured. But the Upanisads conceive of liberation essentially not as escaping the wheel of rebirth, as many later Hindu doctrines do, but as breaking the bonds of finitude and becoming one with everything that there is. As transcendence of finitude means immortality, it naturally also means getting out of the chain of birth and death, but this is a corollary of liberation from finitude, not the prime motive force in the very search for liberation.

I shall now give some quotations to show that contrary to what many critics and commentators have said, moksa, as far as the Upanisads are concerned, does not mean annihilation or diminution of the reality of man; it means rather expansion, or becoming all by abandoning the limited and particular ego that defines man's mortal personality. 'Whoever knows thus, "I am Brahman", becomes this all.'[52] 'This is the highest unborn Self who is undecaying, undying, immortal, fearless Brahman. Verily Brahman is fearless. He who knows this becomes the fearless Brahman.'[53] 'He becomes (transparent) like water, one, the seer without duality. This is the world of Brahma, your majesty. Thus did Yajnavalkya instruct (Janaka). This is the highest goal, this is his highest treasure, this is his highest world, this is his highest bliss. On a particle of this bliss other creatures live.'[54] 'Therefore he who knows it as such, having become calm, self-controlled, withdrawn, patient and collected, sees the Self in his own self, sees all in the Self.'[55] "....Because of his being selfless, he is to be thought of as immeasurable, without origin. This is the mark of liberation, the highest mystery...."[56] 'He who knows the undecaying (Self) in which are established the Self of the nature of intelligence, the vital breaths, and the elements along with all the gods (powers) becomes, O dear, omniscient and

---

[52] *Brihadaranyaka*, I.4.10, p. 168
[53] *Ibid.*, IV.4.25, p. 281.
[54] *Ibid.*, IV.3.32, p. 266.
[55] *Ibid.*, IV.4.23, p. 280.
[56] *Maitri*, VI, 20, p. 832.

enters all.'[57]

It has been remarked by many that the Upanisadic talk about absorption into Brahman means the disappearance of man as a person. No doubt it is true that in moksa, self, the particular ego, is overcome, but a man who becomes Self by entering into Brahman may still be referred to as a person or thought to attain to the Highest Person. 'As these flowing rivers tending towards the ocean, on reaching the ocean disappear, even so, of this seer, these sixteen parts, tending towards the person, on reaching the person, disappear, their name-shape broken up, and are called simply the person. That one is without parts, immortal.'[58] 'Just as the flowing rivers disappear in the ocean, casting off name and shape, even so the knower, freed from name and shape, attains to the divine Person, higher than the high.'[59]

Moksa means real freedom or self-possession, it does not mean loss of man's true being. 'The Self is indeed all this (world). Verily he who sees this, who understands this, he has pleasure in the Self, he has delight in the Self, he has union in the Self, he has joy in the Self, he is independent (self-ruler). He has unlimited freedom in all the world. But they who think differently from this are dependent on others (have others for their ruler).'[60] A man established in moksa is above desire and above suffering, but these are consequences of his conscious search for independence, not a result of escapist withdrawal from life. 'He has the reward of having his bonds (fetters) cut, becomes void of expectation, is freed from fear with regard to others as in regard to himself, void of desire, he remains, having attained imperishable and immeasurable happiness. Verily, freedom from desire is, as it were, the highest prize from the choicest treasure. For a person who is made up of all desires, who has the mark of determination, conception and self-love is bound. He who is the opposite of that is liberated.'[61] 'When all the desires that dwell in the heart are cast away then does the mortal become immortal, then he claims Brahman, here in this very body.'[62] 'When to

[57] *Prasna*, IV.11, pp. 663–664.
[58] *Prasna*, VI.5, p. 667
[59] *Mundaka*, III.2.8, p. 691.
[60] *Chandogya*, VII, 26.2, p. 488.
[61] *Maitri*, VI.30, p. 840.
[62] *Brihadaranyaka*, IV.4.7, p. 273.

one who knows, all beings have verily become one with his own Self, then what delusion and what sorrow can be to him who has seen the oneness.'[63] 'He is not followed (affected) by good, he is not followed by evil, for him he has passed beyond all the sorrows of the heart.'[64]

A man who is liberated is not born again, but this is a consequence of liberation, not the main objective of the search after liberation. 'This has been sung as the supreme Brahman and in it is the triad. It is the firm support, the imperishable, the knowers of Brahman by knowing what is therein become merged in Brahman, intent thereon, freed from birth.'[65] 'He knows that supreme abode of Brahman, wherein founded the world shines brightly, the wise men who free from desire worship the Person, pass beyond the seed (of rebirth),'[66] 'If one is able to perceive (Him) before the body falls away (one would be freed from misery). (If not) he becomes fit for embodiment in the created worlds.'[67] The last two quotations show that Brahman is here being conceived as a Person whom one can worship or 'perceive'. The *Kena* Upanisad even uses the imagery of attaining heaven in describing Moksa. 'Brahman, the object of all desire that verily is called the dearest of all. It is to be meditated as such, whoever knows it thus, him, all beings seek. Austerities, self-control and work are its support, the Vedas are its units, truth is its abode. Whoever knows this, he, indeed, overcoming sin is firmly established in the supreme world of heaven; yes, he is firmly established.'[68] So whoever has difficulty in conceiving of moksa as identity with Brahman here and now is provided with an alternative picture, reaching the divine Person and being established in heaven. And in the Upanisads it has been left to one's choice as to the kind of language and image one wants to use in one's search after liberation.

Non-dualism of Samkara

The Upanisadic insight that the world is nothing different

[63] *Isa*, 7. p. 572.
[64] *Brihadaranyaka*, IV.3.22, p. 213.
[65] *Svetasvatara*, I.7, p. 714.
[66] *Mundaka*, III. 2.1, p. 689.
[67] *Katha*, II.3.4, p. 642.
[68] *Kena*, IV.7–9, p. 592.

from Brahman, conceived as the Self, which constitutes its non-dual essence, was developed by Samkara into the dogma that the multiplicity of the phenomenal world is illusory (maya) and that Brahman exists not as the essence of diversity into which it expresses itself but as the sole reality literally without a second. According to the Upanisads both the statements 'Brahman is Self' (the non-dual essence of existence) and 'Brahman is everything' (the different forms in which the same essence expresses itself) are legitimate. Samkara takes these two statements, 'Brahman is everything' and 'Brahman is Self' to mean that everything is just Self, not as different expressions of it in different name and form, but Self itself, name and form being only seeming. So non-duality here does not mean non-duality of essence running through different forms – as the non-duality of clay in all things made of clay which exist in different name and form – but non-duality of identity, perhaps even of numerical identity, there being just the one thing, the Self, and what have been called manifestations of Self in the Upanisads being essentially or ultimately unreal, illusory or false.

It is possible that Samkara was driven to this position through a problem that can be seen to arise through the definition of Self as being (here it means self-existent being which needs no support), consciousness and bliss. The multiplicities of this world, apparently, at any rate, do not exhibit being, consciousness and bliss, nor does man except in so far as he identifies himself with a part of his being and ignores the rest. Anything that is not obviously identifiable as being, consciousness and bliss, as everything other than Self is not, is then not real, if Self is to be the criterion of reality, and if everything is to be taken as real then all things must literally be found to be identical with being, consciousness and bliss, there being nothing more to them than just this, appearances to the contrary notwithstanding. For how can anything be real except in so far as it satisfies the criterion of reality? If they appear to be there with characteristics that lie outside the criterion of reality such appearances must be illusory, a work of maya that projects them, and of ignorance that accepts such projection as really there, ontologically speaking, and not just as projection having no connection with reality in the way the tricks of a magician or a juggler are projections. So Samkara makes two kinds of statements: (1) everything is literally identical with Self, which comes to the same thing as saying that there is nothing other than the Self anywhere, and (2) in so far as things appear to be not identical with Self, with characteristics other than being, consciousness and bliss, they are the result of a force operating within the realm of appearances, called maya or cosmic illusion, as distinct from an individual illusion such as that of taking the stump of a tree in the dark as a ghost.

It seems to me that if we are to take seriously the Upanisadic pronouncements to the effect that everything is Brahman in different name and form or that they are manifestations of Brahman, we shall have to say that although the essence of Brahman can be conceived to be being, consciousness and bliss, everything that can be said to be Brahman or belong to Brahman need not exhibit this essence in an undiluted form, and that this essence, in an undiluted form, does not constitute the whole of the inexhaustible potentiality of Brahman for being. This essence can transform itself – not the whole of itself but a part of its potentiality[69] – into a differentiated scale of beings and things which have dependent existence, and are not self-conscious or blissful, despite the fact that all things can, because of the presence of this essence in them in a transformed form, gradually move up the scale, and ultimately become identical with Brahman's essence. This seems to pose a problem for Samkara, who asks, how can the eternal and unchanging Self or Brahman change into passing and transitory things without losing eternality and unchangeability? But this is a pseudo-problem, for if Brahman is the inexhaustible source of whatever there can be, which is what is meant by saying that Brahman is all, then all change is within Brahman, so to say, and it does not affect Brahman's reality. Nor does change mean a total transformation of Brahman's essence, as such, from one thing into another. This essence is inexhaustible and it is not at all the case that only a finite quantity of it is available to accomplish a finite number of things. So transformation of a part, speaking metaphorically, of this essence into all things of this world having a variety of qualities and characteristics does not mean that it altogether ceases to be

[69]This was said in the Purusa Sukta of the *Rigveda*, where three-quarters of the sacrificed Purusa remains transcendent while a quarter is transformed into the world.

being, consciousness and bliss. This was already recognised in the Upanisads. As is said in the *Brihadaranyaka* (V.1.1), 'This is full, that is full, from fullness fullness proceeds. If we take away the fullness of fullness even fullness then remains.' To think that change would mean transformation of Brahman from one kind of reality to another is to hypostatize Brahman as an entity with definite characteristics, which can be marked off as a thing different from everything else, while the main burden of Upanisadic thought, when it says such things as 'Brahman is not this, not that' and 'Brahman is everything' seems to me an attempt to wean us away from such habits of thought. Doubtless a question may be asked, 'how can Self transform itself into not-self, these two being radically different from one another?' But Samkara, at any rate, is not entitled to ask this question, for he accepts the authority of the Upanisads, and the Upanisads say that this happens.

Having conceived Brahman as a unitary and perhaps even numerically identical and unchanging substance, and as the sole reality that excludes the possibility of different names and forms, Samkara had to give an explanation as to why we do as a matter of fact experience diversity. The world is certainly not an illusion in the straightforward sense that if we look again or check our observations with those of other people we shall find out that it simply does not exist, as we can find out by looking again that the snake does not exist, it is only a rope. It is in aid of this explanation of the existence of the world which all of us all the time accept as there, not as projection, as the snake exists in the rope by projection, but as lasting irrespective of our activities, that the concept of maya as cosmic illusion was developed. One of the senses in which the term maya is used in the Hindu tradition, beginning with the *Rigveda*, is that of creative potentiality that can bring forth multiplicity out of unity, and this maya constitutes a power of Brahman or God. For Samkara, however, maya does not mean this; maya does not belong to Brahman and it is creative only in the sense that it projects appearances that do not belong to reality, not in the sense that it actualises potentialities that are inherent in the nature of reality itself. Maya is not individual, it is cosmic, for we all suffer from the same illusions and do not even suspect that we can be under illusion when we treat the world as real (except when we are told this by some one who has achieved enlightenment). The question naturally arises that if maya does not belong to Brahman and Brahman happens to be the sole reality, how does it come to be there at all? and this question was already asked by Ramanuja in the 11th century as others before him. Samkara realised that there is no answer to this question and he refused to answer it under the plea that the relation of Brahman to maya is indescribable. This is so because maya is there only as long as we do not know Brahman; as it disappears on the attainment of the knowledge of Brahman we cannot say what the relation is, since there can be no relation between the existent and the non-existent. Some followers of Samkara, such as Prabhu Dutt Sastri in his *The Concept of Maya* even criticises people for asking such a question. Maya is not real, says Sastri, for it disappears on Brahman knowledge; how can you ask what the status is of something that is not real. This, if not hypocritical, is very confused thinking and this confusion is concealed under a doctrine which is designated 'degrees or levels of reality'.

If one asks, how can maya project the world if it is not real, and if it is not real is it itself an illusion, and not just the source of illusion, the answer generally is that maya can do the projection because it has phenomenal reality while having no reality at all at the transcendental level, where both maya and the world simply disappear. This answer is satisfactory only so long as it is not detected that the term 'reality' is being used here in a highly ambiguous sense; sometimes it means that which is there, ontologically speaking, whether or not it is experienced by anyone, sometimes it means that which is experienced without having any ontological being outside experience. If maya has ontological being then it must be accounted for, it cannot just crop up from nowhere without belonging to Brahman and without limiting its sole reality when thought not to belong to Brahman. If maya has reality only in the sense that it is experienced–even if it is experienced by all – without itself having any ontological being outside experience, then it cannot possibly be a power that can project anything. In other words, if maya has no ontological being outside experience, then it itself must be an illusion and so must be lacking in power to accomplish anything. Because it is said that maya has phenomenal 'reality' it looks as if maya has ontological being at the level of phenomenality, while in actual fact phenomenality itself consists of nothing other than the fact that something is experienced; and this makes us accept that maya can be creative at the phenomenal level because it is 'real' at this level. This ambiguous use of the term 'reality' allows Samkara and his followers to believe that they are giving satisfactory answers to our questions when they are not, because their answers involve unwarrantable shifting of grounds that are covered over by the ambiguity of the term 'reality'. Let me try and clarify what the ambiguity is.

Samkara's problem is that he wants to say that Brahman is the only reality and the world is an illusion; and yet, as he does not want to offend common sense he does not want to say in a straightforward way that the world is unreal in the sense in which the hare's horn is unreal (neither exists nor is experienced). Had he said this his doctrine would have been straightaway rejected by all as phantasy, in as much as the world is obviously experienced in common by us all, so in order to accommodate the fact that the world is experienced and yet retain the dogma that it is an illusion he advocates a doctrine that has been called degrees or levels of reality, whereas as a matter of fact it is a doctrine about degrees or levels of experience. The highest level of experience is the transcendental level, and what we experience here, namely, Brahman, is really real. From this point of view the phenomenal or empirical level of experience where we see diversity is nothing other than ignorance and illusion; nevertheless at this level of experience things can be taken to have phenomenal reality because they are not simply imagined by individuals as dream experiences are. And the level of experience to which dreams belong does not have even phenomenal reality, its reality is only seeming. Dream experiences are contradicted by phenomenal experience, so the reality of dreams can be rejected in favour of phenomenal objects. Phenomenal experience of diversity is contradicted by transcendental experience of identity, so the reality of phenomenal objects has to be rejected as illusory in favour of reality of Brahman. What can finally be said about the world is that it is neither wholly real (because it is not experienced at the transcendental level) nor wholly unreal (because it is experienced at the phenomenal level).

The confusion involved in this doctrine is this. If 'real' simply

means 'experienced', then there is no scope for talking about contradiction. Experiences are simply different from one another, one
experience is not another, but it does not contradict it. The question of contradiction arises only if the term 'real' makes an ontological claim that that which is being experienced is there, so that
if one experience says that X is there and the other says that it
is not there they contradict one another. So long as the term
'real' means nothing but experience, we can talk about degrees
or levels of reality, but if 'real' is to be used as an ontological
term, as it must be at some stage, then I do not see how there
can be degrees or levels of reality, especially for Samkara for
whom ontological reality necessarily means being, consciousness,
and bliss.

What does the phenomenal reality of the world mean? It is
not enough for the ordinary man to be told that it is experienced
by all of us, since he knows as much. What he wants to know
is whether it has ontological status and is not just experienced,
and the doctrine of degrees and levels is meaningless with regard to this question. If by reality we mean the ontological status
of something as there, whether or not we acknowledge it (as is
the case with Brahman), then there cannot be degrees of it. A
thing can only be real or not real, that is, there or not there; it
cannot be more or less there. In any case, Samkara does not
think of reality as a sliding scale of diverse entities possessing an
identical attribute in different degrees, so that things which have
more of it are more real than those which have less. Perhaps his
doctrine should be described as levels of reality. But I find that
this too is meaningless in the specific context in which Samkara
uses it. 'Levels of reality' is meaningful when something that we
are experiencing is complex and can be approached from more
than one point of view leading to different descriptions. That
which we describe as colour from the common sense point of
view – this is one level of approach – is described as light wave
from the point of view of physics, and this is another level of
approach. This does not mean that the description of physics is
right and that of common sense wrong. But to say that colour
does not exist from the point of view of physics is a tautology,
in so far as this point of view is formulated by ignoring qualities like colours. Such a tautology does not imply that a man
doing physics will be justified in saying that colour does not exist

in some inclusive scheme covering both physics and common sense.

'Levels of reality' may however imply that some levels of consideration of a problem are more comprehensive than others and so have a better claim to acceptance. A scheme of development of an area will be more acceptable if it approaches the problem not only from the economic point of view but also from the social, moral, and aesthetic points of view as well. But here again 'level' talk is meaningful because the reality involved is complex and lends itself to diverse approaches, some of which are more comprehensive than others. What are called transcendental (that which has unchanging and eternal being) and phenomenal (that which is experienced by all) realities in Samkara's philosophy cannot be brought under one scheme at all – when such a scheme is to have ontological significance – in order to assign them different levels within it. They do not mix and cannot be compared. But despite the fact that levels of experience are different and despite the judgment that these levels contradict one another Samkara does put all the levels together and assess the reality of our experiences in one common scale, as it were, by saying that Brahman is Real, hare's horn is unreal, and the world is neither wholly real nor wholly unreal, which is supposed to give us its precise ontological status in a common scheme of consideration of Brahman, the world and manifest unrealities. But 'neither wholly real nor wholly unreal' cannot be made into an ontological category by computing two levels of experience – the transcendental level where it is not experienced and phenomenal level where it is experienced.

So we find that three kinds of statements are made about the world in Samkara's philosophy and they are constantly mixed up together in a most unwarrantable fashion: (1) the world is real from its own point of view, (2) the world is unreal from the point of view of Brahman, and (3) the world is neither wholly real nor wholly unreal from some mixed up point of view which puts the world and Brahman together. The last is supposedly for the comfort of people for whom it is not enough that the world is real at its own level, since that does not mean any more than that it is experienced. 'Neither wholly real nor wholly unreal' appears to give the world a little more solidity than mere experience, so to say, and it somehow takes the edge off the assertion that it is illusory from the point of view of Brahman. It makes us feel that the world is after all not wholly illusory (as if a thing can be, ontologically speaking, to some degree there but not wholly there), and this makes Samkara's doctrine a good deal more acceptable than if he had said that it is wholly illusory. But in effect, as 'neither wholly real nor wholly unreal' is a spurious ontological category, what the doctrine amounts to is simply this: the world is illusory from the point of view of Brahman, which is the real point of view, but it is experienced by all of us at the phenomenal level, which, however, is a level created by ignorance and illusion (not individual but cosmic). The fact that we do not discover that the world is a result of ignorance and illusion until we have transcendental experience does not make it any less ignorance or illusion, despite the attempt at softening the severity of this doctrine by creating an intermediate category of 'neither wholly real nor wholly unreal'. All it does is to give an unfair advantage in argument to Samkara's followers, who can shift their ground according to convenience and get away with saying things like this : maya can create appearances because it is real at the phenomenal level, maya does not need accounting for because it is unreal at the transcendental level.

Some people have tried to soften Samkara's doctrine in another way. The world is illusory, they say, only when it is considered apart from Brahman, but considered as grounded in Brahman it is not illusory. What is meant by being grounded in Brahman? Is the world grounded in Brahman as diversity? This cannot be so according to Samkara because he definitely says that diversity is superimposed on Brahman by the ignorant mind steeped in maya. This is the famous doctrine of adhyasa. The world is real only if it is divested of all multiplicity and seen as literally identical with being, consciousness, and bliss.

I therefore think that the only way in which we can make sense of Samkara's doctrine is to say that it is axiological, concerned to tell us the comparative value of different levels of our experiences in relation to Ultimate Reality and not ontological, which can inform us of what is there or what is not there, contrary to Eliot Deutsch who puts forward the view that 'containing, then, as it does, both axiological and noetic dimensions that are brought together in a functional synthesis, subration is uniquely qualified, according to Advaita, to serve as a criterion for the making of ontological distinctions.'[70] No doubt Advaita Vedanta does make ontological claims, but I have argued that this claim is confused, and to say that the world is illusory seems to me to amount to no more than exhorting us to undervalue the world in relation to Self if we want to have the ultimate experience of Reality. This axiological dimension of Vedanta claim is embodied in a process which Deutsch calls 'subration'. 'Subration is the mental process whereby one disvalues some previously appraised object or content of experience because of its being contradicted by a new experience.'[71] That is, a man who experiences the non-dual essence of existence from the ultimate point of view comes to *disvalue* the phenomenal level of diversity and because of this disvaluation he treats the world *as if* it were not there, despite the fact that it continues to experience it as long as he lives. This disvaluation he expresses in a seemingly ontological language — 'the phenomenal diversity is not real from the ultimate point of view' — while he should have said that phenomenal reality loses all value from the ultimate point of view (of experience of Brahman as Self). As a matter of fact the term 'reality' is often used in an axiological sense, so that when one says 'this is what is really real', one means 'this is what matters, nothing else does'. Samkara himself uses the term 'false' (mithya) to designate his category of 'neither wholly real, nor wholly unreal' and this is properly a valuational term, not a descriptive one. The phenomenal world is false because it has no importance for our experience of Brahman. But that which has no importance may still be there, and whether or not something has importance depends on our frame of references.

If 'real' is a valuational term then the doctrine of degrees of reality means this. That which is to be valued the most has the highest reality, and anything to be valued less in relation to that has a lesser degree of reality and that which is not to be valued at all has no reality whatsoever. Such a valuational framework in which Brahman is the highest reality and the world is half-real and half-unreal (not to be valued beyond a point) or simply illusory (not to be valued at all) may well be

[70] *Advaita Vedanta : A Philosophical Reconstruction*, p.17.
[71] *Ibid.*, p. 15.

needed if we wish to embark on a scheme of discipline with regard to ourselves and our relation to the world of multiplicity, wishing to realise here and now the non-dual Brahman experience of being, consciousness and bliss. In short, 'the world is an illusion' is heuristic and not descriptive, and Samkara is telling us to look for liberation rather than the pleasures of this world by constructing a supposedly ontological scheme that is not strictly needed, according to me, for liberation to appear desirable. But then it may be that for some minds a literal acceptance of the world as illusory is needed for the acceptance of the goal of liberation. The illusoriness of the world is then a model or picture under which one views the world and the use of this model is needed in order to start one off in the quest for liberation.

Samkara himself was a man of action. In his short life he not only wrote many books but travelled to the four corners of India to establish monasteries. But consistently with his doctrine of the illusoriness of the world he preached that action is not necessary for a true vision of reality, which can be obtained only by knowledge of identity, and such knowledge would lead to the renunciation of all activities in this world. He also insisted that this is the teaching not only of the Upanisads but also of the *Gita*, which one would have thought preached just the opposite doctrine, since it insisted that Arjuna must fight the battle of Kurukshetra if he wanted to remain on the path of liberation. Samkara in his commentary on the *Gita* explained this away as simply due to Arjuna's incompetence or his incapacity to be a man of knowledge. It is because he was a lesser mortal that, according to Samkara, Krishna preached to him Karma Yoga, the path of disinterested action to liberation. A man of knowledge would not only not act in the normal way, he would not follow Karma Yoga either, for to him the world is literally nothing but illusion. No doubt he conceded that action, love and the like may have some usefulness in preparing one for the ultimate illumination, but their value is strictly secondary, and once knowledge is attained all concern about the world, even a disinterested one, is to be renounced, since the world belongs to the realm of maya and not of Reality. In his commentary on the *Brahma Sutra* he acknowledges that as long as liberation has not been achieved man will be justified in continuing to perform all normal activities in accordance with the normal criteria of good and evil, but the underlying feeling is that this is rather a pity and that it would be much better for a man if he were liberated and could renounce all activities.

Samkara's doctrine of maya was severely criticised not only by Ramanuja, who brought forward extremely cogent arguments against this doctrine, but also by a succession of reputed teachers such as Bhaskara, Yamunacharya, Vallabha, Nimbarka, Madhabhacharya and a host of others. As a matter of fact, of all the commentators of the *Brahma Sutra*, and there were a great many Samkara happens to be the only teacher who said that the Upanisads preach the illusoriness of the world. Nevertheless this was the doctrine, with its attendant doctrines of renunciation and inactivity (not just renunciation of the fruits of one's work as in the *Gita*), that came to grip the minds of a good many intellectuals of Hindu India over centuries right down to the twentieth, with disastrous results. Had Samkara preached what he preached as his own reflection on these matters, the effect would not have been so overwhelming, but he insisted that he was delivering the true message of the Upanisads and the *Gita*, the two most important of all Hindu scriptures, and to my mind this meant that these two scriptures were no longer available to the Hindus for guidance as to how to live and act in this world from a religious point of view. But of course the very fact that of all the interpretations of the *Brahma Sutra* and the *Gita* that were available it was Samkara's interpretation that was avidly embraced by many thinkers as embodying supreme wisdom shows that Hindu culture had definitely entered a phase of decadence, to which the message of illusoriness of the world and the need for renunciation of activities was perfectly suited.

Samkara has no monopoly over non-dualism, contrary to what a great many Hindu believe. Sakti tantra as a philosophy, for instance, is non-dualistic, but it fully acknowledges the reality of the world as sakti (power), the relation between Brahman and sakti being rather like that between the ocean and its waves. Nor is it the case that a man who wishes to follow the path of knowledge as opposed to a path of devotion must consider the world as ultimately illusory. Samkara's doctrine has no monopoly over knowledge either. It is a religious commonplace that a man who wishes to experience ultimate reality must not rest content with the multiplicities of this world, but must go beyond them and seek unity conceived either as God or Brahman. But going beyond the world does not require that one should question its ontological status, which is different from questioning its axiological status in the value system with which one is operating for a particular purpose. This is why in the language of the Upanisads the search is for the Real of the real, not for the Real as opposed to the unreal, false or illusory.

Samkarite advaita philosophy involves built-in self-confirmation, as does Marxism and Freudian psychoanalysis. If you disagree with some tenet of Marxism you will be taken to be suffering from bourgeois prejudice; if you disagree with Freudian psychoanalysis you are suffering from some unrecognised sex complex that makes you quite unable to see the truth, and if you disagree with Samkara's doctrine of the illusoriness of the world, you are suffering from ignorance which makes you hopelessly attached to the world of multiplicity. Just to be frivolous, perhaps it was fear of being branded as ignorant that made a large body of Indian philosophers adopt Samkara's doctrines without a question. It is because so many of the intellectual elite adopted it that a myth became current that Hinduism preaches that the world is an illusion, when only Samkara Vedanta, which represents only one trend in a rich variety of trends, does so. The illusion doctrine is contrary to the Vedas, the Upanisads and the *Gita*, not to speak of the theistic systems. No wonder that some Hindus in desperation called Samkara a crypto-Buddhist. As opposed to idealistic Buddhism, Samkara granted, as we have seen, that the world has phenomenal reality and is not just mind-made. But it is too much to expect that an ordinary mind would know how to handle the delicate distinction between phenomenal reality and transcendental falsity, and the tendency naturally is to take the world as illusory in a straightforward sense and not bother with philosophical subtleties. Similarly, the devaluation of love and work as paths to liberation, both of which are preached by the *Gita*, is more likely to lead to an abandonment of these ways on the part of the ordinary man rather than a delicately balanced graded valuational pattern where love and action are given precisely the importance they deserve, neither more nor less.

Samkara's doctrine about the illusoriness of the world profoundly influenced the Hindu intellectual tradition, although the term 'illusory' is often understood by the ordinary non-philosophical Hindu as a valuational term rather than as an ontological term, which it purports to be in Samkara's system. The Upanisads did not preach that the world is nothing but suffering, nor did they conceive of moksa as primarily liberation from suffering. But there were other sources within the general Hindu cultural milieu where the concept of suffering did achieve prominence. Both Samkhya and Buddhism had preached that the world of change and phenomenal existence is suffering, not so much because they despaired of the possibility of obtaining ordinary pleasures of life, but primarily because of the imperfection that is inherent in the very structure of finitude and particularity. Even a life which would normally be thought to offer all possible opportunities for indulging in pleasures of this world, as Buddha's own life did, was identified with suffering from this point of view. The use of the term 'suffering' in 'life is suffering' then does not mean that there are no enjoyments to be had in life, rather as that which are ordinarily called 'enjoyments' and 'sufferings' are both included under the term 'suffering', it expresses a perspective on worldly life which sees it as of no value *in relation to the goal of nirvana or moksa.* It is thus a recommendation to adopt a certain attitude to worldly life to people who would embark on a quest for moksa – life is obviously not all suffering unless one sees it in relation to the bliss of moksa – and it may well be that this attitude helps, at least some people, to embark on the disciplines that are required for the attainment of moksa.

This perspective on life, which is a religious one, was translated into ordinary terms in some Hindu minds, and the actual sufferings of this world, such as pain, frustration, death etc., began to assume increasingly more importance when the terms 'suffering' and 'maya' were used as general descriptive terms, even outside the religious viewing of life. There is a difference between saying that (1) no matter how much pleasures one has in life, a pleasure-bound life is unsatisfactory because it must necessarily involve tension, disquietudes, and frustrations which stand in the way of bliss and that (2) life offers few opportunities for pleasure and enjoyment and it is too full of pain to be worthwhile, irrespective of whether or not one is looking for moksa. The first, according to me, is not pessimistic, while the second is because it expresses a general devaluation of life without any reference to the ultimate goal of bliss. There is no doubt that such a general devaluation of life did develop within the Hindu tradition and that the term 'maya' (illusion) was pressed into service to express it. While 'suffering' and 'maya' (which should be seen as religious terms) are helpful – and may be for some even essential – in getting one into perspective in the context of the quest for liberation, they are extremely unhelpful in the general context of living in the world. The term maya, even if it is not used in the sense of a false imposition on reality, has a connotation of insubstantiality and unsatisfactoriness and to say that the world is maya is to say that the phenomenal world is a place of bondage to pain and suffering, change and decay, and it is insubstantial because it exists in time only, while the true being of man flourishes in timelessness. Such a judgment is significant only for the man who is actively engaged in cultivating timelessness, not for one who lives in time and has no intention of doing anything else.

It is not very clear to people who use the idea of maya whether the world is to be devalued (1) because of the very structure of finitude which ought to be transcended, or (2) because of the quantity of pain, which is always more than the quantity of pleasure to be had in life. The first may be true while the second doubtful. If it is the quantity of pain that bothers one, one should turn to science, technology, social, political, and economic reorganisation, and so on, which can do a great deal to reduce the amount of suffering, rather than to liberation. Liberation is relevant not to the quest of making life more bearable than it is by minimising the scope of suffering and pain that obtains in this world but to that of overcoming the very structure of finitude. The one quest does not contradict the other when undertaken by different people or by the same person at different times or in different contexts. The term 'maya' as a term of devaluation of the world is needed only in the context of search for liberation, and the use of such a term in a non-liberation context may deter one from seeing that a good deal can be done to reduce the amount of pain and suffering that obtains in this world. The man who decides to live within the limitations of finitude may thus be better off without the use of this term. And we shall see that even within a religious context a devaluation of the world such as is entailed in the term 'maya' is not the only attitude to the world that is available to a Hindu for a religious viewing of the world.[72] So general statements to the effect that Hindus believe the world to be an illusion have no validity.

Hindus in general are not any less attached to life than non-Hindus (if attachment is a virtue!) and it is not at all the case that they take no interest in life because it is maya, although some Hindus might have been misled in the past by this term into thinking that no improvement of any kind was possible. What the concept of maya primarily does for a Hindu is to enable him to cope with calamities, hardships and frustrations of life by minimising their importance *whenever it is necessary to do so*. It becomes a little more easy to put up with disasters if one takes up the attitude that, after all, all this is maya and is of no ultimate significance. Perhaps the Hindus needed some such concept, considering the chequered fortune they have had, especially since the Muslim invasion of India, and perhaps it is this worldview which enabled the Hindus, in a paradoxical way, to have enough strength to resist complete disintegration as a culture group in face of tremendous odds. Undoubtedly it also leads to apathy and lack of motivation to improve one's lot in this world, but then there is hardly any concept which helps man that cannot hinder him if he refuses to use his critical faculties.

[72]The alternative is the doctrine of lila which views the world as a spontaneous self-expression of the divine in joy. This will be discussed later.

CHAPTER VI

Samkhya-Yoga Perfectionism

If we define religion in terms of belief in God or gods, then neither Samkhya nor Yoga would qualify as a religion. No doubt Yoga does use a concept of God, who is a free Self and through concentration on whom, it is said, control over the incessant flow of psycho-mental processes can be achieved. But the aim of Yoga as a system is neither to advocate devotionalism, love of God in men, nor to offer union with Him in Heaven at the end of one's career on earth. God in Yoga is the supreme example of perfect and free Self, a status which it is the objective of Yoga to help man to achieve. Samkhya does not even have a concept of God in its system (Vijnana Vikshu, a very late commentator, did, however, in the characteristically Hindu manner, introduce such a concept in his commentary on Samkhya), and it is frankly devoted to the achieving of absolute independence of man as a spirit from phenomenality and finitude, with which a man normally but mistakenly identifies himself. But both Samkhya and Yoga accept the status of man as a spirit, that is, as an absolute and eternal essence which is the source of what is characteristically human in man and if the religious impulse is one that leads man to search for integration with his absolute and eternal source, then these systems do qualify as religion. Moreover, a good deal of Samkhya metaphysics and Yoga technique is now a common heritage of the whole of the syncretistic Hindu tradition, so an understanding of this tradition requires an understanding of these systems.

The concept of perfection in the context of Hindu religion is something quite different from this concept in so far as it functions as an ideal for man in western culture. Perfection of man is thought in the west to lie in the perfection of his physical and mental – intellectual, aesthetic, moral, etc., – attributes as well as in his freedom to develop his uniqueness as a person.

This is not how the concept functions in the Hindu religious context. All physical and mental attributes of man, even those reckoned to be near perfect, are thought by Samkhya to belong to the realm of finitude and limitation, and hence essentially tainted by imperfection. The perfection of man lies in his achieving an unconditioned and absolute status, altogether free from the limitations of finitude, that is, in his becoming a spirit here and now. (This a man already is, but he fails to realise this through lack of discrimination between the essential and the inessential in his personality.) Both Samkhya and Yoga accept that each man is a separate spirit, for what they are concerned with is not what happens to man after death, whether he exists as a separate entity or is identified with some universal Being, but how any particular man can experience himself as unconditioned and free from phenomenal limitations of ordinary living here on earth. In order that a man may become a spirit or realise that he is a spirit he must divest himself of all particularities that normally belong to the concept of the uniqueness of individuals, and become universal in his essence, so to say. Nevertheless, each man is said to be a separate self, for only if he is this can each man realise his own perfection as a free spirit – this can only be achieved here on earth – either through discrimination as in Samkhya or through psychophysical discipline as in Yoga.

All that glitters is not gold however, and before I go on to discuss the philosophical and psychological doctrines of Samkhya and Yoga it is necessary to point out that all that traditionally passes under the name of 'Yoga' in India is not aimed at spiritual perfection and that it is by no means the case that the countless Yogis, Sadhus, Sannyasis, and the so-called 'holy' men of various descriptions who roam around India are perfected souls. In India, being a Yogi can be a career that suits the mentality of someone who would be just a tramp in another culture, but who because he is not ostensibly attached to things of this world is invested with a certain degree of 'holiness' by the ordinary man in India.

In all cultures there are various aberrant personalities, psychopaths, sex maniacs, libertines, saddist, masochists, as well as tramps, who carry on various anti-social or asocial activities and contribute to crime and general social ill-health. In traditional India, because of the diffused character of Hindu religion, some of it bordering on magic and shamanism, and because of its lack of any controlling mechanism, it has always been possible for 'abnormal' personalities to take shelter under the umbrella of religion and attach themselves to various magico-religious practices that are aberrant in various degrees. (A gang of men who would be just plain criminals and murderers in another culture would form themselves into a 'religious' sect, thugs, for instance, in India, thereby creating an impression that thuggism is a form of Hindu religion, which of course it is from one point of view.) 'Yoga' does not necessarily mean, as the term is used in the tradition by all the peoples called 'Hindus', the Yoga of Patanjali. Magico-religious and shamanistic practices involving disciplinary techniques of various descriptions are also known as Yoga. These exist on the fringes of the Hindu tradition, derived possibly from aboriginal spiritual values and appealing to little understood dark and subterranean forces within the human personality. But this sort of Yoga lends itself admirably to needs of abnormal personalities for deviant behaviour which under the guise of religion finds a sanction in society, perhaps not in orthodox circles but certainly from the illiterate masses.

It is a temptation to conclude from this that the Hindu religion is perverse. Actually abnormalities exist everywhere in all cultures, but abnormalities within the Hindu culture can usually find ways of expression that will be acceptable as 'religious' and these will pass off as a part of Hindu religion in the eyes of an observer, even though it may not be generally approved of and there may be only a few people involved. A dead body is unclean and polluting to the Hindu mind, but a man who claims to be doing his sadhana (spiritual practice) by sitting on a corpse will be accepted by some Hindus as engaged in a 'legitimate' activity. But there have never been more than a few people who have indulged in such a practice.

It is by no means the case that all psycho-physical disciplines undertaken by men who command a good deal of reverence even in the written Hindu tradition are aimed at spiritual perfection; some of it at least is aimed at occult power. We find in the Puranas and epics innumerable stories of ascetics who are engaged in what is called tapasya ('tapas' means heat, tapsya therefore means not penance, but disciplinary techniques and austerities for generating heat or power). That these people were in quest for power is shown by the fact that gods in heaven are depicted in these stories as troubled by thoughts of men undergoing severe tapasya lest they usurp the position of the gods through power acquired by such means. (Even in the Upanisads it has been said that Brahman underwent tapas in order to generate power to create.) Also, in these stories the ascetics do not always behave as spiritually enlightened men would; some of them are portrayed as irate personalities who are provoked into cursing others at the slightest obstruction to their purposes – curses that come true because of the magical power they possess.

It is generally believed in the Hindu tradition that there are hidden reserves of power within the human personality which can be tapped by prolonged use of special techniques involving both the body and the mind. This is so because of correspondence between the microcosm and the macrocosm – the energy that is operative in the universe is also operative in the human body, and this can be harnessed and put to various miraculous and magical uses called 'siddhis'. Even Patanjali admits that disciplinary techniques do generate this power, although his Yoga is concerned not with power as such but with spiritual perfection or freedom, and this can be achieved only by ignoring power that automatically comes to men in course of discipline and psychic control. But power and perfection remain inextricably mixed up in the Yogic tradition of India and veneration shown to 'holy' men can be just as much acknowledgement of power as of perfection. And many so-called Yogis, while denying life at one level, are really affirming it at another where it is hoped that possessed with miraculous or magical power they will be able to exercise a good deal of control over credulous minds.

There is no doubt that in India the search for power to accomplish what is normally thought to be beyond the capacity of humans is associated with techniques which are generally thought to be spiritual (tapasya), and activity of this sort commands a good deal of respect in the secondary sources of the Hindu religious tradition such as epics and Puranas. An abundance of myths and legends in these books concerning tapasya of this sort shows that Yoga did not always mean spiritual perfection even in the classical Hindu tradition. Often spirituality and magic have been mixed up in the Hindu mind, and such mixed up notions have given a veneer of spirituality to activities which have nothing to do with freedom from finitude, except in a magical sense. Nevertheless Samkhya and Patanjali Yoga do exist in the tradition and it is to these that I shall now turn my attention.

In a sense, classical Yoga too is seeking power, but it is not primarily magical power, it is power to transcend the control that our own physical and psychological processes have over the functioning of our own personality, since we are normally conditioned to act as these require. It is in effect a process of deconditioning of men which in a sense could be called 'dehumanising', as Eliade puts it. But this will be thought so only if we accept that to be human is to be conditioned, and this Samkhya and Yoga do not accept. On the contrary, they postulate that the highest possibility of man lies in becoming a free spirit, in-dwelling and established in its own essence, by rising above the various conditionings that normally, but mistakenly in their view, define the human status.

The philosophical basis for the largely psychological approach of Yoga to the constitution of a human personality is given by Samkhya. According to Samkhya, there are two fundamental principles – both eternal and absolute in their own spheres – operating in the universe and these are spirit and matter. Matter here does not mean solid, inert, and perceptible substance, rather it is a pure potentiality for physical and psychical happenings composed of three strands of energy (guna), called sattva, rajas, and tamas. These terms have both physical and psychical connotations. Sattva stands for a strand of energy that is responsible for lightness, luminosity or manifestation, but it also represents tranquillity, peace, or harmony in the psychical realm. Rajas represents drive and movement, also conflict and tension, while tamas is inertia, obstruction as well as dullness, confusion and ignorance. In the primordial state of matter as pure potentiality, these three strands of energy are in equilibrium, and although there is constant activity going on in matter, so long as this activity is not of such a nature as to disturb the equilibrium in which the three strands of energy are held, there is no actual manifestation of any physical or psychical being. The presence of spirit as a self-luminous essence in the vicinity of matter, however, disturbs this primordial equilibrium and this leads matter on to a process of evolution into twenty-four categories of being.

Spirit actually does nothing positive to stimulate change in matter, it merely acts as a catalyst, so to say, for matter to undertake its own transmutation. As to why this should be so there is no explanation in Samkhya. Samkhya also says that

transmutations in matter are for the benefit of spirit, which, by
eventually extricating itself from the limitations put upon it by
nature's own forms, can realise its own distinctness. But as to
why spirit should get caught up in matter in the first place, when
it is essentially different from matter, or why unconscious matter
should act for the benefit of spirit, there is no explanation. Anyway, original matter is subtle and imperceptible and its transformation or evolution also proceeds from the subtle to the gross in
progressive steps. The first evolute is intelligence which has both
a cosmic and an individual aspect. Then from intelligence comes
forth the principle of individuation so that one thing may be
different from another; then from it mind, called the internal
sense that synthesises the activities of the senses; then the senses
themselves, five for perception and five for action; then the
subtle and imperceptible essence of elements, water, fire, air,
earth and ether; then the gross elements themselves (here matter
becomes perceptible for the first time), and finally the combination of these elements to form various gross objects of this
world.

The human personality in so far as its physical and psychical
constitutions are concerned is entirely a modification of matter,
the mental being more subtle than the physical, (the subtlety of
a thing is defined in terms of the amount of sattva in its constitution). So all activities that take place in the human personality,
both physical and psychical, are the results of the functioning of
three strands of energy that go to constitute it, but into this highly subtle functioning being, spirit, which in its intrinsic nature is
nothing but pure consciousness, is reflected. The result is that
mental happenings, perception, conception, feeling, will etc.,
going on therein are illumined by the light of consciousness, and
the spirit is misled into thinking that these processes belong to
itself when in actual fact they do not and are just illumined by it.
The real or essential man is the spirit, and not the mental or
physical attributes that belong to matter. The conditioned man
who accepts the limitations of 'his' physical and psychical being
as essentially himself exists through the mixing up of spirit and
the mind-body complex into which spirit is reflected. As spirit
reflected in a finite mind-body complex illumines only the finite
goings on there, man accepts himself as conditioned by these
happenings, so infinite spirit becomes, to all intents and purposes,

a finite empirical man. However, a spirit or Self cannot really become so, it is only mistakenly believed to be so; that is, the empirical man exists by a mistake, so to say. The real man, the spirit, can through a knowledge of his own true being dissociate himself from the activities of the mind-body complex into which he is caught up and thus regain his original independence as pure spirit, absolute in his own pure essence as immutable being.

It seems to me that the real contribution of Samkhya lies in telling man that he is a free spirit, appearances to the contrary notwithstanding, and not in what it actually says, that the real man is nothing but spirit. This kind of reductionism of either variety, idealistic, or materialistic, is an inherent danger in the activity of philosophising, since it aims at systematic thinking, and systematic thinking so often turns into a project of system building. Anyway, the reason why, according to Samkhya, it is necessary to embark on the project of dissociation or isolation of spirit is this. The finite life of man is full of sufferings of three kinds, of the body, of the mind and those brought about by unseen powers, and there is no escape from these as long as man remains finite. These sufferings affect man only because he accepts a finite mind-body complex as himself. If he can disown this, then it would cease to have power over him, thereby losing the capacity to generate suffering. The unconditioned spirit is not subject to suffering, nor need be man if he can identify himself with his essential being, rather than with what is only contingent. Unlike the Upanisads, Samkhya does not say that transcendence of finitude means bliss, all it says is that liberation from finitude means liberation from suffering, so it is really from Samkhya rather than from the Upanisads that what is called 'Hindu pessimism' springs. The Upanisads optimistically believe that man can identify himself with all of existence via the concept of Brahman, and thereby not just transcend finitude but positively gain unlimited bliss, the highest possibility of man's being. All that Samkhya offers is free being, and the mark of freedom is freedom from suffering rather than, as in the Upanisads, freedom to be all in place of one finite, limited being that defines the bound human status. Yoga sides with the Upanisads rather than with Samkhya in emphasising that the peace and harmony of pure being is a state of bliss and not merely absence of suffering. So a perfect Yogi can be expected to be a cheerful man full of good will and sympathy.

As I have discussed in an earlier chapter, Samkhya's limited perspective perhaps results from the specific task that Samkhya sets itself, which is not that of the Upanisads. The Upanisads are interested in cosmic integration, the going forward of the human personality out of itself in order to be identified with all existence. 'Becoming all' is the leitmotiv of the Upanisads. But Samkhya has a different purpose in view. It is philosophical analysis of the human personality in order to isolate that element in it which is spirit or free Self, but which is clouded over by mental and physical happenings of a transitory and conditioned nature. What Samkhya hopes to achieve by this is self-integration or the integration of man with the most enduring and permanent stratum of his own being, that can act as a witness to the constant comings and goings of the psycho-physical being of man rather than be entirely subjected to its demands and then altogether lost sight of. To do this it separates out the two distinguishable strata in the being of man into two radically different things, which may be an extreme device that is deliberately adopted to bring the lesson home to man, or simply a result of inadequate thinking. If spirit is absolute and pure being then it is not really limited by contingent sufferings that characterise the world of becoming. So freedom from suffering is made an essential mark of the being of the spirit. Thus it may be that it is not so much pessimism as the need to demarcate the spirit in man that leads Samkhya to talk about suffering. But whether or not this is so, pessimistic conclusions about the sufferings of man, which can be escaped by escaping life itself, can be drawn from Samkhya, and this has been done by many Hindus.

Self-integration cannot be the final objective of a religious world view. Doubtless each man is an individual and he must realise the possibilities of his own being as such. But no man is an isolated individual and what a self-integrated free man does with his freedom in the world must also count in the realisation of full human possibilities. Samkhya, possibly because of its limited objectives, is silent about this, but the result is that those who within the Hindu tradition take Samkhya's pronouncements as the final word in religious understanding also take it that man has nothing to achieve beyond his own liberation despite the teachings of the *Gita* and the Upanisads that a liberated man would see all things in his own Self and the Self in all beings. This result of the teaching of Samkhya is further accentuated in the Hindu tradition by Samkara's doctrine that the world is illusory and hence not really an object of concern for a liberated man. This conclusion can certainly be drawn and has been drawn despite the fact that Samkara himself did show a good deal of concern about other men and their spiritual well-being. But not every man is a spiritual genius and it is easy for ordinary men to be misled by doctrines which either conceal simple truths by their ambiguities or distort them by a well-meaning but one-sided emphasis.

Yoga takes over Samkhya ontology in its understanding of man, but its special contribution lies in devising a technique by using which man can actually *experience* himself as a free spirit. Yoga does not believe that liberation can come purely by means of discriminative knowledge as Samkhya says. It needs a long, laborious process of step-by-step deconditioning of man and a far more detailed knowledge of how an empirical personality really functions. The absolute and eternal in man cannot be separated and made free of the contingent merely by discriminative knowledge, because the contingent has tremendous hold over man in ways that he does not even know of. The psychological being of man is composed not just of conscious thoughts and feelings but also of subconscious or unconscious drives and dispositions – called vasanas or samskaras in Sanskrit – which even unknown to man make him act such that they may be fulfilled. To gain control of one's own mind and body one must gain control of one s unconscious[1] life, and to do this it is important to know how it comes to exist. Normally we perform an action because we are motivated by an urge to fulfil a desire with which our personality is identified. An action prompted in this manner by an urge or desire, conscious or unconscious, leaves in its turn a psychological deposit in the personality which further strengthens the urge for action that already exists or creates a new one. We are born with a particular psychic bundle that has been created by action in a previous life, and it is this inheritance that initially determines the structure of our desires and our actions follow

---

[1] No distinction will be made here between 'unconscious' and 'subconscious'.

from them. Thus our desires feed our actions and our actions feed our desires further and create the seeds for further actions. It is this determined chain of desires (ultimately rooted in unconscious impressions) and actions that condition our being and make us what we are. To gain freedom from this determined course it is necessary to make the chain inoperative and this can be done by the prolonged use of techniques designed to dismantle the unconscious. Ultimately, however, it requires one to transcend desires that create impressions, for it is not enough to destroy impressions that already exist, the possibility of their accruing to the psychic life at all must also be destroyed at the root.

We must begin by analysing mental states into those which being passional and full of drive are called afflicted (klista) and those which are not afflicted (aklista). Afflicted ones are actuated by anger, envy, jealousy, ill-will, greed, lust etc., emotions which can possess men and make them behave in a selfish manner. Non-afflicted mental states are gentle, non-passional and unselfish, these are expressions of compassion, goodwill, charity, love etc. The first step in gaining self-possession is to engage in an attack on afflicted mental states and whenever in their grip deliberately to try and replace them by non-afflicted ones (to substitute ill-will felt towards someone by a positive feeling of goodwill, for example). In ontological terms what is involved in this process is an attempt to activate sattva elements in one's own being (of which non-afflicted mental states are constituted) and to convert the rajas and tamas elements (of which afflicted mental states are composed) into sattva. This is preliminary to the ultimate goal, the transcendence of all gunas altogether. Anyway, as a man enters this process of self-transformation as a graduated first step to self-transcendence, he begins to make discoveries about his own being that normally lie beyond one's conscious understanding. For it is through the resistance that afflicted mental states offer whenever a man tries to eradicate them that he may for the first time realise that there are forces deep within a human personality that do not follow his conscious dictates, and that on the contrary it is these forces which largely determine what manner of being a person is.

But a deeper analysis is necessary in order that we may successfully deal with affliction. The roots of affliction lie in certain permanent dispositions of mind belonging to the subconscious strata of our personality (called hindrances) and unless we uncover them as the springs of all desire we shall not be able to control surface mental states which are merely expressions of underlying subliminal forces. These are: (1) ignorance, caused by a lack of discrimination between spirit and matter, the latter being the realm to which all physical and mental states belong, (2) egoism, that looks at everything from the point of view of 'I' and 'mine', (3) attachment to what is congenial to us, (4) repulsion from what is uncongenial, and (5) fear of death or thirst for life. These permanent hindrances have to be made ineffective through eradication of desires that feed them, if we want to succeed in gaining control of our life instead of just being carried along by subliminal forces in our own personality that we do not even understand. Control can be gained by a process of Yoga, but for Yoga to succeed we must not only have faith in its efficacy but also such qualities as enthusiam, courage, steadfastness, mental composure and concentration, wisdom and correct understanding. These qualities have to be progressively cultivated and those which cause obstructions progressively eliminated, such as disease, weakness of will, doubt, lack of enthusiasm, laziness, restlessness, attachment to pleasure, feeling of frustration, physical instability and so on. All these are called impurities of mind and body, and eradication of such impurities needs a two-pronged disciplined attack. Constant practice and application with a view to forming stable habits (abhyasa) is needed, backed by a determination not to be swayed by thoughts of pleasure and pain which normally regulate our activities (vairagya). A practising Yogi is even advised to look upon ordinary pleasures of life as painful in relation to the final aim of liberation, in order to break their hold on him.

From the point of view of the degree of control that we have over our mental states, they can be divided into five categories: (1) Distracted, when the mental continuum is in a state of total restlessness, mental states spontaneously generating themselves and flitting from object to object; (2) Confused, or a state of stupor when, overcome by affliction, we hardly know what is what; (3) Semi-distracted, when the mind is able to fix itself on an object from time to time; (4) Concentrated, when we have achieved a good measure of control and can settle our mind on a particular point for a long time at will; (5) Controlled, when we can even decide at will to suppress all mental modifications that bubble up from the subliminal regions of the mind and remain in a state of lucidity without any kind of mental activity whatsoever. The object of the discipline called 'Yoga' is to gradually move to the fifth stage through a step-by-step reversal of normal processes under which our personality functions. As Yoga means a total transformation of the human personality, from a state of acceptance of our physical and mental attributes as ourselves to a state of realisation of our being as essentially free from such attributes, we are required to take total measures such that our thoughts, feelings and actions are subjected simultaneously to a deconditioning process. So discipline and austerities are to be backed up by the study of sacred treatises, and surrender to God. Indeed, the aim is nothing less than to be God-like, so nothing short of total dedication of all our resources to the task will do. This one pointed search is called 'ekagrata'.

Yoga as a technique of discipline consists of eight limbs; (1) yama, (2) niyama, (3) asana, (4) pranayama, (5) pratyahara, (6) dharana, (7) dhyana, and (8) samadhi. Each of these consists in a conscious attempt to reverse the direction of the normal processes under which we live, until finally we can transcend the hold that desires and subconscious latencies have on us, thereby regaining the independence of spirit.

Although the aim of Yoga is not primarily an ethical one, it fully recognises that spiritual independence is unobtainable except through ethical purity, for some of the fundamental sources of affliction and subjection of spirit are forces like envy, ill-will, greed, lust etc. Yama consists of five ethical disciplines: (1) cultivation of non-violence in thought, word and deed, based on the perception that all life is sacred. (2) Adherence to truth, truth here meaning much more than correct statements. Practice of truth needs an attitude of total honesty, and rejection of all hypocrisy and falsity in our dealings with the world. (3) Non-stealing of others' property. It needs both lack of greed and respect for what belongs to others. (4) Continence, sexual abstinence being one of the means of conserving power that can be put to the use of a greater cause, as well as being an obvious means of gaining control over promptings of nature. (5) Non-covetousness of possessions, this being in aid of transcending desires to flourish and prosper in the world. Niyama is a further set of ethical rules that are also required to stabilise the mind and purify it before techniques of control in a narrow sense can be successfully applied. These are cleanliness of mind and body, an attitude of contentment, love of discipline, practice of certain prescribed austerities and the fixing of the mind on God. These preliminaries are just as important for a successful practice of Yoga as techniques of physical and mental control.

With asana starts Yogic technique in a narrow sense. The restlessness of the body has to be disciplined not only in order that it may not constantly thrust itself on one's attention but also in order to reverse one's natural physical mobility into immobility. So one has to learn to sit motionlessly in a certain posture which, however difficult to start with, can with constant practice be managed and even made comfortable. To turn physical discomfort into comfort belongs to the process of deconditioning that has already been started with the attempt to divest the mind of impurities and afflictions. Then comes regulation of breathing (pranayama). According to Yoga physiology and psychology there is a vital connection between the rhythm and rate of breathing and one's psychosomatic functions, and with control of breathing various gross malfunctioning of mind and body due to excess of tamas in the constitution can be eliminated. To make breathing rhythmic and to hold it for regulated periods between inhaling and exhaling is again to reverse our normal propensity to let it function at random without any relation to the total economy of our organic structure. Control of breath is also supposed to do away with distractions of the conscious mind and the restless flitting of subconscious impulses. In short, harmony in breathing is related to the harmony of body and mind.

With the next stage, pratyahara, or withdrawal of the senses from their normal attachment to stimuli that constantly assail them from the external world, the deconditioning process goes even deeper, for here is an attempt to stop altogether by deliberate planning certain functions which are more or less automatic and unplanned in the normal economy of human life. A Yogi practising pratyahara refuses to follow the direction of the senses in his awareness of the world around him, instead he tries to dictate which stimuli he would receive and when, and which not. With the next stage of dharana or concentration a practising Yogi tries to fix his mind on one thing only to the exclusion of the rest. As a man who tries to substitute an afflicted mental state by a non-afflicted one soon discovers that he is not master in his own house, so to say, so a man who tries to concentrate on one point only to the exclusion of the rest also discovers that he does not have quite the sort of say in the running of his own life as he believes himself to have, since myriads of mental modifications, thoughts, feelings etc., bubble up in his psychic field (citta), not because he wants to experience them but because latent impressions have innate strength of their own. One's ability to concentrate depends on one's ability to recognise that this is so and then to subdue and suppress these latencies or make them ineffective by force, as it were. Thus effort at Yogic concentration helps one to discover facts about oneself which are normally not available. Such self-knowledge is invaluable in the task of integration that a Yogi undertakes. Furthermore, it develops the capacity in oneself to play the role of a detached witness in respect of one's own psychic constitution, since a man trying to concentrate cannot but treat mental modifications that spontaneously generate themselves in the manner of an observer.

Dhyana or contemplation is a developed form of concentration when there is an uninterrupted flow of one-pointed mental life without the obstructions that frequently occur at the beginning of one's attempt to fix the mind on one thing only. At this stage the subconscious mind has been sufficiently taken in hand for it not to be able to gain natural control of the psychic field and modify its contents according to its own demands. Dhyana leads to the final stage of Yogic control and discipline, samadhi (enstasis rather than ecstacy is the term used by Eliade to translate it). When meditation comes to a stage wherein one is not even aware of meditating and all distinction that normally obtains between act and object completely disappears, then one enters samadhi. It is of two kinds, with or without support. In the first kind, although the distinction between the mind and the object disappears and all that is left in the citta (the psychic field or mental continuum where modifications are discerned) is a totality without distinction, there is still an object of meditation by the help of which this state is obtained. So the citta has not yet been put completely out of action. In the final stage of samadhi without support there is no object of meditation at all and all modifications of any kind have finally disappeared leaving the citta in a state of undifferentiated emptiness, despite the fact that the Yogi is in a state of lucidity or illumination that cannot be differentiated from pure being. It is at this stage that the spirit comes to possess its own essence and thereby realise itself as autonomous there being nothing in the citta with which it could confuse itself. The man identified with pure spirit has transcended all the gunas of which both psychic and physical existence are constituted; he therefore rises above all dualities, tension, and opposition which inevitably characterise the realm of finitude, since finitude of things and persons consists in their being one thing rather than another as dictated by different proportions of sattva, rajas and tamas in their constitution. Where gunas are transcended, all dualities such as heat and cold, good and evil, thine and mine are also transcended. So the ultimate experience of self-realisation as spirit is also an experience of total peace and bliss, things that the citta does not know.

The citta or the mental continuum of thoughts, feelings and volitions, fed by impressions of the nature of subconscious impulses and drives, is the focal point in terms of which one individuates oneself as a distinct person. In Yoga the unconscious is made ineffective, first through cultivation of unafflicted mental dispositions and then through desirelessness (the unconscious is nourished by impressions that thoughts, feelings and actions governed by desire create), and in the final stage of samadhi the mental continuum is divested of all happenings altogether, through a long and constant discipline aimed at suppression of modifications; yet the person remains beyond all distinctions just as a self-manifest being. Thus the whole being of man is recast, through a gradual process of shedding off everything that normally individuates a man and then turning him inside out, so to say. Then the autonomous spirit becomes established in its autonomy and as pure being is no longer confused with the sheer becomings of the citta modifications.

One of the differences between Samkhya and Yoga seems to me to be this. Samkhya says that when a man has isolated his spirit from the incessant flow of psycho-physical happenings and has gained independence, the world of change will altogether cease to exist for him (not, however, the potentiality of happenings). This has been taken literally by many people in the Hindu tradition, although it seems to be obvious that this is only a figurative way of saying that the world of change might as well not exist for a man since his own being has been made independent of whatever happens there. But those who take Samkhya's pronouncement about cessation of worldly changes at face value believe that a liberated man can have no dealings with the world (since it does not exist for him). Both Samkhya and Samkarite Vedanta encourage men to believe that liberation is not just freedom of the essential being of man from the world of happenings on which he normally takes himself to be dependent for his sustenance, but is total uninvolvement in the world. But it is at least possible to take Yoga, as expounded by Patanjali, as not forcing this attitude on man. For Patanjali talks about various powers with regard to the world that accrues to a liberated man, and for this the world, not just the potentiality for it, must be taken to be there. A Yogi can have knowledge and illumination not only in respect of his own essential being, he can also have knowledge about the subtle constitution of the world by applying Samyoga (the three developed techniques of dharana, dhyana and samadhi practised together is called Samyoga). All happenings in the world are the products of three strands of energy, sattva, rajas, and tamas, the perceptible world being a gross manifestation of these at a later stage of evolution of the potentiality of matter for change. By applying Samyoga at first on gross objects and then concentrating progressively on more and more subtle aspects of material potentiality, a Yogi can have direct perception into the constitution of the normally imperceptible (that is, by the use of human sense organs) subtle potentialities that lie at the root of the world of change. A Yogi can also, by applying Samyoga to mental states such as universal friendliness, compassion, and love, create these dispositions in himself, become a friend to all, and help to remove unhappiness and create happiness (see commentaries by Vyasa and Vacaspati Misra on *Yoga Sutras of Patanjali*, Book 3, para. 3). Although Patanjali does not say that this is what Yoga is for, for in the Hindu tradition a distinction is always maintained between morality and spirituality, the fact that he mentions this possibility as being one amongst the enlarged powers that a Yogi acquires, at least shows that developing these attitudes to other beings is perfectly consistent with the being in the world of a liberated man. He does not have to divorce himself from all concern with regard to the world of change in the context of which most people live.

A Yogi acquires, according to Patanjali, a good many more capacities than these. He can have knowledge of past, present, and future, of his previous births (by applying samyoga to his present samskaras, which are the result of actions in previous births), of receiving stimuli that are normally inaccessible to human capacities; moving through space, walking on fire and water, of becoming small like an atom or big like a mountain or disappearing, of having a good deal of control over all sorts of physical processes. All this because a Yogi has activated sources of power within himself that normally lie dormant within the psycho-physical constitution of man (which are continuous with the sources of energy in the natural world). Since all things are continuous one type of being can be transformed into another by making it more or less subtle in its energy constitution (by stimulating the sattva, rajas or tamas in it). And a Yogi can, by consciously controlling the rajas and tamas elements of his psycho-physical being, make his nature more or less coincide with the sattvic elements (the purest type of energy with the capacity to manifest things, this being obstructed in varying degrees in ordinary man by other strands of energy of far lower degrees of fineness, rajas, and tamas) in his own being and thus become god-like. A 'god' is to be understood as a powerful being with capacities that in relation to normal human capacities would appear as supernatural and not as the creator of the world, the Supreme Being. For Samkhya-Yoga ontology there is no absolute distinction between the so-called 'natural' and the so-called 'supernatural' manifestations of power (such as walking on fire etc.), since both belong to the same sources of energy that make all physical and psychical happenings possible.

These powers would normally be thought to be magical and the Hindu tradition has venerated power as much as it has venerated spiritual perfection. Whether or not these magical powers can be obtained by Yogic disciplines I do not know, although I personally believe that the Hindu imagination being prone to excess – owing to the fact that the mythical and the non-mythical have not been rigidly separated in the Hindu religious writings – a good deal of these descriptions, like becoming small like an atom or big like a mountain, are embellishments on certain extraordinary but limited powers that may come to a 'perfected' Yogi. Anyhow, Patanjali warns that the temptation to exercise these powers will embroil a Yogi again into the world of change, for naturally enough power corrupts – in Yogic terms, by producing a further desire to exercise it for the sake of the gratification it brings, thereby creating fresh impressions. Liberation requires that all past impressions must be made ineffective and creation of fresh impressions stopped at their root by stopping desires. Then only can the Purusa (self or spirit) in man find itself to be different from the limited but ever restless citta, the mental continuum, as this has been brought under complete control by eradicating forces that spontaneously generate modifications – which when generated in this fashion naturally assume dominance on the scene of an individual's mind.

As far as I can see, the value of Yoga is existential in that it helps self-knowledge – an *experiential realisation* that the being of man is in some sense timeless and absolute and that there is an element in him which can witness change but not become subject to it. But in so far as a liberated man lives on in the world he can scarcely remain unaware of the world of becoming and the laws that operate therein. Naturally he will not participate in it out of an urge to fulfil egoist desires, but his freedom is not truly freedom if it is so fragile as to need to be carefully screened from all contact with the world in order to ensure that it may not degenerate into unfreedom. If the goal of life is just not being born again, then a man who has cleansed his citta of all impurities in the form of impressions may concentrate all his attention towards preserving it in a state of cleanliness until death. But if Yoga is to be of existential value which helps man to live in the world in a state of freedom – the sort of Yoga that is preached in the *Gita* – then it cannot be the aim of a liberated man to remain uninvolved, even though he is required to remain unattached. This is why it seems to me that the Yoga of Patanjali, where the aim is specifically the isolation of the spirit from matter and its establishment in its own essence as pure being, needed to be completed in the Hindu tradition by the Yoga of the *Gita*, where self-knowledge, possession, or integration is incorporated in a more comprehensive scheme of living requiring an acknowledgement from man of the life that goes on around him and his participation in it to help maintain what at this level would be considered righteous. And it is this integral Yoga of the *Gita* that brings into play the total resources of man into his life's task that has been preached in the recent Hindu tradition by Aurobindo and superbly practised by Gandhi. But unfortunately for one Aurobindo or Gandhi there remain thousands in India for whom Yoga remains, to some degree at any rate, egotistic, in so far as its aim is set as not being born again and nothing more.

The *Bhagavadgita* conceives of Yoga as non-attachment to the fruits of one's actions rather than non-involvement in the affairs of the world. Renunciation here does not mean renunciation of the world as such, but renunciation of egotism and egotistic desires to prosper without any regard for the well-being of other lives (the term used for this particular concern in the *Gita* is 'lokasamgraha'). In order to attain this state of mind, which is truly Yoga, one may rely on knowledge and discrimination as in Samkhya, or on love of God which consists in seeing all beings in the Self and the Self in all beings, or on cultivation of non-attachment to fruits of action or on the techniques of Yoga. But none of these is meant to be exclusive, and it is expected that although one particular type of practice, love of God, for instance, maybe for a particular man the predominant means of being in Yoga, he will also bring other approaches to bear on his life in order to have a fully integrated perspective. And even if self-knowledge or integration of one's being with what has been called the spirit in man is not by itself the ultimate in our approach to religious reality it has remained one of the prime objectives of the religious quest in India. For it is only a self-integrated man who can be expected to develop the right sort of attitude, of respect and compassion and not just of concern, that he is required to have towards all lives, from a religious point of view.

The fact that the type of Yoga that the *Gita* advocates is lived only by a few, while the vast majority of the people called 'Yogis' in India have literally renounced the world and have refused to feel any responsibility with regard to it in search of a sterile perfection, does not mean that the written tradition of the Hindus does not make room for man's concern for his fellows and for his involvement in their well-being. Even Patanjali allows for this, although being strictly a programme of self-integration only, and not of social and cosmic integration as well, the task it sets itself is primarily to develop the theme of how the spirit can be established in its own being and experience itself as distinct from the fluctuating citta. The *Gita* was preached in the context of an urgent social problem, that of maintaining order and righteousness in social dealings, and naturally its theme is how a man who desires freedom should act in this world. Arjuna's desire to relinquish his claim to his kingdom that was misappropriated by his cousins, and take to begging if only he could thereby escape the need to fight, was put down by Krishna as sheer escapism born out of weakness of will, rather than a genuine manifestation of universal love and compassion. Arjuna was the key figure in the whole preparation of the battle against his unrighteous cousins, and he had simply no right to consider himself free to back out on the eve of the battle, on grounds of scruples he had not so far felt, leaving the whole Pandava side in the lurch. As a kshatriya he had very specific duties, especially in the situation in which he was placed, and these a socially conscious man has no right to relinquish at will. But this does not mean that Arjuna must remain hopelessly attached to a life of pursuit of worldly gain for himself, for the quest for liberation is compatible with worldly action when that action is non-attached. Krishna referred to himself as the model of what a non-attached action means. As God he has nothing to accomplish in the whole world and as he is all, no happening makes any difference to him one way or the other, and yet he is ceaselessly engaged in maintaining the world, even taking a human birth when necessary, for the well-being of creatures. It is the task of Yoga as a discipline to help man to get into the same frame of mind in relation to his pursuits in the world, if he desires freedom, of course. Here self-integration at one level is combined with integration with society at another and beyond that with cosmic integration, since the whole universe is a manifestation of the same divine essence. Yoga becomes a comprehensive quest only when it is incorporated into a wider context than a search for one's own essence and nothing more.

CHAPTER VII

Devotionalism and Qualified Monotheism

Devotionalism : A Distinctive Approach

Among the seekers of religious reality the Hindu tradition makes a distinction between the man of knowledge (jnana) and the man of devotion (bhakti). The man of knowledge seeks the undifferentiated and unchanging Supreme Reality as it is in itself, beyond all attributes (the Nirguna Brahman), while the man of devotion seeks God, a Personal Being endowed with all attributes in their perfection (Saguna Brahman). The man of knowledge is inclined to believe that it is he who knows the truth in its purity, because attributes are only a human way of clothing the conceptually inconceivable with definite characteristics, so that it becomes thinkable within the limitations of the human mind. The man of devotion believes, to the contrary, that it is he who is in touch with truth because God, being the source of everything, must be possessed of infinite attributes and absolute perfection. The attainment of Supreme Reality, according to the man of knowledge, consists in a state of realisation of identity with it – a state which cancels out all differences (the realm of attributes), while for a man of devotion it consists in adoration of and surrender to that which is absolutely perfect in its infinite splendour and power. The pure man of knowledge and the pure man of devotion are however ideal types rather than flesh and blood human beings, and even a votary of knowledge such as Samkara, who in his philosophy claimed that the conception of Isvara or Lord God belonged to a lower plane of understanding, indulged in devotion to gods such as Siva, Krishna, and Devi (a goddess).

So we find that in the Hindu tradition there exists alongside the trend which says that the Highest Reality should be conceived as Saguna (with attributes) or Nirguna (without attributes) another belief which conceives of this distinction as embodying complementary conceptions rather than contradictory ones. It is not so much that the conception of Saguna or Nirguna is a lower or higher category than the other, as some who wish to retain both concepts says, as that they constitute different approaches to the same Ultimate Reality. The man of devotion who loves and adores God as absolute perfection and worships Him with offerings of food, flowers, incense, music etc., brings to bear his emotion and his senses on to his understanding of divine reality, while the man of knowledge, believing only in the intellect, finds these a hindrance in his search for the Ultimate, which, he believes, must remain untouched by human preferences. Even the distinction of perfect-imperfect is an emotion-tinged distinction which man makes to indicate his preferences, and there is no reason why the ultimate category of Being would follow this preference. So Reality, which is Pure Being, must not be qualified by attributes in any way. The trouble, however, is that the man of knowledge is mistaken in believing that his approach is not coloured in any way by what may be called a mere human preference. For the conception of attributeless Brahman, to which nothing that pertains to the world applies, does involve an undervaluing of the world of diversity (which appeals to the senses and the emotion) as insignificant and ultimately worthless; (this is what leads to its rating as illusion). The acknowledged sources of the Hindu tradition, the Vedas and the Upanisads, speak both of the glory of multiplicity (Vedas) and their essential non-duality (Upanisads), and it is already a sign of bias to exalt one set of scriptures, supposed to deal with nothing but unity or non-duality, over the Vedas which quite openly sing the glory of life in its manifoldness – as is done by Samkara.

Already in the *Bhagavadgita* the complementarity of the Saguna-Nirguna distinction is foreshadowed. There are verses in the *Gita* which suggest that Krishna is the same as the Brahman of the Upanisads, a conception to which no attributes are attached, and others which suggest that Krishna is the highest Self (Uttama Purusa), possessed of infinite attributes (as revealed by his cosmic form to Arjuna). It is said in chapter 8, verse 21, 'That which is known as the unmanifest and the imperishable and is said to be the ultimate goal, attaining which one returns no more, know that to be my highest Place'. The next verse combines this with the idea of devotion: 'Dear Partha, that Highest Self in whom all creation exists and by whom all this is pervaded, can only be attained by singleminded devotion.' Chapter 12, verses 2 – 4, combine the two approaches: 'Those who worship me with reverence, with mind concentrated and constantly attached to me, are the best seekers, according to me.' And yet: 'But those who, being equal-minded towards all, devoted to their welfare, and the senses controlled, contemplate the imperishable Brahman – unmanifest, beyond distinctions, all-pervading, unspeakable, ultimate, immovable and unchanging – obtain none other than me.' In chapter 10, verses 20–23, Krishna identifies himself with the best among all categories of being, thereby suggesting the possession of infinite attributes. 'I am Vishnu amongst the Adityas, Sun amongst the celestial bodies, amongst the Marutas I am Marichi, and among the stars the moon. I am Sama amongst Vedas, Indra amongst gods, mind amongst the senses and consciousness amongst men. I am Samkara amongst Rudras, Kubera among Yakshas, Agni amongst the Vasas and Meru amongst the mountains', and so on.

As the *Gita* makes clear, neither knowledge nor devotion is by itself enough, and what is needed, on the part of a seeker, is a combination of both, along with action. Pure devotionalism which attaches itself to a particular conception of God endowed with a specific name and form with specific attributes, without the understanding that Ultimate Reality pervades everything and that there is nothing which is not a manifestation of it, may end in sheer emotionalism, centred around a symbol, dogmatism and fanaticism, while the bare knowledge of identity, unrelieved by any emotional valuation of the realm of diversity wherein the splendour of divine reality has been manifested, can lead to indifference to the world and a purely negative attitude to all that pertains to it. The fact, that from the point of view of knowledge one must see things as not different from the Ultimate Reality, can lead one to the belief that the world of multiplicity wherein differences obtain is utterly worthless and altogether undeserving of one's attention.

I have said that the two conceptions Saguna and Nirguna are held by many in the Hindu tradition to constitute two different approaches to the same reality. The difference may lie in temperament or in purpose. The man of devotion needs to bring into play his emotions, his senses, and his personality, which enjoys being united with the divine but not being identical with it, if it means the exclusion of his own distinct identity from the scene, as this must be there to enjoy the beauty of the relationship realised. As Ramprosad, a Hindu seeker, said, 'I like to taste sugar,

but not to be it.' But to the man of knowledge it is the universal
not the particular, not even the particular which is oneself, that
is valuable, so the complete overcoming of his own distinctiveness as a particular being in the Being of the Supreme Reality,
which is what he is seeking, is to him not a loss but a gain (since
it means becoming universal in place of the particular especially
since he is the type who is not temperamentally attracted by the play
of emotion that is generally involved in the devotional approach.
A philosophical treatment of both the Saguna and Nirguna
approach does of course have the same purpose, understanding of
religious reality.   Still, it is very often the case that the Saguna
approach which seeks to retain the particularity of man in relation to the Divine, conceived as a Person with attributes like
power, mercy, love etc., that can help man, is intimately associated
with man's social existence and his need for justice, righteousness,
harmony in social relations, and so on. This is apparent in the
Gita. The *Gita* does not altogether reject the Nirguna conception,
but it is the Saguna aspect that predominates there. It is interest-
ing that the *Gita* was conceived to have been preached on the
eve of a battle, a social event of great importance, when the need
arose to persuade Arjuna to fight. This was done in terms of
God's will to maintain righteousness and the necessity to surrender all one's action to God in love and devotion. Such a God
cannot be the unmanifest Brahman beyond all dualities; He must
be conceived to be endowed with attributes that relate Him to
the world and its needs in order to elicit the kind of response that
is needed for a religious viewing of social realities. The need for
harmony in social relations is a perpetual human need – whether
this problem arises in the context of war or otherwise – and
in the context of this need God's love for man and His interest
in what happens here below has great importance. So Krishna
advises Arjuna to see all beings in God and God in all beings
even while persuading him to fight for purposes of maintaining
righteousness in the social order. To say that the conception of
God as a Person with attributes is related to man's social needs
is not to say that this approach is inferior to any other approach
or that it cannot be combined with cosmic interests, as is done by
the *Gita.*

The concept of Saguna Brahman, Isvara, or Lord God,
although not totally separated from the concept of Nirguna

Brahman in all Hindu thought, has been developed by many in this tradition as the ultimate religious concept and it has in fact a good deal more importance to the vast majority of the Hindus than that of Nirguna Brahman. The need for this concept of one Supreme Being, the source of all existence and value, a being so conceived that He enters into personal relation with man and ultimately guarantees what he most cherishes, thereby enabling man to concentrate in one centre of power all his need for love, protection and ultimate deliverance from evil and from finitude, is integral to all religious traditions, and Hinduism is no exception. And naturally enough, for it is through the experience of personal relationship, one that involves both love and protection, that man primarily experiences his sense of integration with a reality that is beyond him and yet through relationship with which his own individual existence is preserved and furthered. It is important to emphasise, that in the Hindu tradition the concept of a supreme personal God is at least as important as that of an supra-personal (I prefer the term 'supra-personal' to impersonal) absolute – a concept with which Hinduism is so often identified by people who judge it entirely in terms of the Upanisads. Man's experience of himself as a person who can however exist as a person only through his relationships with other persons is so fundamental to human beings that it would have been surprising if the Hindu religious tradition failed to develop the model of God as Lord – our creator, protector and Saviour, whom we can love, who loves us and in whose love we are united as equals in some sense – in its understanding of religious reality. It is because this need for social harmony supplies one of the basic impulses behind monotheistic religious perception that it is not only that ethical values assume great importance in this context, but heavenly existence itself is conceived under the model of harmonious existence of brothers under a loving father. This model is involved in Lokacharya's comments in his *Tattvatraya*. The Lord, he says, is transcendent. "By 'transcendent' is meant that He is beyond time and is in the further heaven of unbounded bliss where the eternally free souls revel in his presence."[1] It is because this need for social harmony is present in the background of the devotional approach that Narada preaches in his *Bhakti Sutra* the equality

[1] *The Sources of Indian Tradition*, ed. T. De Bary, pp. 339–340.

of all men in the love of God in face of the tradition of caste inequalities in Hindu society. 'Among such devotee there is no distinction of birth, learning, appearance, pedigree, wealth or profession, for they belong to God.'[2] Similar sentiments have been expressed by. many saints and teachers belonging to devotional schools.

The religious impulse behind monotheistic perception is different from that of polytheism, non-dualism and Yogic perfectionism, all to be found in the Hindu tradition. Gods conceived polytheistically are embodiments or representations of archetypal causal or creative agencies, physical, social, moral, and they are supposed to help to sustain man's being in the world in its manifold expressions. Their purpose is not to grant man ultimate peace, bliss and survival on an everlasting scale which only a Supreme Being, monotheistically conceived to be the source of all existence and value, can offer. Polytheistic worship is a means of integration with life and its cherished values here and now, so dispersal of power among a multitude of divinities who help man in a variety of ways to find happiness here on earth is not detrimental to one's perception of religious reality from this point of view. What polytheistic gods offer belongs to this life, even such a thing as illumination of the intellect, not to life after death such as everlasting happiness. So they can be many and share power which ultimately comes from a superior source.

In Upanisadic non-dualism the integration in view is with the cosmos itself, seen as grounded in an infinite and eternal essence, not just with human beings in a social setting. So emphasis on personality at either end of the integrating process, religious reality itself at one end and man's own being at another, is not an important factor in this perception, even when both ends unite through such values as existence, consciousness, and bliss. These are human enough but not particularly personal, which distinguishes one individual from another. So the emphasis here can safely be on the feeling of cosmic oneness rather than on a person to person relationship. Thus the Brahman conception, the divine reality beyond attributes, is not specifically tied up with the social reality of man. However, it is not without all social

[2] *Ibid.*, p. 330.

relevance; if this reality is manifesting itself in everything, one should make no distinction, as the Upanisads preach, between oneself and others, and be equally devoted to everything, man, animals, and nature alike. Nevertheless, since the vantage point from which the search is here made is specifically not man and his social needs, it may so happen that one who preaches the conception of Nirguna Brahman also finds no need for action in the world for man's spiritual fulfilment, as is the case with Samkara (who contrary to his own teachings did act with a view to helping others in finding Brahman, and this is not surprising since man happens to be a social being).

Yogic perfectionism when based strictly on Samkhya principles which preach isolation of the spirit from everything material as the supreme end of man, and when not mixed up with other points of view, as it often is, does not need God's love or grace for the fulfilment of life's purposes. Although the aim is individualistic, self-realisation of the individual in isolation – and this makes the doctrine posit a plurality of spirits – what remains after isolation has been achieved can hardly be called an individual in any ordinary sense of the term. Such perfectionism can have wider significance beyond an individual's understanding of his own possibilities as a spirit only if it is integrated with other approaches, as Krishna suggests in the *Gita* that it should be.

So we see that none of these models can fulfil the need that gives rise to monotheistic perception, and a religious tradition would be incomplete if it failed to produce it. This need is the very human one to feel oneself protected by a love that can only be offered by a supremely beneficent and powerful Person, infinite and absolute in His capacities, whose personal involvement guarantees the harmony of all social and individual values against the pervasive threat of evil and imperfection. But the fact that these other approaches were well-established elements in the tradition meant that monotheism had to compromise both with monism or non-dualism at one level and polytheism at another, or it had at least to exist side by side with these other religious expressions which, serving a need other than that of monotheism, could not be altogether overcome. Non-dualism appeals to the urge felt by some minds to overcome all particularity in the being of absolute consciousness and bliss, and it could not be shown to be a worthless goal. And, because of the doctrine that all of existence is a projection or self-expression of the divine and hence partakes of its nature – a view already set forth in the Purusa-Sukta of the Rigveda – worship of divinities which guard such worldly values as health, wealth, success, learning etc. (these too are aspects of the splendour of the divine) could not be set aside as altogether a mistake from the religious point of view, even if it can be assigned a lower place in the realisation of divine nature. Compromise with these other trends led to the view that monotheism and non-dualism or monotheism and polytheism are complementary approaches suited to different people and their different orientations and capabilities. So it could not be claimed in this tradition that monotheism is the only true expression of the religious impulse felt by man.

But monotheism had to be qualified in another way in the Hindu tradition. In other traditions it has been introduced through the preaching of one founder (or a group of them; as in Judaism) where the belief in one Supreme God has been associated with a distinctive name and form, as related to some historical event or events, and embodied in a dogma or doctrine that required one to reject the attribution of any other name and form to the Supreme Reality as false. The Hindu tradition does not have a founder, and its conceptions of religious reality have come from different sources, originally representing different sub-traditions within one cultural complex; and even when these were, in course of time, amalgamated, three distinct names and forms remained powerful enough for each to find a place within the totality of the tradition. The result is that there crystallised three distinct names and forms of a montheistic God, Vishnu or Krishna (or some other name and form identified with Vishnu, such as Rama), Siva and Devi or Sakti (a goddess also variously known as Kali, Durga, Uma etc.). Each is worshipped by his sectarian devotees as the only Supreme Being to the exclusion of the rest and all of them are accepted by non-sectarian Hindus, who constitute the majority of the Hindu population, as different expressions of the same Divine Being.

Because of this blurring of edges in the tradition we sometimes find it difficult to delineate where monotheism ends and monism or polytheism takes over, especially if we consider the philosophical and popular religious literature such as the Puranas.

Kashmiri Saivism in its philosophy, for instance, ultimately identifies Siva with Brahman beyond name and form, with which Krishna is also identified, at times at any rate, by the *Bhagavata Purana*. In *Saundaryalahari*, one of the texts in which the conception of the Goddess (Devi) being the highest reality is put forward, Devi is identified with Paramabrahman. Again, in sectarian Puranas a name and form which is treated elsewhere as the Supreme God, be it Krishna, Siva, or Devi, is relegated to an inferior position appropriate to a god in a polytheistic complex (powerful but not the supreme being). In some religious philosophy centred round a monotheistic God, Siva, Krishna, or Devi, liberation (eternal life) is so conceived that it can more appropriately be called identity with Brahman, rather than union with God – a language which only fits in with monotheism as generally understood.

This is because in the Hindu tradition speculative approach to the divine, as distinct from the practical one involving ritual, worship, devotion etc., has from Vedic times, (speculative monism exists side by side with ritualistic polytheism in the *Rigveda*), involved non-dualism as a powerful trend of thought, and this insists that religious reality is inexhaustible beyond all name and form, (even the name that one may cherish oneself), that it permeates all of existence so that there is no insurmountable distinction between man and God and that man's final aim in life is to realise that he is nothing different from this reality. So spiritual experience is envisaged as an experience of identity and not as one in which two persons stand over against each other, separate in their distinct identities even if united by a bond of love. Not only polytheism but even monotheism could not totally escape this trend of thought so that it is possible to discern an undercurrent of monism in several forms of Hindu monotheistic philosophy which claim that God, the Supreme Self, is in all beings, and all beings are in the supreme self. Identity with God, of course, is sometimes qualified, in the interest of the devotional approach, as identity-in-difference, where the relation between man and God becomes somewhat ambiguous, neither total identity nor total difference. In any case, man must finally find God in his own being and not just out there. That is, God is internalised after He has been posited as transcendent for the purposes of devotion, and then the difference between theism and monism becomes rather thin in so far as continuity between men and God is re-established through internalisation. However, again in the interest of devotion, some monotheistic philosophy emphasises that in the experience of indentity-in-difference man becomes godly and divested of all the limitations of finitude, but not God, since liberated souls do not acquire creatorship.

I therefore find it more illuminating to talk about monistic, monotheistic, and polytheistic treatment of religious reality in the Hindu tradition rather than of monism, monotheism and polytheism with their suggestion of being exclusive descriptions of this reality. But monotheism elsewhere than in the Hindu tradition will be resistant to such language, for there what monotheism says stands for the nature of religious reality itself and not for one of the ways of conceiving this nature. This is why I am labelling this chapter 'Qualified Monotheism' rather than just 'Monotheism'. This is not to say that one cannot find Hindus who are monotheists in the ordinary sense, that is, who accept one name and form of God as being the only true one to the exclusion of the rest. But as I am here concerned to study the tradition as a whole I believe that 'Qualified Monotheism' is a better description of it than just 'Monotheism.'

Devotionalism, as a characteristic approach to religious reality, is a specific human need and, as Krishna says in the *Gita*, love and devotion to a personal God is the most easily acceptable and workable of all paths to the divine. So we may surmise that long before the *Gita*, which so far as the written tradition of the Hindus is concerned first elaborates in detail the idea of love of God with all its ramifications, there were many ordinary people (outside the closed circle of Vedic aristocracy dominated either by ritualism or contemplative practices) who had always expressed their religious impulse through devotional cults of various sorts. The centre of these cults may have been some deified tribal chief or holy man, some semi-legendary hero or a mystic personality adopted as a divine being for its symbolic value, or even a human relationship symbolically approached and deified, such as the cult of the mothers. A good deal of love and affection were probably being showered on these deities in an exclusive fashion, who, conceived as persons presiding over the domestic domain and its welfare, became intimately associated with the daily life of man. These eventually combined into three distinct types of divine images, with their somewhat different symbolic connotations, which were assimilated to the Vedic tradition by way of cognate conceptions found in the Vedas – in the figure of Vishnu, Rudra-Siva, and the Vedic mother Goddess. It seems to me that the reason why all of these three images finally survived is that they not only embody three distinct but characteristic perception of life and its possibilities, each of which can legitimately claim to fashion a divine image from the standpoint of its own understanding of life, but also represent somewhat different emotional needs all of which can be found in the context of the religious search. In short, they satisfied three types of distinct personalities through their characteristic forms, images, rituals, symbols, and philosophies, and as there was no church or order within the tradition entrusted to regulate the whole of man's religious life, they all survived.

Vishnu in the Vedas is comparatively a minor deity, but he does stand for an important principle, as by taking three steps he not only creates the domain for Indra's royal activities but also points to the transcendent sphere where the third step leads us. He is called the pervader and as a solar deity associated with Indra he could easily become the source of life and light here on earth as well as hereafter. Also, because of his association with Indra he came to represent grandeur, magnificence, joyousness, friendliness, and generosity, qualities which fitted him for being the symbol of all positive excellences admired and adored by men. He could then become the central point around which Vasudeva, Gopal Krishna, Narayana and similar cults, all of which conceived the divine in his benign aspect of creation, preservation, and protection, crystallized and eventually combined to produce – through a process of synthesis and refinement – a supremely lovable monotheistic God, endowed not only with omnipotence, omniscience, and omnipresence, but also with surpassing beauty, sweetness, goodness, glory, joy, and splendour of every sort. Vishnu, as the pervading principle whose very presence preserves and enhances life, appeals to all that is optimistic, joyous, and harmonious in man's life. He is therefore particularly suited to act as the symbol of the divine to those people who are drawn to a religious perception of life through the appreciation of the sunny side of life – in its beauty, splendour and goodness, and not through what is enigmatic, mysterious, inscrutable, or fearful.

But life is not all sunshine and there are minds which are more keenly sensitive to what is mysterious and terrifying in life than what is pleasant and beautiful, and to them divine power may appear not only awesome and fearful but actually destructive when it deals with men, disease, and death. If a man is impressed by the incomprehensibility of what appears to him as divine wrath and is struck by the mystery of it all, he is likely to project the image of a God who, although to be loved with all one's heart, nevertheless appeals, even if subconsciously, to the dark, subterranean, and dimly understood anxieties and insecurities of the human mind. Thus arises the picture of a God who is mysterious and enigmatic, because on the one hand he holds in his power all the destructive potentialities which terrorise mortal men, and on the other he is supremely beneficent and saves man by bestowing grace. It is only by attributing both creative and destructive attributes to the Divine and emphasising them equally, so that the image embraces a comprehensive picture of life, that some men come to terms with the fierceness of life and its disturbing possibilities, along with divine grace and love.

Rudra in the *Rigveda* fills the role of a god with destructive and terrifying potentialities but who at the same time is conceived to be a protector of men and beasts. He is both a dealer of disease and a healer. Outside the Vedic circle there was the Indus valley god who was also enigmatic and whose phallic symbol was the embodiment both of supreme self-restraint in Yoga and of fertility and exuberance of creation. Then again, there was perhaps the god of mountain tribes, dressed in skin, possibly a vagrant and a frequenter of cremation or burial grounds, but at the same time a protector of beasts and a friend of man. All these were put together as Siva, a supremely mysterious being who transcends all distinctions and yet combines in his being all dualities, such as good and evil, creation and destruction, vagrancy and lordship over the world, sexual potency and supreme self-restraint. In short, Siva is the expression of an inscrutable principle in the world which symbolises eternal life in death, and his destructive potentialities at the phenomenal level are no bar to devotion, once the devotee accepts that he too must transcend phenomenality by surrendering to God. Acceptance of such a God means acceptance of terror and suffering which cast their inevitable shadow in life along with divine love and ultimate protection.

But the divine has also been conceived in the Hindu tradition as a female principle, variously called Devi, Sakti, Kali, Chandi etc. The goddess is the embodiment of the dynamism and energy of the creative principle in the world, and here the creative and preserving role of the human mother in generating life and steering it through helpless conditions full of danger and insecurity to safety, provides the symbol for the divine nature and function. Devi, like human mother, generates the Universe out of her own being, nurtures it through good and evil and finally sees it through a stormy passage to its rest in the transcendent principle of bliss and quiescence. There are cognate ideas of a mother goddess in the Vedic and non-Vedic religious traditions in India. The Vedic mother goddess was a benevolent figure, an embodiment of productive energy and understanding in the world, but the non-Vedic mother goddesses were fertility symbols and as such were probably representatives of life and beneficence as well as of the awesome and unpleasant aspects of generation and destruction that demand suffering as a price of life. Accordingly, the composite figure of the mother goddess in the Hindu tradition has two faces, one beneficent, loving, and graceful, the other fierce, and black with powers of death and destruction. The same goddess who mercilessly destroys evil and scatters death all around graciously protects those who take refuge at her feet. So those who have the courage and imagination to penetrate through the apparent terror and unloveliness of the goddess to her transcendent beauty and grace are supremely rewarded with bliss and eternal life.

The mother goddess appeals to the imagination of those who find the mother-child rather than the father-child relationship as revelatory of divine involvement in the world. The all-embracing love of the mother for a child offers an instinctive security which the more distant care of the father does not. Also the love of the mother has an organic intimacy about it which the love of the father lacks. Thus those in the Hindu tradition who long for an all-enveloping love in surrendering to which one can find absolute and utter security – like a child in relation to his mother in total trust – find the image of a mother goddess much more congenial for the expression of their religious impulse than a male god. But of course religious motivations are complex like other motivations, and as the Mother Goddess is the embodiment of energy one may be drawn to her figure through adoration of energy and strength rather than through a feeling of helplessness. After all, it is also the function of the mother to help the child grow from dependence to self-sufficiency and to some people, at least in the Hindu tradition, the mother is the embodiment of strength and wisdom, and not just of love. However, the mother for many is a symbol of closeness, since one can make demands on the mother for unconditional help, as it were as a matter of right – and we find that in the songs of the devotees of Kali demands are actually made on her that she should help her children to realise the divine – whereas one has probably to prove oneself worthy of receiving grace before one can appeal to the father, who is likely to be more demanding. It has been suggested, and perhaps rightly, that the unimportance of the concept of sin and guilt in the Hindu religious complex as compared to other monotheistic traditions is owing to the wide currency of the image of the Mother Goddess as the Supreme Being in this tradition. A child makes instinctive demands on the mother without having to worry himself about whether or not he merits to be loved and cared for, while by the time an articulate father-child relationship grows up the child is made aware that in certain matters at any rate what he gets from his father depends on how he behaves. Hence the importance of the concepts of sin and guilt.

The problem of evil and suffering everywhere poses a major problem to the religious mind because it is incomprehensible and unacceptable to human beings, and there have been different ways of dealing with it. In non-Hindu monotheistic traditions, suffering starts with disobedience and opposition to the will of God who is all good, and had originally given man perfect happiness, even in the created realm. This was lost through sin of disobedience, so it is man who is responsible for the presence of evil and suffering in the world, not God. The Hindu tradition generally traces everything from the same source, both good and evil, joys, and sufferings – this is why some of its gods are gods of destruction or at least have destructive functions among others.

The Infinite and Absolute Being manifests itself in the realm of finitude and relativity through different names and forms in order to enjoy itself as multiplicity and diversity. The very nature of finite things is to be limited in space and time and in their limitation they are opposed to the nature of other things similarly conditioned. As everything finite must come into being and eventually go out of existence, it is subject to change and decay, and its opposition as a particular thing to other particular things similarly limited gives rise to tension, conflict, and consequent suffering, when it comes to human beings. The imperfections of the phenomenal world are a temporal expression in multiplicity of what is at the transcendent level, timelessly one, and God enjoys both transcendent bliss and phenomenal joys and sufferings (out of his own choice). If there is to be a phenomenal world, there are also to be the limitations which are inherent in the very structure of finitude, and man has to accept this basic fact as God does in his decision to be many. However, God is present in man, who being self-conscious can come to find his identity with infinite existence and thereby transcend the limitations of the phenomenal world. This is the attitude man is required to take as regards his own suffering. When the suffering of other people, who have not transcended the world, is concerned, one who finds God in everything would endeavour to minimise its scope through charity, compassion, non-violence, and where applicable through the righteous ordering of social phenomena (one of the reasons given by Krishna to Arjuna for the need to fight was this), without however suffering the illusion that the finite world can be turned into absolute perfection.

It may be said that if evil and suffering are built into the world, and these happen through God's choice to savour Himself as the limited many in the sphere of change and finitude, then one should just accept these and do nothing to make the world a better place. This will be a misunderstanding about the nature of the world as constituted of prakriti with its three gunas expressing God's lower nature. These gunas are sattva, representing goodness, equalmindedness and harmony, rajas, representing drive, energy and desire for accomplishment and excellence, and tamas, representing dullness, ignorance and inertia. Everything in this world, including human beings, are constituted of these in different proportions. In so far as there is sattvic goodness in human beings they will by their own inherent nature feel charity, compassion, and concern for the well-being of all creatures within phenomenal existence, and in so far as there is rajas in them they will desire to accomplish many things by exerting themselves. So concern for welfare of the world and attempt to achieve it are not contrary to the constitution of the world and these are perfectly in accordance with God's nature as displaying itself within phenomenality. Men may not overcome the inevitable limitations of finitude within the phenomenal sphere, but if there are suffering and evil in this sphere which can be counteracted by man's actions, then there is nothing in the concept of God's play and self-enjoyment in multiplicity which forbids this – on the contrary, man's actions of this nature are part of this play and self-expression, just as much as anything else. But ultimately to conquer suffering one must finally transcend it. The way to it is knowledge, as in transcendentalism (Yoga and contemplative non-dualism) which tells man that his essential nature is infinite and immortal beyond the limitations of space and time with which he identifies himself only through ignorance, or love as in devotionalism, where man learns to cope with his own sufferings through surrendering his own will to God's and respond to that of others through serving them as reflections of God.

The fact that the Hindu tradition accepts suffering as part of the concept of finitude does not mean that it is not sensitive to it. In fact, suffering has loomed so large in the Hindu consciousness that it has not been able to project an image of the divine which is devoid of all connotations of destruction. The popular image of Krishna is of a sweet, loving, friendly, and gracious God, who is entirely non-terrifying. But Vaishnava philosophy makes God the creator, preserver, and destroyer of the world. In both Saiva and Sakta popular myths, legends and imagery, suffering and destruction (mainly caused by the evil actions of Asuras, Daityas, and Danavas, who are enemies of the gods) have been integrated into the very drama of life and hence a part of the conception of the divine image projected. No doubt divine destructiveness is aimed at evil-doers, and not at the virtuous. But the fact that there had to be stories of this nature and not just incidents describing God's loving kindness is indication that the darker side of human existence did not escape the attention of the myth-makers. No doubt the Supreme Being brings peace and eternal life to man in the end, but the way to it is not easy and the price may be heavy in terms of evil and suffering. Suffering is thus the other side of the coin of love and bliss which will be offered to the devotee who is not frightened to die in order to live. Hence the terrifying figure of the Goddess Kali, with her garland of severed human heads, bloodstained tongue and death-dealing sword, does not stop the Hindu from finding her adorable and lovely, particularly as with one of her hands the goddess offers refuge to all who may seek her. (I am of course not talking of all Hindus; sectarian Vaishnavas did object to both Siva and Kali.)

Devotionalism follows a path that is more directly satisfying than either ritualism or contemplative-mediative practices, being capable of a more direct and immediate emotional impact on the personality. Hence the need to conceive of divine reality as a person and to represent this person in a concrete image with a definite name and form. The image enables one to treat God as a person through loving adoration offered in the specific form of Hindu worship called the 'puja'. Devotion, however, is a mental attitude and it is not specifically tied up with image worship, although it is normally directed towards a God with a name and form brought to the level of personal existence through embodiment in myths and legends. By devotion (bhakti) what is meant is primarily love, a permanent emotional disposition towards God. As Narada says in his *Bhakti-Sutra* (Aphorism on Devotion), 'Devotion consists of Supreme love of God. It is also supremely delectable like ambrosia. On obtaining that man has achieved everything, he becomes immortal, he is completely satisfied. Having got it he desires nothing else, he grieves not, he hates nothing, he delights not in anything else, he strives for nothing, having realised which man becomes as if intoxicated and benumbed; he delights in his own intrinsic bliss.'[3] Love of God does not need cultivation of qualities other than those man already possesses, but to release a man from his normal state of ignorance it does need complete and exclusive absorption in God and indifference to things of this world. According to the *Bhagvata Purana* the characteristic of pure devotion to the

[3]*Ibid.*, p. 327.

Supreme is that it has no motive – as distinct from motivated worship of lesser divinities in a polytheistic complex – and is incessant, involving a total transformation of the personality and not just temporary states of emotional exuberance.

According to Lokacharya, God's 'personality' is in his form and qualities, something which He can take on according to His own desire and for the benefit of his devotees. Many writers on Bhakti emphasise that God can take on whatever personality a devotee wishes to ascribe to Him. The controversy on the question of God's personality, whether it has a specific name or form or specific qualities is thus futile, for God can take on a personality with specific form and qualities at will. Certainly personality is not beyond God and the forms in which this personality can be conceived are manifold. According to Lokacharya, 'The Lord's form is five-fold; the transcendent one (Para), the manifestations (Vyuha), the incarnations (Vibhava), the immanent spirit (antaryamin) and images (arca).'[4] The function of an image is to give concrete content to the idea that God is a person and can be approached as such, so long, of course, as one knows that the image is only a symbol by the help of which a tangible relationship of love to the divine is to be established and that God is not confined to the image. Offering puja to the image is a way of establishing this relationship. According to the *Bhagavata Purana*, 'When the devotee's whole being has become pervaded by My form, which is the inner soul of all beings, the devotee shall, having become completely immersed in Myself, make my presence overflow into the image etc. established in front of him, and then with all the paraphernalia, conduct My worship....

'With clothes, sacred thread, jewels, garlands, and fragrant paste, My devotee should decorate My form suitably and with love. With faith, My worshipper should then offer Me water to wash, sandal, flower, unbroken rice, incense, light, and food of different kinds; also attentions like anointing, massage, showing of mirror etc., and entertainments like song and dance, these special attentions and entertainments may be done on festive days and even daily.'[5]

[4]*Ibid.*, p. 337.
[5]*Ibid.*, p. 336.

But although the image enables man to conceive of God as a beloved person to whom he can offer concrete acts of love and care, image worship can degenerate into ritualism and then the worshipper may fail to realise that God is everywhere and in everything and not just in the image, which is after all an aid to cultivating a permanent disposition of love through practical means. So the same *Bhagavata Purana* adds: 'I am always present in all beings as their soul, and yet, ignoring Me, mortal man conducts the mockery of image-worship. He who ignores me resident in all beings as the soul and Master and, in his ignorance, takes to images, verily pours oblation on ash [i.e., worships in vain]. The mind of the man who hates me abiding in another's body, who, in his pride, sees invidious distinctions and is inimically disposed to all beings, never attains tranquillity. Blessed lady, when the worshipper is one who insults living beings, I am not satisfied with his worship in My image. Doing one's appointed duty, one should adore Me, the Master, in images and the like, only so long as one is not able to realise in one's heart Me who is established in every being.[6] The *Purana* goes further: "To look upon all beings as Myself, and to shape one's conduct towards them accordingly, in thought, word and deed – that is the best method of worship.'[7] So love of God cannot really be separated from love of man where He is said to be most manifest. And it seems that the best way to cultivate love of man is to love the Ultimate Reality as a Supreme Person who resides in the heart of all men.

Vaishnavism, Saivism, Saktism

In this section I shall briefly examine the three distinctive types of devotionalism that resulted in the specific approach to religious reality in the Hindu tradition that I am designating 'Qualified Monotheism'. Each of these involves a specific name and form for the divine Being, who is iconographically represented in a particular fashion and worshipped at home and in temples, various myths and legends to be found in the epics, the *Ramayana* and the *Mahabharata*, and in the literature called

[6] *Ibid.*, pp. 331–332.
[7] *Srimad Bhagavatam*, trans. Swami Prabhavananda, p. 303.

the 'Puranas', that give concrete content to the personality of the divine Being, and make him or her stand out as a distinctive character to the popular imagination, and a philosophy (or philosophies) which expound to the more sophisticated mind the philosophical implications as to the nature of the world, man and the ultimate reality that devotion to these deities regarded as the Supreme Being imply. While at the popular level the specific form attributed to the deity, and myths and legends woven round him, are taken to be literally true, at the philosophical level these are often symbolically interpreted and understood at the level of principles rather than that of the concrete particular where the question whether or not there is actually to be found such a person as is iconographically represented to be Krishna, or whether or not the various events narrated around him actually did take place, becomes relevant. A philosophical treatment of religious questions, however, does not demand what is called demythologisation, for it is generally believed by Hindus that myths even if taken literally can function to open the mind to the divine – through playing on the emotions rather than the intellect – which it is their function to do. Those whose minds are oriented in such a way that their intellect demands that it must be ascertained whether certain stories are in fact literally true, before they can be made to function in any way, can make their approach to the divine through philosophy rather than mythology. But there are in fact a great many people for whom philosophy is too abstract and who find mythology much more congenial to their mental make up; that is, they respond to the divine through mythology as they would not be able through philosophy.

The point is not just to know the legends as so many pieces of information about God and his activities, but to feel closeness to God through repeated subjection to hearing about Him as a person. This is why in the old Hindu tradition repeated narration of myths and legends by village bards or visiting story-tellers to gatherings on festive occasions or even regularly at temple precincts and dramatic presentations of stories about gods by folk theatrical troupes formed an important cultural activity. Hindu theistic religious philosophy therefore does not reject the myths and legends that have gathered round the name and form of a Deity but freely makes use of them for its own purposes, without feeling called upon to settle the question of their truth value in historical terms. This is possible as the Hindu religious tradition is not bound up with historical events whose authenticity needs to be ascertained in order to assess the religious value of the stories told. The popular mind no doubt takes the stories as real events, but no insuperable damage to the tradition will be done if the events are ultimately found to be imagined rather than flesh and blood happenings, particularly as some of these take place in spheres other than this world – in various lokas where reside gods, sages, semi-divine beings etc. – or in heaven itself. I shall in this section be concerned more with philosophy than with mythology, except in so far as myths bear on the model which is being used to conceive of divine nature in relation to man and the world.

VAISHNAVISM

The term Vaishnavism etymologically refers to the god Vishnu who, however, is now worshipped more in his incarnations as Krishna or Rama than as the Vedic pervader who is later defined as the embodiment of the quality of sattva – the cohesive tendency which holds the universe together – and iconographically represented as a god with four arms symbolising his divine powers. Some Hindu mythologies conceive the divine function as threefold – creation, preservation, and destruction – and attribute these to three different gods, Brahma (creation), Vishnu (preservation) and Siva (destruction), these three gods being referred to as the Hindu trinity. As monotheism developed all these functions came to be vested in one supreme God – Siva, Vishnu, or Devi – who had replaced Brahma as a major God. However, as Vishnu was originally conceived to be the principle of preservation, this was a suitable concept around which to weave the Hindu doctrine of incarnation, the descent of the godhead into the phenomenal world to preserve its righteous order against the forces of evil. In accordance with Hindu cosmology which conceived time to be cyclical, in which there are different ages with different needs, incarnation is thought to be a repeated occurrence rather than once and for all. Some mythologies give a definite number for the incarnation of God on earth, ten being most commonly accepted, but the *Gita* puts forward the idea that God incarnates himself whenever there is a need for divine intervention in the preservation of the world order against forces of disintegration. The *Bhagavata Purana* also supports the *Gita* in this: 'Just as from an inexhaustible lake thousands of streams flow on all sides, so also from the remover of sorrow (Hari), sum of all reality, come forth countless incarnations; the seers, the law-givers, the gods, the human races, the lords of progeny, all are parts of him.'[8] Again, 'whenever the truth is forgotten in the world and wickedness prevails, the Lord becomes flesh to show the way, the truth, and the life to humanity. Such an incarnation is an Avatar, an embodiment of God on earth.'[9] This idea of multiple or countless incarnations goes well with the Hindu concept of creation. God is present in everything, but his essence is manifested more in some things than in others – things which possess excellence or perfection to a striking degree. As Krishna says in the *Gita*, 'Whichever entity is endowed with glory and with majesty and is verily full of vigour – each such entity do thou know to have originated from a fraction of my splendour'. And it is said in the *Srimad Bhagavatam*, 'Wherever there is power, beauty, fame, prosperity, modesty, sacrifice, concord, fortune, strength, fortitude or knowledge – there I am manifested.' An incarnation is thus a person who manifests God's power to an extraordinary degree and who works to preserve the world from moral or physical disaster.

However, both the *Gita* and *Bhagavata Purana* concentrate on a specific incarnation, Krishna, who is ultimately identified with God Himself and who replaces Vishnu as the object of the Vaishnava devotee's love. Some Vaishnavas no doubt worship the figure of Rama rather than Krishna as the incarnation of God, but as Vaishnava philosophy is elaborated round the concept of Krishna-Vishnu I shall here take Krishna as the key figure in the monotheistic devotionalism that is known as Vaishnavism.

[8] *Bhagavata Purana*, 1.3. 26–27, trans. A Danielou, in *Hindu Polytheism*, p.164.

[9] *Srimad Bhagavatam*, trans. Swami Prabhabananda, p. 6.

It is Krishna among all the monotheistic Gods who has a complete life-story from birth to death, and this suggests that there was probably a historical figure who was at first made into a 'deva'[10] and then gradually elevated to the position of the Supreme God. This, however, does not mean that all the events that are attributed to the life-story of Krishna actually belong to history or to one life. The Hindu tradition is cumulative and agglomerative, and has gathered material from different sources and put them together to make a connected story – a process which resulted in some inconsistencies and a good deal of fanciful embellishments that were needed to fill in the gaps. But as nothing hangs on Krishna's being a historical figure, the mixing up of fact with fancy did not have to worry anyone. There was probably a chief of the Vrishni tribe called Vasudeva Krishna – a hero-king who killed the tyrant Kamsa and other kings of evil disposition and who established a kingdom at Dwaraka, in the west of India. This Krishna may also have been the disciple who is mentioned in the *Chandogya* Upanisad as having learnt Upanisadic wisdom from a teacher, Ghora Angirasa, or who is identified with him. For Krishna appears in the role of a great teacher in the *Mahabharata*, where in the *Bhagavadgita* he synthesises the teaching of the Upanisads with devotionalism (probably as a result of himself being the centre of a devotional cult). This adored hero-king and teacher (or these two figures put together) was deified and then made into an incarnation of Vishnu and Narayana (a deified sage who had himself been identified with Vishnu). But Krishna's life story as mentioned in the *Harivamsa* (an appendix to the *Mahabharata*) and *Bhagavata* and other Puranas also brings in an entirely different kind of trend, far removed from the picture of Krishna the king and the teacher. There he is also shown as a child god, being reared by parents who are dairy farmers and spending an idyllic childhood and adolescence among the herdsmen and herdswomen of Vrindaban, a life that is full of marvellous exploits of various kinds, including amorous ones. This pastoral Krishna (incidentally being reared by people of a

---

[10] 'Deva' (a god) means a shining being and as everything in Hindu theology partakes of the divine essence, a being who is found to be particularly shining for some reason, is made into a divinity without any great difficulty.

vaishya occupation and himself following the same), the darling of the cowherd community amidst which he lived, is of a quite different cast from the heroic Krishna, the kshatriya, and so it may be that legends about the boy Krishna came from a different source – perhaps from some cowherd tribe who pastured their herds in the woodlands called Vraja and had a cult of a boy God. However that may be, in the life-story of Krishna these incidents are shown as an interlude[11] in his life, between his birth – immediately after which he was removed to Vrindaban for reasons of safety – and his later exploits as a kshatriya and a righteous ruler.

It seems that there is an unconscious process at work in the putting together of all these diverse myths and legends to build up the model of a God-man, an incarnation of God who was fully human. The image that was finally projected of Krishna shows him to be involved in life at every level from childhood to a ripe age, participating in the diverse functions of life to the full in many different capacities. He was born a kshatriya, that is, one who by birth belonged to the social category of warriors and rulers, and did all that was required of a perfect kshatriya. He put down the tyranny of unjust rulers, himself ruled righteously, and even founded an entirely new kingdom in the west to give his subjects better conditions of life than obtained at Mathura because of the constant incursions made by powerful enemies who did not forgive Krishna his killing of the tyrannical Kamsa. But in his childhood he was brought up in a village among the ordinary folk, and as a boy himself grazed cattle with cowherd companions, towards whom he displayed a most affectionate friendship. He is shown to be a delightful infant, full of childish pranks, and fond of teasing his adopted mother while enjoying a most tender relationship with her (once while ostensibly leading her on to punish him for having done something rather naughty he opens his mouth and shows her that the universe is within him). But his relationships were not confined to his family or friends of the same sex. Full of grace, charm, and beauty, and superbly skilled in playing the flute, he conquered the

---

[11] For some Vaishnavas, however, it is this part of his life-story which has the greatest spiritual significance being all a display of love.

hearts of all and sundry around him in the village, including the cowherd girls. Krishna is not only not shown to be above sex, he is portrayed as alive to feminine charm and the beauty of romance in the same way as he is sensitive to all other aspects of life, and there are charming tales (which to a mind which finds sex sinful would no doubt appear offensive) of his romantic and amorous associations with young girls of the village, particularly with one called Radha, with whom Krishna is involved in a most intense and passionate romance. Their love is interpreted on different levels, the physical transcending itself into the spiritual. (In later Vaishnava literature Radha's love for Krishna becomes the symbol of the soul's intense passion for God.) In short, at this stage of his life, Krishna is shown as involved with love at all levels, mother-child, comradeship and friendship, romance, and even love of nature and animals, and he is one with it all, giving himself graciously and unstintingly to all, whichever way they desired and loved him.

The same Krishna is then turned into a kshatriya, serious about his mission and responsible, entrusted as he was with the difficult job of vanquishing tyrannous rulers and establishing righteousness in the social order, and he performs all his tasks very much as a kshatriya conscious of his duty should. He even goes to live with a teacher for his allotted time of studentship to acquire sacred and other knowledge, and on his return marries and starts a family as befitting the stage of a householder. And this kshatriya Krishna later appears as a teacher, in the role of a brahman, as it were, who as the friend of man (Arjuna) imparts to him supreme wisdom. He is involved in the great war of the Mahabharata, but his job there is not to fight but to offer wise counsel to both sides and act as the ambassador of peace from the Pandavas to the Kauravas, who pay no heed to his proposal, and finally to offer himself as the chariot driver to the main actor of the drama, Arjuna, who happens to be a very dear friend. But his love for Arjuna did not induce him to take an active part in the war, for that would have been against the rules of impartiality to which he was committed as a relation and friend to both sides of the family. He even lent several thousands of his own soldiers to the other side so as to counterbalance the advantage that Arjuna was going to have through having Krishna at his side, even if in a non-fighting capacity.

After an extremely active, varied, and eventful life, Krishna died through being hit by an arrow from a hunter who mistook his body resting in the woods for that of an animal. He died in peace and in a state of Yoga, granting liberation to the man who killed him. He died in the same spirit in which he had lived, with a capacity to transcend events in which he was fully involved. Krishna's life is a full life, and fully human, not perfect in the sense that he never did anything to which the slightest objection can be taken, for he would then be above humanity – indeed he is shown as having to take recourse to subterfuges when exigencies of tricky situations demand it– but in the sense that he lived life on all fronts and savoured it in every possible way. Nothing human was foreign to his nature, nothing too low to be beyond the range of his interests, and this great warrior who had himself accomplished magnificent heroic deeds thought nothing of offering himself as a mere chariot driver to another in friendship. Too often a disproportionate amount of interest is shown by critics in Krishna's varied love-life which is thought to be quite unbecoming in a 'good' man, let alone in God. But if we view these incidents in relation to the whole pattern of his life, we should find that they fit well into the model that is here being offered of a life that God, who projects Himself into diversity in order to enjoy it, would live. This life is a full life which denies neither its joys nor its responsibilities, but not a 'good' life, in the sense that it is not strictly confined to activities which normally pass as virtuous, although upholding righteousness in the world was one of its manifold functions.

Krishna is a full human being towards whom all attitudes of love are possible, including romantic attachment between sexes. Hence his life-story must show this important aspect of life in action as it must show others equally significant for the living of human life. No doubt the excesses of the Hindu imagination have probably blown some of the tales beyond the bounds of 'propriety', at least for the orthodox mind, but the Purana stories make it perfectly clear that Krishna's love-life was manifold, not because he was a particularly licentious young man who could not be easily satisfied, but because many women desired him from the romantic point of view – his appeal was great in this field just as it was great in the matter of friendship with men – and Krishna as God offered himself in whichever way he was approached. It would have been opposed to the idea of his plenitude of being if he were to restrict himself to some, or to certain relationships only. The stories are of course given a spiritual interpretation and no doubt such an interpretation is perfectly valid, particularly as many of his escapades took place when he was still in his early adolescence (according to some Puranas at any rate). But we should remember that according to the ancient Indian tradition there is nothing sinful about sex (renunciation of worldly life, when it took place, was to overcome not sin but ignorance), and in order to paint Krishna's life on a large scale he was shown capable of giving romantic happiness not just to one woman but many. All other activities of his life were on a grand scale as well, which is easily overlooked in one's preoccupation with sex.

The projection of a full life, which a man gifted with all sensibilities and qualities proper to a man, from physical beauty to spiritual illumination, would live, as a model of life for the divine on earth, accords well with the doctrine of lila that goes with Vaishnava philosophy. According to this doctrine, creation means a spontaneous self-projection of the divine, out of sheer joy and fullness of being, into multiplicity in order to savour itself in manifold ways – and this creative activity is called sportive because, like a sport, it is its own purpose and indulged in for the pleasure of the activity itself and not for an extrinsic purpose. In theistic language, the Lord sports with Himself in and through creation, which Krishna in the *Gita* calls his lower nature, and those who can participate in it as sport (which does not mean that one must not take it seriously, for players usually take their activities quite seriously) can also participate in the joy that underlies creation. Or it is said that God is an artist and creation is a work of art (art too is spontaneous self-expression). Krishna's life itself is a portrayal of lila in miniature.

Zaehner misinterprets this concept of lila when he says that according to this doctrine creation is a kind of joke as there is no purpose behind it. What this doctrine does, however, is to conceive of creation as a whole from the aesthetic point of view rather than the moral, but that does not mean that one could not take up a moral attitude to happenings on earth from a more limited and sectional point of view. This concept is an elaboration of the Upanisadic teaching that the created realm is an expression of Brahman's essence and it is not produced out of nothing. But the fact that God has no purpose in creation other than being many does not mean that there can be no purpose within the created realm for limited creatures like men, who must make distinctions of good and bad, right and wrong and uphold what is good against what is evil. Indeed, such purpose is a part of the conception of God's lila in being many, and if this were not so there would be no point in the doctrine of repeated incarnations which goes with the doctrine of lila. Incarnations are supposed to take place when there is too much evil and unrighteousness in the world, which God comes down to put right and this is part of His lila. One has only to read the Vaishnava literature, the *Bhagavata Purana* for instance, not to speak of the *Gita*, to see how much importance it lays on moral virtue – service to mankind, charity, compassion etc. – without the cultivation of which, it is said, one does not become pure enough to feel love of God.

It is only at the level of the totality where, as the *Vishnu Purana* says, God is both the demon and the demon killer that the distinction of good and evil is not significant. At any level lower than this where such distinctions obtain it is essential to uphold good against evil for one's moral and spiritual health. The door through which man must pass in order to finally transcend good and evil is constituted of good, never of evil. This much is made clear by all Hindu scriptures, including the Yoga darsana which does not aspire beyond man's self-realisation as spirit. And this is only to be expected, because it is only through forces of good (sattva) that one can rise above selfishness (the root of all moral evil) and identify oneself with all, and as God is all identification or union with God cannot take place without identification with all. However, what the lila doctrine emphasises is not that he who loves God is good and virtuous, but that life for him is bliss and full of delight. 'To the man who finds delight in me alone, who is self-controlled and even-minded, having no longing in his heart but for me, the whole universe is full of bliss.[12] It is only the moral man, as against the immoral, who can come to this perception of the world as God's lila and find bliss in this perception, but when he perceives this he also transcends morality. That is, he, like God, achieves spontaneity in action. 'When thou hast gained knowledge and wisdom and canst feel unity with all embodied beings, when thou dost know the Self and dost find delight in the Self, then art thou free from all limitations. Thou shalt go beyond both good and evil. Good actions will proceed from thee without any thought of merit and thou shalt desist from evil actions naturally and not through a sense of evil.'[13]

It seems to me that inherent in the doctrine of lila is a positive and healthy attitude to life which would find joy both in participation in it and contemplation about it. There is a story about Nikasha, the hundred year old mother of Ravana, who was fleeing when Rama's army entered Lanka on Ravana's death. She was asked why at her age she should be so afraid to die. Her reply was that it was not that she was afraid to die but she wanted to live on to see more of God's lila. Anyway, even if a limited egocentric life does not quite offer the kind of joy that lila talks about one ought to find it, consistently with this doctrine, in participation on a bigger scale, which includes life all around. That is, the quest for liberation for a man whose devotion to God is inspired by the lila doctrine should consist not in renunciation of worldly activity but in activity on a grander scale, aimed at the welfare of all beings and not just oneself. Liberation here means joys of the infinite which however is manifesting itself in the finite, meaning God and his lila, and not the purely negative and essentially selfish aspiration of not being born again. According to Bhagavat Kumar Goswami, the Satwata Bhakti cult in Ancient India, that is, the cult centred around the love of Vasudeva-Krishna, did preach the type of higher bhakti which involved this positive understanding. Referring to a saying in the *Bhagavata Purana* which condemns the life of gods and sages who seek their own liberation by living a solitary and silent life in

[12] *Srimad Bhagavatam*, trans. Swami Prabhabananda, p. 241.
[13] *Ibid.*, p. 208.

the wood without any concern for the well-being of others as miserly, he says, 'The man of self-culture and meditation must live and act as a cultured and thoughtful man of action. If the whole universe is in his full knowledge and full life he must live for all life. It will not do for him to lead a silent unconcerned life in pursuit of his self-contained salvation. It will be a standing reproach against him if he chooses to keep aloof from the world of sinfulness, ignorance and misery.'[14] Also, such wide participation in life is required for joy. 'Life in the pursuit of life is a life of untainted joy. The bhakta pursues such a course of life. He seeks to induce others to follow the same ideal. To him therefore life is joy, pure joy. He wants not to retire from the world of life and live the life of a religious recluse. He seeks to live in the midst of a great organization of life....In the society of fellow men he enjoys his life to the full, by doing good to all, self and others.'[15] Further, 'The fact is that when true life is indicated in the world, true joy is indicated along with it. The Bhakti cult of the Satwata recognises this and boldly preaches the doctrine that life is worth living and enjoyable if only one knows how to live it. To 'live it is to live for it and to know it to be everywhere. The joys of such a life are unquestionable.'[16]

However, with the decadence of Hindu culture such positive and bold valuations of life and its possibilities more or less disappeared from the Hindu mind, or at least ceased to influence it on a large scale, and the concept of renunciation in its purely negative interpretation, recommending as little participation in life as possible rather than its opposite, came to dominate even the bhakti movement. It seems to me that the doctrine of lila is a continuation in an altered context, (that is, monotheistic rather than polytheistic) of the original Vedic perception of life, the Vedas, especially the *Rigveda* being composed of hymns in praise of the fullness, beauty and glory of life itself, as manifested in such adorable things as health, wealth, beauty, long life, freedom from sin, intellectual understanding, and spiritual illumination. It is a misunderstanding

[14]*The Bhakti cult in Ancient India*, by Bhagavat Kumar Goswami, Chowkhamba Sanskrit Series, Vol. LII, p. 222.
[15]*Ibid.*, p. 235.
[16]*Ibid.*, p. 236.

to interpret Vedic hymns as prayers for the fulfilment of essentially selfish desires. These prayers are in the form 'Give us, O Agni' etc., rather than 'Give me', and this shows, to my mind, a valuation of things like wealth, long life etc., for human beings rather than a desire to appropriate the good things of life for oneself. Anyway, it seems to me that a positive understanding of what lila implies needs a socio-economic and cultural environment which is on a phase of expansion rather than of contraction, and as the Hindu society had been for many centuries on a contracting phase, it is hardly surprising that the retention of the concept of lila did not mean the retention of the ideal of fullness of life, including of course the joy of spiritual understanding, such as is represented by Krishna's lifestory.

As to the relation between the world and God, says the *Bhagavata Purana*, 'as the spider weaves its thread out of its own mouth, plays with it and then withdraws it again into itself, so the eternal and unchangeable Lord, who is formless and attributeless, who is absolute knowledge and absolute bliss, evolves the whole universe out of itself, plays with it, and again withdraws it into itself'.[17] Again, 'There is one absolute existence; on its surface appears the myriad forms of the phenomenal world like bubbles on the ocean. For a while they stay, and then they disappear. The one absolute existence, the abiding reality remains.'[18] This reality may be understood from three different points of view, as Brahman, Paramatman, and Bhagavat – Brahman, in so far as it is all transcending and attributeless, Paramatman (the highest Self) in so far as this Self dwells hidden in all beings as their innermost reality, and Bhagavat (Lord God) in so far as He is possessed of infinite attributes, majesty and power.

The same Reality is thus conceived in this Purana as both attributeless and possessed of attributes. Brahman, the attributeless, becomes Paramatman, and Bhagavat in relation to the phenomenal world which forms a part of Brahman's essence. 'The one existence, the absolute reality, the Brahman which transcends mind and speech, becomes divided into two, the

[17] *Srimad Bhagavatam*, trans. Swami Prabhabananda, p. 222.
[18] *Ibid.*, p. 259.

maya or the creative power, and the possessor of the power; of
these one is known as Prakriti, which is cause as well as effect,
and the other is called Purusa, whose nature is self-luminous.'[19]

This is the same doctrine as preached in the *Gita* by Krishna
about his higher and lower nature, Purusa (Self), Prakriti
(nature), and it does not differ from the Upanisadic teaching that
Brahman is everything, except that by bringing in Prakriti it
explains how individual selves with a material body come to
exist as separate beings. However, Brahman is in all beings, not
only in its aspect of Prakriti, but also as Paramatman, the Self,
which in its self-luminous nature is most manifest in human
self-consciousness. This is why human beings can consciously realise their identity with Brahman, which in a devotional context
becomes union with God (symbolised here by Krishna) in love.
So says Krishna to Uddhava, his disciple, 'Whatever is acquired
through work, austerity, knowledge, detachment, yoga or
charity, or through any other means of discipline, can be attained easily by my disciple through love of me and devotion to me.
Heavenly enjoyment, liberation, my dwelling place– all are within his easy reach, should he care to have them.'[20] Further, 'those
who follow my teachings to the attainment of my being dwell in
my blissful state which is unity with Brahman'.[21] It would thus
appear that according to the *Bhagavatam*, the experience which
in devotional language would be expressed as 'dwelling in the
blissful state of Krishna' can also be described as unity (or identity with Brahman), perhaps by a man who follows the path of
knowledge. Or, it would be better to say that what is being talked about is not so much the same experience as two types of
experience directed to the same abiding reality in which everything has its being. And the language one uses in respect of religious reality is determined by the kind of person one is as well
as by the background of one's experience.

But not all devotional Vaishnava philosophy accepts the concept of attributeless Brahman or the goal of identity with it. If
we take Ramanuja and the philosophers of the Caitanya school
as broadly representative of the Vaishnava approach we find

[19] *Ibid.*, p. 283.
[20] *Ibid.*, p. 268.
[21] *Ibid.*, p. 268.

that they prefer to think of Brahman—which they identify with Vishnu-Krishna – as possessed of infinite attributes rather than as attributeless. Brahman is still the whole of reality but this reality is not to be thought of as undifferentiated pure consciousness beyond mind and speech, such as was advocated by Samkara. According to Ramanuja, Brahman or God is possessed of eternal attributes representing the values of truth, beauty, goodness, holiness, and bliss. As creation is not out of nothing, He is still the immanent ground of the universe, which constitutes His body. Individual human beings are attributes of God from one point of view while being substances themselves from another. So while they are not separate from God they remain as distinct entities within His differentiated unity. It seems to me that Ramanuja conceives of God essentially in his role as creator; that is why He is thought of as having the universe as his body, while the *Bhagavata Purana*, while fully acknowledging the creatorship of God in relation to the world, assigns to Him a being independent of creation, such as abides even when creation is taken back into God's essence at the time of dissolution when all differentiation ceases to exist.

However, Ramanuja accepts the Upanisadic picture of creation that God wanted to be many and by His own inner creative power differentiated Himself into the space-time world and the myriads of individuals in it, while at the same time remaining his transcendent Self. The Being of God being inexhaustible, He is not to be equated with the manifested world which forms only a part of Him. God transcends the world in this role of the creator, controller, and the goal of the world process. Individual human beings are a part of God and liberation consists in union with God and not identity with Brahman. In this union man is divested of his space-time limitations and becomes godly, but not identical with God Himself. Ramanuja accepts the doctrine of lila but suggests that this lila has built into it the purpose of creating a world such that it is found suitable for the spiritual progress of man. The world as the body of God and a field for the spiritual development of man is real and not at all illusory. Ignorance consists in not knowing that it has its being in God, not in believing in its reality.

In accordance with the dominance of the concept of creatorship in respect to God in Ramanuja's thought he stresses the aspect of God's power. This power is very often conceived in Hindu thinking as a feminine principle. So Vishnu-Krishna as God is thought of as coupled with Sri or Lakshmi, the feminine principle that represents God's energy. Godhead is represented by the union of Vishnu in his essential being with his power that creates, that is, Sri. It seems that this union is necessary, because the essential being of God may conceivably be imagined outside the context of creation – it will not do to say that the being of God is constituted solely of his creative power. But such a God will not serve the devotional purpose which is to adore God as our creator, preserver, and liberator. So Ramanuja couples God with his Sakti (creative power) in order to integrate his creatorship with the concept of His very being, and this means that he did not have to say that God has no abiding reality except through the aspect of his creativity. Unless God is seen in his aspect of creativity – it is in relation to the created realm that we come to conceive of such attributes as perfection, love, power etc. – He may easily become the changeless, attributeless Reality beyond all name and form. This may serve the purposes of knowledge, even of bliss of being (Sat), but not of love, in so far as by love is meant a relationship between persons. Those who want to follow the way of love must therefore insist on the creatorship of God and the attributes that are required for such a function.

It is thus clear that Ramanuja's philosophical principles fit the requirements of devotionalism according to which the highest stage of religious realisation for man consists of love of God although for Ramanuja this love is not just an emotional state and it includes as an important component in it knowledge about the nature of God and man. This is why he subjects Samkara's concept of the undifferentiated attributeless Brahman to severe criticism, and when he himself uses the term 'Brahman' it functions in exactly the same way as does the term 'God' in religion – that is, as a Person with infinite attributes. Devotionalism, based on the experience of love of God, also requires that man should retain his distinct identity, capable of experiencing this union, even if that is not separate from God's being. This identity is also necessary for receiving God's mercy and grace, on which finally depends the dawning of the kind of love for God that is a way to the liberation of man. It is not that individual effort is not needed, but this effort is best directed to surrendering to God. However, this surrender needs preparation through karma and jnana. So Ramanuja advocates Yogic practice, meditation, purification of the body as the temple of God, detachment, contemplation of God as the inner self, service to all, practice of such virtues as charity and non-violence etc. Final liberation, however, comes only after death when, free from empirical life, one attains to the transcendent realm of Narayana or Vishnu.

Caitanya's devotionalism differs from that of Ramanuja primarily in that in place of Vishnu and Sri in their heavenly abode of Vaikunta it takes Krishna and Radha in their union in Vrindaban as the model of divine existence and love. In Ramanuja God in his majesty, greatness, and glory remained somewhat distant, particularly as the image of God projected was placed in heaven rather than on earth, despite Ramanuja's acceptance of the fact of incarnation. Caitanya and his followers stressed Krishna's lila (play) at Vrindaban in his role as child, friend, lover, etc., so it is not so much the majesty of God in His transcendence as his love and companionship which formed the keynote of this particular brand of devotionalism. As a result, the emotional content of love became much more important in this devotional movement than the aspect of jnana emphasised by Ramanuja. But the philosophy that Caitanya's followers developed does not substantially differ from that of Ramanuja, in that it too rejects the concept of attributeless Brahman and thinks of God as possessed of perfect beauty, majesty, strength, glory, plenitude etc., and not just love.

The world is not an illusion, it is a manifestation of God's power (Sakti), and here too God, united with his power, Krishna and Radha, is the ultimate reality, rather than God by Himself, otherwise creativity would have to be a defining concept of God and not just his power. God in his completeness is conceived as duality-in-unity, symbolised by Krishna and Radha, bound to each other by inseparable bonds of devotion, love and affection.

God in this philosophy is said to have his sva-rupa, his essence, which is not identical with his powers. Nevertheless his powers are not really anything different from him, so the relationship of God's essence with his powers is said to be a kind of unthinkable difference-in-non-difference. Among the manifestation of God's powers are jiva sakti (power that is manifested in men), maya sakti (power that is manifested in nature) and cit-sakti (the power of illumination that belongs to consciousness). But God also has what is called Sva-rupa Sakti, of which consists his essence and whereby He is conscious (samvit sakti) of his own being (Sandhini Sakti) as joy (hladini sakti). This is the same as the old Upanisadic idea of Saccidananda (Being, Consciousness, Bliss). Samkara used this concept to denote the essence of Brahman, in so far as this can be done at all, and he distinguished this essence from attributes such as creatorship which belong to the phenomenal world and not to the essence of reality. Vaishnava philosophy, however, rejects the idea that the essence of God is something totally separated from his powers even though these two terms may not mean the same thing. The Sva-rupa sakti or essence of God is present in his activity of self-positing, whereby He realises Himself as a spiritual unity-in-difference as Krishna and Radha, distinct and yet not different from each other in the realisation of love and in the delight involved in such realisation. But apart from such essential powers called antaranga (intrinsic) God has other powers called bahiranga (extrinsic), which however belong to God just as much as does his essence. These extrinsic powers are called maya sakti, the power of creation consisting of self-limitation of God in nature, and jiva-sakti, the embodiment of God's power into innumerable monads who share in both spiritual and material being.

The relation between God and man is like that of fire and spark, and like the spark man shares in a fragmented form in the nature of the source. However, man is not always aware that this is so and the reason for his ignorance is his enslavement to the material world. This does not mean that the material world is illusory, it is fully real as a manifestation of God's power, but it does offer men allurements which keep them from realising their divine heritage. The way to counteract this danger is bhakti, complete self-giving of man to God in love. This love is a state of intoxication with emotion for God; however, its emotional content and the attendant excitement varies depending on the particular attitude that the devotee adopts towards God. Of this there are five important variations: Santa (peaceful), dasya (that of a servant), Sakhya (that of a friend), vatsalya (that of a parent or a child), madhurya (that of a beloved). No matter what attitude man adopts God as Krishna is ever close to man, he is ready to bestow his love on the devotee, remove ignorance, and allow him to enjoy the bliss of divine love. It is with this divinely bestowed love that a true understanding of the nature of God and man comes not before, and when it comes, man enjoys companionship with God. It is through this companionship that man realises the bliss of God's own nature. Bhakti can no doubt be directed to God without form, but realisation of God as with form is better than without form, as it is a richer experience with concrete content. The best devotee, however, is he who is not just devoted to a particular form but who perceives God in all beings and all beings in God (who is revealed in one's own being).

The Caitanya school believes in jivanmukti, enjoyment of liberation, even whilst in the body, a state in which man is established in the true knowledge of himself as part of God. He is still, physically speaking, subject to the fruits of Karma already done but he is no longer bound to these. The culmination of the state of liberation lies in the revelation of the true nature of God and participation of man in the joy of God's being. But here one does not become joy, one experiences it.

The concept of love in Caitanya's devotionalism, being based on the Radha-Krishna model, is a good deal more tinged with emotion than that of Ramanuja, for whom love was more like a state of quiet contemplation of God accompanied by surrender of will, rather than a state of ecstasy and thrill. So for Ramanuja the state of mind that is called 'love of God' is not by itself liberation, it only leads to liberation after death. But for Caitanya, love of God itself is an emotional state of bliss, wherein man finds complete fulfilment in feeling united with God as a part of him. So love of God itself is liberation and it happens in life itself and not after death.

SAIVISM

The image of Siva as the almighty lord presents quite a different picture from that of Krishna-Vishnu, the embodiment of sweetness, beauty, romantic passion, and universal benevolence. The god-making impulses do not all stem from the same roots and some minds are more keenly sensitive than others to the mystery of the incalculable and unpredictable powers in the universal which bring devastation, disease, death, failure, and incompleteness along with life and its joys. No doubt beauty, love and generally anything that produces joy in human experience can lead to a sense of mystery and wonder at the unfathomable depths from which springs life, but when a sense of mystery is coupled with the dread of the unknown, especially when this unknown appears suddenly to emerge from nowhere to destroy what man holds most dear, it leads to a different kind of perception of the divine than a sense of mystery which is rooted more in the appreciation of the plenitude of life. One may wonder why the fierce and fearful should at all be looked upon as divine, which should rather be thought of as merciful, gracious and loving; but if by divine is meant power which is the source of all existence and value and which abides in and by itself beyond all change and manipulation, then the impulse to link all facets of human experience, including those which men would rather not have, to this source cannot but be thought to be legitimate.

Certainly the divine cannot be pictured as *nothing but* fierceness, danger, death and destruction, for it is not only the ground of all existence but also of value, and the human fear of disintegration and aversion to evil can by themselves do no more than reveal psychological attitudes, which speak only of the inner being of man. The search for the divine is a search for integration and completeness – the linking of the inner being of man with the ground by which all manifestations of being in the universe are supposed to be sustained. So a religious perception of life is inevitably coloured by a perception of the wholeness of life and its total fulfilment, notwithstanding the fact that this wholeness has to triumph over forces of disintegration that constantly threaten it. Therefore the mystery of the divine consists not just in the mystery of death, but also in that of life in death, not just in disintegration and dispersion, but also in creation and sustenance which eventually win their victory over everything that tends to diminish life. So divine power becomes enigmatic and paradoxical and eventually its mystery comes to be identified not only with the opposition of dualities, such as good and evil, that pervades life, but also the transcendence of all such dualities in the inscrutability of divine existence.

The recognition of dualities of life wherein one force is opposed by its contrary which appears to refute it in some fashion, is fundamental to a characteristic Hindu world-view. However all dualities are also thought to be complementary, so that the tension that is generated by their opposition at one level is also thought to be solved at another level of higher perception where opposites combine to produce a rich unity-in-difference. Dualities such as the cosmic male and female principles in the creative urge, of Purusa (self) and Prakriti (nature), creation and destruction, good and evil, cohesion (sattva) and dispersion (tamas) – in this instance mediated by a third force, the thrust of energy involved in all activity (rajas), – knowledge (vidya) and ignorance (avidya), and liberation (moksa) and life in bondage (samsara) pervade human existence and supply the tension that is integral to the functioning of life itself. Only with the perception of their fundamental unity, which embraces the duality and transcends it, that an integral view of the totality of existence comes, at least according to what I believe is the most perceptive of Hindu attitudes. Take, for instance, the duality of liberation (mukti or moksa) and life in bondage to the world (samsara). At one level the opposition is complete, liberation is liberation from samsara, the typical worldly existence of man. Yet the goal of life is not heavenly existence of unalloyed pleasure which is accessible to man through good and virtuous deeds, but transcendence of both good and evil here in life through an experience of unity or identity with the ground of all existence, God or Brahman, leading to bliss beyond pleasure and pain. So we come to the conception of jivan-mukti, liberation in life which combines life with liberation by transforming one's perception of samsara itself from a place of bondage to a place of release. And release can only be obtained here in life by man. So the life of man on earth, despite the possibility of bondage, is valued by many thinkers above that of gods in heaven, and even if man goes to heaven in the course of his career of transmigration through various forms of life he must in the end be born on earth as man to obtain liberation. Thus the opposition of liberation and life is finally transcended by a process of transformation through which only a perception of the full possibilities of human existence in its totality is achieved. This insight is more forcefully expressed in Mahayana Buddhism which finally equates Nirvana with Samsara, but I think that the jivan-mukti conception of the Hindus, especially as it is expounded in the *Gita*, also embodies this, even though many Hindu thinkers, who glorified the liberated life on earth as a life of non-activity and non-involvement (as distinct from non-attachment) rather than as the life of the Bodhisattva, the man of universal compassion in Buddhism, failed to draw out the full implications of this perception.

I have gone into this question here because the crystallisation of Siva as the great God (Mahadeva) in the Hindu tradition is very much related to this initial acceptance of paradox and its final transcendence as true wisdom on the part of some Hindu minds. This perception may have something to do with the peculiar nature of the clash of cultures in ancient India between the Aryans and the non-Aryans, neither of which tried to submerge the other, the Aryans, the dominating group, being content to demarcate separate spheres of cultural and religious activity for themselves and others, rather than to impose their own pattern of values on everyone. The non-Aryans, or at any rate, those who were marked off as such by the device of calling them the non-twice-born sudras, were excluded from the Vedas and allowed to go their own ways in religious matters, it being unlikely that they were forcibly debarred from having any kind of religious life at all. This eventually resulted in the mingling of the two cultures, the initial opposition having been transcended in a totality which embraced both in varying degrees of synthesis. As it is through this process that Siva, especially Siva of all Hindu conceptions, emerged as a dominant religious figure, the image that is projected of him in the mature Hindu tradition reflects this understanding of the presence of opposites in divine existence as well as of their transcendence.

We have a conception of divinity in the Vedas, Rudra, who is marked off from the rest as being wrathful, fearsome and dangerous, who paradoxically is both a destroyer of cattle and men and their protector. It is this complexity of Rudra, stimulating both fear and reverence for his two-edged power, that separated him from the rest of the deities of the Vedic pantheon, who were beneficent forces catering for the well-being of man. Rudra did not belong either to earth, atmosphere or heaven, the spheres where belonged the respectable deities, the guardians of the cosmic order. He was a mountain God, almost a stranger, but who nevertheless was fascinating in his strange combination of power and wildness on the one hand and kindness and graciousness on the other. If he is a slayer when his anger and will-ill are aroused he can, when propitiated, bring health and well-being, not only to the human but also to the animal world. This incalculability of Rudra made men approach him with caution, in a tone of respectful distance, rather than one of easy intimacy in which men during sacrifice called upon Indra and other gods to be in their midst and share their bounties with men.

This Rudra of the Vedas was found to have something in common with the proto-Siva of the Indus Valley complex, in the matter of their interest in the animal world and its lordship. They had an affinity also in their strangeness and paradoxicality. The proto-Siva sits apparently in a yogic position of supreme self-control but paradoxically with an erect phallus suggesting a state of excitement. In this yogic posture the proto-Siva is uninvolved in the world, but through the symbol of phallus he is also its generator. It is therefore not strange that the particular impulse towards the divine in the Hindu tradition which erupts out of a sense of the awesomeness, mystery, and paradoxicality of existence, would put the cognate ideas in both the Aryan and non-Aryan traditions together to form the image of a God who would be supremely mysterious in his combination of opposite qualities and who would stimulate that particular view of love which includes as an essential component of itself the sublimation of fear. The myths and legends that were gathered from all the different traditions that eventually merged into what is called Hinduism, the Aryan, the Dravidian (if this is the name for the people who created the Indus Valley civilisation) and the aboriginal, to create the complex character of Siva, confer on him all possible attributes of the most widely divergent kind and these in their sheer juxtaposition of opposition force the mind in its perception of the divine to go beyond the limited human perspective.

I have no wish to suggest that there was a planned and conscious construction of legends or their deliberate amalgamation in order to prove a point. As in the Krishna stories, the process of amalgamation and selection was unconscious, but as we know, the unconscious is also directional. Anyway it can cogently be surmised that all the three originally distinct religious traditions in India, the Aryan, the Dravidian and the Aboriginal (including mountain tribes) involved conceptions of gods who were in some ways strange, fierce, or incomprehensible because the projection of the unknown and fearsome possibilities on to the divine plane is a common human way of coming to terms with the unpredictability and mystery of life. Nothing was more natural than that these should all come together under one umbrella to produce an enormously complex conception of divinity whose ambiguities seemingly defy comprehension and yet who appeals to the imagination as a true symbol of the inscrutability of the divine.

We have already talked about the association of the concept of destruction with Siva, and this meant stories which adorn him with skulls and snakes, make him a frequenter of graveyards and cremation grounds, where Siva hobnobs with demons and other evil spirits — he is even made their Lord — and which extol blood sacrifice as a means of his propitiation. On the other hand Siva is a symbol of purity and many hymns and songs in praise of Siva emphasise his matchless beauty, his shining limbs, and brilliant form with the crescent moon adorning his forehead and which picture him as the mildest of deities who needs no more than a *bilva* leaf to satisfy him. Siva's wrath, which can easily be aroused, can bring forth the most gruesome and hideous apparitions like Bhairava and Virabhadra whose ruthlessness is beyond measure and yet he is equally easily appeased and more than ready to grant boons whenever approached, whether by gods, men or demons, with whatever purpose.

Siva is the lord of the Universe and there is nothing that happens here except on his wish. And yet he is pictured as a vagrant, smeared with ashes, clad only in a tiger skin, with no possession other than his trident (which replaces the Vedic bow and arrow). Having no home to call his own he roams about alone in mountains and forests away from habitations (some of these stories probably came from legends of mountain tribes). The *Vamana Purana* makes him say to his wife: 'I am, oh lovely one, without a shelter, a constant wanderer in the forest. My beloved, I have no riches for the erection of a house nor am I possessed of ought else than an elephant's skin for a garment and serpents for my ornament.' For all that, his wife is Annapoorna, who fills the universe with food.

Siva is the arch yogi who sits at the mountain top in oblivion of the world, rapt in meditation and yet it is through the rhythm of his dance that the universe is unfolded. But if this dance creates, it also destroys. The Nataraja form of the dancing Siva is itself a study in contrast. The drum in his upper right hand is sound, the first element of creation, and fire in his left hand is annihilation. Thus Siva holds in his hands creation and destruction in equal poise. The other two hands grant boon and offer refuge so as to suggest eternal life beyond all vegetative and biological processes of generation and annihilation. In this figure the rhythm, of his swaying limbs, representing time and change contrasts with the absolute stillness of his face representing eternity and Siva himself, paradoxically holding together time and eternity in his total activity and total passivity, becomes the absolute beyond description. The lesson too is paradoxical, the triumph of the joy of existence, to be savoured, no doubt, on an aesthetic plane, in the very heart of disaster.

This arch yogi is also the most ideal of all husbands in Hindu mythology, in his domesticity, sexual potency, loyalty, and love to his marriage partner (Krishna represents youth, romance, wild passion, Siva loyal and steadfast devotion).[22] However he is also conceived as the Hermaphrodite, half male and half female in one body.

Again there is the contrast between Siva the sage, the fount of all wisdom, who delivers to Parvati, his wife, knowledge of the secret of all existence and Siva the wild hunter, given to drinking, dancing, and revelry of all sorts (some of these stories probably came from aboriginal sources).

Siva is supposed to represent tamas, the disintegrating

[22]There are however conflicting accounts of Siva in the Puranas. While some Puranas represent him as a faithful husband, others tell stories which how him in the role of an adulterous seducer.

tendency in the Universe and yet his symbol is the phallus, the instrument of creation of life in the biological world.

Siva possesses the third eye, the eye of knowledge to which the whole universe is instantly present in utter lucidity, and yet he is the lord of sleep, the symbol of oblivion and rest from experience. And there is a good deal more of this nature which suggests the unfathomable depths of his being as the Great God who is finally identified with the totality of the universe.

Unlike Krishna, Siva has no connected life-story and he is generally reckoned not to have incarnations despite the attempt of some Saiva Purunas to give him some. This fact also reflects his remoteness and transcendence. Siva is not made to behave like one of us sharing in human joys and sorrows on a human scale (except in stories in sectarian Puranas which, in order to prove the superiority of their own favourite god, present him as an inferior being), as his activities mostly relate to cosmic happenings involving battles between gods and demons. (This shows that unlike those of Krishna, Siva stories are not built on human models.) And in these happenings his destructiveness is generally aimed at the demons who constantly threaten the sovereignty of the gods, although there are also instances where gods too suffer from his violent temper when found to have done something disagreeable. He destroys the sacrifice of Daksa, a minor divinity, because Daksa invited all the other gods but Siva to the ceremony. He reduces Kama, the god of love, to ashes because Kama tries to disturb his yoga, with a view to bringing about his union with Parvati (whom he eventually marries after she had undergone prolonged asceticism). But in keeping with his dual character he also does things which are supremely beneficial to gods and men. He drinks the poison that comes up when gods churn the ocean in search of ambrosia and thereby saves the world from impending disaster. He holds the onrush of the river Ganges when she descends in a wild torrent from the Himalayas in the locks of his matted hair, taking the first blast, so to say, on to himself, so that men on earth can have the benefit of her life-giving current. There are many such stories but I hope I have said enough to bring into relief the distinctive conception of God that the term 'Siva' signifies. He is indeed Rudra-Siva, the terrible-auspicious

God, the name by which this divinity was known in the Vedic-Upanisadic times.

When Siva is elevated to the role of the Great God he no longer remains the god of destruction, the role assigned to him in the conception of the Hindu triad. He becomes the source of all three functions, or Brahma the God of creation and Vishnu the God of preservation, become his distinct manifestations. And the Puranas begin to identify him with the totality of creation through such doctrines as his five faces and eight forms. Each of these is given a name and a separate function and it is possible that by this device many independent local divinities were successfully combined into one cult. His five faces are Isana, Tatpurusa, Aghora, Vamadeva, and Sadyojata and his eight forms, Sarva, Bhava, Pasupati, Isana, Bhima, Rudra, Mahadeva, and Urga. The five faces are rulers of five directions which, taken together, represent the totality of spatial extension, and the eight forms represent the five elements – ether, air, fire, water, earth – the sun, the moon, and jiva (self). There is no doubt that these doctrines are attempts to represent Siva as the pervading principle of the Universe, as in the form of five directions and eight constituents of the world Siva provides the corporeal frame and the animating essence (in the form of jiva the self) of the totality of existence. It would seem that Siva is here conceived as the material cause of the Universe, from which it would follow that God and the world are one. This would however, be denied in the later philosophy of Saiva Siddhanta which makes Siva Lord of the world but different from it in essence, in the interest of devotion. However devotion to Siva is preached in the *Svetasvatara Upanisad* which not only makes him both transcendent and immanent, as does the Saiva Siddhanta, but also both the material and efficient cause, an idea which the Siddhanta rejects. To quote from the Svetasvatara: 'The God who is in fire, who is in water, who has entered into the whole world, who is in plants, who is in trees, to that God be adoration, yea, be adoration.'[23] 'He by whom this whole world is always enveloped, the knower, the author of time, the possessor of qualities and all knowledge,

[23]*The Principal Upanisads*, trans. Radhakrishnan, p. 724, *Svetasvatara Upanisad*, II, 17.

controlled by Him (this) work of (creation) unfolds itself, that
which is regarded as earth, water, fire air and ether.'[24]
'He indeed is the God who pervades, He is the first born and
he is within the womb. He has been born and he will be born.
He stands opposite all persons, having his face in all directions.'[25] Thus the Purana doctrine of Siva pervading all
directions and as constituting all elements, fire, water etc., comes
from here. Also possibly the doctrine of five faces. 'We meditate
on Him as a river of five streams from five sources, fierce and
crooked, whose waves are the five vital breaths, whose original
source is fivefold perception, with five whirlpools, an impetuous
flow of five pains divided into fifty kinds of suffering with five
branches.'[26] This God in *Svetasvatara* is Rudra-Siva. 'He who is
the source and origin of the gods, the ruler of all, Rudra, the
great seer who beheld the·golden germ (Hiranya-Garbha) when
he was born. May he endow us with clear understanding.'[27]

The Saiva-Siddhanta school of Southern Saivism in developing
its philosophy about the nature of God, man and the world
makes a distinction between the idea of immanence of God
and his being the material cause of the world and affirms
the former while denying the latter. I believe that this is
because despite the insistence on immanence it is the transcendence of God that is really the key concept in this particular
approach. God must be conceived as being something different
from man and the world, not just in the sense of being more,
but in the sense of being different in substance or kind, which
would not be the case if the relation between God on the one
hand, and man and the world on the other were to be thought
in the analogy of the relation between gold, the universal
substance and the various ornaments made of it. As we have
noticed, a continuity of kind between man and God has been
maintained in Vaishnavism in so far as men are thought to
be attributes of God as in Ramanuja or as parts of him as
sparks are parts of fire, as in Caitanya.

Saiva Siddhanta is unable to accept this account of the

[24]*Ibid.*, p. 743, *Svetasvatara*, VI, 2.
[25]*Ibid.*, p. 724, II, 16.
[26]*Ibid.*, p. 713, 1.5.
[27]*Ibid.*, p. 735, IV, 12.

relationship and the motivating reason seems to me to be the following.

The history of the Siva concept has contained a connotation of danger and fear which the inscrutability of God presents to man. The other side of this perception is the thought of some radical defect in man, believed here to be a sort of congenital impurity adhering to man as a finite being, which makes him subject to suffering (and possibly also justifiably deserving of God's wrath). Between a man of this nature and God there cannot really be any continuity of essence or substance, however close be the relationship which is claimed to be intimate enough to merit being called non-dual, not in the sense of any fusion between man and God either on the plane of existence or that of thought, but in the sense of a realisation, induced by love, on the part of man that he is not separate from God. This non-duality is thus based more on a psychological state of the devotee, who feels himself to be unseparated from god, rather than on any ontological bond such as that of being of the same essence or substance as is generally thought to be the case in the Hindu tradition. In the psalms of the Saiva saints one comes across the idea of sin and worthlessness of man – a feature which is not particularly prominent in the Hindu tradition generally, which believes that the trouble with man is ignorance rather than sin. A man who approaches the omnipotent Lord for redemption out of a sense of his own worthlessness and sinfulness must not only make God different from man in substance, it must also emphasise man's existential distinctness in order that he may receive grace and be saved. So in this system man cannot be a part of God.

Paradoxically this system which insists on the utter dependence of man on God in the matter of liberation also gives man some kind of ontological independence. And this is how. In the Hindu tradition the soul, having originally been conceived, as in the Upanisads, as identical with Brahman or at least sharing in the essence of God, has always been thought to be eternal by its own intrinsic nature and its eternality is not something that is conferred on it as a matter of grace. This continued to be the case in the Saiva-Sidhanta view, and this means that souls are not created by God. Being neither created by God, nor a part of His essence, they seem to me to gain a kind of ontological independence (that is, their being there is not mediated by God). However, this may not be crucial; as God in this system is conceived to be the Lord of souls from eternity this ontological independence of souls does not mean their religious self-sufficiency or independence, just as the ontologically independent existence of subjects in an absolute monarchy (or dictatorship) does not mean their independence in matters political. It seems that although souls can manage to exist, as hopelessly enmeshed in threefold impurities, they cannot manage to divest themselves of these impurities and by extricating themselves from the cycle of birth and death come to experience their godliness, without His love and grace. As far as devotionalism is concerned what is of importance or interest is not man's existence as such; what one seeks to enjoy is existence above the limitations of an impure, sinful or worthless life, and this can be achieved only by grace.

This picture of Lord God conceived as one who rules over the world and men in his transcendent goodness and love, rather than as one who produces the world of multiplicity out of himself in order to enjoy himself as many, also led to the conception of a radical discontinuity between the world and God. God is not here the material cause of the world. This cause is maya (world-creating potentiality). But whence comes maya? Is it part of God's Being, something that belongs to God's intrinsic essence, or something independent? I believe that the general tendency of this system is not to think of maya as belonging to God's essence (Krishna says in the *Gita* that maya is his lower nature), or his inherent power as it is believed that in that case the impurities of the world would affect God. Thus maya can only be assumptive, a power that is taken on for a specific purpose (parigraha Sakti), as admitted by Suryanarayan Sastri in his article on Saivism in *The Cultural Heritage of India*. Now, either this maya is already there to be taken on by God, in which case the world potentiality has an ontological existence independently of God, just like souls, or, if it makes no sense to talk about the pre-existence of maya before God assumes it, what this doctrine comes to is creation out of nothing, since it is neither creation out of some pre-existing material, nor out of God's own being. In that case there is really no material cause of the world at all.

This, of course, does not affect God's lordship of the world as it does not affect his lordship of men. And it is this lordship which is important in the context of man's need for being saved by God, who has power to dispense things such that men can be divested of the impurities they suffer from, and thus released from the cycle of birth and death, rather than a logically irrefutable doctrine about ontological relationships involved. For, someone who approaches God primarily via a sense of the powerlessness of man, induced by cosmic factors – which is very much the spirit in which Southern Saivism does approach God – is bound to lay a good deal more stress on the power of God with its redemptive significance, than on anything else. This is clear from the three primary categories adopted in this system, Pati (Lord), Pasu (the creature), and Pasa (bondage). Man becomes Pasu, the creature, despite the fact that souls are: eternal and all-pervading, because of threefold impurities in which they are involved by the very act of creation. These are (*i*) maya mala, imperfections and defects resulting from creation by the power of maya which is limiting in its function; (*ii*) Karma mala, impurities induced by actions performed by men; and (*iii*) Anava mala, impurities that necessarily adhere to transmigrating men and make them appear like finite jivas by veiling their true nature. Bondage happens because of these impurities which only God's power can remove, as they happen to be there through his will. Hence the need for grace.

However, God has other functions as well, which are fivefold: creation, maintenance, destruction, veiling of the true nature of things by maya, and grace. But grace is still the most important in so far as in this system God creates the world in order to give opportunities to bound souls to work out their Karma and find release from the cycle of finite existence through love of God. One may ask why souls which in their inherent nature are eternal and infinite should first be bound and then released? To this the answer is that it is God's lila (play). But lila here does not mean what it means in Vaishnavism, which is that God sports with Himself in and through being many (that is, he suffers and enjoys as many), because the world and the souls are not part of God's essence and are external to Him.

God is formless, but he can take up whatever form the devotee wishes to see Him in. This form will consist not of physical elements, but of spiritual potency such as is expressed in Mantras (sacred incantations). Man's relationship to God is typically that of a servant to master although deepened it can approach friendship. As God is united with all souls, love of God means love of men, according to many Saivite teachers. A released man would thus help others to find God and not remain in splendid isolation. Cultivation of love of God can be divided into four stages, from activities which are external to those which are more internal, depending on the competence of the devotee and the intensity of his desire to find God. These are: (*i*) Carya, like clearing the temple and serving devotees; the aim being to live in the vicinity of God (Salokya); (*ii*) Kriya, intimate service of God in the form of worship, the aim being nearness of God (Samipya); (*iii*) Yoga, meditation on God, the aim being to acquire the form of God (Sarupya); and (*iv*) knowledge and contemplation, the aim being union with God (Sajujja). In the latter stages the devotee thinks of God not just as the master, but also as a friend. God reveals himself to devotees in various ways, again, according to their readiness; in the human teacher (Guru) who directs the soul towards God, as deities in the form of which the devotee worships God, and finally as inner light within oneself. It is only through grace and God's love of man that liberation comes—and it can happen while still in the body—the experience being one of being united with God and not of being identified with Him.

Thus in this system Siva becomes the God of love par excellence whose very activity of creation and destruction (which is to give souls temporary rest from rounds of rebirth) is actuated by a desire to help souls. Nevertheless it seems to me that in the structure of this system some traces can be found which are influenced by the original idea of Siva as mysterious and rather dangerous. God's action of binding free souls and then releasing them is supremely mysterious and the original idea of danger can be seen particularly in the relative remoteness, ontologically speaking, of God, as well as in the belief that the most appropriate attitude of man towards God is that of a servant to a master, whose most appropriate title is 'Lord', with its connotation of power. Also the idea of the basic impurity of man (anava mala) and the sense of sin and guilt induced by the thought of this impurity may be the indirect reflex of the idea of an incalculable power with dangerous connotations. The insistence on a certain distance between man and God even in liberation despite the fact that the relationship is called 'non-dual' might have had originally something to do with fear, fear of irreverence involved in claiming to be part of God, and not acknowledging His total superiority over creatures like men (who is Paśu, just an animal). However, Siva as a God as imagined by Southern Saivism arouses just as much fervent devotion as Krishna as imagined by the Puranas, even though the character of the emotion involved may be different. It appears that as far as the ability of a model of God to arouse intense religious devotion is concerned it makes little difference whether one thinks of Him as transcendent or immanent, as Lord or lover, as creating the world for play and enjoyment or solely for the solemn purpose of saving souls. The difference rather lies in the field of psychology in so far as some people, constituted as they are, may be able to respond better to one conceptual scheme than to another. However, most people's choice in this matter, as in anything else, is socially conditioned and it is only on rare occasions that a free and purely individual choice is made.

I shall not discuss here in detail Kashmiri Saivism which brings back in to the field of love of God the old idea of the non-duality in essence between man and God as well as the idea of creation as the self-projection of the divine into the field of multiplicity out of sheer joy and fullness of being. Its philosophy in these respects is not substantially different from that of Vaishnavism with its doctrine of lila although it has details peculiar to itself as to how the originally one reality beyond manifestation becomes many. Also there is a doctrinal difference between this Saivism and Vaishnavism in respect of liberation. Liberation does not mean complete identity of existence between man and God in Vaishnavism, whereas Kashmiri Saivism does imply this. Accordingly, it makes a difference between the concept of Siva and Parama Siva, the latter being, so it seems to me, the same as the ground principle of immensity (Brahman) of the Upanishads. Identity with this principle is no doubt achieved through devotion to Siva (the concept of devotion here, as with Ramanuja, includes contemplative understanding of the nature of Reality). But it does not make much difference whether this is called Paramasiva (Parama meaning ultimate) or Parama something else unless it be that it is only through devotion to Siva as God (Isvara) that one can be led to the Parama principle. For liberation does not here happen merely by one's own effort, it requires grace of Siva (Sakti-pata). This particular school endeavours to combine the needs of devotionalism which demands a personal God with a distinct name and form, such as is provided by Siva, so that there can be a relation of love between man and God, with that of the contemplative approach (called the way of knowledge in the Hindu tradition), for which the highest stage of spiritual realisation is an experience of identity with the divine principle itself. Perhaps a feeling of identity with the divine principle does not necessarily detract from love, as in some contexts of experience the divine may appear as endowed with personal attributes. However, the characteristic emotion involved in experience of identity is bliss, and although this is an emotional state, it is perhaps not quite the same emotion which is called 'love'. For bliss is a blissful consciousness of being, where one's own being has merged into the being of everything else on an infinite scale, whereas love requires two distinct persons between whom union is effected. Perhaps the divine can elicit both kinds of response, depending on the context of experience and the one does not preclude the other. In any case Kashmiri Saivism seeks an experience of bliss through devotion to Siva who is conceived both as a Personal God and as the Supra-personal Infinite Consciousness (Paramasiva).

SAKTISM

It is very often assumed that the idea of a Mother Goddess in the Hindu tradition has its origin in the non-Aryan strand of this culture, and there is no doubt some truth in this, as many of the names under which the Goddess is worshipped in different parts of India are not traceable to the Vedic literature. This, however, is a half-truth and, just as in the case of Siva and Krishna, some elements of the complex concept of the Goddess do come from the Vedic sources – elements which are of no mean significance in the understanding of the Goddess as the Supreme Reality, particularly in its philosophical aspects. There are several female deities in the Vedas, of which Vac is the most important as being the goddess who offers inspiration and illumination to seekers after truth. This Vac is also conceived in what is called the Devi-Sukta (*Rigveda* X. 125) as the energy (and this was later deified as Sakti, the generic name of the Goddess in the Hindu tradition) which moves the gods and the world. In view of the importance of the concept of energy in the Hindu image of the Mother Goddess – that by which everything, including self-realisation, is accomplished in this world – it is necessary to cite this hymn here in full in order to made it perfectly clear that the philosophy behind the Mother Goddess, even if not details of her name and form, is perfectly Vedic :

I move with Rudras and with Vasus, I move
    with Adityas and All-Gods by my side,
And both Mitra and Varuna, I support,
    I support Indra, Agni and the two Asvins.

I upheld Soma, the destroyer of the foe,
    I sustain Tvastri and Pushan and Bhaga,
I reward with wealth the offer of oblation,
    And the devout worshippers pouring the soma.

I am Queen the gatherer-up of treasurers
    'The Knower', the first amongst the Holy ones.
The Devas have established in many places
    Me who live on many planes, in many a form.

The man who sees, who breathes, who hears what's spoken,
    Through me alone obtains his sustenance.
There are those who dwell by my side but know not.
    Hear thou who has hearing: I tell thee the sacred truth.

Yes, I myself say this – and these my words
    Must needs be welcome to the Devas and men—
One whom I love I make mighty—make of him
    A Brahmana, a Rishi, a gifted man.

For Rudra I stretch out the strings of his bow
    To slay the fierce enemy of the holy man,

And for the people I engage in battle,
   And through the earth and heaven I spread

And on the summit I bring forth the Father,
   My home is within waters, in the ocean,
From where I entered to all existing worlds,
   And yonder heaven I touch with my forehead.

And it is I who, like the wind, breathe forth,
   And set all existing worlds in motion.
Beyond heavens and beyond the earth am I,
   And all this I have become in my splendour.[28]

As for the Upanisads, a particular name of the Mother
Goddess, Uma, occurs in the *Kena*, where she appears to reveal
to the puzzled gods the real source of their power, Brahman.
And in the *Mundaka* three names of the Goddess, Kali, Karali,
and Dhumavati, are mentioned as amongst the seven flaming
tongues of Agni, the fire-god (one can see here the beginning of
the later association of Kali with a destructive force), some of
whose functions were later incorporated in the concept of Siva,
whose energy or Sakti the Goddess is commonly conceived to
be. Also, the name Durga appears in the Taittiriya Aranyaka. It
is indeed true that amongst the findings of the Indus-valley
civilisation, there are female figurines who were probably
worshipped as goddesses and there is a seal depicting a fertility
or vegetation deity from whose womb a plant is shown to be
issuing. It would be a mistake to jump to the definite conclusion, from these evidences, either that this civilisation was
matriarchal or that a female deity (or deities) was the exclusive
object of veneration of the Indus Valley people. For we know
that male deities also occur in this complex, including the
Proto-Siva. The fact is that polytheistic cultures, Aryan, Dravidian, or Aboriginal, generally include various conceptions of
divinities representing different functions and values, some of
which are naturally pictured as male, some female, based on the
human experience of the function of these two principles in life.
And it is only to be expected that cognate ideas found in coexisting but different cultural complexes would eventually be

[28] *Hymns from the Vedas*, A. C. Bose, p. 307.

synthesised in a tradition that aimed at preserving all valuable insights as well as all styles of expression of the religious impulse, coming from all the different strata of the population, who, willy-nilly and despite the caste system, formed part of one social order.

It is believed in some quarters that some features of the Sakta religion, such as the use of meat, wine and sex in a sacred complex, come from a non-Vedic source as Brahmanism, representing Vedic wisdom, is abstemious, if not totally ascetic, in its taste. This is a mistake and when believed by Hindus themselves shows a tragic ignorance on their part of their own Vedic tradition. The Vedas, if anything, are unashamedly life-affirming and the delight these books show in enjoyment of life is beyond question. The Vedic Indians sacrificed animals to their gods and partook of the meat (including beef) as potent sacrificial offerings (to augment their effectiveness as human beings) along with soma which, apart from being conceived as a god itself, was also offered to other gods to increase their power and potency. The delight they took in the beauty of the female body is shown in the hymn to Ushas whose awaited arrival in the sky was conceived under the image of the exposure of the female body to admiring eyes. Not only in the Vedas, but post-Vedic literature such as the epics, the *Ramayana* and the *Mahabharata*, and the Puranas mention innumerable incidents of the partaking of meat and wine by the people of those times, not low-caste people, but those belonging to the highest aristocratic cycles (such as Rama himself, an incarnation of God, and his wife Sita). *Manusmriti*, supposedly the most venerable law book of the Hindus, expressly says that there is nothing wrong with the eating of meat or drinking of wine, even if abstention helps to accumulate merit.

As for sex, two of the most highly prized Upanisads, *Brihadaranyaka* and *Chandogya*, conceive of the sexual act as a sacred rite or sacrifice. *Brihadaranyaka* obviously believed that the image of the embrace of men and women in love and the transcendence of separation therein is a fit symbol of the supreme unitary experience (iv. 3.21), which is also called fulfilment of desires. The fourth Brahmana of the sixth chapter in *Brihadaranyaka* is devoted to treating the sex act as a sacred sacrifice. To quote the third verse: 'Her lower part is the (sacrificial) altar: (her) hairs the (sacrificial) grass, her skin the soma-press. The two labia of the vulva are the fire in the middle. Verily as great as is the world of him who performs the Vajapeya sacrifice (so great is the world of him) who, knowing this, practises sexual intercourse.'[29] And it says in the *Chandogya*, section 13, 1-2, chapter 11, 'one summons, that is the syllable *him*. He makes request, that is a *prastava*. He lies on the woman, that is the *pratihara*. He comes to the end, that is the *nidhana*. This is the Vamdevya chant woven on sex intercourse. He who knows thus this Vamdevya chant as woven on sex intercourse comes to intercourse, procreates himself from every act, reaches a full length of life, lives well, becomes great in offspring and in cattle, great in fame. One should not despise any woman. That is the rule.'[30]

Many of the Puranas like these two Upanisads frankly treat sex as a symbol of spiritual union in devotion, and some of them have achieved notoriety in depicting Krishna as a young man who aroused and fulfilled sexual passion in a variety of women.

In view of all this it seems to me that the Sakti Tantras, in their philosophy and outlook at any rate, if not in every detail of the conception of the Goddess, do belong to the early Vedic tradition as opposed to ascetical Brahmanism that views the world to be a mere illusion to be carefully bypassed, and their claim to be re-interpreting this tradition according to the needs of the Kali Yuga seems to be substantially valid. They are life-affirming like the Vedas and the worship of the Goddess can be not only for liberation or love of God but also for enjoyment of the things of this world (conceived as divine gifts) just as the Vedic sacrifice was conceived to be both for illumination and enjoyment of life. Ascetical Brahmanism represents neither the Vedas nor the early Upanisads which too, contrary to the Brahmanical and ascetic interpretation of Samkara and his followers, are full of the concept of joy even though joy of Brahman is incomparably superior to the joy of ordinary life (which is not thought to be joyless, as the life of an accomplished and handsome young man with a beautiful wife is taken

[29]*The Principal Upanisads.* trans, Radhakrishnan, p. 321.
[30]*Ibid.,* p. 368.

to be one unit of joy).

Now the sense of mystery in which the religious impulse is rooted can be kindled by the productive activity of generation and growth that goes on around life, not only in the human but also in the vegetative and the biological world, and because of the obvious role of women in bringing forth life out of the substance of her own being, so to say, the power of the female as a productive force can come to have a sacred and divine aura about it. The affirmation of the mystery of the female as divine is affirmation of life in its spontaneity, fecundity and plenitude and because Nature exhibits these characteristics she too becomes a female and a semi-divine force in the context of a religious appreciation of life. Thus the power manifested in life becomes a female principle and since all power is creative and productive power as such becomes a female divinity. This is why all male divinities in the Hindu pantheon, at least of the Puranic age, are endowed with a wife who is called the God's Sakti (energy). As the father is powerless to bring forth life on his own, and it is the mother's activity in nurturing the child not only in the womb but afterwards through its helpless years, that makes it possible for life to establish itself and thrive, so too God is powerless without his Sakti in the discharge of his divine functions. The point is that the male principle in the world in the context of generation and immediate maintenance of life is rather distant and uninvolved, compared to the constant presence and participation of the female principle in its growth and nurture. So it is through God's Sakti, the female principle, that divine activity in the world is manifested, Purusa, the male principle of divinity being transcendent. And one could not fail to recognise the presence of these two principles in the world, opposed and yet in complete union, if one is struck by the mystery of life itself, that appears as the result of the union of the male with the female, develops and thrives as an individual for a time, and then eventually disappears in the great womb of nature herself, who both brings forth life and receives it back into nothingness.

Although both Siva and Vishnu or Krishna have Saktis the Mother Goddess as Sakti could best be integrated with Siva because so it seems to me, the Siva concept already involved the mystery of polarity and their transcendence and was thus a most suitable image for exhibiting the duality and unity of the male-female (linga-yoni) principles in the world. And because of her association with Siva the Devi (Goddess) comes to participate both in his fearsome and destructive and in his gracious and beneficial aspects when she is elevated to the rank of the supreme divinity on her own. And in this capacity she is looked upon not simply as the Sakti or power of a god (though she remains the wife of Siva) but as Divine Power as such, conceived as the Universal Mother; the love relationship between the mother and the child now becoming the symbol of man's relation to the divine reality rather than the relation of Lord to the servant or that of lovers, friends etc.

As the wife of Siva, Sakti or Devi shows two faces, just as does Siva. She is, as Uma and Parvati, pictured as a beautiful, gracious, gentle, and devoted wife. But as Kali and Durga she is represented as a destroyer of evil and, as Kali, even as horrific and apparently repulsive in her blackness and blood thirstiness. Devi, when she emerges as the supreme divinity in her own right, is more often pictured as Durga and Kali than as Uma and Parvati, because the former images lend themselves to the portrayal of the mystery of existence, with its polarity of creation and destruction, on a much deeper level than does the picture of a gentle goddess portrayed in her wifely devotion. Devi is power, and although this power is conceived as feminine it needs a far greater sphere of operation – indeed one that is of cosmic significance involving fight between good and evil, life and death – than the domestic hearth, to show itself in all its splendour and effectiveness.

Devi Mahatmya (the greatness of the Devi) also known as *Sri Chandi*, a treatise on the origin and function of the Devi, inserted into the *Markandeya Purana*, shows the Goddess in this splendour and brings out the wider implications of the concept of power (Sakti) that moves the world as a female principle. Mahisasura, a king of demons, became so powerful that he conquered the gods and drove them out of heaven. This was reported by the gods to Vishnu and Siva who became very angry on hearing this. The power of this anger issued forth from their faces as concentrated energy. To this was added the energy which emanated from the bodies of other assembled gods, equally angry, and all these came together as a flaming mountain of brightness out of which emerged an incomparably beautiful woman. This was the Devi (Durga) who was to kill Mahisa-sura and deliver the gods from their servitude. The female principle is here represented as the embodinemt of the concentrated essence of male power which, when functioning as female, can accomplish what energy in its pure male form cannot, in the maintenance and preservation of order in creation. For the distinctiveness of the Goddess was in aid of re-establishment of order and peace that had been disturbed by the typically male power of arrogance and wilfulness. The power that maintains the world is not just brute force, heedless and haughty, but it is a force that is tempered by beauty, graciousness, and charm, with which the Goddess was amply endowed through the combined gift of the gods, so much so that one of the chiefs of the demon army proposed marriage to her even while knowing that she was an adversary. The female principle represents the best that is in men, because it brings into its task greater ease, more tact, and better understanding, while being no less forceful in the execution of its business. This is shown by the Goddess bringing forth from herself many forms and shapes of female divinities, more or less terrible, more or less benign, according to the needs of the circumstances during the terrible battle she fought single-handed with several hosts of the demon army. The Devi is said here to be created and yet it is made clear at the very beginning of the *Devi Mahatmya* that she is eternal. So the story of her creation shows not so much a temporal fact as the very structure of her being, representing the best that is in gods as sources of power.

Some Hindu scriptures such as the *Devi Bhagavata Purana*, *Saundaryalahari*, supposedly written by Samkaracherya, the advaitist, and some Sakta Tantras, elevate Devi above Brahman, Vishnu, and even Siva whose wife she is, and they are supposed to owe their existence and their function to her. She is even identified with Paramabrahman (the unmanifest beyond the manifest) of the Upanisads, as in the *Mahanirvana Tantra*. The *Saundaryalahari* too, when treating her as female subjugates the masculine principle to her but ultimately goes on to suggest that she is both soul (masculine) and nature (feminine) and as the neuter – Brahman of the Upanisads – beyond both masculinity and femininity. Devi thus becomes the absolute non-dual principle of the universe, a position that is or can be held by Krishna in Vaishnavism and Siva in Saivism. Such a Devi cannot be identified with mere destructiveness, which is only a part of the divine function and must herself be credited with all the three traditional divine activities of creation, preservation, and destruction, and this is what actually happens. Even Kali who is commonly represented as a black (black being the symbol of tamas, the disintegrating tendency in the world) goddess, standing on the corpse of Siva, with her garland of skulls, girdle of severed hands, and protruding tongue dripping with the blood she has drunk, possesses two hands offering refuge and boon.

In the context in which Kali is worshipped as the Supreme divine power, such as by the 19th century saint Sri Ramakrishna, she becomes subject to more than one interpretation, as befitting the Supreme Being who is really all. According to him Kali as Sakti or manifest energy is nothing different from Brahman, the inactive, unmanifest principle, and it makes no difference if one calls her Krishna or Siva, as divinity is no more of the female sex than of the male, being beyond all polarities. Nevertheless, for the devotee, Kali is the mother for it is as mother that divinity can evoke purest love and utter self-surrender that are needed for self-transcendence. Kali plays in the world in various ways. She is Mahakali, one with the great all-consuming darkness before all creation, called Mahakala. Shyamakali is her form as the gentle protectress of men in their life at home. As Rakshakali she protects from collective dangers like epidemics, famine, earthquake, drought and flood. Kali of the cremation ground is her form as the destructress, it is she who is pictured with a garland of skulls and when universal dissolution takes place she collects the seeds together for future use in another creation (destruction and creation being two sides of the same coin). Kali appears black only because she is viewed from a distance, just as the sky looks blue because of the distance. She really has no colour being beyond the gunas and for the devotee even when pictured as black she illumines the lotus in one's heart and fills one with divine love. This is so because the true devotee is not dismayed by the processes of decay and death that are inevitably interwoven with the processes of creation and maintenance of a changing world, and accepts them as part of God's supreme act of love in becoming all this and suffering change. Kali is Mahamaya, creator of the great illusion which keeps men tied to the world of her play but she can, if she wishes, offer liberation and lead men beyond play to the transcendent eternal reality. But the sweetness of love for her within the realm of play is so utterly fulfilling for man that one may prefer, once one has known the unchanging divine essence beyond all manifestations, to remain within the boundaries of lila and continue to taste this sweetness. For a devotee continued experience of divine love is even superior to knowledge which takes one to the realm of the changeless essence and he would rather have bhakti (love) within the sphere of mother's play, than mukti (liberation) which takes one beyond.

Sri Ramakrishna was not a Sakta in the sense that he would refuse to accept other divine names as equally applicable to God. Songs sung in praise of Krishna would bring about in him tears of joy or samadhi (ecstasy) just as easily as the name of Kali. Yet Kali was in a sense his chosen divinity for the mother-child relationship gave him the fullest scope for the expression of his personality and his specific type of religious impulse. This enabled him to establish a relationship of intimate right (as that of a child to the mother) with God which could dare to demand that the Goddess should fill him with love for her to the exclusion of everything else, as Ramprosad, who also thought of God as the mother, had done before him. This felicity in establishing a relationship in which one can rely on the Divine Being as being the more eager in bringing about a transformation or as being one from whom such eagerness can be naturally demanded is one of the reasons for preferring to think of this Being as the mother rather than the father with his relatively transcendent role.

But this is not the only insight that goes into the conception of divine power as a female principle, for the power involved is not just the transforming power of a mother's love but the generating power in general, functioning in the universe, which is also conceived as female in analogy with women's function in giving birth. Sakti then can be not just the Divine Mother but the female partner with whom one does Sadhana (spiritual practice) in order to arouse the dormant energy that is in oneself, ready to be used for a far greater vision and understanding than that to which human energy is generally put. Sakta philosophy as developed by the Tantras deals with this aspect of all-permeating energy including that of sex and its use for spiritual illumination. Tantras are, of course, not philosophy books, they are treatises on Sadhana (practice) but a general philosophical outlook can be gleaned from the various assumptions that are implicit in the Sadhana prescribed and this is what I shall attempt now in brief.

Devi is manifest energy (Sakti) that is expressing itself in all the processes of the world, physical and psychical – in nature, animals and men. But beyond this manifest energy is the unmanifest source (often pictorially represented by Siva, the static corpse, under the dynamic Kali, whose symbols represent manifestations of energy both in its creation and destructive potentials) and this is of the nature of Pure Consciousness (Consciousness not mediated by the mind and body as is the case with the empirical consciousness of the jiva, the finite man). This pure consciousness is also power, Cit-Sakti (consciousness-power) infinite and absolute by its very being, but formless. Ultimate power is thus power of consciousness which holds within itself all possibilities of manifestations of power in the universe in both of its aspects, gross (solid, substantial matter) and subtle (potentials of matter called tanmatras, as well as psychical power such as intelligence which are not open to observation by gross physical organs). This reservoir of all-embracing power, which is a plenum containing within itself the seeds of all existence, can by the exercise of its own power of will (iccha), knowledge (jnana), and action (kriya), bring about the manifold universe in order to savour, so to say, its own possibilities in the world of name and form, and experience in the process the delight of becoming. The world of form and becoming thus arises out of the formless world of pure being through a process of concentration that takes place with a view to self-expression. The Devi as Sakti is this concentrated energy of the divine that expresses itself in all the manifold processes of the formed universe.

Thus appears the first polarity in the world, between the unchanging inactive Brahman who, conceived as Siva, the transcendent, is thought to be male, and the dynamic activating energy arising in the bosom of Brahman itself, Devi, who is female. And nothing can take place without the polarity and union of these two principles. For dynamism or activity must ultimately draw its sustenance from the plenum of pure being at rest, while rest by itself will naturally not be productive of changing forms. This means also the polarity of 'I' and 'this' within the unity of Brahman, consciousness and object of consciousness, a distinction which is only vaguely perceived in the primal state of readiness of energy to evolve into form, but which is gradually turned into the duality of subject and object in all experience. But in the original being of consciousness-power, out of which all differentiations arise, the 'this' of experience is not anything different from the 'I'; and ultimate realisation consists in the perception of this unity. All other polarities are also implicit in their original bifurcation, for instance between eternity or timelessness and time, the form of change.

The concentrated energy, which is called the bindu, the point-limit, has no magnitude, but it is the beginning of potentiality for form in the subtle sphere of existence that first emerges out of formlessness. From this limit of existence and form gradually emerge all tattvas or principles, from the most subtle to the gross–from cosmic intelligence, for instance, which makes distinction of one thing from another possible to sense organs to receive forms, and from akasa (ether) the formless expansiveness without distinctions, to gross material objects occupying a particular space and possessing distinctive qualities. But there is perfect continuity between the subtle and the gross, the mental and the physical. Also the power that is inherent in matter and the power that is mind are continuous with the ground power of consciousness of which these are evolutes for the purpose of manifold expressions in name and form. The more we move from the subtle to the gross, from the psychical to the physical, the more is the power of consciousness (cit-Sakti) veiled in it, nevertheless they are not different from it except for the fact of contraction involved in their very possibility. Thus there is nothing in the universe, mental or material, which does not have involved in its very being the power of consciousness, the ultimate source of all power.

The Tantras are not philosophy books devoted to an abstract analysis of the nature of the world for its own sake but books concerned with spiritual practice and their interest in understanding the constitution of the universe arises out of a desire to know how best to treat the world from a religious point of view and use it, particularly for the purposes of spiritual illumination. And the great lessons they learnt are these. Both man and the universe which he inhabits are energy systems between which there is perfect correspondence – man as a microcosm is a reflection of macrocosm. But these energy systems are not just material or psychical ones, they are expressions of the divine energy of consciousness in varying degrees of density and veiledness. This being the case, man can utilise the energy that is implicit within him and the universe to gradually uncover the divine energy that is also resident therein, both in the realm of form as Devi and as formless Being and Bliss in which even the distinction of devotee and god disappears. But existence as such is divine – even though it is not understood in this way except in spiritual illumination – so there is nothing wrong in man's enjoyment of the world (bhukti). Indeed the Tantras, like the Vedas, believe that it is perfectly permissible, from a religious point of view, to ask for enjoyment of the world to the divine being since the world is an expression of his power, and enjoyment is an aspect of divine delight in creation. So the Tantras say that Mother or Sakti can be approached both for enjoyment (bhukti) and liberation (Mukti) although, no doubt, the man who asks only for enjoyment is a man of low spiritual competence compared with the man who asks for mukti or prema (divine love). Furthermore, liberation itself can be sought for through the enjoyment of things of this world, food, drink, sex, which can be turned into a sacrifice, so to say – and here again there is a similarity to the early Vedic approach – under the guidance of spiritually discerning men and thus made liberating rather than binding. Indeed man can use anything, sight, sound, patterns, colours, his own body in his search for the divine with which he wants to integrate himself, for the divine is in everything and the correspondence that exists between all orders of being allows him to treat one thing as the symbol of another and thus gradually ascend the scale to its ultimate perfection in Pure Consciousness.

The divine energy is in man, permeating his physical, vital, mental, and spiritual functions. But most men do not utilise the great fund of energy that is available within themselves. This fund is called the Kundalini, the representative of Sakti in the body, which normally lies coiled at the base of the spine more or less unused. Kundalini can, however, be aroused and gradually led through the grosser centres of power in the body to the more subtle ones and ultimately to the highest centre of all at the top of the brain where man becomes Pure Being, Consciousness, and Bliss. Kundalini yoga is thus one form of Devi worship whereby man can become, with the help of Devi herself, one with Brahman.

The centres of the body represent different kinds of power manifest in the world and they are seven in number, from the bottom of the spine to the top of the brain, each progressively more subtle. The body to which they really belong is the subtle body made of impressions and tendencies and not the gross body visible to the eye, although they are imagined in terms of their location and formation on the gross spinal cord. The lowest centre is muladhara (the root support of energy) located at the bottom of the spine and it is the home of the gross physical energy that is represented by earth. The next is swadisthan, the centre at the back of the genital organ, which is the home of the physical energy that is represented by water. The name of the third centre is manipura situated at the navel and it is constituted of the energy of fire. These three centres mainly represent power that are predominantly physical and their main contribution would be in the enhancement of physical health and vigour. The fourth centre, anahata, is situated near the heart and although it represents the power of the physical element, air, it is subtle enough for the first stirring of the spiritual impulse when Kundalini enters there. The next is Visuddha, at the throat, representing the power of ether, the most subtle of all matter and even if it is still a material centre it represents – mind and matter being continuous – the beginning of knowledge which matures at the next centre, ajna, between the eyes, which is composed of the energy of the mind. The presence of Kundalini here means spiritual understanding. It is when Kundalini reaches the top of the brain and as Sakti unites with Siva, the transcendent, that spiritual realisation in the form of experience of pure being, consciousness and bliss takes place. Needless to say, all dualities and tensions in the lower realms of the body so far traversed by Kundalini in her ascent are transcended in the supreme realisation of one's identity with the divine.

Thus both Siva and Sakti, the transcendent and the immanent powers of divinity are actually in man himself or at least they are realisable in his body, which instead of being devalued and subjected to repressive ascetical practices is to be divinised and used for the highest of all purposes. There is no absolute distinction between matter and spirit and because of the correspondence between the microcosm and the macrocosm the body itself can be a vehicle for the happening of the bliss of union between Siva and Sakti.

The ritual of Tantra is developed also on this understanding that all energy systems in the Universe are part of one fundamental plenum of divine energy, pure being. The devotee, before he offers the deity food, flower, incense, water and other objects for adoration and welcome, should by certain prescribed movements place the spirit of the deity in various parts of his body and thus purify it and make it harmonious with divine energy. He, then, should utter in a continuous rhythm certain sacred syllables which contain in seed from the sound pattern representing the power of the deity. This is based on a certain theory of the nature of sound as the basic constituent energy of the universe and the correspondence of the vibration of sound with various other energy patterns. According to the Tantras tension in the all-pervading energy that is ether gives rise to certain fundamental vibrations, representing certain root sounds or sound potentials which later emerge, at a more gross stage of manifestation, as articulate sounds that form the very basis of language. This sound potential is unstruck sound as distinct from the struck sound, conveyed by air to the ear drum, and this goes unheard except by yogis. The sacred syllable 'om' is a symbol of this unstruck sound, produced by spontaneous vibrations in ether, caused by its own stresses and strains, but it is below the threshold of the capacity of our sense organs to receive it. The energy of this sound lies at the very basis of all patterns of energy that are formed enough to be actually conveyed to us in experience. Thus vibrations of energy that constitute the fundamental sound-substratum is here conceived to be the basic formless (relatively) material out of which the universe, as an energy system, at different planes of manifestation of form is evolved. This is also known as Sabda Brahman, Brahman as Sound. According to the Tantras sound vibrations at a certain level of manifestation are transformed into vibrations of light which through receiving certain patterns give rise to enclosed space. Anyway sound syllables that constitute a mantra are supposed to embody a pattern of sound vibration which is a suitable symbol for the energy of the deity who is being invoked. This is why the uttering of these syllables is supposed to help the devotee to get in touch with the spirit of the deity.

The devotee can also use enclosed space, another configuration of energy, in the form of a Yantra, a particular spatial design constituted of triangles, circles, and squares to symbolise the dynamism of energy that goes into the constitution of the world. Concentration on a Yantra can ultimately lead the mind from the realm of the manifest to the unmanifest, from the formed, abstractly represented by geometrical shapes, to the formless beyond, and its geometrical design is specifically created for this purpose. It is constructed with the help of a series of nine triangles four of which have their apex up and five down, surrounded by several concentric circles framed in squares with a door on each side. Downward triangles represent Sakti the female principle and upward ones Siva the male. In the centre of it all is the Bindu, the point-limit. When one concentrates on this geometrical symbol, one is supposed to be able to experience in an apparently static medium the dynamism of opposing forces that go into the constitution of the world and which ultimately unite into the Bindu, the point-limit. The Bindu itself which stands at the threshold of the formed and the formless finally leads the mind into the void beyond all manifestations and unites it with Brahman, which is both the void and the plenum.

Finally we come to the five M's, (Pancha Makara), a particular ritual of Tantra which uses five things, the enjoyments of which are specifically forbidden by ascetical Brahmanism, particularly to the spiritual aspirant who must negate the world in order to reach Brahman. These are meat, fish, wine, parched grain, and sexual intercourse. This shows the revolutionary and daring character of Tantra which believes its ritual to be fit for a hero (vira) who, instead of anxiously screening himself from all temptations that enjoyment of life offers will openly and courageously use this very temptation as a means of his spiritual unfolding. Tantra believes that there is nothing on earth which does not partake of the divine essence and it depends on the vision of the devotee whether it appears sacred or profane. There is no need to say 'no' to pleasure, particularly for one who is still at the stage of temptation, although there is need to transform this pleasure from a thing of purely selfish enjoyment (representing the profane attitude to pleasure) to something of cosmic significance via offering it as a sacrifice to God, whereby one's personal pleasure becomes a part of divine joy that lies at the very basis of the urge for creation. Sex particularly can be seen as the vehicle of union with the divine, as in the act of sex two separate pleasures can be mingled into one which reaching beyond the tension of opposition can reveal the secret of being in bliss. Of course, one needs a certain spiritual orientation and preparation for approaching sex in this fashion. But what Tantra teaches is that pleasures, in which the ordinary man indulges in any case, can be seen as sacred rather than profane, thereby enriching one's being in the world. For the opposition between pleasure and liberation, with which a man has to live, does interfere either with liberation – if one opts for pleasure – or with the appreciation of life as a thing of joy and beauty, if one aspires after liberation. Tantra teaches that this opposition can be overcome and pleasure, when seen integrated with divine existence, can lead one towards liberation.

But one must have the daring and the vision of the hero to play successfully with danger. There are three types of men, according to Tantra, the sattvic, the rajasic, and the tamasic. The sattvic man is already advanced on the road to spiritual unfolding and is no longer tempted by desire to forego his quest for the divine. There is thus no need for him to worry about self-fulfilment through satisfaction of desire. So he can internalise the divine and offer worship that is purely mental. The rajasic man is a man of the world with all the basic desires that go with human nature, but endowed with enough energy to be able to use his desires in a constructive way, thereby redirecting the energy that goes into fulfilment of desire towards his search for the divine. The tamasic man must keep his desires in check through prohibitions and taboos, for otherwise indulgence in pleasure would lead, in his case, who lacks the vision and the courage of the hero, to sheer dissipation and waste. And not having the sattvic man's capacity for internalisation his worship must be conducted through conventional ritual, institutionalised and safe. Worship of the divine is an individual thing and it must be in accordance with the capacities and inclinations of the devotee in order that it may be really of help in one's spiritual unfolding. A man who is a hero by nature will be lost if he wants to start in the sattvic way, although he may eventually become sattvic, as would be the tamasic man if he adopts the hero's path.

The revolutionary character of Tantra is also shown by the fact that it went further than other bhakti movements in categorically rejecting the validity of caste within the religious context. This may be owing to the fact that a good deal of Sakti worship at the level of practice does probably come from the sudras – although the philosophy developed by Tantra is Vedic – and even the brahmans who systematised the Tantras could not possibly leave the sudras out of a form of worship which was already predominantly theirs, unlike the Vedic sacrifice. These two aspects of tantra, worship of the divine as energy and rejection of caste, seem particularly relevant for the Hindus today, for what stand in the way of the Hindus' recovery from decadence, in which they have been steeped for centuries, are inertia and caste.

I have in the above sections treated the worship of Krishna, Siva, and Kali as a qualified form of monotheism. It is qualified, for while some Hindus may worship only one of these as God, others accept all three as a suitable symbol for the Supreme Being. And while sectarian Hindu scriptures, such as some Puranas, speak in the name of one of these symbols only, others being reduced to the status of inferior beings, there are to be found many pronouncements in various Hindu scriptures to the effect that it makes no difference whether one calls God Siva, Krishna or Kali (or indeed Jesus or Allah as in the Gospel of Shri Ramakrishna), for it is the same God only conceived in a different name and form. If there is one God, then no matter what the name one uses, worship, if sincere, must reach the same destination. Any one of these can, of course, be adopted as one's own chosen medium of divinity (Ishta-devata) but this need not lead one to deny the validity of other people's choices. Even sculpturally Siva and Krishna are sometimes made into one God. Hari-Hara, and so are Siva and Sakti in the representation of Ardhanarisvara (God, half male, half female). Some legends dwell on the identification of even Krishna and Kali, who apparently belong to different spheres. Furthermore, worship of God as the Supreme Being does not invalidate contemplation of Brahman beyond name and form – these two being different approaches to religious reality, suitable to different temperaments. And, lastly monotheism does not rule out polytheism with its different purpose in a religious approach to life. Thus monotheism in the Hindu context does not have the same connotation as monotheism elsewhere and I have used the name only to convey the fact that it is the idea of one divine reality, who is represented as a person, that has inspired bhakti movements in the Hindu tradition.

CHAPTER VIII

Truth and the Hindu Religious Tradition

'Truth has many aspects. Infinite Truth has infinite expressions. Though the sages speak in many ways they express one and the same Truth.'[1]

'There is a tank with 3–4 approaches. The Hindus drink water out of this tank, through a particular approach and they call it "jal", the Muslims drink through another approach and they call it "pani". Through yet another the English drink water and they call it "water". The three are the same, only the name is different. Someone calls him Allah, someone God, someone Brahman, someone Kali, also Rama, Hari, Jesus, Durga.'[2]

In the first quotation the term 'truth' has two meanings, one ontological and the other epistemological, that is it means both Being and statements about it. The Sanskrit for Being is 'Sat', and a derivative of it, 'Satya', may mean either Being (ontological) or a valid understanding of it expressed in language (epistemological). As far as the ontological category of Being or Truth (Sat or Satya) is concerned, which refers to what I have labelled 'religious reality', it is being claimed that there is only one Truth, but with infinite aspects that may be approached in diverse ways and this means that there may be many truths about it when truth means an epistemological category which applies to the expressions of our understanding of it.

But it may be questioned whether there is an objective religious reality 'out there' at all in the same way as there is a physical reality open to inspection, and its ontological status is just taken for granted by referring to it as Being or Truth – an unwarrantable procedure. It must first be proved by means of clinching arguments to be there, before we can proceed to discuss the validity of our statements about it. Now, it is believed in the Hindu tradition that the objective and ontological status of religious reality is revealed not by argument but by experience. But this situation is not peculiar to religious reality. No domain of experience, including that of physical reality, can be

[1] *Srimad Bhagavatam*, trans. Prabhabananda, pp. 270–271.
[2] *Srisri Ramakrishna Kathamrita*, Part I. p. 52.

proved to be there merely by argument and at some stage or other we have to fall back on experience. Arguments and processes of ratiocination can analyse what is involved in experience and show that some of the things that we say are there are not there, or something that we do not believe to be there is there, and we say what we say because we have confused one thing with another and so on, but it cannot establish the objective status of a *whole domain of experience*, as this can only be founded on experience itself. This is why the sceptic or the solipsist can always insist on maintaining, as far as argument is concerned, that the external world has not been proved to be there.

Religious experience, unlike sensory experience, is not something that happens to one simply because one is there, and this is because of the nature of religious reality, which transcends the spatio-temporal framework within which ordinary experiences are cast. Religious experience may, of course, be of more than one kind. But in so far as the domain of religious experience may be said to constitute a realm of its own, as distinct from domains of other characteristic kinds of experience, such as scientific, artistic etc., it has peculiarities of its own, which, negatively speaking, mark it off from other domains. (The distinction that is being made here between different domains is for purposes of analysis; it is not being suggested that these domains can be encountered in life in a state of unmixed purity.) That is, religious reality is reality which impinges on one as not being one particular spatio-temporal thing distinguishable from other particular things by virtue of certain inspectable attributes, the existence of which is related to other things similarly conditioned. The unlimited nature of this realm of experience can thus only be referred to by such terms as 'infinite' and 'absolute' (because it does not have the character of finite and conditioned things). This is not to say that the positive character of this experience may not differ from one person to another. Again, religious experience is an experience of not being separated from this reality, which, positively speaking, may be described in more than one way.

The infinite and absolute character of what is here experienced is expressed by the term 'Being', meaning Being as such which is not conditioned and limited by anything else, and so neither comes into being nor goes out of existence (the sort of thing which is described in western theology as 'necessary existence'). So Being is the same as Truth, for if it is experienced it is experienced as indubitable. Whether or not such a reality is there can be judged not by those who never had religious experience but by those who did, that is by mystics and other seekers after religious truth. These people may try to verify the authenticity or otherwise of their experience in ways which are recognised amongst seekers of religious truth in a community as marks of genuineness. In a religious literature which has studied religious experience in detail, with a long record of people who have realised religious truth, one can find mention of various signs and marks which would characterise the attitude and behaviour of those who had had genuine encounters, and one may, if one so wishes, judge people who claim religious experience by these recognised signs. But it is obvious that in this domain demonstration of the objective reference of one's experience to whoever may demand it is impossible, since religious reality cannot be presented for one to gaze at it; it is not that sort of thing. Even if a mystic manages to have another experience on demand this will not help the non-experiencers in the least, who, unable to participate in the experience, will be no further forward. To someone who had had religious experience, however, the 'out-there' character of religious reality is undeniable. No doubt illusory experience is possible in this domain as anywhere else, but there is no *a priori* reason to postulate that all experiences in this domain must be illusory. The difficulty of a non-experiencer in accepting this reality on trust is, however, genuine, if experience is ultimately the basis for the understanding of something as given.

I believe that it is not the job of a philosopher to decide whether or not certain characteristic kinds of experience, including religious experience, have objective reference. Within each domain of experience there is an inter-subjective language, understood by people who talk such language, and certain characteristic signs and marks accepted by those who use this language and understand what is being talked about as evidences of genuineness and authenticity. And it depends on the nature of the domain what kind of evidence is available as evidence – what is available in the domain of sense experience is not available elsewhere. A philosopher can only examine the language that is used in respect of a domain to see what is involved in the use of this language, including the language of truth used as both ontological and epistemological categories, and I shall confine my investigations to this. In the Hindu tradition while Truth, in the sense of the Being of religious reality, is said to be absolute, truth in the sense of the epistemological status of the statements we make about it is not claimed to be so, so it is not the case that only one statement about it can be accepted as true while others must be rejected as false. What, then, is meant by truth in this sphere?

We have seen that religious language in the Hindu tradition is not of one kind but many, polytheistic, monistic or non-dualistic, monotheistic (qualified), and even that of self-realisation as spirit (the language of Samkhya-yoga). They do not all say the same thing about religious reality and yet all these are accepted as valid explorations of this reality by most Hindus. This is why I have used the term 'religious reality' rather than 'God', as the intended objective reference of all these languages, since 'God' fits only one kind of language, the monotheistic.

The term 'religious reality' is used here in a way in which the term 'physical reality' may be used to demarcate a characteristic domain of experience from other domains. This domain itself may be complex – indeed it is said to be infinite – just as the domain of physical reality is, which may be approached from many different points of view, such as commonsensical, artistic, scientific, technological and so on, depending on the purpose we have in mind. Even in the field of a specific scientific approach, say that of physics, there may be more than one framework of enquiry and alternative formulations of truth which complement or supplement one another, rather than 'the truth' being embodied in one statement or theory alone which requires us to reject all other statements made in this field. As Kuhn remarks in *The Structure of Scientific Revolutions*, 'there is no one answer to the scientist's quest in his study of physical reality which has been set by Nature herself in advance, so to say, as opposed to all other answers, and there is no need to think that there is some one full objectively true account of nature and that the proper measure of scientific achievement is the extent to which it brings us closer to that ultimate goal.'[3] The nature of physical reality, as revealed by the study of science, requires us, according to Kuhn, to give up the idea that every revolution in science that results in a new theory carries us closer and closer to 'the truth', for there is no such thing as an absolutely neutral and objective report on the given as it is in itself. Many people believe that the scientific method is such that when it is applied to a given set of phenomena that appears puzzling in some way it will come up with the only one legitimate answer. This is not the case. 'Instructed to examine electrical or chemical phenomena, the man who is ignorant of these fields but who knows what it is to be scientific may legitimately reach any one of a number of incompatible conclusions. Among those legitimate possibilities, the particular conclusions he does arrive at are probably determined by his prior experience in other fields, by the accidents of his investigation, and by his own individual make-up.'[4]

The remarkable progress of scientific knowledge in recent centuries makes many people believe that the immature condition of pre-modern science is a result of lack of correct scientific objectivity and method, which were not available in those days. This, according to Kuhn, is a mistake. Ancient and medieval science embody 'a number of distinct views of nature, each partially derived from, and all roughly compatible with, the dictates of scientific observation and method. What differentiated these various schools was not one or another failure of method – they were all "scientific" – but what we shall come to call their incommensurable ways of seeing the world and of practising science in it.'[5] If Kuhn is right in saying that there is not something available called 'the scientific method' by applying which it can be found out which of the various ways of seeing the world is the correct one, then the choice between these available alternatives is dictated not so much by the nature of the 'given' as a neutral entity as by historical factors which create a scientific community with certain specific purposes and objectives in view. And when two competing theories,

[3]*The Structure of Scientific Revolutions*, Chicago, Paperback, p. 171.
[4]*Ibid.*, pp. 3–4.
[5]*Ibid.*, p. 4.

neither of which can be said to be conclusively verified beyond all possibility of doubt, vie for men's allegiance it may even be personal make-up that decides which theory one will accept.

This is not to say that some theories cannot be better than others in being more comprehensive (able to solve a wider range of problems or connect a greater variety of fields previously thought to be distinct) and hence intrinsically more acceptable at a certain stage of historical development of science. But all available scientific theories in respect of physical reality cannot be graded in this fashion, since they may involve different perspectives or framework of enquiry – the study of light from one framework may make it appear like a wave and from another framework as particles. There is also the fact that no theory solves all problems which can be seen to arise, even within the perspective of the theory in question. Hence however better it may be than other theories in certain respects, the truth it possesses cannot be claimed to be absolute.

Now Kuhn's account of scientific theory and practice has laid him open to charges of subjectivism, irrationalism, and relativism. This may be a misunderstanding, if I understand him right. That there is a physical reality the existence of which is not in anyway relative to any particular kind of scientific practice is not in dispute. But what Kuhn is saying, as a result of his studies in the history of science, is that this reality is too complex for anyone to size it up *just as it is in itself*, by means of one theory, which can be seen to be absolutely true by seeing that it alone corresponds to the 'given'. For interrogating nature, which is complex, requires a certain framework of enquiry, the formulation of which depends on certain historical factors, and there may be more than one framework of enquiry, none of which can be shown to be the right framework by referring it to physical reality itself, antecedently given as such and such. Being complex it can be given in more than one way, depending on the questions we ask of it. That the answers we get are relative to our framework, of which there can be more than one, need not, however, mean pure relativism in the sense that there is nothing given of which we need to take account and which determines the answer that we come upon. All it need mean is that what is given is complex and its givenness as such and such, that is to say, in a determinate sort of way, may only become apparent to us when we ask a particular question from a particular framework of enquiry, not independently of it. Nevertheless, the possibility of our finding this answer is there, independently of us.

A certain assemblage of lines, curves, dots etc., can be seen as a duck, a rabbit, or just as a complex configuration representing nothing in particular, depending on how we look, but all these possibilities are there to be viewed. They are not relative to us *per se*, that is, what is relative to us is not the fact that we see a rabbit, it is rather that we see the *whole thing as a rabbit rather than as a duck*, both of which are genuine possibilities, the given being what it is. Again, formulating a certain framework of enquiry is not subjective in the sense that there is nothing given of which a scientific researcher need take any notice in trying to find an answer to his question. It need only mean that the possible questions that may be asked of nature and the possible frameworks of enquiry from which these may be formulated are more than one, and at least one explanation why one researcher asks one question rather than another may lie in psychological and subjective factors. Since what we find in nature depends on the questions we ask, this psychological and subjective aspect is not totally irrelevant to our understanding of what goes on in science. Lastly, the development of scientific knowledge is irrational, not in the sense that observation, experiment and logic do not determine the outcome of scientific research, but only in the sense that an explanation of why a community comes to ask questions of nature that lend themselves to scientific treatment, or why a certain question which leads to a great expansion of our understanding of nature is asked at a certain time, may lie in historical factors which are not rationally determined.

I have gone into this discussion of physical reality here in order to draw certain parallels with religious reality, particularly with regard to the question of truth. It is now being recognised in science that there is no such thing as the absolute truth in the scientific understanding of nature although there are many truths, and the situation is the same in respect of religious reality in the Hindu tradition. I have said that this is because physical reality (or any reality) is complex and it cannot be sized up as it is in itself without adopting a certain framework of enquiry which qualifies it, and this too applies to religious reality. The idea that reality is complex or, better, many-sided (anekanta), and that all statements that we make about it are from some particular standpoint or other (naya) — the many sidedness of reality making it impossible for us to talk about it as it is in itself — to which the truth of the statement made is relative, was developed in India by a Jaina logical doctrine called 'Syadvada' ('may be it is' doctrine). According to this doctrine statements from one point of view do not contradict statements which appear to be opposites, if they are made from different points of view. Many arguments in which people indulge could be avoided if they were aware of the fact that there is a point of view involved to which the truth of their statement is relative, for they could then see that their opposing statements are not really making the same claims. So any categorical and absolute claim of the form 'X does exist' is false, because it involves that the existence of X can be asserted without any reference to any point of view whatsoever. Even 'X exists' is not enough if it just admits that there is a point of view involved and it is only 'somehow X exists' which is logically satisfactory because here the assertion of the existence of X is being made relative to its own standpoint (X may not exist from some other standpoint).

According to this logic, the multiple possibilities of predication with regard to the same thing from different points of view, giving rise to apparently contradictory statements, can be schematically represented by seven types of predication (all equally admissible), some of which involve just one point of view, some a combination of points of view:

1. Somehow (meaning from a   S is P
                  distinct point of view)
2.   ,,   ,,   S is not P
3.   ,,   ,,   S is both P and not P
                                          (where P and not P are
                                          contraries and not contra-
                                          dictories)

4. Somehow (meaning from a distinct point of view)	S is indescribable (not in every way but in so far as the ascription of P or not P is concerned)
5. „ „	S is P and it is indescribable (representing a combination of the 1st and 4th points of view).
6. „ „	S is not P and it is indescribable (2nd and 4th)
7. „ „	S is both P and not P and it is indescribable (3rd and 4th)

This doctrine of sevenfold predication (Saptabhangi naya) makes several points :

1. No statement can claim to be talking about reality as it is in itself because it is made from a particular point of view, others being available.
2. Apparently contradictory statements are not really opposed to one another if they are made from different points of view.
3. Truth of a statement is relative to its own point of view, that is, if made from a different point of view it may be false.
4. A multiplicity of points of view can be brought to bear on the same thing, some of which are simple (involving only one point of view), some complex (involving a combination of points of view). All this, however, does not mean that either the many-sidedness of reality or its very existence is relative to man's activity of predication.

Although this doctrine is Jaina, it seems to me exactly the kind of logic that can illumine the Hindu belief in many truths in the realm of religious reality, some of which appear to contradict one another, such as polytheism and monotheism, or monotheism and monism. That religious reality is many-sided is a belief that has been long held in the tradition, from the time of the *Rigveda*, and it was particularly stressed by Sri

Ramakrishna. He used to illustrate this by certain examples. In a tree there dwelt a chameleon which several people saw at different times. And they argued without agreement as to its colour, some insisting that it was red, some green, and so on. Then they met a man who lived under the tree and had seen the chameleon under different circumstances and he explained that all of them were right because being a chameleon it had all those colours and many more besides. Thus the dispute was settled. Another story is that of an elephant and four blind men. The four blind men felt different parts of the elephant's body and kept arguing as to what it was like. One said that the elephant is a winnowing basket, as he had felt one of its ears; another said that it was a pillar because he had felt one of its legs; and so the other two, according to their experience. Those who argue about the nature of religious reality and insist that it must be described in one way only are like these blind men, according to Ramakrishna.

The domain of religious reality is the infinite and it is the source of all existence and value. Although it is inaccessible to sense experience or to inference through intellection it is possible for men to have experience of it in the form of a mystical or intuitive illumination. It is far from the case, this reality being infinite, that all experiences in this domain are carbon copies of one another; nevertheless, they must all be characterised by an understanding that religious reality is free of the spatio-temporal limitations of finite existence. Furthermore, all such experiences involve this realisation that man's own reality is linked with this domain of existence in an enduring way. But when it comes to expressing these realisations in language some difficulties are encountered. Language is a tool which is specifically used for the purpose of noticing similarities and differences between a multitude of particular things spatio-temporally conditioned in their nature. So it is not found to be adequate for expressing the nature of something which is above spatio-temporal particularities, and one has inevitably to resort to metaphors. Added to this general difficulty is the fact that whenever man formulates his understanding of religious reality, he does so from a particular point of view as defined by a certain purpose or framework of enquiry that there is at the back of his mind in undertaking the job of formulation and explanation. Furthermore, religion is not just a matter of theoretical understanding. As I said religious reality impinges on one as being something with which man's own reality is linked. But this link is not felt by most men most of the time. So explorations of religious reality have a practical aim, that of making man aware of his relatedness to a dimension of reality above that of finitude. But here again the kind of relatedness one seeks is defined by the purpose one has in mind and this purpose is not of one kind but many, at least in the Hindu religious tradition. However, when it is seen that these purposes are different the different formulations arrived at are no longer seen to be contradictory, as Jaina logic points out. One may, of course, psychologically speaking, prefer a certain approach to others available and hence adopt it exclusively in one's religious search, but one would not be justified on this ground in asserting that other approaches are false.

Polytheism, for instance, has the purpose of relating man's ordinary living here on earth, in its pursuit of wordly happiness, to this reality. Religious reality then appears as a multitude of divine beings with power to confer gifts on men (this expressing in the realm of worldly pursuit the general religious belief that all existence and value are grounded in religious reality). Polytheistic cultures do not lack the idea of one Supreme Being who has created the world in the first instance, or a supreme principle of which everything is an expression. But this is thought to be too remote and exalted for the purposes of the fulfilment of man's day-to-day needs. Hence in this complex lesser divinities, embodiments of power in somewhat limited fields, receive worship and prayer, and the purpose here is to be linked with sources of power that subserve men's day-to-day needs of sustenance and fulfilment. Polytheism thus constitutes a specific kind of approach to religious reality as defined by a specific kind of purpose that one has in making the approach. It is religious because it involves a belief in the reality of a domain of existence which is beyond the limitations of man's finite existence and to which man is linked in such a way that he may receive from it what he needs through appropriate ritual, by means of which the link can be felt to be there. Ritual can thus transform the profane into the sacred with which integration is achieved in the context of ordinary living.

Non-dualism involves an entirely different kind of purpose and point of view. Religious experience is an experience of an infinite mode of being. As it happens to an individual he may experience this infinitude within his own being as well as outside, that is, as something out there but also within oneself, if the purpose of one's search is understanding of one's own being as well as integration with all of existence. One then formulates religious reality as Brahman, characterised by Being, Consciousness, and Bliss, which pervades everything and with which one's inmost being is found to be non-dual. Here contemplation of Absolute Being and one's own identity with it replaces ritual as it is better adapted to bringing about the required kind of understanding and integration.

Self-realisation as a spirit has a more limited objective, integration with a level of one's own being which is here and now free of the limitations of finitude. Religious reality here is not understood to have any reference beyond one's own being, so the infinite mode of being encountered in religious experience is thoroughly internalised from the point of view of understanding one's own enduring essence. So the religious search becomes a programme of self-realisation, when self is the infinite.

Monotheism is a perspective from which our link with the infinite mode of being is perceived as a social relationship between two persons bound by love. So religious reality is conceived as God, an Infinite Being, but who nevertheless is a Person because He enters into a relationship which only persons can enter into. The purpose of this approach is not to secure a transitory good life on earth (which intermediate divinities have power enough to confer), but an everlasting life bestowed by God through which man achieves integration with the source of his existence. But as befitting a conceptual model of a relationship between an all-powerful Being and a finite person, man's salvation from finitude and integration with religious reality are here thought to come about through being received as a gift from the merciful and loving God.

All these formulations of religious reality apparently contradict one another, but, as the Jaina doctrine of Syadvada points out, if we become aware that they are approaching religious reality from different perspectives and with different purposes in view we shall find that there is really no contradiction. Rather they are complementary views none of which can claim exclusive or absolute validity, although each one has validity in relation to its own point of view. There may be historical reasons why a certain purpose or framework of approach is adopted by a religious community at a certain time, with its appropriate practice for effecting integration. That is, a certain approach may serve the felt religious needs of a community better than others at a certain time. Also there may be psychological reasons, (intellectual and emotional) why an individual may prefer a certain approach to another, both of which are available to him.[6] But from the point of view of philosophy all one can do is to bring out the logic involved in each form and show how the truth it claims is relative to its purpose. But this kind of understanding of religious truth is possible only if it is accepted that this truth is a human truth, that is, attained by the human mind in its search after religious reality and not something that has been handed over from another source, beyond man. It is true that revelation is claimed by people in the Hindu tradition in respect of the Vedas and Upaniṣads, but the compatibility of these scriptures with every shade of religious opinion, as the history of the Hindu tradition shows, makes it clear that the truths of the Vedas were revealed to Vedic seers through their own search and their own capacity for religious experience, insight and illumination; they were not received from above. No doubt an understanding or illumination in respect of truth not apparent to the senses, particularly when it belongs to a dimension not normally available in experience, may involve a feeling of revelation, as if an aspect of reality not hitherto understood suddenly lays bare its secret to one's wonder-struck gaze – one who feels more like an observer than a discoverer. This happens because a moment of understanding a truth of this nature is not a moment of intellection – however much intellection may have gone into it – but a moment of intuition when truth just happens. This is however not peculiar to religion, and many scientific discoveries happen in this way as well. But revelation in this sense remains

[6] I have already discussed in Chapter IV the different orientations and needs that are involved in the formulations of the three monotheistic models of Krishna, Siva, and Kali.

human, even if we decide to say that it happens through that element in man which is divine.

But it may still be asked, in what sense is polytheism (or anything else) true? Are there really divinities called Indra, Agni etc., who have power to confer gifts on men? Now it seems to me obvious that propositions of a religious nature which are apparently descriptive (saying that God or a god is such and such) are not descriptive in the straightforward sense which allows verification by means of correspondence. I have in the previous chapters used the term 'model' to refer to the various distinctive approaches to the divine in the Hindu tradition, including certain characteristic kinds of world-view, doctrines about the nature of religious reality, rituals, disciplines etc., as are invovled in polytheism and so on. As we have seen, all these involve a distinctive framework of approach, as defined by a certain purpose, for religious search in the last analysis is a practical activity which aspires, to realise in actual experience the link that is understood to be there between the ultimate reality beyond spatio-temporal limitations and the world of finitude. But the term 'model' may be misleading, and it may lead us to expect more information than it can give us if it is taken to be a descriptive model of the type that is used in science.

A theoretical model in science is used to make intelligible certain fundamental properties and relationships of a certain field of investigation on the basis of an analogy that is found to exist between a familiar and well-understood phenomenon and the object of one's study which defies understanding and description in a direct manner and without the help of the analogy — for example, the wave model for the study of behaviour of light which exhibits properties and relations that can be best understood (at the present stage of enquiry, at any rate) if one conceives of it as a wave (since there are certain features in common between the way a wave functions and the way light behaves). The analogy is not perfect; if it were light would be a wave and not just to be understood under the model of a wave, and there are respects in which the analogy breaks down. The fact that there are positive and negative analogies between light and wave shows that the use of the term 'wave' is here metaphorical and not literal. It is felt that the use of the model can be a help not only in understanding certain characteristic features which are being exhibited but possibly other relationships which an extension of certain properties of the model to the field of study might unravel. (It is in trying to do this that negative analogies are found.) Nevertheless the ultimate aim of science is to dispense with models and metaphors at some stage of progress of inquiry into a certain field. For as Mary Hesse says, in her 'Role of Models in Scientific Theory'. The purpose of using models is to make them unnecessary by so familiarising ourselves with the new field of discovery that it can be described by means of its own language without comparison with something more familiar.'[7]

Now models used in religion, like models in science, help us to understand a certain field of investigation the structure of which is not apparent in its own terms and can only be understood by means of metaphorical extension of language drawn from another field. But models in religion do not have all the properties of models in science which, in however limited a way, have a descriptive purpose that can be demonstrated. This is because in science there is a recognised field of investigation shared by many people in common in which some facts and regularities have been established. So it is possible to show where precisely lies the analogy between the model and the field of study and where it does not, so that the metaphorical extension of language does not lead us beyond its field of applicability. Nevertheless models do help to establish further facts and regularities because of their descriptive function. Models in religion do not have this sort of descriptive function. The field of religious reality, being about a domain which transcends spatio-temporal characteristics, does not have established facts and regularities. So the analogy between the model that we are using and religious reality itself is vague, being based on an indeterminate perception (the link that one experiences with religious reality is indeterminate, which may be understood under the metaphor of union, or identity, or something else), rather than on an examination of details available in both fields. Nor do models here help to establish further facts and regularities. The greatest difficulty in talking about

[7] *Philosophical Problems of Natural Science*, ed. Dudley Shapere, p. 106.

religious reality is that it has no language specific to itself, except a few terms that indicate this reality but do not describe it, such as God, Brahman, the Infinite, or the Absolute. These terms can be made intelligible only by using models and metaphors drawn from other fields of experience, and these bear a greater burden in this sphere than they do in the sphere of science. They give a shape or form to an experience which in itself has not got a shape because it is above spatio-temporal determinations, and if we cease to use models and metaphors we shall have to cease to speak, unlike in the field of science where models can be used as temporary measures.

Religious models thus appear to me to be formative models rather than descriptive ones and their metaphorical character remains with them throughout. There are positive and negative analogies involved in scientific models, and it is very important to remember these negative analogies if one is not to be misled into reading into one's field of study properties, via those of the model, which do not belong there. It seems to me that in the use of models in religion this careful analysis of positive and negative analogies has far less significance because models here do not aspire to lead one to an eventual literal description in a language that is no longer metaphorical. Religious models remain metaphorical and there is no help for it. Analogies involved in these metaphors are not clear-cut and they bear the stamp of the purpose that leads one to find them, their function being to create a certain kind of picture drawn from a field of experience familiar to human beings and project it on to the field of religious reality in order that we can talk about it at all and act in regard to the fulfilment of the purpose we have in mind in approaching the divine. They have thus a formative creative function, not creative of the field of religious reality itself, but of a certain determinate form which this field can be seen to have in relation to certain purposes.

According to Max Black, 'A memorable metaphor has the power to bring two separate domains into cognitive and emotional relation by using language directly appropriate to the one *as a lens for seeing the other*; the implications, suggestions and supporting values entwined with the literal use of the metaphorical expression *enable us to see a new subject matter in a new way*.'[8] Metaphorical thought, says Max Black, is a distinctive mode of achieving insight and this insight is achieved by using the metaphor as a filter (through which our approach to a certain object of understanding is processed, as it were, to give it a certain shape). He takes as an example the metaphorical expression 'man is a wolf'. 'The wolf-metaphor suppresses some details, emphasises others — in short, *organises* our view of man.'[9] Any argument as to whether a man is a wolf or not as futile; what the metaphor does is to suggest that we might find it illuminating to look at man in this way. (If we do not do so we need not use the metaphor). Thus 'man is a wolf' is what I have called a formative metaphor or model — rather than a descriptive one — which makes us look at man in a certain way which will not be available without the use of the metaphor itself. (All metaphors, or for that matter language, may be said to be formative, as is done by Cassirer but within this general creativity a further distinction between formative and descriptive metaphors and models may be made to demarcate distinctive functions.)

Perhaps the distinctive forms of approach to religious reality that I have referred to as 'models' should better be called 'archetypes' (in order that wrong things may not be demanded of them), another term used by Max Black. By an archetype I mean a systematic repertoire of ideas by means of which a given thinker describes, *by analogical extension*, some domain to which these ideas do not immediately and literally apply.'[9] Archetypes are not true or false in the same way as literal descriptions can be. They make us see things as such and such, when this is not apparent, but seeing things in this fashion may enable us to come to grips with certain things which would remain inaccessible otherwise, hence their value. The value of the archetypes in religious fields is twofold. (1) Intellectual. It is only by using these metaphors that we can at all talk about the field of religious reality, which will remain inaccessible otherwise. We would be reduced to silence if the purely metaphorical character of religious language made us feel that it was highly

[8] *Models and Metaphors*, p. 236 (emphasis added).
[9] *Ibid.*, p. 41.
[10] *Ibid.*, p. 241.

unsatisfactory to use it, being unwilling to let these metaphors do what they can for us beyond the level of articulate thought. But the use of language to give literal information is not its only use, as the existence of metaphorical language shows. What metaphorical language does, or can do, is to bring the hearer to a point where he has to transcend language itself and intuitively apprehend a domain of reality for which literal descriptions are not available. Language here functions as a kind of dialectic ladder which must be used in order that we may reach a certain height but which must also be thrown away after the height is reached. People may not of course use metaphorical language in this way, being unable to transcend the literal level. But as a domain of reality remains inaccessible to man unless he uses language in respect of it, even a literal misrepresentation of metaphorical language is perhaps better than refusal to use language at all. That the metaphors used to talk about religious reality are unsatisfactory, if they are taken on a literal level, of this there is no doubt, and many mystics, having described their experience in terms of these available metaphors, insist that religious reality is ultimately indescribable. Nevertheless they persist in using language to describe the indescribable, for the alternative is for man to deprive himself of all contact with the divine. (2) Pragmatic. By organising our thoughts, emotions etc., in a determinate way these archetypes enable us to pursue a definite course of discipline or religious practice whereby we can positively link ourselves with religious reality. And this is what religion is ultimately all about; so although verification by correspondence is not available, some kind of validation by pragmatic test is. And this means that if the use of an archetype enables us to find religious reality and integrate ourselves with it then it is valid or true in this field. In order to do this, of course, an archetype must be such as to be capable of unveiling, to some degree, the mystery of religious reality. It is in this sense of 'true' that there are said to be many truths in the Hindu religious tradition. As the *Srimad Bhagavatam* says, 'Ignorant is he who says "what I say and know is true; others are wrong". It is because of this attitude of the ignorant that there have been doubts and misunderstandings about God (meaning religious reality). This attitude it is that causes dispute among men. But all doubts vanish when one gains self-control and attains tranquillity by realising the heart of Truth: thereupon dispute, too, is at an end.'[11]

As I have said, archetypes are not true in a literal descriptive sense (there are not literally speaking beings called 'gods' who reside in heaven or wherever. But we can see the powers that affect us as gods if this helps us to integrate ourselves with life and with religious reality). But they have nevertheless intellectual and pragmatic value, both of which are indispensable for man's contact with religious reality. However, all archetypes do not have that same value for everyone. Some archetypes may have value for some people, but not for others who may find it entirely unhelpful in their religious search. But for those who can use it, it remains valid. Polytheism is defended in the Hindu religious tradition by saying that it may be the only religious search that is available to some people – since the context of search is here and now values of life – people who are not ready to pin all their hopes on an everlasting life after death but who nevertheless can see themselves integrated with a larger reality through their ordinary search for happiness here on earth. Furthermore, a particular archetype may have value for a man at a certain stage of his life which it may subsequently lose, when another archetype comes to have a greater revealing power for the man concerned with change of purpose. But as far as the Hindu religious tradition is concerned no archetype which helps man to integrate himself with the divine (the source of all existence and value) in any way can be said to be invalid. Because the divine is all, the seeing of it as so and so – so long as this does help one to achieve the integration that it is the function of religion to bring about – is perfectly valid. There is then such a thing as religious truth, and archetypes which cannot serve the purpose of bringing about integration between man and the domain of religious reality are false. There is of course no absolute truth, and acceptance of some available truths can be mediated by psychological (one's own competence, intellectual and emotional) and social factors (the archetype used by the religious community in which one is born and brought up).

[11]*Srimad Bhagavatam*, p. 271.

But the fact that even in the field of science some people are discarding the idea of 'the absolute truth – in view of the manysidedness of reality which can only be interrogated from some framework of enquiry or other – and increasingly recognising historical and individual factors that go into the determination of what is accepted as true, makes it possible to consider the specific doctrine of truth that is implicit in the Hindu religious tradition as intellectually respectable.

Finally, I shall look at the metaphors that are involved in the various models or archetypes available within the Hindu tradition. Religious reality, I have said, is free of the spatio-temporal limitations of finitude and from the point of view of religious experience man is linked with this reality, his very existence being grounded in it. If the purpose of religious search is integration of man's instinct for happiness on earth, through fulfilment of various desires, with divine existence, then the divine can be filtered through the metaphor of powerful beings, beyond earthly limitations, however, and hence conceived as gods, who can confer happiness on man, provided he qualifies through moral purity, intellectual understanding, and social concord (things which are actually found to be elements in a good life on earth, besides satisfaction of desires). Man's link with the divine realm, modelled after an assemblage of powerful beings, is then found through the use of other metaphors, those of order and exchange. Men and gods actually belong to one cosmic order, rita, and this order can actually be reproduced through the ritual means of sacrifice. Sacrifice is also a means of exchange whereby the acts of men can augment the power of gods. Thus the model of a give and take relationship (whereby men are joined together in society) is projected on to the divine realm and by means of this a religious meaning is found for life in its everyday dimension. If we believe that man's relatedness to the divine concerns him in all that forms a part of his life and that religion has relevance not just for a projected life after death but for enjoyment of life here on earth it cannot be denied that polytheism, as a specific model of approach to the divine, has validity.

But the realm of religious reality can be universalised rather than particularised, as in the conception of gods, and since it involves an experience of being sustained by this reality the metaphor of one common essence running through all things known by the same name, as gold in all things made of gold, may be found by some minds as illuminative of the nature of religious reality in relation to man and the world, if one's purpose is to understand the highest principle of existence, one that is naturally beyond that of finitude, by reference to which all things can be explained, including man's consciousness. Thus one comes by the notion of Brahman, beyond all name and form, albeit characterised by Being, Consciousness and Bliss, of which all things are manifestations at various lower levels of existence (illustrated by the metaphor of a spider weaving a web out of its own substance). And when integration with this reality takes the form of a feeling of one's own identity, and that of everything else, with it, (identity rather than union – since all things are of the same essence, insistence on the separate existence of things is not important), the metaphors one finds significant are rivers entering the sea or various sparks coming off from the same fire.

This reality and man's relatedness to it is also seen under the metaphor of a loving Lord or master (or father or mother), giving rise to the conception of a personal God who, unlike gods, is possessed of infinite and absolute power, able to confer eternal life beyond all blemishes of finitude and not just transient happiness on earth. Consistently with the use of this social metaphor in clarifying one's conception of religious reality, one's link with this reality too is grasped under another social metaphor, that of love. Eternal life is then seen under the model of a perfect social existence, minus the limitations of finitude, projected on to the religious plane. The difference between the social metaphors used in this archetype and those of polytheism (which are also of a social nature) is that the purpose here is to ensure everlasting life, while polytheism is concerned with the here and now values of life.

When the experience of religious reality, the domain of infinitude, is not found to extend beyond the realm of personal consciousness, the metaphor one uses to understand the relation of the infinite to the finite is reflection as in a mirror – the infinite Purusa (Self) being reflected in the finite Prakriti (nature) and caught up in it – if one's purpose in religious realisation is nothing beyond that of understanding oneself as spirit (infinite rather than finite matter. The link with the infinite which is to be found within oneself is then sought through the metaphor of isolation (Kaivalya), the separating off of the infinite in oneself from the finite, in order to be established in one's own essence.

It is perfectly possible to judge the greater or less satisfactoriness of these various models or archetypes in relation to some accepted goal, and even to reject some as not being worthy of one's endeavours. But the validity of the model in relation to its own framework is not thereby impaired for those who find the framework acceptable. As frameworks are many, truths are said to be many, although any given person may not find them all equally acceptable. According to the Hindu tradition the spiritual competence of people, just as their competence in other respects, vary, so one should adopt a model which is suitable to one's inclinations and make-up and which will therefore help one most in finding one's link with the divine. That which, abstractly considered, sounds like the highest goal, may just be waste of time for someone, when adopted, if he is not ready for it emotionally and intellectually. Also, it may well be that what helps one will hinder another, so the avilability of alternative models is thought to be a good thing. If there is only one model available some people who find it difficult to respond to it because of psychological reasons (intellectual or emotional) may well be deprived of all thought of the divine, which, it is possible, may not happen if a model of a different kind is there for them to respond to. Sri Ramakrishna used to say that a wise mother does not prepare the same dish of fish for everyone of her children if their tastes and digestive capacities vary—for one she prepares stew, for another curry, for the third fried fish and so on. But it is the same fish that is being enjoyed by all of them, however differently.

CHAPTER IX

Moral and Spiritual Values in the Hindu Tradition

In the Hindu tradition Ultimate Truth (Being) is often said to be beyond good and evil and all other distinctions, and realisation of this Truth is thought to dawn on one through an eventual transcendence of these distinctions rather than merely through doing or being good. As is said in the *Brihadaranyaka Upanisad*, 'This eternal greatness of the knower of *Brahman* is not increased by work nor diminished. One should know the nature of that alone. Having found that one is not tainted by evil action.'[1] This however should not be taken to mean that the knower of Brahman, because he has reached a goal beyond all distinctions, would act in evil ways. For the teaching quoted above continues thus: 'Therefore he who knows it as such, having become calm, self-controlled, withdrawn, patient and collected, sees the Self in his own Self, sees all in the Self. Evil does not overcome him, he overcomes all evil. Evil does not burn (affect) him, he burns (consumes) all evil. Free from evil, free from taint, free from doubt, he becomes a knower of Brahman.'[2] The knower of Brahman is not guided in his understanding of ultimate reality by the categories of good and evil, but his transcendence of these categories also means his overcoming of evil, because he sees the Self in his own self and sees all in the Self. Such a man would naturally not be tempted by evil, the root of which lies in the distinction between 'mine' and 'thine' – said to be a work of the gunas. As long as man makes this distinction he cannot overcome finitude and reach the ultimate beyond all distinctions. Ceasing to make this distinction is also ceasing to be tempted by evil.

To talk about reality in a religious context is to talk about what is beyond the categories that men use in order to mark off certain distinctions within the sphere of their experience, including those of good and evil. Man calls whatever serves the purpose of human happiness 'good', and whatever obstructs,

---

[1] *The Principal Upanisads*, trans. Radhakrishnan, p. 280.
[2] *Ibid.*, p. 280.

diminishes and destroys it 'evil', and this is a perfectly valid distinction that human beings must make in order to live as satisfactory a life on earth as obtainable. From this point of view there is also the need to do whatever will add to happiness and prevent unhappiness, and while man is instinctively ready to see this where his own happiness or unhappiness is concerned he has to be exhorted to learn to view other people's happiness or unhappiness in the same way as his own and act accordingly. Indeed, so basic is this need for a moral point of view for the continuation of society, let alone its happy functioning, that there is no human society which does not adopt it. It would be suicidal to say that this point of view should be transcended if that were to mean that a society should find this distinction between good and evil meaningless in respect of the purpose which it serves, or abandon the pupose itself.

Reality as looked at from an ultimate point of view cannot however be conceived to be fashioned specifically according to man's need for happiness in a finite existence, for it is the ground of all value and also of all existence, including what men call 'evil'. All things in the realm of finitude, including human beings, are composed of three gunas, the sattva, rajas, and tamas of Prakriti in different proportions. Interaction between these gunas necessarily involves possibilities of conflict, tension, and disharmony between one finite existence and another. Man has of course this advantage that he is made not just of Prakriti but also of Purusa (Self) and he can, through his conscious understanding of how things are, do something to prevent discord and unhappiness. This possibility is as much a part of Reality as the limitations of finitude and it cannot itself be understood as either the one or the other. Rather it must be seen as transcending this distinction and other similar ones, in order that we may grasp its full possibilities as the source of all existence and value. The Hindu tradition conceives of the spiritual goal of man as an actual experience of this Infinite and Absolute Reality, whether in the form of love of God or in the form of identity with Brahman. A corollary of this experience is the realisation of oneself as a reflection of this Reality, and hence *essentially* free of the limitations of finitude. This goal, being a matter of experience, is an individual one, something to be had or looked for for the fulfilment of one's own possibilities as an individual being, and not for social or communal well-being. Thus a distinction is made between spiritual realisation, and doing good to other people, an ethical value; one is not the other, despite the fact that they are closely related. Man's religious life no doubt begins with ethical considerations and values, but its goal is spiritual realisation. A spiritually realised man is thought to transcend an ego-centric existence and become a friend to all, tranquil, and equal-minded. But virtue, righteousness, and concern about other people's well-being still remain distinct goals from that of the ultimate experience of the infinite, with which an individual can find himself linked in an enduring way.

It is because ethical and spiritual goals are different that we find that many spiritual treatises, such as the Upanisads, concerned to elaborate what spiritual realisation involves, do not specifically instruct people to do good to others. [The *Bhagavadgita*, which while being a spiritual treatise is also concerned with the maintenance of the righteous order of society, does talk about the intrinsic importance of performing one's duties by society and generally of doing good (lokasamgraha and lokahita) under the label of Karma Yoga.] Nevertheless it is a mistake to assert, as some writers on Hindu religion do, that the Upanisads are totally lacking in an ethical dimension. What they do however is to give what is ethically good an instrumental value *in the perspective of realising ones spiritual goal, not in the perspective of realising the maximum potentialities of man's social existence*, with which they did not concern themselves. Social and ethical values have been treated in the Hindu tradition as ends in themselves in treatises called *Dharmasastras*, of which there are quite a number available, not in what are called *Moksa sastras*, treatises specifically concerned with spiritual realisation. And as far as guidance of man's life in society is concerned these Dharmasastras had greater importance in the classical religious culture of the Hindus than the Moksa sastras.

The Upanisads, being Moksa sastras, do not dwell at length on ethical values. However they certainly do mention some of these values as prerequisites for the cultivation of the spiritual goal. Section 17, chapter III of *Chandogya* conceives of man's life as a sacrifice and says that one should offer as dakshina (payment to the priest) such virtues as austerity, alms-giving, uprighteousness, non-violence, and truthfulness. That is, presence of these virtues is thought to be required in a person in order that he may achieve spiritual fulfilment, of which sacrifice is a symbol. And in *Brihadaranyaka*, chapter V, second Brahmana, when the threefold offspring of Prajapati, gods, men, and demons, asked him to instruct them in virtue he told gods to practise self-control, men to give or be charitable, and demons to be compassionate. According to Radhakrishnan, 'The three injunctions require us to go about doing good even though we find ourselves in a world of evil. Self-control is necessary, for we must not be elated by success or deterred by failure. Daya or compassion is more than sympathy or intellectual and emotional feeling. It is love in action, fellowship in suffering. It is feeling as one's own the circumstances and aspiration to self-perfection which we find in others. The practice of these virtues will preserve, promote and enhance the values of life.'[3] It cannot then be said that the Upanisads were blind to ethical values, even if these were conceived as aids to spiritual realisation. These same values were emphasised in Smriti scriptures, such as the *Mahabharata, Bhagavatam,* and *Yajnavalkya Smriti.* According to the last (1.4.122) the values men should seek on earth are non-violence, truth, non-stealing, cleanliness, sense-control, charity, austerity, compassion, and peace to all.

In the Santi Parva of the *Mahabharata,* Yudhisthira asks Bhisma why Narada among all the sages is so highly respected. Among the highly esteemed qualities mentioned was: 'He loves all and he is certainly always employed in doing good to all people.' Then he is instructed thus: 'They that are possessed of knowledge look with an equal eye upon a Brahman possessed of knowledge and disciples, a cow, an elephant, a dog and a chandala (outcaste)...when a living creature beholds his soul in all things and all things in his own, he is said to attain to Brahman.....He that can always realise the identity of all things with his own self certainly attains to immortality. The very gods are stupefied in the track of that trackless man who constitutes himself the soul of all creatures, who is engaged in the good of all beings and who desires to attain to Brahman which is the final

---

[3]*Ibid.,* p. 291.

refuge of all things.'⁴ It is not only for realising Brahman but also for obtaining happiness on earth that ethical values are recommended. 'He succeeds in obtaining happiness who practises abstention from injuring (others), truthfulness of speech, honesty towards all creatures, and forgiveness and who is never heedless. Hence one exercising one's intelligence should dispose one's mind after training it to peace towards all creatures. That man who regards the practice of the virtues enumerated above as the highest duty, as conducive to the happiness of all creatures, and as destructive of all kinds of sorrow, is possessed of the highest knowledge and succeeds in obtaining happiness.'⁵ The moral teaching of the *Mahabharata* can be summed up, according to Tuladhara, the righteous vaishya, to whom Jajali was sent for instruction, as 'the ancient wisdom known to all, universal friendliness and beneficence to all creatures'.

Indeed, doing good to others in the form of alms-giving and charity was in ancient India built into the very concept of dharma according to castes and stages of life, by which one was supposed to live. A householder was required to offer a libation prayer everyday for the happiness of all creatures dead and living. 'Having repeated this prayer the householder should devoutly throw food on the ground for the benefit of all beings, for the householder is the supporter of them all. He should also disperse food on the ground for dogs, outcastes, birds and all mean and degraded persons.'⁶ Further, 'if a guest comes he must be received with all hospitality, he must be offered a seat, his feet are to be washed, food must be respectfully given to him, he must be spoken to with all kindness and civility and when he goes away the friendly wishes of the host must accompany him.'⁷ Also, 'The householder should pay attention to that guest who comes from another place and whose lineage is not known.... He who feeds himself, neglecting a guest who is poor, who is not his relation, who comes from another place and is desirous of eating, goes to hell. The householder should receive his guest regarding him as the golden embryo, without enquiring his

---

⁴*The Mahabharata*, trans. P.C. Roy, Santi Parva, Vol. IX p. 195.
⁵*Ibid.*, p. 110.
⁶*Vishnu Purana*, trans. Manmatha Nath Dutt, p. 202.
⁷*Ibid.*, p. 203.

studies, his schools, his practices or his race.'[8] In the Manusmriti also, charity, at least in the form of alms-giving, has been
made obligatory on householders, and it is conceived as both a
social and religious duty.

In *Srimad Bhagavatam*, Krishna declares to Uddhava, his disciple, that his incarnations on earth are for the good of all and
those who wish to attain to him must work in the same fashion.
'My devotee is compassionate towards all beings, he bears enmity
towards none, he is forbearing, his only strength is truth. Free
from impurities, he looks with an equal eye upon all beings, and
works for the good of all. His heart is unsullied by desires; self-
controlled, sweet-tempered, pure, free from consciousness of ego,
serene, temperate, a master of his mind, having me as his refuge,
he meditates on me steadily.'[9] And such virtues were not thought
to be the preserves of this brahmans alone: 'Avoidance of injury
to all beings, love of truthfulness and chastity, abhorrence of
stealing, refraining from anger and greed, striving to be of service to all beings – these are the universal duties of all castes.'[10]
Finally: 'One must be pure in heart to enter into the life of the
spirit and follow the yogas. To achieve purity of heart one must
observe cleanliness, practise austerities, be compassionate
towards all beings and perform the appropriate duties of life.
Work becomes consecrated and purifying when it is done as service unto me.'[11] Even Yoga, the aim of which is the perfection
of man as spirit and not union or identity with anything beyond
himself, advises cultivation of universal friendliness and compassion as necessary aids to the entering of the life of the spirit.

But, as already remarked, doing good was not to be equated
with spiritual realisation itself. Also in this tradition there are
other paths to this realisation, such as knowledge, Yoga, and
devotion. The Upanisads emphasise knowledge, but they do not
preach non-action (at least the early Upanisads). *Isa*, for instance,
says that always performing works here one should wish to live
a hundred years and that neither those who adore knowledge
alone nor those who adopt action without knowledge can enter
liberation. As for the *Gita*, it categorically rejects the idea that

[8] *Ibid.*, p. 203.
[9] *Srimad, Bhagavatam*, trans. Prabhabananda, pp. 230–231.
[10] *Ibid.*, p. 252.
[11] *Ibid.*, p. 269.

there can be a life of total inaction – inaction is also said to be a form of action – and instead advocates performance of action without attachment. But there did develop in later times an idea that all action leads to bondage and therefore those who desire liberation must take to the life of a sannyasin with no interest at all in what goes on in the world, that is, not just renounce fruits of one's actions but action itself. This is because by then liberation had come to mean nothing beyond liberation from rebirth, and as all actions, both good and bad, were thought to create subtle impressions in the mind – the seeds of another life – not to be involved in activity was thought to be of the greatest importance for a man, for he would otherwise be caught up in another life and not be liberated. No doubt one finds scattered throughout the vast religious literature of the Hindus the sentiment that one would rather be born again and again than be liberated if one could thereby help others to achieve liberation. But it seems to me that by and large the fear of being born again and the desire to find a way of stopping this from happening supplied, at some stage of Hindu history, the most dominating motives behind the search for spiritual values. And as other paths than good works have traditionally been available such as knowledge, Yogic self-control, and cultivation of love of God, fear of action could grow without one's feeling that one is thereby cut off from the path of spiritual endeavours.

It is thought in the Hindu tradition that spiritual realisation, whether it is conceived as union with God or identity with Brahman, can be achieved by man only if he can transcend desires for happiness in the world. And as happiness in the world was understood to be a natural desire which could not be just discarded, as one can discard an old garment, it was thought that a substantial part of man's life should be devoted to search for happiness in the world in order that he may eventually become ready to transcend desire for happiness and devote himself exclusively to spiritual fulfilment. Desires must be transcended because they are expressions of the ego and the ego is a finite limited thing composed of the three gunas of nature. As long as one accepts the ego as oneself, one is caught up in finitude and its limitations. With the acceptance of transcendence of desires as a goal one come to accept oneself as a potentially infinite being which is veiled over by the finite characteristics of the ego. This is important, as it is because the self, of man is infinite in all systems Hindu, theistic or monistic, that a realisation of the Infinite and Absolute Reality, whether called God or Brahman, can happen to man. The theistic systems acknowledge the importance of God's grace in removing obstacles to man's understanding of his infinite status, but they too claim, equally with non-dualistic systems, that the self in man is infinite, although not identical with God. This spiritual realisation depends on a transformation of man's inner being and his acceptance of himself as substantially different from what is normally taken to be the limits of human possibilities. This is a tall order and it needs that a good deal of work should be done on oneself through Yoga and spiritual disciplines of various kinds (both devotional and intellectual). Even if transformation comes through God's grace, spiritual disciplines, at least of a devotional kind, such as repeating God's name, offering worship etc., are needed to make oneself a fit recipient of grace. So in the Hindu system there are specifically spiritual requirements demanding a certain kind of purity and tranquillity of the inner being of man, which comes from not asking for wealth, pleasure, name, fame etc., for oneself, quite apart from any ethical requirement such as is involved in the idea of doing good. It is not the case that there is a contradiction between the demand for self-transcendence and doing good to others; on the contrary it can even be said that it is only a man who has transcended himself who can really do good to others through selfless service. Equally one may come to transcend oneself through trying to do good to others. But it is still the case that self-purification and preparation needed for spiritual life do require one to give a good deal of attention to oneself, all of which cannot be diverted to one's fellows, and spiritual disciplines adopted for self-purification – a means towards transcendence of the ego-may become ends in themselves, drawing up all the energy that one has available for spiritual endeavours, and then the whole exercise can end in self-absorption rather than self-transcendence. When this happens the virtue of charity, compassion, and working for the good of others can cease to have any significance for man's spiritual unfolding, despite the fact that these have been repeatedly recommended in ancient Hindu scriptures. (Of course, doing good to others by itself may only be a means of self-fulfilment – fulfilment of the ego's desire to establish itself in the world through altruistic means – rather than of self-transcendence, which is required for spiritual realisation.)

Thus the distinction between the ethical and the spiritual, the availability of multiple paths, and the emphasis on specifically spiritual disciplines in the tradition do present a danger, that of people forgetting the ethical dimension altogether or of not giving it the importance it deserves, especially as there is no such thing as preaching in the Hindu tradition, whereby what is best in the tradition is brought to the notice of the people, (nor is there the *general* practice of reading the scriptures as found in other religions, and the fact that there are many scriptures of many different varieties does not help). So acceptance of the spiritual goal may just mean adoption of certain techniques of discipline or ritual observances, or it may mean repeating the name of God and listening to religious discourses and so on without the cultivation of charity, compassion and universal friendliness. This danger is aggravated by the teaching already mentioned which, by undervaluing action, if not totally condemning it, has minimised the importance of the specifically ethical way of the spiritual unfolding of men, as was taught by the *Gita*. Lastly, there is the danger to the ethical dimension that is presented by the caste system. A rigid and hereditary system of caste, where the traditional privileges of the higher castes have been given a religious veneer by identifying high caste status with purity and low status with impurity, certainly restricts sympathy and concern for one's fellow beings. However much bhakti movements within the tradition preached the equal worth of all castes in a religious milieu, this could not eradicate the deeply entrenched attitudes of arrogance that are implicit in a hereditary caste structure, which forbade not only inter-marriage but also inter-dining. A social structure like this, with its emphasis on ritual purity, makes it difficult to realise in practice the high values that were placed on compassion, charity, and universal friendliness as prerequisites to a life of the spirit.

Critics of the Hindu tradition often say that it is the goal of renunciation, at best an asocial value, that makes for the shortcomings of Hindu culture in the worldly sphere. It turns away man's attention from social and moral problems by preaching that life is fundamentally bad and should be abandoned, the wisest course for a man to adopt being his individual salvation. There is no doubt that Hindu religious culture posits the renunciation of the life of worldly ambition as the highest achievement of man, not a life of manifold attainments, not even a life devoted to the welfare of one's fellow beings, if this is not based on renunciation. Renunciation is expected to lead to compassion and concern for the good of all, but it is not in itself a socially oriented value. And for those for whom renunciation does not extend beyond its negative aspect, that is, attempt at control of the ego's instinct for pleasure and happiness in the world, the goal of life can, and often does, remain self-centred. Nevertheless, in the early days of this culture renunciation was not preached on the ground that life is fundamentally bad, rather it was thought to complement man's long involvement in the world during the first two stages of life by enabling him to devote himself to that which is of enduring significance within himself and which is a part of a bigger reality beyond man and the finite world. Renunciation is necessary because this aspect of man is veiled over in a life of strictly worldly pursuits, whether purely individual or social in nature. One has only to read such Hindu scriptures as the Laws of Manu, which accepts renunciation as the final goal of life, to see that there is no suggestion here of life being fundamentally bad, or of the necessity of escaping it. Renunciation was not preached as a lifelong goal, nor as the only goal of life; it was to be adopted at the last stage of life after a man has paid all his debts to society, family, ancestors, gods, and so on.

But all things are subject to corruption, and when liberation came to be thought of in terms of not being born again, rather than in terms of the joy of the infinite, some people did begin to paint life in as dark a colour as possible so as to make it appear that any happiness here on earth is quite unobtainable. It is far from the case that such preaching was widely successful in persuading people on a large scale to give up the world; the effect was far more insidious. People remained busy as ever in satisfying their desires as well as opportunities permitted, but it perhaps hampered the development of the thought that chances of happiness can be enhanced by improving things here on earth. When people who have neither the desire nor the capacity to renounce nevertheless accept that life has not much to offer, they belong neither here nor there – neither able to live one's life as best one can within its finite limitations, as people who wrote such treatises as Dharmasastras, Arthasastras, and Kamasastras thought one should, nor able to give it up in quest of the infinite. The basic realism and good sense of the classical Hindu tradition are against such extreme positions. Nevertheless a pessimistic and fatalistic attitude towards life did develop at some stage and, being well-suited to decadence, gained a good deal of prominence during certain periods of Hindu history.

According to the best teachings of the Hindu tradition there is no need to think that the world is an illusion or a place for suffering for one to embark on a quest for renunciation at some stage of one's life, despite the fact that renunciation, at least of the fruits of one's actions and of the desire to establish oneself in the world, is enjoined in the tradition on a serious spiritual aspirant. It seems to me that those who are persuaded to renounce the world because of its sufferings do so for the wrong reasons, or at least not for the best of motives, which in the words of *Chandogya* should be the joy of the Infinite. The *Isa Upanisad* even believed that far from renunciation being in aid of abandonment of enjoyment of the world, it is the best means of doing so; so it says, 'enjoy the world by renouncing'. Renunciation is renunciation not of the world as such, but of the ego and its desire-based ego-centric universe. To give it up is to be open to the wide world that lies outside the little circle within which one lives while engaged in pursuit of worldly happiness for oneself. And traditionally such renunciation has been thought to require a high degree of purity of heart which cultivation of such virtues as charity, compassion, non-violence and truthfulness help to bring about; and naturally enough, for renunciation is renunciation of the ego, which is the hardest task that one can impose on oneself. Charity, compassion etc., are ways whereby one learns to free the ego from the confines of its own shell and spread it across a wide sphere. Even such a system as Yoga, which is primarily based on a discipline of self-control, was forced to recognise that the understanding of oneself as infinite spirit can be considerably helped through the cultivation of universal friendliness and compassion.

In the old conception of the four stages of life, the renounced life of the wandering mendicant was admittedly not thought to be one of active engagement in promoting the welfare of the people in a social context. Even so, it seems to me that such a life can be seen to have a social significance. The mendicant wanders around being a living example of unattachment and freedom from selfishness to people who normally live a narrow life of self-interest. Because of the traditional acceptance in this culture of the life of renunciation as the ideal life, the living example of such a life can bring to people a fleeting relief from the pressures of self-interest by opening up a wider vista of dispassionate existence. Thus even though the renouncer is outside all social norms, he nevertheless has a function which by reminding people of the folly of too exclusive an interest in one's own well-being can contribute to social health. Quite apart from this indirect effect on society at large, the renouncer is also traditionally accepted as being supremely qualified to help others who may seek spiritual illumination. In a culture where spiritual fulfilment is given a high value, the social contribution of the renouncer is not thought to be negligible, even if what he furthers is not a social goal as such. Indeed, he acts as a guiding light for many who remain within society. And in a society which accepts dharma (righteousness), artha (political and economic well-being), and Kama (pleasure) as legitimate goals, for certain periods of man's life at any rate, the eventual goal of renunciation need not have the kind of devastating effect on society as it is thought by many to involve, as a matter of necessity, so to say.

While it is true that a high value is placed on renunciation, both the fruits of one's actions and of worldly life itself, it is by no means the case that this tradition preaches renunciation to all and sundry. Both Rama in the *Ramayana* and Yudhisthira in the *Mahabharata* had expressed a desire to renounce the world and both were dissuaded from that course by people who were renouncers themselves because it was thought that their place was in society. The sage Vasistha, Rama's teacher, tells him that liberation can be attained neither simply by renunciation of activity, nor merely by activity in the world. It comes from realising that we are ever living in the ocean of bliss and this realisation may come to a person fully engaged in worldly activity and escape one who has officially renounced. *Yoga-*

Vasistha, the book in which Vasistha's teaching to Rama is
embodied, tells the story of a king Sikhidhwaja who renounced
his kingdom and went to live in a forest in search of liberation, leaving his wife Chudala to rule over the kingdom. The
king could not attain peace of mind or liberation in his solitary
existence while the queen obtained it in the midst of her busy
life. And it was she who finally helped the king to find it too.
In the Santi Parva in the *Mahabharata* Yudhisthira is told by
Vyasa that the highest religion, as declared by the scriptures,
depends on the duties of domesticity. The gods, ancestors,
guests, servants, all depend for their sustenance upon a person
living a life of domesticity and it was his duty as a ruler to support them all. Thus those who have a social task to accomplish, as both Rama and Yudhisthira had, are advised to remain
in the world and do their duties. It would thus appear that for
men who can do great good to society by acting within society,
it would be a form of selfishness to renounce. They can still
pursue liberation, whilst acting for the good of society, by practising such virtues as non-violence, truthfulness, justice, compassion, self-restraint etc. For liberation is in the last analysis
in the mind.

I thus find that the religious values of the Hindu tradition,
correctly understood, need not lead to grave ethical and social
shortcomings, even if it is the case that a certain kind of misinterpretation of these values can lead to social and moral apathy.
But then all things are subject to misuse because of what the
Hindu tradition calls the 'forces of ignorance', which must be
constantly fought in order that the ideal may be realised. The
fact that the Hindu tradition, whatever its shortcomings,
emphasises spiritual experience and realisation, here and now, as
a distinct goal, which is to be understood as a thing distinct from
all social goals, can be seen as one of its strong points. Man is
a social animal and his culture does not consist of religion alone,
being organised on many levels, social, political, economic, and
so on. So he has many means and institutions available for the
furtherance of his social goals, including moral ones. Religion
is *specifically concerned*, so it seems to me, to help man to be
integrated with a source which is beyond man and society, that
is beyond our individual and collective goals as social beings,
despite the fact that this integration also involves a realisation

that there is nothing here which is not rooted in this Reality. By insisting on spiritual realisation, that is experience, not just faith in some doctrine about the nature of religious reality, it keeps alive a sense that man's self-fulfilment cannot be measured entirely in terms of worldly fortunes, not even in terms of moral virtues, however desirable. Man seeks happiness in the world as a matter of instinct, and he can be taught to find collective happiness desirable and, as I said, there are many means available in society to further these goals. If there is a religious reality, then it seems right and proper that religion should teach man to ask for something other than this happiness (or at least see this happiness as rooted in something beyond man, as in polytheism). And as long as it does not positively obstruct man's search for happiness in the world, which remains accessible for all who wish for it and as long as they wish it, its teaching that man's *final* fulfilment lies in something other than this happiness need have no detrimental effect on society and its fortunes, for only those who feel a definite need to go beyond the search for happiness will turn to this teaching and that too when they feel it.

Religion in a narrow sense, that is, not in the sense of a whole way of life, but as concerned with the realisation of man's relationship with ultimate reality, is only a part of man's culture and not the whole of it. Man creates his culture and its manifold expressions in order that he may realise his various possibilities with the help of the concepts, institutions, practices etc., which these cultural forms engender. Religion is one of these forms, – one may wish to say the most important of these forms – since it fulfils the highest possibility of man (liberation from finitude), but it is still one form among others and it should not be expected to fulfil all needs that man may feel either as an individual or a social being. If all men at all times were engaged in the quest for liberation, the dire consequences that are feared from the religion undervaluation of the world would naturally follow. (Polytheism from within a religious perspective acts as a counter-balancing force to this undervaluation.) But in the Hindu tradition at least all men at all times are not expected to be engaged in liberation, and there is no reason why an attitude to the world which is specific to this quest should be adopted by all and sundry, even when engaged in living a worldly life. Indeed the attitude to worldly values that is involved in the specific approach to religious reality called 'polytheism' is, as a matter of fact, opposite to that which is involved in the quest for liberation. Hindu culture has always been a pluralistic culture, and other values than str ctly spiritual values have traditionally been recognised as part of this culture. Even within the realm of spiritual values many paths have been preached, some of which, such as disinterested work, are not only consistent with but conducive to the preservation of social and moral values. The greatest weakness of this culture, however, is the hereditary caste system, which according to me, has undermined its social and moral structure, by making it impossible to introduce or even conceive of changes that were needed to keep the Hindu tradition in a state of health. This system, unlike the concept of renunciation, had all-embracing repercussions on all sphere of life for everyone, and it made customs and regulations geared to the preservation of this system have priority over all other consideraitons, however urgent. In so far as this system has been given a religious sanction its shortcomings may very well be considered shortcomings of the Hindu religious tradition. Nevertheless its virtues, if virtues these be, multiple models of religious reality suitable for different purposes and different types of personalities, its doctrine of many truths and many paths in the practice of religion, including those other than the Hindu, its acceptance of religious values as complementary and not contrary to other values of life and its insistence oñ religious practice and experience rather than doctrinal purity and faith as the kernel of religious life, can function without the benefit of the caste system.[12]

It is another matter of course if we mean by the Hindu tradition that which is now being lived by Hindu peoples, for excessive ceremonialism and ritualism with its emphasis on external rather than internal purity, verging on superstitious adherence to a multitude of performances–more social in their nature than strictly religious–believed to have magical value (insofar as their

[12]The fact that caste distinctions of some sort can be found even among the Christians and Muslims in India show that this system is not so much a part of Hindu religion which the Christians and Muslims have discarded as of the Hindu culture and way of life which they continue to share in some ways in spite of being converted to another religion.

non-performance is thought to cause harm or lead to religious demerit that would be counted against one), vitiate for the majority of the Hindus any significant appreciation of the religious life. Ritual and Hindu worship through images have importance because they constitute vital means of practising integration with the divine. But when ritual becomes almost a thing on its own, which it tends to be when excessive importance is given to the correct performance of elaborate ritual rules (believed to help one to acquire religious merit) of many descriptions, it can defeat its own purpose. It seems to me that this particular weakness of the Hindu tradition, sociologically speaking, can also be explained by the caste system. The existence of a hereditary caste of priests whose livelihood depended on the performance of various rituals by individuals (the practice of Hindu religion being mainly a matter of various observances performed mostly by individuals with the help of the priest, rather than of community events) ideally created a situation where more and more emphasis could be placed on rituals of various descriptions – the more the better for the priest – especially as the same caste had monopoly of leadership over all moral, intellectual and spiritual matters. The result was that in this tradition ceremonial and ritual observances came to relate not just to matters strictly concerned with religion (worship etc.), but to almost all spheres of life which were hemmed in by elaborate rules requiring the services of a priest (whereby they acquired a religious connotation). So the practice of Hindu religion often comes to mean nothing more than correct observances of ritual practices in all matters – social as well as narrowly religious – traditionally brought under their domain. But then this represents Hindu religion insofar as it is a way of life, not in so far as its philosophy is concerned. And perhaps the Hindu religious tradition is not the only tradition where there is this gap between the ideals to be found in the tradition and what is practised by the people at large.

CHAPTER X

Conclusion

Religion as a culture form has two distinguishable aspects. One of these speaks in the name of values that are universal, that is, not tied up with a specific type of social practice – such as love, compassion, self-transcendence (or unselfishness), and so on. The other is institutional, related to specific types of social practice, justified in its name, and varying between different religious communities. It is this institutional aspect of religion that makes possible the social use of religion as a means of integration of people in distinct communities. This aspect of religion is ultimately justified, if a question of justification does arise, in terms of universal values, even though the practices themselves may, in fact, be determined as much by historical circumstances – social, political, economic – as by considerations of a strictly religious nature. But since religion speaks in the name of something higher than man it has integrative power, in traditional societies at any rate, that is lacking to other culture forms. And man has used religion, directly its institutional structure and at a remove its universal value norms, to justify social practices which, being filtered through religion, come to acquire an added importance.

The institutional aspect of the Hindu religious tradition in its social dimension is represented both by the caste system and by its elaborate ritual structure which has acquired an autonomous existence of its own, being built into the traditional Hindu conduct of life from birth to death. It may appear that the caste system is more properly an instrument of social division than of integration. But as this system was the only large-scale organised institution available within the Hindu cultural milieu for the social use of religion – there being no church, no organised priesthood, no one conception of God and no one sacred book – it had to be used in the role of a socially cohesive force via such ideas as the law of Karma and rebirth, which gave justification for the practice of caste distinctions. So this system has played a paradoxical dual role in the history of the Hindu tradition: on the one hand it led to the social immobility and cultural degeneration of the Hindu society, on the other hand it was the only cohesive social force built into the very pattern of Hindu existence, which could save the Hindu society from total disintegration during its long period of decadence.

Now I have criticised both the caste system and excessive ritualism of a superstitious kind (especially its taboos) as negative aspects of Hinduism which it could do well without. But several questions arise. (1) Can the Hindu religion survive if the caste system disappears? Can it then have any social use as an integrative force, since it is the caste system itself which provides this? (2) What is the relevance today (in terms of modern perspectives) if any, of Hindu religious values to the conduct of Hindu life on a social plane? (3) If ritualism is discarded along with caste Hinduism ceases to have all institutional embodiment and in that case nothing can save it from disappearance (which some Hindus feel will be good riddance).

Now modern perspectives developed in the West because certain historical developments, like the growth of scientific methodology, technological inventions and industrial production, and cultural phenomena such as the Renaissance and Reformation led to fundamental questionings about the nature, function, purpose, and justification of social forms and practice. So Western societies developed, over centuries, various new justifying concepts of a non-religious nature embodying values that men claimed to be based on rational and utilitarian conceptions rather than on divine commands, in contradistinction to traditional societies where institutions and justifying concepts remained religion-based. Secularisation of social life, however, was not complete in the west either, since religious justification of the new institutions and concepts were not slow in developing. Nevertheless, human history in the west entered its modern phase where values that integrate human communities took a predominantly secular form, more or less released from their religious moorings, although by no means completely.

The Hindu society did not enter this phase on its own initiative, steeped as it was for centuries in orthodoxy and decadence. But western impact on traditional Hindu life has meant that its present social, political, and economic norms, as conceived by its elite, at any rate, are largely inspired by secular values developed in the west. But such values are yet to become an integral part of the Hindu tradition as they have become a part of the western way of life through several centuries of thought and practice. Hence they cannot, as yet, play the kind of integrative role they have played in western societies. Hindu ritualism and the caste system which give to the common man his values and norms in social practice thus largely retain their role as socially cohesive forces. Nevertheless as a good deal of these traditional practices clash with such modern values as, progress that includes the common man in its scope, social justice and a degree of material well-being for all that is essential for the cultivation of higher human faculties, they will eventually have to go if modernisation is to be successful. In other words, the institutional structure of the Hindu religious tradition has to be radically reshaped by incorporating modern institutions and methods that make possible the implementation of modern values. This may well take a long time, as tradition cannot be built in a day (it was not in the west either), and there will be a long transitional period when new values backed by organised institutions gradually replacing caste will have to compete with traditional mechanisms for social integration.

But will this not mean the disappearance of Hinduism as a religion if the institutional structure which gives it concrete content disappears? Now it has been my contention that however integral caste is to the total Hindu way of life it is not logically inseparable from Hindu religious values of a universal nature, both ethical and spiritual, and provided alternative institutions – political, social, economic – capable of embodying communal values, and more in consonance with the aspirations of modern man take root and are eventually integrated with the Hindu way of life, disappearance of caste need not be fatal to Hindu religion. Of course new institutions will have to be justified by showing that they are in accord with universal religious values held within Hinduism, if necessary through a reinterpretation of traditionally available Hindu concepts, in order that they may eventually become a part of the Hindu tradition. (Religious justification of social values that have developed on non-religious grounds occurs even in *modern* western societies). But this is not asking for anything unusual. In a society which is not completely stagnant (as the Hindu society has been for a long time) changes take place as a result of pressures that originate elsewhere than in religion, but these are subsequently justified in terms of religious concepts, which are suitably reinterpreted if need be. This is true of the development of the institution of caste itself. In other words, the role of religion in respect of social institutions has always been justificatory rather than originative at least so far as the Hindu tradition is concerned. There is then no logical reason why there cannot take place a radical reconstruction of the social base of the Hindu way of life under modern pressures, which will eventually become a part of the Hindu tradition, and even an institutional expression of this religion itself.

But need religion retain today the social role that it has traditionally played? Would it not be better to discard it altogether if institutions do develop on non-religious premises ? It seems to me that a complete break with religion even if desirable is scarcely possible, especially for a culture like the Hindu that runs into thousands of years. Traditionally, Hindu culture has not made a total separation of its profane activities – dharma, artha, kama, moksa were put together in one schema of existence – from the divine order with which it is thought to be continuous, being an expression of it in time. This does not mean that this culture views all social arrangements as directly instituted by divine command, or that it believes that the passage of Hindu culture in time shows a plan that God has conceived for man. The ahistorical character of Hindu religion and its relativism make such claims quite out of place. But it does mean that in this culture the divine is thought to be present here on earth, in the temporal order itself, and so living one's life in this order is not thought to be totally divorced from timeless truths. What we do here is thus seen to have religious significance, not in the sense that we have been commanded by God to act as we do, but in the sense that what we do (social relations, etc.) may be conducive or not, or more or less conducive, to the understanding of the presence of the divine in the temporal order. Hence the importance of the belief that social institutions and values are not completely divorced from religious values and this being the case the social absorption of new institutions in India can be facilitated if they are seen in this light rather than otherwise. In any case, one can hardly proceed on the hope that a complete break with tradition will take place, which is only possible through a violent revolution and a totalitarian organisation of social life. Such things may or may not develop in India.

Furthermore, it seems to me that the religious impulse is a genuine human impulse – which is not to say that every single individual feels it or feels it in equal measure – and this is rooted in the need to see life as of enduring significance going beyond man's individual and collective goals of a transitory nature. And even when broken down by deliberate effort this impulse seems to erupt here and there, under the most uncongenial circumstances. It is better than to think in terms of its enlightened direction in social life for the furtherance of values that are rationally acceptable than to pin one's hope on its total disappearance. That is to say, new democratic institutions that are being created in India or, one hopes, will be created, may profitably be given their ultimate justification in religious terms (as they always have been), as in accordance with the self-expression of the divine in time, rather than exclusively on utilitarian principles, if the orientation of the Hindu religious tradition is to be used constructively for social purposes.

This does not mean that the institutions involved will be seen as specifically *Hindu* institutions or that they will be brought about exclusively for the benefit of the Hindus in India. Their development will be primarily on secular considerations, such as good life, health and worldly happiness of all, Hindu and non-Hindu, and they will come to exist through secular means. But once they develop they will have to be shown to be in accordance with the enduring values of the Hindu tradition in order that this tradition may come to incorporate them successfully. This task of the transformation of the concept of the Hindu tradition in its details can only be performed by Hindus themselves. Can this transformation take place? I think it can in principle, although whether or not it will in practice depends on the courage, imagination and the creative vigour of the leadership that the people of this tradition are capable of providing, which fortunately is no longer confined to a particular caste. It seems to me that the Hindu religious tradition has certain in-built advantages which may be suitably exploited for the task of reconstruction. First of all, what is called the Hindu religion is more properly a tradition than a fixed dogma and being a tradition, it is, in its theoretical structure, at any rate, open-ended. Any proposed innovation can be given a religious justification as long as it can be shown to have some link with 'sacred' utterances in old books, and this is not too difficult to find. The Hindu tradition, theoretically speaking, does not clash with scientific ideas some of which it conceived on a mythical plane (which means, unfortunately, without the benefit of a scientific methodology). So introduction of scientific concepts in the reorganisation of life in India poses no break with the theoretical underpinning of the Hindu world-view. Secondly, Hindu culture is assimilative and it has not generally found it impossible to incorporate elements that are technically of a 'foreign' origin into its existing structure, of which they eventually became an integral part. Indeed it grew to be what it is by such a process.

Assimilation of institutions that have originated outside the Hindu context may also be justified by the doctrine of non-dualism which preaches that all things that exist in the universe are expressions in different name and form of the same divine essence. That the universe extends beyond India was fully acknowledged in the Puranic times. Thirdly, various floating ideas are available within the tradition which can be constructively used to justify and accommodate changes that are already taking place. For instance, Yudhisthira's comment in the *Mahabharata* that institutions are man-made, and they are but imperfect manifestations, according to time and place, of eternal values which are hard for man to know. Or, take the doctrine of Yugas according to which human organisations take different shapes at different phases of a cycle – everybody is a brahman in satyayuga, the first phase of a particular cycle of ages – and this is recognition that institutions do not have a fixed character irrespective of changing times. Again some dharmasastras mention, without of course giving this much weight, human happiness and conscience, along with tradition and custom, as the sources of dharma (law and righteous conduct), so presumably change is justified if required by these considerations. Finally, and most important of all, caste itself can be given, by using ideas and examples from the Vedas and the Upanisads, a functional interpretation in place of a hereditary one and then the idea of the importance of performing one's caste duty for the well-being of society can be squared with open opportunities to find out who belongs to which caste. According to an accepted tradition, in case of conflict between primary sacred texts, called sruti, and secondary texts, called smriti, sruti should prevail, and it is not difficult to show that it is only in the secondary sources, called dharmasastras, that the hereditary nature of the system has been emphasised, not in the primary sources such as the Vedas and the Upanisads. The unimportance of caste for religious purposes has been emphasised by the initiators of the bhakti movement, and this is also reflected in the fact that a renouncer is reckoned to have no caste. These imply that caste is a social institution created by men for their own convenience rather than something that is required from a religious point of view. Officially, caste is no longer recognised in India as the basis of social functioning. Wise use of religious ideas gleaned from the complex and rich religious tradition of the Hindus can help towards transforming this official stand into a social reality. All this is important, as the energy and the emotion of the Hindu masses can be tapped much more easily if one speaks for change in the name of religion than as a revolt against it.[1]

India of course is not exclusively Hindu. But to show that certain institutions – which have developed in any case through secular means – are in accordance with the values of the Hindu traditions does not mean that one must insist that they are not in accordance with the values of other religious traditions. The best in the Hindu religious tradition have always said that all religions are searching for the same goal, so that all values that Hindus live by do not have to have an exclusive stamp of 'Hindu' on them; some, at any rate, can very well be shareable by all religions. Of course, there will remain in India non-Hindu beliefs and practices side by side with those that are specifically Hindu. However, the Hindu religious tradition has this advantage that it preaches many conceptions of religious reality and many paths of approach to it. And this makes it relatively easy for Hindus to accept non-Hindu beliefs and practices as having equal validity with their own. Hindu religious ideas can thus be used to justify even the pluralistic structure of Indian social and religious life.

---

[1] It seems to me that the mass enthusiasm and capacity for sacrifice shown in India during the independence movement – features which have since disappeared – can be explained, partly at any rate, by the semi-religious motivation that inspired it.

As for ritualism one must admit that its relatively formalised structure remains, outside of caste, the only institutional base for the practice of Hindu religion and for the social cohesion of the Hindus as a religious community. If and when caste loses its importance Hindu ritualism will remain as the only candidate for the social expression of what is characteristically Hindu. To ask for the total abolition of Hindu ritual is then to ask for the complete secularisation of the Hindu way of life. What one can legitimately ask for, however, even within a religious approach to social life, is the shedding of the junk of superstition that has been accumulated over millennia under the protection of the overall need for ritual practice of some sort, particularly as it is this which stands in the way of a rational approach to human problems. Unfortunately, that which constitutes the strength of the Hindu religious tradition from one point of view, the fact that it does not have an organised ecclesiastical structure, which gives it resilience in the face of change, also constitutes its weakness from another point of view, since it means that there exists no pruning mechanism whereby what is found to be a hindrance rather than a help can be eliminated in a planned way. So rationalisation of the extravagant ritual structure of the Hindu tradition, harbouring under itself many superstitious rites, can happen only through spread of education whereby practices fed by ignorance and fear can be gradually discarded. That is, ritualism will have to find its own level of rational tolerance that does not clash with the achievement of modern values and the introduction of modern methods in the management of social affairs. However, the Upanisads and the *Gita*, and other texts besides, can be used to expose the folly and futility of excessive ritualism.

My object here in talking about the social aspects of Hinduism has been to see if the Hindu religious tradition does or can have any relevance today, in face of the need for modernisation of Hindu institutions. I have said that the Hindu tradition can absorb the changes by means of their religious justification and this can serve the purpose of social integration. But as we have noticed, this tradition has highly developed concepts which cater to extra-social religious needs of man, such as cosmic and self-integration, needs which are private and individual rather than social. If a religion comes to lose its social relevance it is a debatable point whether or not these private and personal aspects can prove enough for the survival of a distinctive religious tradition. But even if a religion survives purely by virtue of these aspects, it then becomes a matter of pursuit exclusively for the elite and is no longer available to a man of average religious capacities for the purposes of integration with a reality that is beyond man. It has sometimes been said that religion ought to be a matter for private pursuit with no institutional trappings attached to it and this is an attractive view. But religion could become a purely personal and private matter rather than a thing that concerns whole communities on a corporate basis only if all members of a community could operate at this private level, without feeling any need for institutional support on the social plane. This, perhaps, is not the case. So a need remains for both the social and personal dimension of religious belief and practice, at least for societies that are traditional. By 'social dimension' I mean primarily a communally shared ritual expression (such as is involved in the method of worship, marriage customs etc., and these affect human relationships in a social milieu to some degree) of how a distinctive religious tradition perceives the divine rather than political, economic and social institutions (such as class or caste), which must be ultimately based on rational considerations of human happiness, even though they are justifiable at the same time in terms of universal values which all religious traditions more or less share.

Index

Aborigines, 3, 129, 252
Absolute truth, 275, 287, 292, 298
Academic mud-slinging, 37–38
Adhirakiveda doctrine, 43, 78–80
Affliction, 188–89
Agni, 55, 102, 109–11, 118, 126, 252 282
Aitareya Upanisad, 145
Alexander, 8
Alms-giving, 75, 295, 296
Ananta concept, 45
Animals
  Hindu attitude, 13–14
  Sacrifice, 253
  Vedic hymns, 114–15
Animism, 22
Ardhanarisvara, 268
Arjuna, 173, 198, 200, 202, 213, 223
Arthasastra, 7n, 38, 74n
Aryans, 3–4, 21, 29, 129–30, 238, 239, 252
Asana, 190, 191
Asceticism, 159–60
Asimove, Isaac, 53, 54
Asoka, 38
Asur kings, 21
Asvamedha sacrifice, 137
Atala, 48
Atharvaveda, 26, 39, 90, 91, 108, 110, 115, 118, 119, 150
Aurobindo, 197

Bauls, 34–35
Beef-eating, 11, 27
Beginning, 65, 68, 144–45, 234
Bhagavadgita, 40, 41, 76, 99, 128, 154, 173, 174, 175, 200, 205, 208, 220, 221, 293, 296, 299, 314
  God-world relations, 229–30
  Incarnation doctrine, 220, 226
  Saguna-Nirguna distinction, 200–202
  Yoga concept, 196–98

Bhagavat Purana, 44, 207, 215, 216, 217, 220, 226, 227, 229, 231
Bhairava, 240
Bhakti movements, 268, 299, 313
Bhakti Sutra (Narada), 203, 215
Bhaskara, 174
Bhirgu, 155
Bhisma, 294
Bhuvar-loka, 48
Bible, 132
Black, Max, 284-85
Bliss, 138–39, 158–59, 169, 211, 215, 234, 262, 280, 289
Bloomfield, 120
Boddhisattva, 73, 238
Bose, A.C., 39n, 89n, 110n, 120, 252n
Bose, D.M., 15n
Brahma, God, 19, 33, 43–44, 219
Brahma Sutra, 173, 174
Brahmans, 6–7, 9, 10, 117, 126, 128, 132, 135–36
Brihadaranyaka Upanisad, 23, 88, 89, 108, 120, 137, 138, 139, 140, 141, 143, 144, 145, 146, 147, 148, 166, 253, 291, 294
British rule, 11–12
Buddha, Gautam, 176
Buddhism, 1, 10, 37, 73–74, 81, 138, 175, 176, 238
  Academic fights, 37–38

Caitanya, 230, 233, 235, 244
Caste hierarchy, 6, 55, 299, 306
Caste system, 3, 4, 5–6, 7–9, 16–17, 55, 71, 72, 96, 97, 117, 135, 299, 305 306, 307, 308, 309, 310, 312–13, 314
Chandi, Goddess, 211, 256
Chandogya Upanisad, 88, 142, 144, 146, 149, 221, 253, 254, 293, 301
Chandragupta, 8
Charity, 295, 296, 301

Christ, 23
Christian beliefs, 15, 17
Christianity, 1, 15
Christians, 132
Christmas Day, 129
Chudala, 303
Compassion, 294, 301
Consciousness, 85, 169, 234, 280, 289
Conversion, 129-30
Cosmic integration, 88-97, 186, 198
Cosmology, 43-54
Cows, 26, 115
Creation, 47-49, 52, 65, 68, 231, 243, 247

Dadhyac, Rishi, 89
Daityas, 48
Daksa, 242
Danavas, 48
Danielou, A., 220n
Daya, 294, 301
Dead body, 181
Death, 125
De Bary, T., 203n
Desires, 297-98
Deutsch, Eliot, 171, 172
Devi, Goddess, 199, 206, 207, 211, 219, 256, 262
  Faces, 256
  Representaion, 256-57
Devi Bhagavata Purana, 257
Devi Mahatmya, 256, 257
Devi-Sukta, 251
Devotionalism, 33, 179, 199-268
  Distinctive approach, 199-217
Dharma, 190, 191
Dhavamony, 120
Dhruva, 48
Dhumavati, Goddess, 252
Dhyana, 190, 191-92
Dionysus, 20
Dissolution, 52, 58, 65, 68
Divine destructiveness, 214
Divine years, 51-52
Down, Goddess, *See* Usha, Goddess
Dravidian civilization, 4, 5, 7, 21, 129-30, 239

Dravidians, 3, 252
Durga, Goddess, 26, 33, 106, 206, 252, 256, 257
Durga Puja festival, 106
Dutta, Manmatha Nath, 13n, 295n
Dutta, N.K., 11n
Dwapara Yuga, 46, 50, 51
Dwaraka, 221

Earth, 48, 90, 92
  Atharvavedic hymns, 113-14
Edgerton, 139
Eliade, 183
Ethical values, 293-94, 307, 308, 309
Evil and suffering, 213-14, 215, 292

Folk religion, 130
Folk superstitions, 131
Fortunes and sufferings, 57, 58, 71
Freudian psychoanalysis, 175
Friendliness, 118-20

Gambhastimat, 48
Gandhi, M.K., 197
Ganges river 12-13, 242
Gautama, 141
Gayatri Mantra, 120, 139
Ghora Angirasa, 221
God
  Concept, 81-82, 199
  Dependancy on men, 102
  Form, 216
  Functions, 247
  Humanisation, 105
  Numbers, 108
  Personality, 216-17
  Puranic stories, 102, 105
  Relation with world, 229, 234-35, 248
Gods' years, 51-52
Gopal Krishna, 209
Goswami, Bhagavat Kumar, 227, 228n
Great dissolution, 52, 53
Greece, 143
Greek gods, 105
Greeks, 8, 20
Griffiths, 122, 123

Griswold, 120
Guests, 295-96

Harivamsa, 221
Heaven, 46, 56, 108, 120, 136, 181, 256
Hell, 48, 56
Henotheism, 103
Heracles, 20
Hermaphrodite, 240
Hesse, Mary, 283
Hindu cosmology, 43-54
Hindu culture
   Decadence, 2-3
Hinduism
   Institutional aspect, 307-12, 314-15
   Sanskritisation, 22, 29
   Term meaning, 16, 22
Hindus
   Conversion to Islam, 10
   Sectoral quarrel, 37
   Trade relations, 10-11
Hladini Sakti, 234
House foundation laying, 26-27
Human life
   Previous stages, 45-46, 54, 66-67, 76-77
Human values, 12-14, 33, 108
Hume, 57n

Illusion, *See* Maya
Images, 101, 306
Incarnation doctrine, 219-20, 226
Indra, 55, 93-94, 103, 107, 110, 118, 121-22, 124, 126, 151, 209, 282
Indus Valley civilisation, 3, 210, 239, 252
Infinite truth, 269, 292, 298
Interdining, 5, 9, 11
Intermarriage, 5, 6, 11
Isa Upanisad, 140, 155, 296, 301
Islam, 1, 7, 37, 129

Jaina logic, 276-78, 280
Jaivali, Pravahana, 141, 144, 295
Janaka, 141, 161
Janaloka, 51

Janardana, 50
Jews, 103
Jivanmukti, 235
Judaism, 206

Kali, Goddess, 26, 33, 34, 206, 211, 212, 215, 252, 256, 258-59, 267, 268
Kali Yuga, 46, 50, 51, 254
Kama, 242
Kama Sutra, 13, 74n
Kamsa, 221, 222
Karali, Goddess, 252
Karma doctrine, 18, 43, 54-80, 173, 293, 307
   Social dimensions, 72-73
Katha Upanisad, 88, 144, 148, 156
Kautilya, 7n, 38, 74n
Kena Upanisad, 155, 163, 252
King
   Caste duties, 8
   Cultural duties, 8
   Functions, 10
   Religious duties, 38
Koran, 132
Krishna, Lord, 6, 20, 26, 33, 34, 40, 76, 107, 122, 128, 160, 173, 198, 199, 200, 202, 205, 206, 207, 208, 213, 214, 218, 219, 240, 246, 249, 250, 255, 258, 259, 267, 268, 296
   As child god, 221-222
   Life story, 221-24, 229
   Lila, 233
   Love-life, 44-45, 225-26, 254
   Myths and legends, 221-22
   Personal God, 154
   Puranic stories, 102
Krita Yuga, 46, 50, 51
Kshatriyas, 7-8, 135, 136
Kuhn, 272, 273, 274
Kundalini yoga, 263

Lakshmi, Goddess, 232
   Collective worship, 91
Lemaitre, G.E., 52
Libation prayer, 295
Liberation, 56, 65, 73-74, 75, 76, 77-78, 140, 158, 160-63, 173-74, 175, 176-77, 185, 186-87, 207, 224,

227, 235, 237–38, 245–46, 249, 259, 262, 297, 302, 304, 305
Lila doctrine, 225–28, 231, 233
Lokacharya, 203, 216
Lokaloka mountain, 47

Macdonald, 119
Madhabhacharya, 174
Magic, 22, 131, 180
Magico-religious practices, 180–81, 195
Mahabharata, 6, 10, 20, 21, 96, 136, 219, 221, 223, 253, 294, 295, 302, 303, 312
Mahanirvana Tantra, 257
Mahapralaya, *See* Great Dissolution
Mahar-loka, 49, 51
Mahatala, 48
Mahisasura, 256, 257
Maitreyi, 157
Maitri Upanisad, 73, 138
Man
    Components, 59
    Dual nature, 85
    Social values, 92–96
    Unity with nature, 89–90
Manu, 7n, 8, 26, 74n, 75
Manusmriti, 253, 296, 300
Markandeya Purana, 256
Marxism, 175
Mathura, 222
Matter, 34, 183, 184
Maurya dynasty, 6
Maya, 137–38, 144–45, 147, 151–52, 164–78, 233, 234, 246, 247
Mehta, P.D., 119n, 123n
Mendicancy, 75
Mental states, 188
    Control, 189-90
Misra, Vacaspati, 194
Mitra, 28, 93, 118, 119
Moksa, *See* Liberation
Moksa sastras, 293
Monism, 22, 30, 86, 87, 91, 133, 137, 205, 208, 272, 298
Monotheism, 33–34, 81, 82, 87, 91, 103, 107, 121, 133, 134, 208, 219, 280

Monotheism, Qualified, 199–268, 272
Moral values, 291-306
Mother goddess, 211-12, 250-52, 262
Muir, J., 11, 49
Müller, Max, 103
Mundaka Upanisad, 88, 145, 252
Muslim rituals, 129
Muslim rulers, 8, 9–10, 178
Muslims, 14, 132
Mysticism, 33, 135
Myths and legends, 218–19

Naipal, V.S., 13n
Narada, 203-4, 215, 294
Narayana, 209
Nature, 12,112–14
Nikasha, 227
Nikhilanda, Swami, 36n
Nimbarka, 174
Nirguna Brahman, 152, 199, 200–3, 205
Nitala, 48
Niyama, 190–91
Non-dualism, 86, 135–178, 200, 204, 205, 206, 207, 214, 249, 272, 280, 312
    Samskara's doctrine, 163-78
    Upanisadic, 135–63

Organ, Troy Wilson, 45

Pantheism, 22, 30
Parjanya, God, 106
Parvati, 241, 242, 256
Patala, 48
Patanjali, 181, 182, 198
Patanjali Yoga, 181, 182, 194-96
Perfectionism, 86, 179–98, 204, 205
Personal God, 30, 31, 33, 40, 80, 98, 154, 156–57, 199, 200, 250
Physical reality, 269, 272–75
Polytheism, 19–22, 28–29, 38–39, 86, 91, 101–34, 135, 137, 204, 205, 206, 207, 208, 252, 272, 282, 279, 287, 304–5
Prabhabhanada, Swami, 41n, 60n, 217n, 220n, 227n, 229n, 269n, 296n,

Pradhaba, 47
Prakriti, 47, 52, 53, 152, 230, 289, 292
Pralaya, *See* Dissolution
Pranayama, 190, 191
Prasna Upanisad, 144
Pratyahara, 190, 191–92
Priests, 126, 135
Pushan, 94

Races
    Equality, 4
    Extermination, 4
    Mixed with culture, 6–7
    Prejudices, 4–5
Radha, 223, 233, 234, 235
Radhakrishnan, S., 57n, 69n, 138n,
    139n, 140n, 142n, 143n, 157n, 243n,
    291n, 294
Raikava, Sage, 143–44
Rajdharma concept, 38
Rama, Lord, 206, 219, 220, 227, 253,
    302, 303
Ramakrishna, 36, 258–59, 267, 278,
    290
Ramanuja, 153, 156, 167, 230–32, 244,
    249
Ramayana, 217, 253, 302
Ramprosad, 201
Ravana, 227
Reality, 81–100, 146, 168, 169–72,
    232, 233
Rebirth, 18, 54–80, 307
    Memory, 60–63
Redeath, 57
Reincarnation, 42, 54–80
Religion, Definition of, 15, 16, 85–86
Religious beliefs, 14–16, 18, 19, 31,
    43–80, 101, 129, 130, 315
Religious ceremonies, 95–96, 128–29
Religious models, 283–88, 290
    Metaphors, 288
Religious reality, 81–100, 124, 134,
    152–53, 156–58, 199, 202, 208, 269,
    270, 272, 275, 278, 280–81, 285,
    288–89, 291–92, 304, 313
    Approaches, 86–87
    Cosmic integration, 88–91, 99, 186
    Domain, 278–79

Levels and dimensions, 86–87, 170,
    172
    Self-integration, 97–99
    Social integration, 91–97, 99
Religious tradition, 1–42
Renou, Louis, 46
Renunciation, 197, 299–303, 305
Rigveda, 17, 27, 30, 36, 38, 40, 41,
    90, 91, 92, 93, 94, 102, 106, 107,
    111, 113, 114, 116, 117, 119, 122,
    123, 124, 125, 139, 150, 151, 166,
    207, 210, 229, 250, 277
    Gods praising hymns, 24–25, 27–28,
    31
Rita, 55, 112, 116
Ritualism, 33, 35, 125–27, 128, 135,
    136, 215, 279, 306, 307, 308, 314
Rivers
    Rigvedic hymns, 114
Roy, P.C., 295
Rudra, 26, 29, 50, 209, 210, 238–39,
    242–43, 244

Sacrifice, 125–27
    Magical potency, 31–32
Sadhana, 181, 259–60
Saguna Brahman, 153, 199, 200–3
Saguna-Nirguna distinction, 200–1
Saivism, 214, 217–19, 235–50, 258
Saivism, Kashmiri, 207, 249–50
Saivism, Southern, 94, 244, 247, 249
Sakti, Goddess, 206, 211, 232, 262,
    264–65
Saktism, 174, 214, 217–19, 250–68
Samadhi, 190, 192, 193
Samaveda, 150
Samkara, 140, 147, 153, 156, 194,
    199, 205, 232, 254
    Gita's interpretation, 139, 173
    Maya doctrine, 137–38, 144–45,
    151–52, 163–78
    Non-dualism, 163–78
Samkaracharya, Sri, 139n
Samkhya philosophy, 34, 67, 73, 176,
    205
Samkhya-yoga, 86, 179–98, 272
    As differed from Yoga, 193–94
Samyoga, 194

Sanatkumar, 150–51
Sandhini Sakti, 234
Saptabhangi naya, 277
Saraswati river, 114
Sartre, 158
Sastri, A. Madhava, 139n
Sastri, Prabhu Dutt, 167
Sastri, Suryanarayan, 246
Sattva, 183
Satwat Bhakti cult, 227
Satyakama, 5–6
Satya-loka, 48
Saundaryalahari, 207, 257
Scientific models, 282–84
Sea-crossing, 11
Seal, B., 15n
Self, 64, 65, 88, 97–98, 99, 107, 140,
    147, 157, 158, 159, 161–63, 164,
    187, 291
Self-control, 294
Self- discipline, 97
Self- integration, 97–100, 186
Self- manifestation, 64
Sensory reality, 83
Sex, 253–54
Shamanism, 180, 181
Shapere, Dudley, 283n
Siddhis, 182
Sikhidhwaja, 303
Sita, 253
Siva, Lord, 20, 26, 29, 33, 34, 94,
    199, 206, 207, 210–11, 219, 235,
    250, 252, 255, 256, 259, 260, 264,
    267
    Destruction concept, 240
    Faces, 243
    Forms, 243
    Nataraja form, 241
    Puranic stories, 102, 142–43
    Tamas representation, 241–42
    Third eye, 242
Sky, 48, 92
Social customs, 16–17
Social gatherings, 95–96
Social integration, 91–97, 99
Social values, 293, 309–10
Soma, 101, 106, 108, 121
    Vedic hymns, 122–24

Spirit, 34, 59, 155, 183–84
Spiritual values, 291–306
Srimad Bhagavatam, 41, 60, 220,
    230, 286, 294, 296
Subration, 172
Sudras, 5, 21, 117
Sun, God, 110, 116-17
Superstitions, 115–16
Supreme reality, 199
Sutala, 48
Suturdri river, 114
Sva-rupa sakti, 234
Svetaketu, 141, 142, 149
Svetasvatara Upanisad, 151, 152,
    243, 244
Syadvada doctrine, 267–68, 280

Taittriya Upanisad, 138, 139, 141,
    142, 143, 144, 145, 252
Tantra, 30, 99, 260, 261–67
    Rituals, 262–66
Tapaloka, 48
Tapasya, 181–82
Tattvatraya (Lokacharya), 203
Temples, 101
Thales, 143
Theism, 22, 33, 109, 207, 278
Time
    Cycle theory, 45
    Measurement, 51–53
Trade relations, 10–11
Trade tools, 115
Transcendentalism, 214
Treta Yuga, 46, 50, 51
Tribal belief, 15–16
Truth, 269–90
    Meanings, 269–70
Tuladhara, 295

Uddalaka, 142, 149
Uddhava, 220, 296
Ultimate reality, 171, 199
Ultimate truth, 291
Uma, Goddess, 206, 252, 256
Universal values, 307
Universe, 32, 48, 154
    Creation, 52–53

Eternality theory, 53, 68
Upanisadic sages, 135–37, 140–41
Upanisads
  Non-dualism, 135–63
  World's material constitution,
  143–44
  Ushas, Goddess, 90, 105–6, 116–
  17, 253

Vac, Goddess, 26, 251
Vairajas, 48
Vaishnavism, 214, 215, 217–19, 219–
35, 244, 249, 258
Vallabha, 174
Vamadevya cult, 254
Vamana Purana, 240
Varna-caste confusion, 6-7
Varna system, 4, 6, 7, 96
Varnasrama dharma, 43, 74–80, 301–2
Varuna, 28, 40, 55, 103, 106, 110,
118, 119, 120–21, 122, 124, 155
Vasistha, 302
Vasudeva, 209
Vasudeva Krishna, 221
Vata (air)
  Rigvedic hymns, 113
Vatsayana, 74
Vedanta philosophy, 64, 67, 171–72,
175
Vedas
  Gods praising hymns, 24–25
  Sacredness, 23
Vedic gods, 27, 28, 30, 105–6
  Loss of status, 32
Vedic sacrifice, 101–2, 128
Vedic worship, 101–2
Vijnana Vikshu, 179

Vipa river, 114
Virbhadra, 240
Vishnu, Lord, 47, 49–50, 156, 206,
209, 255, 256
  Incarnations, 67, 219
Vishnu Purana, 13, 44, 47, 226
Viswamitra, 7, 114
Vitala, 48
Vrindavan, 221, 233
Vrishni tribe, 223
Vyasa, 6, 303

Water
  Rigvedic hymns, 113
Wilson, H.H., 47n, 48n, 50n, 51,
54n

Yajnavalkya, 108, 140–41, 147, 157,
161
Yajavalkya Smriti, 294
Yajurveda, 89, 110, 112, 114, 115,
117, 150
Yakshas, 48
Yama, 125
Yama (Yogic technique), 190–91
Yamunacharya, 174
Yoga, 160, 179, 210, 214, 224, 226,
230, 232, 296, 298, 301
  Aim, 179, 190
Yoga-Vasistha, 302–3
Yogic perfectionism, 86, 179–98,
204, 205
Yogic techniques, 190–94
Yudhisthira, 294, 302, 303, 312
Yugas, 46–47, 312
  Measurement, 50–52
Zaehner, 225,

around us. The rain tapped faintly on the window-pane. Miranda lit two cigarettes and gave me one. Soon the smoke rose like a diaphanous mist, through which her hands fluttered like doves in flight.

One day I shall tell the strange tales that Miranda told me as a prelude to our symphony of love. Here I only wanted to tell how, after following her all over the world, as well as in my dreams, I found the Lady of the Green Jade Lamp.